Cent Banking, Monetary Theory and Practice

Central Banking, Monetary Theory and Practice

Essays in Honour of Charles Goodhart, Volume One

Edited by

Paul Mizen

Reader in Monetary Economics and Deputy Director, Experian Centre for Economic Modelling, University of Nottingham, UK

Edward Elgar
Cheltenham, UK • Northampton, MA, USA

Published by
Edward Elgar Publishing Limited
Glensanda House
Montpellier Parade
Cheltenham
Glos GL50 1UA
UK

Edward Elgar Publishing, Inc.
136 West Street
Suite 202
Northampton
Massachusetts 01060
USA

A catalogue record for this book
is available from the British Library

Library of Congress Cataloguing in Publication Data

Central banking, monetary theory and practice: essays in honour of Charles Goodhart, volume one/edited by Paul Mizen.
p. cm.
'This volume and its companion have been compiled from the proceedings of a two-day Festschrift conference in honour of Charles Goodhart at the Bank of England, 15–16 November 2001'—Preface.
1. Banks and banking, Central—Congresses. 2. Monetary policy—Congresses. I. Title: Essays in honour of Charles Goodhart: volume one. II. Goodhart, C.A.E. (Charles Albert Eric). III. Mizen, Paul.
HG1811.C4586 2003
332.1'12—dc21 2002034706

ISBN 1 84064 614 4 (cased)

Printed and bound in Great Britain by MPG Books Ltd, Bodmin, Cornwall

Contents

Figures

Tables

Contributors

Charles Bean, Chief Economist and Executive Director, Bank of England, UK
Sudipto Bhattacharya, Arizona State University and London School of Economics, UK
Alec Chrystal, Sir John Cass Business School, City of London, UK
Stanley Fischer, Vice-Chairman, Citigroup, and President, Citygroup International, USA
John S. Flemming, Warden, Wadham College, Oxford, UK
Charles Freedman, Deputy Governor, Bank of Canada, Canada
Benjamin M. Friedman, Harvard University, USA
Marvin Goodfriend, Senior Vice President, Federal Reserve Bank of Richmond, USA
Charles Goodhart, London School of Economics and Bank of England, UK
Mervyn King, Governor designate, Bank of England, UK
Nobuhiro Kiyotaki, London School of Economics, UK
Paul Mizen, University of Nottingham, UK
John Moore, Edinburgh University and London School of Economics, UK
Edward Nelson, External Monetary Policy Committee Unit, Bank of England, UK
Adam S. Posen, Institute for International Economics, Washington, DC, USA
Martin Shubik, Yale University, USA
Anne Sibert, Birkbeck College, London, UK
Lars E.O. Svensson, Princeton University, USA

Preface

This volume and its companion have been compiled from the proceedings of a two-day Festschrift conference in honour of Charles Goodhart at the Bank of England, 15–16 November 2001. The conference would not have been possible without the participation and efforts of a large number of people. The contributors of papers are listed on page ix and my thanks are extended to each and every one of them for producing exceptionally high-quality papers. My thanks must also be extended to all those who chaired the sessions: Mark Gertler, Roger Alford, Leslie Dicks-Mireaux, Sushil Wadhwani, Anna J. Schwartz, Lord Desai, Peter Cooke, and David Webb, the discussants and those who provided comments from the floor. In some cases contributors and discussants went to considerable lengths to attend despite the commitments they were obliged to keep to other events on different continents the following day. My thanks are extended to them all.

As with all great enterprises there is a large number of people whose time and energy has been devoted to the task of putting the arrangements in place. I would particularly like to mention a few who took on the greater part of the task. The organisation of the conference at the Bank involved a number of people including Charles Goodhart, Mervyn King's office and especially his two Personal Assistants at the time, Mark Cornelius and Phil Evans, and the conference organisers, Debbie Nyman and Maureen Black. Ryan Love and Raoul Minetti undertook the task of writing detailed notes summarising the presentations and the subsequent discussion, for which I am very grateful. My own secretary, Jill Brown, at the University of Nottingham took on much of the administrative work and Tara Lehane at the Financial Markets Group, London School of Economics, handled the financial affairs. We are most grateful that the conference was generously supported by the Bank of England and the Financial Markets Group, London School of Economics. The publication of the two-volume set has been organised by Edward Elgar under the oversight of Dymphna Evans and Caroline Cornish who have been supportive and encouraging as always. My thanks are extended to them all for their patience and help.

Paul Mizen

Acknowledgements

The publishers wish to thank the following who have kindly given permission for the use of copyright material:

Banca Nazionale Del Lavoro for article: 'Whither Now', Charles Goodhart, *Quarterly Review*, 203, December 1997, Banca Nazionale Del Lavoro, 385–430.

Introduction

> He accumulated a vast and various collection of learning and knowledge, which was so arranged in his mind as to be ever in readiness to be brought forth. But his superiority over other learned men consisted chiefly in what may be called the art of thinking, the art of using his mind – a certain continual power of seizing the useful substance of all that he knew, and exhibiting it in a clear and forcible manner; so that knowledge, which we often see to be no better than lumber in men of dull understanding, was in him true, evident and actual wisdom . . . His maxims carry conviction; for they are founded on the basis of common sense, and a very attentive and minute survey of real life . . .
>
> (James Boswell's *Life of Samuel Johnson*, p. 511)

Ben Friedman refers in this volume to Charles Goodhart as the Samuel Johnson of Monetary Policy – and how true a statement that is. The extract quoted above was written by James Boswell of Johnson at the end of his life in 1784 but could equally have been written of Charles's academic career in 2002. Like Johnson, Charles Goodhart has written extensively in many styles and has become synonymous with his subjects of monetary economics and central banking. Although I am not aware that Charles has ever produced a dictionary, he has made substantial contributions to the literature in his field and has on many occasions been the influence that has altered its direction at crucial junctures. He has also been a helpful critic and commentator on other authors' work, an encouragement and a source of wisdom to many younger colleagues. He has combined these features with a great deal of wit and amusement, and I am sure Charles would not mind if I continue to quote from Boswell, who states, quite accurately I believe, that 'Though usually grave, and even awful in his deportment, he possessed uncommon and peculiar powers of wit and humour; he frequently indulged himself in colloquial pleasantry; and the heartiest merriment was enjoyed in his company.'

This volume and its companion are a testimony to the high regard and good will that exist among his fellow economists. Not every economist deserves a Festschrift upon retirement from academic life, since a Festschrift is a mark of distinction reserved for the outstanding academics of their generation. It is an indication that they have made a significant contribution to the development and understanding of their subject. The quality of the economist can be judged by the excellence of the contributions, and there is no doubt that this volume and its companion, that have arisen from a two-day conference held at the Bank of England on 15 and 16 November 2001, have a stellar quality about them. It was a delight to find that the Governor of the Bank of England, Sir Edward George, was able to make time in his diary to open the conference, despite its close proximity to the IMF–World Bank meetings the following weekend. His opening address summed up this point exactly when he said 'I hope the MPC – and the Bank staff who provide us with such wonderful support – will not misunderstand me when I say that I cannot remember ever before having had such a galaxy of academic economist and central banking superstars gathered together under one roof!' As the Governor went on to say 'that is just how it should be as we meet to pay tribute to Charles who has given such a huge amount to his twin professions throughout his working life'.

The comments of the contributors, discussants and members of the audience all confirmed this view. Those who attended the conference were given privileged access to some of the outstanding minds in the vast fields of monetary economics, central banking, financial regulation and exchange rate economics. In view of the outstanding quality of the contributions it was a high priority to make them available to the wider profession. For this reason the original conference papers have been drawn together into two volumes with the help of Edward Elgar, to ensure that they reach a broader group of professional economists, central bankers, academics and students of monetary economics.

It has been difficult to know how to divide up the contributions by the various authors into two volumes. All the chapters refer to subjects that have been major research topics in Charles's wide-ranging portfolio, and all are interconnected. It would have been possible to reorganise the chapters in many other ways, and no doubt there will be some who would wish that chapters on certain subjects had been put in the same volume. Indeed the order of the presentations in the conference was different from the order that the chapters now appear, but the timing of the chapters in the conference was driven by the diaries of many busy people. The printed volume is free from these constraints and we have sought to draw together the chapters that have the most in common with each other. All the chapters highlight the contribution that Charles has made to their field whilst also offering a contribution of their own in terms of a summary of current thinking and insights into the latest controversies. The benefit that this volume offers the reader is a summary of subjects from the full range of modern monetary economics. Hardly a single issue is omitted and all the topics blend the clarity of academic thinking with the practicalities of policy; whether that falls into the realm of central banking, financial regulation or international finance. We encourage the reader to read beyond his or her own interests and draw the full benefit from this collection of chapters by economists who are eminent in their field. It is to be hoped that the readers will appreciate them as much as those who heard the presentations at first hand.

The first volume contains contributions relating to monetary policy, central banks and financial regulation. The first chapter is by the Governor designate of the Bank of England responsible for Monetary Policy, Mervyn King, with the title 'No money, no inflation – the role of money in the economy'. King begins by showing that the onset of the Great Inflation came about because money was ignored by the economic establishment, and that the reduction of the high inflation was largely attributable to the fact that control of monetary aggregates was put at the centre of monetary policy in the late 1970s and early 1980s. The idea that central banks abandoned monetary aggregates in the mid-1980s is not the truth, however, since as the Governor of the Bank of Canada is quoted as saying 'we didn't abandon the monetary aggregates, they abandoned us'. More recently, King goes on to show the decline in interest in the role money plays in the economy despite the very strong correlation between money and the price level. According to King, the simplistic methodologies employed by some econometricians has not served to shed more light on this paradox. Over-simple models of the relationship between money and inflation can be criticised for their failure to specify the monetary transmission mechanism clearly, if at all. The solution, he argues, to understanding money and inflation does not lie in simplistic reduced forms, rather it lies in opening up a new line of enquiry in which monetary and portfolio theory are integrated. The bridging of the gap between the finance theorist and the monetary economist is a clear area where more work would be illuminating. King conjectures that (a) the fact that transactions costs are important in determining asset prices and (b) that money reduces transactions costs will be two pillars in the new literature that makes the breakthrough between finance and monetary economics. Potentially, this is a new line of research that could reintroduce money into monetary economics of central banking and could reassert that money does matter after all.

The second chapter is by the Deputy Governor of the Bank of Canada, Charles Freedman, who is particularly well placed to discuss the issue of his chapter, namely 'Central bank independence'. Freedman starts by introducing the canonical Kydland/Prescott model of time inconsistency and inflation bias using a social loss function defined as a weighted average of squared deviations of output and inflation from target levels. According to the model, the central bank does not choose a value of inflation equal to the target level because it lacks a precommitment technology in this framework. But Freedman criticises the model on several grounds. First, it cannot explain how or why we saw high inflation in the 1970s and is essentially 'ahistoric' since it assumes that inflation is endemic even though the experience of the 1950s and 1960s suggests otherwise. Second, the basic assumptions are not applicable in the central banking business and are disconnected from the reality of monetary policy-making. An example includes the assumption that the desired level of output is higher than the full employment level. This is crucial to the model, otherwise we still achieve the first-best solution where inflation is equal to its target even when we do not have a precommitment technology. But this is not the way that central banks operate and Freedman cites a number of prominent senior central bankers who disagree with the basic premises of the time inconsistency model. Helpfully Freedman offers some reasons that support central bank independence without relying on the time inconsistency framework. His arguments are built on three central tenets: that monetary policy involves lags in transmission, that there is considerable uncertainty in the decision-making process, and that monetary policy operates over long horizons – longer, that is, than those of most government horizons. Freedman quotes approvingly two papers by Alex Cukierman presented in recent working papers and conference proceedings that embed these very ideas. It remains to be seen whether these models will begin a shift away from the time inconsistency emphasis towards a more realistic view of the policy-making process in central banking. Ultimately it may offer more secure theoretical foundations for independent central banks.

The final chapter in this group is given by Benjamin M. Friedman of Harvard University entitled 'The use and meaning of words in central banking: inflation targeting, credibility and transparency'. Friedman begins by explaining the reasoning for targeting a nominal variable. Since long-run real outcomes depend on real factors such as preferences and technologies, only nominal values (prices) are dependent on monetary variables. Hence the authorities target nominal rather than real quantities. However, in any discussion on inflation targeting, it is quite possible for the public to conclude that monetary policy-makers have no concern for real outcomes such as output or employment. This is unfortunate since if the monetary authorities only care about inflation, and inflation moves from its target level due to some economic disturbance or policy error, then the authorities will try to bring inflation back to its target immediately, irrespective of the adverse effects such actions will have on real variables. Friedman argues that this is clearly not the case.

Friedman also discusses the related topics of policy transparency and credibility. A commitment to inflation targeting, he argues, achieves credibility 'by keeping out of the discussion those considerations that would reveal that commitment to be qualified', that is, by not even talking about 'real' factors there is little basis for outsiders to doubt the central bank's commitment to achieving its inflation target. In this way he demonstrates that the language of the debate controls first what is said and then what is thought. The use of inflation targeting language draws the central bank fraternity to consider price stability and inflation control, rather than real objectives, as their primary aim. This has certain advantages in defining the purpose of central banks. Friedman concludes by considering the opposing view, questioning whether policy-makers should act in such a way as to disguise their 'real' preferences. Although inflation targeting can achieve credibility and transparency of policy, it hides from the public the policy-makers' 'real' preferences and also fosters the belief that real outcomes are unimportant. This, Friedman argues, is not what monetary policy should be about.

The first discussant of this group of chapters is John S. Flemming, Warden of Wadham College, Oxford. When reviewing King's chapter, he suggests that one can only observe a correlation between money and prices but not (Granger) causality between the two. He argues that while money is driven by nominal income and interest rates, money itself drives nothing at all. The one concession to money, he argues, is that it may be among the choices available as a nominal anchor, which recent history has taught us we need. Flemming's reaction towards the main message of Charles Freedman and Ben Friedman is favorable. The time inconsistency model he regards as highly stylised and unrealistic, and he is prepared to take most of Freedman's reservations on board. Likewise, the verbal theme of Ben Friedman's paper is accepted, although the critique of inflation targeting is stronger than this discussant would be willing to support.

Stanley Fischer, formerly First Deputy Managing Director of the International Monetary Fund and now Vice-Chairman of Citigroup, offers comments on the same group of chapters. Assessing the critique of Charles Freedman, Fischer suggests that the summary of the great inflation tallies with his recollection of events and offers a convincing and rich description of the monetary policy problem. However, he argues that the Barro–Gordon model does what every good model should: it provides the essence of an important problem even if it omits some of the details. With Ben Friedman there is substantial agreement about the problems of conveying concern for inflation and the reality of the output–inflation trade-off in the short-to-medium run. Fischer concludes that it it not clear what should be done about this problem, but the compromises that have been made by prominent central banks seem to be sensible. The main point, he suggests, is that an inflation-targeting framework is the right one for central banks, and precision in this area is worthwhile even at the expense of obscuring the output–inflation trade-off to a degree. Taking Mervyn King's chapter last of all, Fischer agrees that monetary indicators still have a role to play, although the role of monetary aggregates as guides for policy-makers is receding fast. This, he argues, takes us a long way from the days of 1968 when Milton Friedman lectured the American Economic Association about the importance of monetary magnitudes and the dangers of interest rate rules. The crucial difference these days is that the interest rate is tied to an inflation target as the nominal anchor for monetary policy.

The next three chapters consider monetary policy issues relating to the theory of inflation targeting, the practice of central bank accountability and lastly an overview of monetary policy experience in the United States over the period 1987–2001. The first chapter considers 'The inflation forecast', and is written by Lars E.O. Svensson of Princeton University. He discusses the practical issues surrounding the idea of the monetary authorities targeting the inflation forecast and, in particular, the differences between his views and those of Goodhart. Svensson assumes that the authorities try to minimise some intertemporal loss function, a discounted sum of squared deviations of inflation from target and of the square of the output gap. In this context he argues that central banks behaving with discretion are not prone to 'over-ambitious output targets' exceeding potential output and hence the inflation bias problem arising from the Barro–Gordon framework and the Kydland and Prescott model does not emerge (a point made earlier in the volume by Charles Freedman and Ben Friedman). Svensson argues that the distinction raised by Lawrence Meyer between 'hierarchical' and 'dual' mandates for central bankers is mute in these circumstances and is a misunderstanding of flexible inflation targeting. The sticking point with Charles in the business of inflation forecasting in practice is whether a specific loss function should be specified and whether a constant or a time-varying interest rate forecast should be used. Goodhart has two arguments against a specific loss function based on the problem that it may 'abrogate the right to select its own (short-term) goals' and because he believes it to be difficult for the monetary authorities to agree on the functional form of the loss function, due to changing membership of the MPC over time for example. Svensson believes that the Bank of England Act 1998 is 'completely consistent' with an explicit statement on the loss function, which could be reviewed by the Chancellor in any case, and could be agreed between MPC members in the same way that forecasts and minutes are hammered out before publication. Svensson argues that a quadratic loss function has the great advantage of symmetry and simplicity since it amounts to the choice over a single parameter (the relative weight between inflation and output). Practical implementation of such a policy would involve the MPC staff generating feasible inflation and output gap paths and choosing the one that 'looks best', that is, one that returns inflation to target and output gap to zero in a 'reasonable' time frame, so minimising the intertemporal loss function. This will then generate an optimal targeting rule. Svensson therefore suggests that a time-varying interest rate path could and should be implemented, as opposed to Goodhart who believes there to be no better alternative to a fixed interest rate rule due to the difficulties of implementing such a time-varying policy.

The second chapter, given by Adam S. Posen of the Institute of International Affairs, Washington, DC, offers 'Six practical views of central bank transparency'. As the title suggests the chapter takes central bank transparency from a practical perspective rather than from a theoretical point of view. Posen argues that transparency has 'gone from being highly controversial to motherhood and apple pie (or knighthood and fish and chips for a British audience)'. But the concept of transparency is varied and what transparency actually means is still a matter open to debate. Like Charles Freedman, Posen argues that the monetary framework based on central bank types, time inconsistency and credibility sheds little light on the practicalities of transparency for 'real world' central banks. Transparency, as this chapter shows, has much to do with real issues such as inflation persistence, financial market responses to central bank announcements, and influence over private sector expectations more generally. To bridge this gap, Posen puts six views on central bank transparency, ranging from the 'reassuring' view where communication of monetary policy can allow a central bank to be more flexible when responding to economic shocks since the public know what the authorities are doing, to the 'irrelevancy' view of transparency, which suggests that talk is cheap and only actions matter. An announcement, rather than actual implementation, of a policy change should have little effect in the latter case. Posen concludes with some bold policy recommendations that are sure to generate interest and comments from the academic, policy framing and central bank communities. These are that two claims can be eliminated from the literature: first, that transparency inhibits central bank independence and second, that transparency provides sufficient accountability for central banks to be justifiable in democratic countries. He argues that accountability and transparency should increase and central banks with control over their goals (goal independence) should not continue to have this privilege.

Marvin Goodfriend, Senior Vice President of the Federal Reserve Bank of Richmond, makes a practical assessment of monetary policy by discussing 'The phases of US monetary policy: 1987–2001'. Goodfriend chronicles US monetary policy into six episodes on the basis of the policy problem facing the Fed in each period. The six periods fall into phase 1: the October 1987 stock market crash to the outbreak of the Gulf War; phase 2: the 1990–91 recession, recovery and fall of inflation; phase 3: the approach of the Fed to tackle inflation pre-emptively; phase 4: the 'Goldilocks' period of seemingly unending boom; phase 5: the tightening of policy to rein in growth; and phase 6: the recession and post-September 11 slowdown. With the exception of the very beginning, the six phases reflect the Greenspan era, an unprecedented episode of successful monetary management.

Goodfriend has a tough task to document the very varied experiences of the six periods, but the resulting overview is admirable. Of particular note was the period of rising interest rates (1994–95) during the economic expansion, for which the Fed received much criticism. However Goodfriend argues that this was a textbook example of pre-emptive monetary policy. Following 1995 the Fed was learning to cope with having achieved credibility for maintaining low inflation. This slow learning process, together with the high productivity growth at the time, which necessitated high real interest rates, resulted in insufficient monetary tightening and laid the foundation for the boom of the late 1990s. Goodfriend concludes by considering the current economic situation, suggesting two possible scenarios. First, the downturn could last a lot longer (previous unemployment increases have always been accompanied by further rises and there is little leeway for further monetary easing). Second, the recession may not be as deep as some commentators make out, partly because of the pre-emptive action already undertaken and also because this recession, unlike those seen previously, was not caused by the Fed trying to achieve low inflation. On this point the Fed has already achieved credibility.

When discussing Goodfriend's chapter Charles Bean, Chief Economist at the Bank of England, concentrates on the Fed's achievement in obtaining credibility for low inflation. He argued that it is important for monetary policy not to be 'too successful' as that would lead the public to believe monetary policy to have no real effects. (Perfectly stable output associated with changing monetary variables). With respect to Svensson's chapter, Bean argues that the choice of the relative weight of activity to inflation in the central bank's loss function ought to be a matter for the Chancellor of the Exchequer rather than the Monetary Policy Committee, although there are difficulties in framing an algebraic term with the precision required by economists into a legislative document. After rehearsing the arguments against constant interest rate projections Bean agrees with the conclusion offered by Svensson that there should be a time-varying forecast. But he also argues that a simple forecast has value as a teaching aid and an explanatory tool for the public. This may be right but in many respects this returns to the theme of Ben Friedman's chapter that points out that while simplicity avoids confusion, it can also over-simplify, despite repeated caveats and qualifications. The logical conclusion he draws is that both should be published and discussed as they are at present. The chapter by Adam Posen picks up on this point, since it considers the extent of disclosure of information. While Bean does not offer unqualified support for any of the six views of central bank transparency he does eliminate some as unconvincing. He also offers a practitioner's view of the pros and cons of each, the value of which is that we are able to see the issues that are relevant among the remaining feasible options.

Edward Nelson of the Monetary Policy Unit of the Bank of England follows up Marvin Goodfriend's analysis of the phases of US monetary policy with a corresponding analysis from the perspective of interest rate rules for the UK. The chapter illustrates that once again Charles Goodhart was a vital contributor to the development of a new research field, which in this case was the literature on policy reaction functions with the short-term nominal interest rate as the instrument. The focus of the chapter is primarily empirical and it splits the sample period 1970–2001 into distinct monetary regimes and then estimates interest rate reaction functions for each regime. These are then compared with the Taylor rule. The approach differs from the usual route which estimates the Taylor rule for the full sample and compares the actual interest rate to the one that would have been in force if a Taylor rule had been used to set monetary policy. Nelson shows that the 'Taylor principle', namely the objective of dealing aggressively with inflation whilst maintaining a concern for output in relation to its capacity, appeared to apply only in the inflation targeting period (1992–97). This finding confirms the evidence reported for other countries, which have also conformed to the 'Taylor principle' during the inflation targeting episode.

The discussion is provided by Paul Mizen of the University of Nottingham, who appreciates the approach that distinguishes policy regimes and estimates reaction functions separately for each sub-sample. It is pointed out that the advantages of regime-specific reaction functions need to be weighed against the disadvantages in that the sample periods are often short, requiring the use of monthly rather than quarterly data. Taylor rules at high frequencies exhibit greater instability in the coefficient estimates. Paul Mizen argues that Taylor rules are good *ex post* summaries of central bank reaction functions but not good *ex ante* guides for monetary policymakers.

Charles Goodhart is probably best known by non-monetary economists for Goodhart's Law. In the chapter by Alec Chrystal of City University Business School and Paul Mizen of the University of Nottingham, an account is given of 'Goodhart's Law: its origins, meaning and implications for monetary policy'. Chrystal and Mizen first summarise what Goodhart's law is and especially dwell on its connection and differences from the Lucas

Critique. They dispel some of the myths that have emerged surrounding the definition and its application to monetary policy by discussing a number of historical applications of Goodhart's Law, starting from its origins in competition and credit control policy, known affectionately as 'the Corset' in the 1970s. They go on to show that it is equally applicable to monetary targeting, and interest rate targeting, or any mechanistic rule based on a 'statistical regularity'. It is its application to monetary economics that is probably the distinguishing feature of Goodhart's Law with respect to the Lucas Critique.

In his discussion Charles Goodhart reminisces about the development of events in the 1970s, when the Bank introduced competition and credit control at the Prime Minister's request. It fell to him to devise a sufficiently complicated form of regulation to contain monetary growth without raising interest rates, and to do this without appearing to reimpose the restrictions on the credit market that had been removed very publicly shortly beforehand. It was in this period that Goodhart's Law emerged as an observation on the practice of monetary policy, at a conference hosted by the Reserve Bank of Australia in 1975, although it was in the later period of monetary targeting that it received greater prominence. Charles notes that the distinctive feature of the Law is that it applies to the public sector as well as to the private sector response to changing economic conditions. The Lucas Critique is essentially an observation about private sector behaviour.

The next chapter shifts into pure monetary theory. Nobuhiro Kiyotaki of the London School of Economics and John Moore of Edinburgh University and the London School of Economics presented 'A cost of unified currency'. At the conference, we were told by Nobu in delightfully humble terms that, in a joint course taught by Kiyotaki and Goodhart at the LSE, the students often asked questions to which Charles seemed to have ready answers but Nobu was left asking 'do I know the answer?' The topic of this chapter arose from just such a question, which cuts to the heart of a current academic debate. The question is: 'Is a unified currency always better than having separate national currencies?' There are many types of goods and people in their model, and money exists to overcome the double coincidence of wants. People meet randomly and trade using money, often accepting it not for its own sake but as an intermediary between selling and buying goods. These same people have a choice over whether to produce a local good or a generic good, which is acceptable internationally. It turns out that this choice generates different conclusions from the previous literature. Kiyotaki and Moore present a theoretical framework showing how a switch from national currencies to a unique currency can lead to a welfare loss. The intuition underlying the analysis is that the introduction of a single international currency can spur the diffusion of international consumption goods whose utility is lower than that of domestic goods. The authors show that, if the utility of the international good is neither too high nor too low, the unique currency will circulate in equilibrium and the diffusion of the international good will generate a welfare loss.

The discussant, Sudipto Bhattacharya, from Arizona State University and the London School of Economics, praises the clarity of the chapter and the intuition behind it. He points out that models of trading processes with frictions, useful as they are, ought to be subjected to robustness tests in order that the generality of their conclusions can be ascertained. The chapter that is presented by Kiyotaki and Moore offers just such an analysis of these models where there is some *ex ante* heterogeneity in the tastes and endowments of the participating agents. In his discussion of the Kiyotaki–Moore contribution Bhattacharya has some robustness tests of his own. He shows that the argument that a specialised outcome, where each country produces a product for its own market, is not a Nash equilibrium with a single currency, can be subjected to changes in the frequency with which a seller might meet foreigners from the other country. This argument is given 'flavour' by use of an illustration involving Marmite sellers from Britain and goat-cheese spread sellers from Norway! Bhattacharya produces a model in which he can contradict the critical assumptions of the Kiyotaki–Moore model and demonstrate the Pareto dominance of specialised production even under a single currency. In other words there is no welfare loss from a single currency. Last of all, Battacharya suggests three avenues for future research which introduce (i) agents with convex preferences over local and generic goods; (ii) costs of currency exchange due to bid-ask spreads; and (iii) meeting patterns that vary according to the gains from trade.

The final chapter in this volume is provided by Martin Shubik of Yale University. The topic is a general one, and deals with questions that are necessarily hard to answer. Two of the central questions are 'What are the basic distinctions between money, near-money and money substitutes?' and 'What role do information and networks play in monetary theory?' These require a detailed examination of the features and properties of assets along a spectrum and the properties of information networks are considered in detail. In this regard a great deal of statistical information is provided to identify networks and structures in terms of ratios between firms, government, households and the financial sector. From these characteristics Shubik extracts features of a credit economy and offers some models of the networks behind them. It is shown that a perfect world, like Thomas More's Utopia or the Arrow–Debreu model, in which all information is known and shared such that there is perfect trust, eliminates the properties that create the need for networks and credit. Each individual is observed sufficiently well to be able to issue his or her own money without resorting to any other money-issuing authority, so that everyone becomes their own banker. It is when we have imperfections in information and other frictions that different levels of trust and enforcement against default are necessary.

Anne Sibert of Birkbeck College offers an appraisal of the chapter. Her discussion affirms that much of what is said is interesting and useful providing 'a storehouse of ingredients for concocting theoretical and empirical models of financial networks'. These are useful for the analysis of a number of new developments, such as e-money, that have implications for technological and regulatory control. Where Sibert disagrees with Shubik is over the notion that all money is credit. The argument is made, citing the recent literature extensively, that the ultimate feature of fiat money is that the issuer does not offer to convert it to anything else. In this sense money is special and different from other types of near-money and credit, and the analysis of the phenomenon of networks and information, while useful for the latter, may not be so useful for the former.

A Central Bank economist

Charles Goodhart[1]

1. INTRODUCTION

I doubt whether I rank as an 'eminent economist'. I have become a leading figure in a limited number of special areas, notably central banking and monetary policy and, later on in my career, the microstructure of the foreign exchange market; but I have added little, or nothing, to the body of accepted theory, and my role as policy adviser, though frequently exciting and fulfilling, has mostly been at too junior a level to count as eminent. Nevertheless vanity affects us all; having been asked to contribute to the series on distinguished economists arranged by the Banca Nazionale del Lavoro, and published in their *Quarterly Review*, and thereby become a member of the elect, who am I to refuse on grounds of unworthiness?

I should, nevertheless, like to use my experiences in the four main phases of my career: learning at Cambridge(s), 1958–65; policy advice at the Bank of England, 1968–85; teaching at the London School of Economics, 1966–68 and 1985–2002; and membership of the Monetary Policy Committee, 1997–2000, as a springboard for discussing some ongoing issues in economics, to wit the treatment of expectations, the use and role of economists in the City, the analysis of markets, central bank autonomy, the process of decision-making in (Monetary Policy) Committees, and finally financial regulation.

2. BIOGRAPHY (1936–58)

I probably come from a more privileged background than any previous contributor. My paternal grandmother was a Lehman, of the great New York Lehman family.[2] Besides the bankers and the bank, that family had the distinction of providing simultaneously one of the most famous Governors and Senators from New York (Herbert) and its Chief Justice (Irving). My paternal grandfather was a senior stockbroker on the New York Stock Exchange.

My father, Arthur Lehman Goodhart,[3] was sent by his parents to Trinity College, Cambridge, to study economics in 1912. At that time there were no economists at Trinity, and – as my father told it – he was advised *not* to go next door to Kings College to study under the young Keynes because his advisers at Trinity doubted whether Keynes was quite 'sound'. Anyhow, he turned instead to the study of law with a young Trinity don called Harry Hollond, and that was the start of his life-long academic career as a lawyer, specialising in Jurisprudence.

My father returned to New York in 1914 to practise and then, after a spell in the Artillery in World War I and a more important period as a junior legal adviser in the US commission to Poland (1919) to investigate ethnic, essentially anti-semitic, problems there, which became the basis of his first book,[4] he returned to Cambridge on a more permanent basis becoming a law don himself at Corpus Christi College, Cambridge. From there, he moved his family to Oxford, where he had become Professor of Jurisprudence, in 1936 (the year of my birth), and became Master of University College, 1951–63.

Although my father's American family is Jewish, many were not by that time strictly observant, and my father was not a religious believer. While at Cambridge he married an English girl, Cecily Carter, daughter of a Birmingham accountant, who was a staunch member of the Church of England, and brought up her three sons as such.

The Anglo-American theme was reinforced in World War II. As an outspoken opponent of Nazism, my father was on the Nazi black-list. With many close New York relatives, my two elder brothers and I were evacuated to the USA, my brother William (aged 6) and me (aged 2) under the command of a Norland Nanny, since my parents remained in Oxford. My mother had to be pointed out to me on the boat-train platform when we returned after the war was over.

Since American primary schools then taught no Latin, a major requirement for entry into British public (that is, private fee-charging) schools, little French, and the 'wrong' history, my brother was scholastically several years 'behind' his English contemporaries (though in fact intellectually brilliant). Anyhow the only (fee-paying) British preparatory school that would accept him was the St Leonards branch of the (Oxford) Summerfields School, intended for those intellectually too weak to go to the main Oxford school. I was given the choice of staying at home with my parents as a day boy at an (excellent) Oxford school, or accompanying my brother to the boarding school; since he was the only constant in an otherwise kaleidoscope world, I chose to go with him.

Intellectually challenged or not, it was a lovely place, but in its sixty years of existence it had had but two scholarships to any school, and although there was some thought given to trying to prepare me to sit a scholarship exam, when the time came I was too far behind.

My father, despite his academic career, was a worldly man, comfortable with, and interested in maintaining, the power to influence events. He wished to pass that on to his children. So, he put us all down for Eton, the dominant English public school. If you did not obtain a scholarship to College (as a King's Scholar, KS), you had to be accepted by an ordinary House Master (as an Oppidan). Owing to the War, my father had been late in putting us on the list. The only reason that I was accepted was that I was then good at cricket, and the prospective house master (Whitfield) wanted above all to win the house cricket cup. Alas, my eyesight then deteriorated rapidly, and I could not see fast bowling!

Whitfield's house was far from an academic milieu. One was encouraged to avoid being 'too clever by half', a serious failing in Oppidan eyes. Nevertheless the teaching was excellent, and the streaming by ability meant that we were always stretched academically. However, the English education system specialises far too early, and I concentrated on history (plus languages) from the age of 16, giving up all the natural sciences and maths, before I had even started calculus!

As in many other fields of English life, Eton has been a major source of leading figures in Economics (though no economics was taught there before the 1970s). Keynes and Dennis Robertson were both Etonians (KS), and in my own generation Richard Layard (KS) and Nick Dimsdale have made a mark. Someone should do a note on the contribution of Etonian economists.

When I went up to Cambridge in October 1957, after two years' compulsory military National Service,[5] I put myself down to read Economics. This was not because I wanted to become an economist then; instead it was part of my father's grand design for his three sons. My eldest brother, Sir Philip Goodhart, Conservative Member of Parliament, Beckenham (1957–92), was already embarking on a political career; my elder brother, William Goodhart, QC (now Lord Goodhart), was the cleverest of us three; my father saw him as a worthy successor to his own work in the (academic) legal field. But academics and politicians do not earn much money. My father had me typed to go into finance, probably as an investment banker, probably in New York, in the footsteps of many other members of my extended New York family: Altschuls, Lehmans, Loebs, Morgenthaus, and so on.

I did not work very hard in my first year at Cambridge, and expected to get a moderately good exam class. To my astonishment, and delight, I got a First. That changed my life completely. I had never been top of anything before (except the Summerfields, St Leonards School, which does not really count). Now I had found something which I could do. Moreover, economics was fun and a challenge because it seemed so unsure of itself (so bad). Despite the formal models, no one really knew, or knows now, what determines the level, or rate of growth, of most of the key economic variables. In all my previous education there had been one correct pronunciation, one correct date, one proper proof; and the main exercise all too often was just to learn how to regurgitate that. To find a subject wherein one's teachers admitted that there were several possible answers, and that *none* of those yet developed might be correct was profoundly liberating. I believed as a result that I might be able to contribute, *and* to do so in a socially worthwhile manner.

Despite the particularities of my earlier experiences, a comparison of these with those of other previous contributors reveals some common threads. First, there are my Jewish connections; why have Jews been so clearly predisposed to Economics? This strikes me as a stylised fact, but one which most commentators purposefully overlook. Second (perhaps related also to Jewishness?), is my feeling of *not belonging* to any group/religion/country in depth, but sharing a broad international (but essentially Atlantic) culture in general. Third, there is the common tendency to come to Economics from an outside specialisation, there being two main streams, the first from Maths and Physics, the second from History, together with the other Social Sciences and Humanities. The interaction between these two separate strands provides most of the personal creative tensions in the subject. Maths, without understanding of the institutional/social/political background, will just lead to empty formalism. Historical and institutional knowledge, without a hard theoretical core, will be wordy, vague and often wrong. I have always known that I needed more Maths to become a really good, rounded economist, but time was always too short, my aptitude too slight, and too many other fascinating exercises to work on to undertake the necessary investment.

3. THE CAMBRIDGES, 1957–65

The Cambridge (UK) economics faculty was dominated during these years by the triad of Kaldor, Kahn and Joan Robinson. Kahn seemed a reclusive, and somewhat sinister, figure (to me at least), who never lectured and had little contact with undergraduates, but who was supposed to be the *eminence grise* maintaining doctrinal purity. Joan Robinson was in her Chinese period, and the contrast between the fantastically beautiful silk robes, reputedly given to her by Mao personally, in which she lectured, and her yellowing teeth was remarkable. She was ferocious and strident in debate, but *much* more so with other academics, especially with the neo-classicals, than with undergraduates; if we were obviously making an effort, Joan would be really quite kindly to us (though I am glad that she was never my own supervisor). Nicky Kaldor was far the most approachable, and in my view the best economist of the three. He had a fount of original ideas (of admittedly varying quality), with enormous enthusiasm for all of them, and for economics in general. Nicky used to doze (feign sleep?) during seminars, and then come alive with a sharp, and usually apposite, interjection.

The ideological front maintained by these three dominated Cambridge; Piero Sraffa was a charming, but largely invisible,[6] figure in the Marshall Library; Austin Robinson appeared a minor, self-effacing attachment; James Meade was yet to be invited to come, and Dennis Robertson had just retired; though the dominant triad managed successfully to marginalise any serious competitive challenge from these latter two. Dennis invited me to tea, with his cats. I still remember my embarrassment when I immaturely suggested that his exchanges with Keynes over the *General Theory* must have been stimulating, and saw the expression of pain in his face.

The best lecturers, however, were the younger economists, and Cambridge had another trio of these, Michael Farrell, Frank Hahn and Robin Matthews. Of these, Robin Matthews gave the clearest lectures; Frank Hahn was the most technically advanced; but it was Michael Farrell who struck me as the most original. His early death was a great loss. Of course, Cambridge had a much larger faculty with experts in many other fields, for example Robin Marris in Industrial Economics; and Dick Goodwin on Trade Cycles (though no-one, after Dennis Robertson, was really much good in monetary economics). At that time economic history formed an integral part of the tripos, and was generally taught exceedingly well.[7] By contrast, the statistics course was elementary and rudimentary; there was nothing recognizable as econometrics; any mathematics for economists or mathematical economics was just optional, and an option that few, and not me, took.

In any case lectures did not form the main basis for education at Cambridge; the lecture course/class system was unknown. The lecturers often did not set the exams. Many, probably most, lectures were poorly attended, the more so as the term went on.[8]

Instead the main form of instruction was via tutorials. This is enormously labour-intensive, representing a one-on-one, or a one-on-two, hourly meeting between tutor and undergraduate, at which the undergraduate reads out his essay and the tutor then comments. Sometimes the tutor would have read it in advance, and sometimes not. It is almost certainly too labour-intensive to endure. Nevertheless at the time the selection, associated reading and writing of the weekly essay formed the main work of the term. Tutors mostly came from the College at which you were. My first two tutors were, therefore, Trinity economists, Robert Neild and Maurice

Dobb. Dobb was supposed to be a communist, but he was useless as a tutor, since he refused to criticise, take up any position and would barely even comment. He seemed rather a retired gentleman than a communist economist.[9] My best tutor, by far, was not from Trinity, but Michael Posner (from Pembroke College). Michael would often profess to know less about an essay subject than you, but would then, apparently guilelessly, slip in a couple of apparently 'simple-man' questions that would make one have to reconsider the whole subject from a new light.

In my final year, I was paired in tutorial with a student who had just moved over into economics from pure Mathematics. His name was Jim Mirrlees. Jim and I got on well together, though our approaches and aptitudes were quite different. I recall being rather put out that our tutor in that year, David Champernowne, clearly preferred Mirrlees, despite his slight background then in Economics and my two prior Firsts. Subsequent events demonstrated the acuity of Champernowne's preferences, with Sir James receiving the Nobel Prize in 1997.

The main figures in the faculty also ran an evening seminar for undergraduates who had done best in the first (and second) year economics exam, usually about 12–15 undergraduates. Those asked to join in their second year would deliver a paper to this seminar in their third year. The other undergraduates would draw lots, with the lottery determining the order in which you *had* to comment on the prior paper, if you drew a number at all. Faculty members attended, often in surprising numbers, but kept any brief comments right until the end.

While I have now forgotten the essay which won part share of the Adam Smith essay prize, I remember my paper to the Marshall Society rather well. It was a rendition of Shackle's theory[10] of how agents approached the uncertain future, with the potential surprise function, three-dimensional graph (made by me out of multi-coloured plasticine), et al.

Shackle claimed that people would in practice concentrate their attention on a single focus gain (or focus loss) that might result from a decision, where the focus (gain/loss) was a function of the potential surprise of the outcome together with the intensity of anticipation of that outcome. Where the two variables interactively reach their maximum is the focus (loss/gain); people would then compare the focus gain with the focus loss and come to a decision. When the outcome is on an either/or basis (for example I will either catch new-style CJD from eating beef, or I will not: either my next plane trip will end in disaster, or it will not), this kind of approach still seems reasonable. Indeed, outcomes with intensely felt anticipations (as in the examples above) frequently induce much stronger behavioural reactions (airports became almost deserted after the Lockerbie disaster), than rational probability analysis would have suggested made any sense (after the

BSE/CJD scare, beef consumption fell as sharply in Germany, where no cases of BSE had occurred, as in the UK!).

This approach, of trying to simplify the decision-making process to a comparison of two focus values, is less appropriate when the outcome can take a continuum of values, as is the case with most economic variables, for example prices and quantities. But, even so, Shackle would argue that the exercise of trying to build up an expected probability distribution would be excessively time-consuming (and thus not utility-maximising), especially when we are still uncertain of what confidence we can attach to our subjective probability distribution. There is an infinite regress of what probability we can attach to the probability we have attributed to an outcome.

As in the Grossman/Stiglitz paradox, shortage of time and the costs of acquiring information make it rational to stop short of trying to incorporate all available information into our expectations' formation process. The simplest, and most obvious, way of economising on time and effort is to try to learn (for example about probabilities, about outcomes, about models, and so on) from others who may possess more, or better, information than oneself. The 'representative agent' paradigm may make computation and analysis easier, but is patently invalid for any analysis where expectations are important. While we do learn from our own, and others', mistakes, we learn much more from the arguments, ideas and behaviour of other people.

Given that people are heterogeneous and fallible, and that everyone is always learning, both from events and from everyone else, the concept that 'everyone' knows the true model of the world is ridiculous; no one knows the 'true' model. Even the logically more seductive idea that one should assume model-consistent expectations, that is, that in setting out a model one should assume that all the agents will behave as if that particular model were correct, is not only false in reality, but is also likely to lead to an underestimate of the extent to which learning by observation of others is likely to lead to 'herding' in behavioural response and, apparently irrational, sudden shifts in market behaviour, and so on.

Whereas the minimalist form of rational expectations, that is, that people will not persist indefinitely in making systematic errors, is mostly correct (you cannot fool all the people all the time), the more ambitious extensions of that theoretical approach, whether expressed in terms of the extent of information assimilated, or of common knowledge of a 'true' model, go too far. A preferable approach would be one stressing bounded, or near, rationality in a static context, and learning processes (in a world itself subject to change), in a dynamic context. There is still much to be done to improve our understanding and analysis in this field. Shackle will, I expect, go down in the history of economic thought as an idiosyncratic pioneer; his work was stimulating and enjoyable for a young but enthusiastic undergraduate.

It took me about thirty years before I stopped having nightmares about sitting exams, and the (self-induced) pressure of Finals was severe, but I got my First Class result – though not the starred First for which I had hoped; and then I turned to the US for the graduate training that a professional academic needs. At that time (1960), there was none to be had in the UK. It had been thought that a well-trained undergraduate could move directly into research. But since undergraduate courses in economics then included only relatively low-level, and optional, courses in maths and econometrics, this meant that entrants into economic academia in the UK would only carry with them the technical aptitudes learnt earlier and on other courses; and I had none.

I chose to go to Harvard. The subject on which I wanted to do research was trade cycles. There was an inconsistency between the *models* of such cycles, which predicted lengthy periods of slump/stagnation as excess capital slowly got worked off and brief booms – checked by capacity ceilings – and *real* economic experience, which was that slumps were much shorter than booms (usually). In particular I wanted to work with James Duesenberry, whose work on macroeconomic subjects, notably on the consumption function, was exciting.

But first I had, and wanted, to do course work on maths and econometrics. The maths mostly involved difference equations, but not calculus, and attempts to teach myself calculus (on the boat trip over to the USA – to the annoyance of my newly-married wife, who complained of being left alone – and subsequently in a maths class at Harvard), proved largely unavailing. The econometrics course was more comprehensive, taking us nearer to the professional front-line. At that time the print-outs from the latest IBM were done by a typewriter on top of the mainframe, whose striking arms moved by electronic command; it really looked like the ghost in the machine.

Most of the other courses, however, covered ground already taught at undergraduate level in Cambridge, UK, since economic majors at US universities had far less exposure to courses on economics than economic specialists at Cambridge.[11] Anyhow the thought of doing another two years of repetitive material was deeply depressing, and the Chairman of the Faculty, Arthur Smithies, allowed me to telescope the normal two-years Masters into one, which I managed to do.

Research started the next autumn – after the only long vacation my wife and I have ever had, touring most of the coastlines of North America – and was enormous fun. There was an initial glitch. I had intended to try to explore why the US economy had rebounded so sharply after the 1907 collapse, but had failed to do so in 1929. But to do that exercise properly, higher frequency national income data (quarterly and monthly) were needed, and these were not available for the 1906–09 episode, which was my starting point. Instead there was a copious wealth of high frequency (for instance call report) data on money and banking. The question of the interaction between regular seasonal financial fluctuations (in a banking system without a Central Bank) on the one hand, and cyclical and other shocks on the other, was quite intricate and central to the history of the 1907 crisis.[12] Moreover, prior studies had, I believed, got much of that analysis wrong. Everything went swimmingly. My PhD thesis (1962) was completed within the year, by June 1962; and a Harvard Economic Study book (1969) and a *JPE* article (1965) followed shortly thereafter.

While young married life in Cambridge, Mass., was delightful, and I had had dual nationality (US/UK) until army national service had forced a choice (in 1955), I had become essentially English over time, and my wife was even more so. So in 1962 we returned to Cambridge, UK, to a Prize Fellowship at Trinity College and an Assistant Lectureship in the Faculty. Having successfully (to my own satisfaction) reinterpreted US (1900–14) monetary history, using a high frequency data base, the obvious continuation was to try the same trick for the UK. Monthly banking data were also available (though heavily window-dressed in some respects) in the form of the monthly reports of the London Joint Stock Banks, which the Chancellor of the Exchequer, Goschen, had required to be collected and published, following the first Baring crisis in 1890. The problem was that no one had previously systematically collected, checked, and analysed these. So the better part of two years (1963–64) was then taken up with primary historical research, collecting, checking and assembling as much monthly banking and macroeconomic data as existed into usable time series format. This was a tedious chore. With these data published in *The Business of Banking, 1891–1914* (1972), nobody should ever need to repeat that exercise.

In the early 1960s the Cambridge faculty was embroiled, with the dominant US mainstream, on questions over the measurement and definition of capital (for example the re-switching issue), and on growth theory (see Harcourt, 1972). Bob Solow visited on sabbatical, and he and Joan Robinson used to go at it hammer and tongs. Although intellectually intriguing at the outset, through constant repetition of the arguments, the debate became (to my eyes) both strident and sterile; I have cordially disliked and distrusted growth theory ever since.

But while I quietly kept out of the main academic squabbles in Cambridge, I found it more difficult to avoid administrative duties. Traditionally the Secretary of the Faculty was a post taken for two years by a junior faculty member. It was (is) a hideous job. The faculty chairman, Ken Berrill, led me to believe that my chances of tenure depended on taking it, and in a weak moment I agreed. When I realised that I had sacrificed two years of decent academic work to faculty administration (and in Cambridge!), I sought the first good job outside.

In 1964 an incoming Labour Government (after 13 years of Conservative misrule, so the slogan went) was keen to introduce indicative planning (French style) in order to try to speed up the (comparatively low) UK growth rate. They set up a new Ministry, the Department of Economic Affairs, under George Brown, with Sir Donald MacDougall as Chief Economist, to promote that; though its relationship with the Treasury, which continued to wield all the levers of demand management, was never clear. Anyhow they needed economists, and working in the DEA, albeit not in my own area of research, was preferable to being an administrator at Cambridge.

The 'National Plan' in the event turned out to be a non-starter, because there was a black hole where the balance of payments was supposed to be, and the Labour Government was neither prepared to countenance devaluation (until later in 1967), as almost all its senior economic advisers advised (in private), nor to retreat to a siege economy with quotas on imports, and so on, as some of the Left advocated. Instead it fumbled along from crisis to crisis, as beautifully described in Cairncross (1996). That was hardly conducive to planning.

Fortunately I was not involved in the wider, macroeconomic policy discussion. Instead, the plans, for example for future growth, of each of the main sectors needed to be made consistent with the overall Plan target growth rate (4 per cent). So the DEA needed economists who would assess sectoral/industrial plans/forecasts/objectives for such consistency. I worked under John Jukes, a sensible economist and nice man, on the Energy sector, where a White Paper was under preparation, and on Housing and Construction. This was quite interesting, but not enormously intellectually demanding, and with the DEA and the National Plan clearly heading for the rocks, it was time to return to monetary economics.

After Dennis Robertson retired, monetary economics was not a leading field at Cambridge. By contrast the London School of Economics had made monetary economics a specialty. In the more institutional/historical wing, there were Richard Sayers (a key figure in the 1959 Radcliffe Report), Leslie Pressnell and Roger Alford; while on the analytical/theoretical wing, Alan Walters had passed through, being followed by Harry Johnson (holding a joint Chicago/LSE chair), plus there were several lively younger monetary economists (Morris Perlman and Laurence Harris). Harry's weekly seminar was *the* key feature of LSE. So I was happy to go there as a lecturer (in 1966), and pick up the traces of my monetary research. This involved trying to complete the work on the pre-1914 UK banking system (though I had to bring work on the operation of the gold standard to a premature end in 1968 when I moved to the Bank of England), together with several other (new) research exercises, of which two stand out. The first was a study on current monetary policy in the UK, commissioned by Holbik of FRB Boston for a comparative study of *Monetary Policy in Twelve Industrial Countries*. This was completed in 1967, but Holbik was so inefficient at putting pressure on co-authors that it was not published till 1973, by which time a 'postscript' was, to my annoyance, required. For the second, I did, I believe, the first serious empirical article in the field of 'political economy' regressing political popularity, as measured by Gallup poll data, on a series of macroeconomic (for example inflation and unemployment) and political cycle variables (in *Political Studies*, 1970).

By comparison with the spacious and gracious living conditions at Cambridge, LSE was (and remains) an inner-city slum – though the inhabitants have a vibrant intellectual life. In 1968 conditions at LSE worsened sharply, as the students there became infected with the contagious epidemic of revolt that had spread from Berkeley, via Paris, to LSE. In the winter term of 1968 the atmosphere at LSE was hysterically febrile, and unconducive to any form of civilised academic activity. So I was glad to get a call from the Bank of England to join them for a two-year temporary secondment.

4. THE BANK OF ENGLAND AND THE FORMATION OF MONETARY POLICY

4.1 The Battle of Ideas: Monetarists and Keynesians

The Bank had begun a policy of inviting young monetary economists to come into the Bank on a two-year secondment, one at a time, earlier in the 1960s. Roger Alford, Tony Cramp and Brian Reading had been my immediate predecessors when I arrived there. When I became installed, I discovered that I was effectively the only person there reasonably expert on the latest developments in monetary theory, especially what the Monetarists (led by Milton Friedman) were arguing.

The Bank had earlier recruited two economists with some background in monetary economics, Kit McMahon, whose specialty was in international monetary economics, and John Fforde, who had written a book on the history and workings of the Fed (Fforde, 1954), but these now had senior positions, on the international and domestic monetary policy side respectively, and did not have the time (or perhaps the inclination) to go into the minutiae of the academic debate. The executive director responsible for economics in the Bank was Maurice Allen, who was sharp but, by then, quirky, and while his experience of, and feel for, monetary affairs was excellent, his formal training had been many decades earlier. Meanwhile the head of the Economic Intelligence Department, Michael Thornton, was a man of great charm and ability, but not a professional economist, and his chief economist, Leslie Dicks-Mireaux, had been a general macro and labour market specialist.

Readers may think it odd, as I did, that the Bank then had no resident expert in monetary theory, but it was somewhat symptomatic of attitudes in the Bank at that time. Economists in the Bank were generally content with, and supportive of, the Keynesian economic analysis as outlined in the Radcliffe Report. The crucial requirement for domestic stability was, they believed, an appropriate fiscal policy, perhaps supported at times of crisis by an incomes policy of some kind. Without good fiscal policy, monetary policy by itself (at least within the bounds of practical politics), so it was argued, would be unable to stem the tide; variations in interest rates could be used for a time to counter speculation and to protect the balance of payments, but the essential requirement was to use fiscal policy to keep the economy in balance. The paper on 'The operation of monetary policy since the Radcliffe Report' (Bank of England, 1969a), largely the work of Kit McMahon, provides a very fair picture of attitudes at that time.[13] Sometimes it felt as if the Bank considered its (private) advice to the Chancellor on fiscal policies to be its main input into macro policy.[14]

But the Radcliffe/Keynesian view of the role and functions of monetary policy was under threat and attack from the moment that I had arrived. The devaluation of 1967, so long resisted by the Government, did not seem, in 1968, to be working successfully to improve the trade balance. Speculation against sterling restarted, and the IMF were called in for support. Under the influence of Jacques Polak and Marcus Flemming they had developed an international monetarist approach, and they attributed our problems in the UK in part to an unduly lax monetary stance.

Their (IMF) approach to a country in balance of payments difficulties was then broadly as follows. Discuss, and agree, planned future objectives for output, prices, the balance of trade, and the broad context of fiscal policy, and interest rates, with the country involved. This would give an estimate of future nominal incomes, consistent with a desired recovery in the trade (and fiscal) balance. Then feed those estimates of nominal incomes (and interest rates) into a demand for money function. Given the expected (forecast) external contribution to monetary expansion, that demand for money calculation then led directly to a figure for domestic credit expansion (DCE) consistent with the achievement of the agreed forecast. Subject to some margin for error, those (quarterly) DCE forecasts then became the IMF's ceilings, which the deficit country had to achieve in order to receive further tranches of loans from the Fund. The idea was clear: any unplanned domestic expansion would raise nominal incomes and (via the demand for money function) increase DCE, which would then have to be cut back by some deflationary action (fiscal, interest rates, debt sales, credit ceilings); only if the expansionary impulse arose from (unexpectedly large) inflows from abroad – a larger external monetary component – could it be accommodated.

Much of this was a novel concept to British economists, especially the key role of an (assumed predictable) demand-for-money function, and antipathetic to many – recall that the Radcliffe Report had denied the stability, or even the usefulness as a concept, of velocity. So my first role at the Bank was to try to explain the concept and role of DCE, both within and without the Bank.[15] Actually we had to go further. To protect British *amour propre* there had to be some pretence that we, in the UK, had thought up this wonderful new wheeze, rather than had it foisted upon us, out of weakness, by the IMF.

Anyhow I had already found a niche in the Bank,[16] which was to try to explain internally to the Bank what the outside (monetarist) economists were arguing, while at the same time trying to explain to those same outside economists what the Bank's viewpoint was. This meant that within the Bank (and perhaps the Treasury) I was perceived as almost the resident 'monetarist', while to the monetarists outside, notably at the Konstanz Conferences organised by Karl Brunner and Allan Meltzer, I was seen as an 'unreconstructed Keynesian'.

It was obvious that a, perhaps *the*, crucial difference between the Monetarist and the Radcliffe camps (though not so much in the case of the neo-Keynesians under the leadership of James Tobin in the USA) lay in the question of the predictability of the demand for money. So the Bank next set me the task of assessing this empirically for the UK, under the supervision of McMahon and Dicks-Mireaux, and with the assistance of Andrew Crockett, now the General Manager of the Bank for International Settlements (BIS). This resulted in the *Quarterly Bulletin* (1970) paper on 'The Importance of Money', together with Andrew's paper (1970) on whether money was a leading indicator for subsequent movements in output and prices.

The results suggested an econometrically quite stable relationship, both for broad money (£M3) including interest-bearing as well as non-interest-bearing deposits, as well as for narrow money, M1. Largely because the movements in £M3 could be analysed in terms of the credit counterparts (and DCE), it was preferred as the main measure for assessing monetary conditions.

The main clearing banks in the UK had been subject to direct credit controls, more or less continuously, since 1939, and the Bank, especially John Fforde, rightly argued that such constraints were both increasingly deleterious to the efficiency of the system and, over time, became more and more ineffective, via disintermediation. The Bank used my work as one argument against maintaining such controls. If the demand for money function was stable *and* there was a significant negative coefficient on interest rates, then you could rely on interest rate adjustments – and did not need direct credit controls – to maintain monetary stability.

The Treasury, then under Sir Douglas Allen, were cautious, and worried about the likelihood of a credit explosion if controls were to be lifted. But after extensive discussions,[17] mainly in 1970, they relented, and 'Competition and Credit Control' appeared in 1971, just in time for the 1972/73 boom, and subsequent bust.

In the event, bank lending and broad money accelerated very sharply in 1972/73, far faster than consistent with current and prior nominal incomes and interest rates, which were raised to 13 per cent in the autumn of 1973. 'My' demand-for-money function broke down within a couple of years of being estimated! What had gone wrong? Unduly lax monetary policy – a supply shock – said the critics. My own view is that a large part of the explanation is due to the regime shift encouraging banks to compete in offering much more attractive deposit liabilities, notably CDs, with much more competitive, money-market-related interest rates. Indeed, the ambience of the time, with a boom and rapid expansion, led the banks to compete so strongly for market share that they were prepared to raise interest rates on wholesale deposits, relative to lending rates, to a point where 'round-tripping' arbitrage, whereby some well-placed borrowers took the loans just to reinvest the money in such bank deposits, became (arguably) profitable.

Meanwhile, however, the demand-for-money function of M1 remained well-behaved and stable, and M1 growth slackened as interest rates rose in 1973. What was intriguing during these disturbed years, 1972–74, was that previously estimated demand-for-money functions (for example Goldfeld's in the USA (1973)) generally misbehaved in most developed countries, but almost always it was the function for that definition chosen by the Central Bank as its preferred monetary indicator that broke down most emphatically. When the Reserve Bank of Australia invited me to a Conference in 1975, as the third visitor in a trio alongside Jim Tobin and Dick Cooper, I used that observation (see Goodhart, 1984, p. 96), as the basis for a jocular footnote about 'Goodhart's Law', that, 'whenever a government seeks to rely on a previously observed statistical regularity for control purposes, that regularity will collapse'. To the British Press and wider public, that quip, which was picked up and seems to lead a life of its own, is the only memorable thing about my work! While this 'law' does have its serious analytical side (q.v. the Lucas Critique), it does feel slightly odd to have one's public reputation largely based on a minor footnote.

But whether or not the data for £M3 were artificially inflated, it is impossible to deny that the boom, especially the bubble in housing and property prices, in the UK in 1972/73 got out of hand. Ex post, policy was far too weak. Even though the demand for money function in 1972/73 broke down, the fact that the surge (1972/73) and subsequent fall-back in the growth of £M3 preceded the surge and fall-back in inflation, led virtually all UK monetarists, and most outside commentators in the country, to reinforce their conviction that broad money was *the* key monetary aggregate.[18]

The Prime Minister, Ted Heath, had sought to rely on incomes policy in 1973 to hold the line on inflation. Having interest rates rise (an input cost to businessmen) while prices were supposed to be held pegged, was an obvious embarrassment. So, towards the end of 1973[19] an edict reached the Bank that the continuing fast growth of the monetary aggregates must be curtailed *without* any further rise in interest rates. That could only mean a resort once again to direct credit controls. John Fforde asked me to spell out the options, and I wrote a note stating that we could place a limit on either the level or the marginal increase of either loans or deposits. The option which both I and John Fforde preferred was a limit on the marginal increase of *interest-bearing* deposits. No limit on non-interest-bearing deposits could be applied since banks could not refuse them. But they could discourage additional interest-bearing deposits by cutting the interest rate offered. Since much of the previous rise in £M3 had been engendered by 'excessive' competition between banks to offer ever more attractive interest rates, the punishment seemed to fit the crime. The banks could hardly scream too loudly about a measure aimed at raising the spread between loan and deposit rates. Moreover, and for some the clinching argument, the 'corset' (as my colleague Gilbert Wood christened the scheme) was sufficiently different from, and rather more complex than, simple direct controls on bank lending to the private sector. So its imposition did not appear to be such an abject reversion to the *status quo ante* 'Competition and Credit Control'. In fact its initial imposition worked rather well; the £M3 bubble burst, and its growth slackened rapidly.

There were a number of bubbles in the UK economy in 1973, including a property and housing price boom. These burst towards the end of 1973, leading to the fringe bank crisis and 'lifeboat' rescue scheme, with which I was not involved. Indeed the downturn in 1974/75, somewhat exacerbated by the incoming Labour Government's fiscal squeeze on the company sector, led to a period of comparative calm on the monetary policy front. Moreover, the 1976 external crisis and speculative attack on sterling was not, I believe that history will tell, much related to the conduct of domestic monetary policy.

Instead the main subject of interest in my field was analytical in form. Following the breakdown of the Bretton Woods system, and the disturbed and unhappy experience of 1972–74, the monetarists were arguing that domestic monetary targets should become the centrepiece, and rule, for monetary policy. While not accepting the full panoply of monetarist theory, neither the rigidity of rules nor the use of monetary base control as an operating mechanism, Central Banks around the world were tending to describe themselves as 'pragmatic monetarists', and to publish monetary bands as general guidelines and indicators against which the conduct of monetary policy could be judged, beginning with the Bundesbank in 1974 and continuing with the Fed in 1975 (see Goodhart, 1989b).

Opinions in the UK were mixed. Advisers of the new Conservative opposition leader, Mrs Thatcher, such as Gordon Pepper and Brian Griffiths, were strongly in favour of monetary targets. Many of the Keynesian, and the more left-wing, advisers of the Labour Government were vehemently against. Meanwhile the new (June 1973) Governor of the Bank, Gordon Richardson, was listening to his Central Bank colleagues in his regular meetings with them in Basle, especially perhaps Governor Bouey of Canada. But there were also differences of view within the Bank. While the experience of the breakdown of the £M3 demand-for-money function had made me unwilling to advocate the acceptance of rigid rules, whereby monetary policy would be conducted solely on the basis of a quantified monetary target, I could see the benefits of an indicative quantified forecast of how the monetary aggregates could be expected to develop consistent with the Government's objectives for the growth of nominal incomes.

Christopher Dow arrived in the Bank, coming from the OECD, just about the same time as Richardson took over, and became Executive Director and Chief Economist when Kit McMahon moved from that position to becoming Overseas Director in October 1972.[20] I believe that the Governor saw Christopher as someone who could warn him whenever the Bank might be moving in such a way as to inflame the sensibilities of the Labour Government and the Left. Anyhow Christopher was much more suspicious and sceptical of monetary targetry than me. The Governor's, and the Bank's, pronouncements on this subject, such as the Governor's (1978) Mais lecture, usually followed a lengthy process of redrafting after redrafting, partly, but only partly, to reconcile the differing analytical standpoints of Christopher and myself.

As usual, events decided, and the pressures of the 1976 sterling crisis led to the publication (by the Government) of quantified monetary targets, first in a normative, subsequently in a positive, manner; and the 'corset' was reimposed, though (as usual with direct credit controls) by now the banking system was better prepared to disintermediate through the 'bill leak', a technicality whose details are not worth restating here.

In practice the tightened policy measures (mostly fiscal) taken in 1976, once again under IMF tutelage, slowed the economy less than had been expected – especially by the more hysterical members of the Labour party. The period 1977–79 was again one of relative calm for domestic monetary policy,[21] in some part because the rapport between Governor and Chancellor, Denis Healey, was then particularly close.

As earlier noted, the new Conservative leadership, Mrs Thatcher and Keith Joseph, had espoused many of the tenets of monetarism. One facet of monetarism which I believed to be unworkable in practice in a monetary and banking system, such as existed in the UK, is monetary base control.[22] So I felt it desirable to make these arguments known and public, before they might be regarded as contrary to the expressed views of an incoming Conservative Government. This was done in a paper jointly written with Michael Foot and Tony Hotson, in the *Quarterly Bulletin* in 1979.

The Conservative Party duly won the 1979 election, and shortly thereafter reaffirmed a target for broad money, £M3, which target then became the centrepiece of their Medium Term Financial Strategy (HM Treasury, March 1980); the best analytical account of the strategy is to be found in the Zurich speech given by Nigel Lawson (1981), then Financial Secretary to the Treasury. The new Government was warned by the Bank, not least by myself, that the presumed underlying stability of the relationship between £M3 and nominal incomes was *not* sufficiently reliable for the weight being placed upon it. In order, however, to make their new policy seem firm and credible, specific quantified targets for £M3 were nevertheless promulgated, with no caveats.

From the outset circumstances led to great pressures being placed on the monetary target. The second oil price shock led to sharp upwards increases in input costs; the new Government had felt bound to allow a negotiated (post-incomes-policy type restraint) surge in public sector pay to proceed unchallenged; the Chancellor had announced a major shift from direct income tax to VAT, raising it from 8 per cent to 15 per cent in his first Budget in June 1979. All this led to sharp price increases in 1979/80. At the same time, however, the UK's new position as a prospective large oil exporter, confidence in Mrs Thatcher's policies, and the tightening of monetary policy, with interest rate increases, were putting very strong upwards pressure on the UK nominal exchange rate. So real exchange rates were going through the roof and the competitiveness of the tradable goods sector, essentially manufacturing, was being put to the sword.

While this conjuncture was causing consternation among many economists, for example the famous letter to *The Times* of 364 economists (March 31, 1981), the pace of monetary growth was right at the top end of the target range. It was shortly to go way over the top in embarrassing circumstances.

Exchange controls had been summarily discarded in October 1979, with no adverse effects (given the concurrent sharp upwards pressure on sterling). But once exchange controls had been dropped, it was hardly possible, or sensible, to continue with direct controls over domestic bank expansion, since they could now be avoided by simple disintermediation abroad. The 'corset' was still in place, but was accordingly to be removed in the summer of 1980.

The difficulty lay in predicting how large had been the prior build-up of disintermediation that now might come flooding back into bank deposits and £M3, after the corset's removal. My colleagues and I at the Bank made a rough stab at a prediction, predicting a rise of somewhat over 2 per cent in £M3 in the month of June, 1980, data becoming available in late July. That would have been bad enough by itself for meeting the target. In fact the rise in the month was more than double our prediction, nearly 5 per cent. But such a huge jump, when published, would make a nonsense, a laughing-stock, of the recently established (with much fanfare) monetary centrepiece, the target for £M3, in the Medium Term Financial Strategy. There was a great need (from the Bank's viewpoint) for some urgent quiet diplomacy. It did not receive sufficient. It was the start of the holiday period, and almost all the key senior *dramatis personae* were away on holiday. Mrs Thatcher was on holiday in Switzerland, and discussed the British monetary surge with some monetarist experts in Switzerland, before the Bank had had a proper chance to talk with her about it. Anyhow she returned unsure whether the Bank were fools or knaves; the Bank was well and truly in the dog-house.

We, in the Bank, had to explain at regular intervals why we were so ineffectual in slowing monetary growth, and we were regularly chastised for our shortcomings. To her credit Mrs Thatcher never considered reverting to direct controls. When we pointed out that any market-oriented method for slowing monetary growth would involve raising interest rates yet further, the tone of such discussions always changed abruptly. As it happened, the surge in £M3, and its subsequent fast growth in the remainder of the early 1980s, were not accompanied, or followed, by a similar surge in nominal incomes; indeed the upwards trend in the velocity of £M3 broke precisely in 1979; though, of course, in the early 1980s we were not to know that, and for several years we waited anxiously for the 'overhang' of excess money balances to feed through into expenditures – as it had (or so it is believed) in 1973/74.

Instead, the high level of interest rates, and especially of real exchange rates, and an increasingly tough and determined willingness to confront the unions, was bringing down inflation at just about exactly the rate which the Government had always wanted.[23] And with real output going through a brief, but sharp, deflation, this was hardly the time to raise interest rates further, even for monetarist purity. Moreover, doubts were increasing about what such monetarist purity actually entailed. Milton Friedman had been critical of the UK choice of target.[24] Even more important, Alan Walters returned to the UK as Mrs Thatcher's adviser, and he encouraged Jurg Niehans to do a study (1981) on UK monetary policy. Their advice was that the narrow monetary aggregates were a better guide to policy than broad money, and that by those standards monetary policy between 1979 and 1980 had been, if anything, too tight rather than too lax![25] Alan and the Bank were in broad agreement on that.

Against this background the Government, and the Bank, retreated to a multiplicity of target aggregates, narrow and broad. But with the relationship between the original cynosure £M3 and nominal incomes having become patently unreliable, and with uncertainty about which was the proper aggregate to target anyhow, the Government's earlier confidence in this approach was ebbing fast. This matched, and was reinforced by, similar problems that the Fed was having in steering by M1, with the operational method of non-borrowed monetary base control. As John Crow, Governor of the Bank of Canada, quipped, 'We did not leave the monetary aggregates; they left us.' That meant Nigel Lawson, who became Chancellor in 1983, was faced with the problem of finding some alternative anchor for steering monetary policy towards price stability. His subsequent attempts to find such an anchor in a link with the Deutschmark and the Bundesbank, via the ERM, against the wishes of Mrs Thatcher (and Sir Alan Walters) is, however, another, often-told, story almost entirely played out after I had left the Bank.

As earlier recounted, Mrs Thatcher's personal economic advisers (for example Griffiths, Pepper, to a lesser extent Walters[26]) were, I believe, all strongly in favour of trying to move operationally to a system of monetary base control. But the Bank, the banks and the City viewed the proposal with horror (certainly including me). As I recall, the Treasury tried to keep out of this argument (on the one hand . . . on the other hand). The details of the subject were, however, quite arcane, and the issue did not have as much resonance with Mrs Thatcher and Keith Joseph as the monetary targets/Medium Term Financial Strategy had had. So the defenders of the status quo won the day, as I have described at greater length (1989b). A truce was declared with the publication by the Bank of England of new arrangements for monetary control in August 1981 (Bank of England, 1981), which actually left the Bank's basic modus operandi unchanged.

4.2 Structural Developments at the Bank and the Use of Economists

When I arrived at the Bank, there was more relative attention then given to the analysis of economic events abroad and less to domestic economic concerns, with the economists split between the Economic Intelligence Department (with responsibility also for financial statistics – including seasonal adjustment techniques – and the *Quarterly Bulletin*), and the Overseas Department. I was in EID. Our job was forecasting, analysis and policy simulation for internal Bank consumption, and published commentary, mainly for the *Quarterly Bulletin*. One question that kept on being repeated throughout my time at the Bank was whether we should have our own model, or just rely on the Treasury's for forecasting and simulation purposes. A key concern was that, if the Bank was to publish its own forecast projections, the press would concentrate their attention on differences, however minor, between the Government's and the Bank's outlook. Such a focus on (minor) differences in forecasts was felt to be unhealthy. So discussions with the Chancellor and Treasury were, almost always, held on the basis of their (HMT) set of consistent forecast figures – though the Bank contributed to (and discussed aspects of) HMT's forecasts, particularly on the financial side.

HMT economists not only had the advantage of playing on their home ground on the forecasts, they also had immediate access to the Chancellor and Treasury Ministers. So, whenever there might be a debate on purely analytical economic matters between HMT (and their economists) and the Bank (and its staff), HMT would be the likely winners. Not surprisingly, therefore, the Bank's main card was usually its practical experience of market responses. 'I must warn you, Mr. Chancellor, that whatever the academics may claim, the markets would not be happy with policy X.' With the pound endemically weak, and with an uncomfortably high borrowing requirement, Chancellors were often frightened by such warnings.

The Bank saw its main strengths, therefore, 'as a Bank, not a study group'.[27] Economists were necessary as a potential counterweight to economic analysis elsewhere, for expressing the Bank's views and policies in an academically acceptable light (PR), and for forecasting purposes. They were, when I first joined, not welcomed into the operational areas of the Bank. In the case of monetary (and to a slightly lesser extent, the gilts) markets, this gap between academic/analytical advice and operational decisions narrowed greatly during my time at the Bank. This was partly because it was perceived that the senior executives in the Bank needed to combine proficiency in the language of monetary/macro economics with practical/practitioner command over operational activities.[28] Ability as a practitioner was partly a matter of personal aptitudes, common sense, unflappability, and so on, and partly a matter of on-the-job training; but the discipline of economics required professional university training. Hence the recruitment policies of the Bank shifted consciously towards gifted young economists. Usually these high flyers (for example Andrew Crockett, Lionel Price, Michael Foot, Tony Hotson, Bill Allen, and many more), first passed through my Monetary Analysis and Forecasting Sections, before moving on to the next (operational) stage of their careers in the market management part of the Bank. Over time the personal and analytical intertwining of economic analysis and market operations grew stronger.

The same was not true, during my time at the Bank, on the supervisory/regulatory side, but has become so since, as I shall discuss later. The 1973/74 fringe bank crisis and 'lifeboat', noted earlier, led to a mushroom-growth of Bank formal supervisory functions. But the principles on which this worked initially were strictly practical and, apparently consciously, eschewed academic input (though, in fairness, there was not much useful input then to be had); instead the idea was that you should find out what was widely accepted as 'best practice' among the banks, and other relevant financial institutions involved, and then chivy the laggards into abiding by such better behavioural norms.

Despite the greater formalism of economics now, and the effects of the IT revolution in enabling us to access and analyse mountains of data, we do not really understand much more about, or feel any better able to predict, the macro-economy than in the 1960s. Indeed almost the reverse; in the early days of (computer-assisted) macro-modelling, we (that is, macro-economists in the public sector) really felt that we were enhancing our ability to understand *and* control the economy. Since then the Lucas Critique, the rational expectations revolution, and the failure of the large (Keynesian-type) forecasts, have thrown forecasting (and parts of the previous canon of macroeconomics) into disarray.

What has, instead, developed with great success has been the study of finance and the analysis of the relationship between risk and asset prices, and the determinants of risk, for example variance, co-variance, fat-tailed distributions, risk factor analysis, and so on, and so forth. From the Black/Scholes option pricing formula onwards, it became clear that the design, analysis and pricing of assets, and the measurement and assessment of risk, lay in the domain of the economist.

The rational expectations hypothesis explains why anyone, whether economist, chartist, or soothsayer, is bound to fail to predict the movement of asset markets at all well (since they will be mainly driven by unanticipated news); together with the Lucas Critique, it also explains why the economist will have perennial problems even in predicting those parts of the economy subject to inertia, rigidities, and so on. So the primary use of economists, in the public sector and in the City, as forecasters exposed them to circumstances where they would be inherently fallible, treated as witch doctors one minute, and derided as charlatans the next. Such a condition was (is) exacerbated by the unwillingness of the audience for forecasts to accept, or for forecasters to insist on the provision of, probability/confidence bounds for those forecasts. The inflation fan forecast in the Bank's *Inflation Reports* is one of the few praiseworthy exceptions. So the treatment of City economists as mainly forecasting/PR merchants has not, in my view, been helpful to the profession.

Where economists really can help is in the analysis of risk. There are much more systemic and predictable fluctuations in the *variance* than in the *level* of asset prices (variances often follow an ARCH process – mean levels are, close to, random walk). Thus where City firms really would get the best out of their economists is in the risk control areas – and in the regulatory/supervisory areas in the public sector, which in the 1970s and much of the 1980s was mostly a 'no go' area for economists. All that, however, is now changing fast, and very much for the better. The growing partnership between academic work in financial economics and practical operations in risk management in the City is one of the most encouraging developments of recent years, but it largely post-dated my stay in the Bank.

In the early 1970s, following Competition and Credit Control, there was a systematic formalisation of our analysis of monetary developments, and their subsequent discussion with the Treasury and Chancellor. This was structured around the arrival of monthly balance sheet data from the banks. After processing and analysis, the data were presented to the Monetary Review Committee, chaired by John Fforde, the Home Finance Director. I was responsible for (most of) the papers going to MRC and was its first Secretary. Following the discussion in MRC, a summary of (considered) views on these monetary developments was put to the Governors and Executive Directors, and formed the basis for subsequent regular discussions with HMT officials and, if felt necessary, between Governor and Chancellor.

With monetary developments playing an increasingly large role in determining what the market operators were asked to achieve through the 1970s and 1980s, and the perceived resultant need to unify analytical advice with market operation, I myself formally moved into the Home Finance division, under John Fforde and alongside Eddie George (gilts market) and Tony Coleby (money markets) in the early 1980s. All that created something of a gap for complementary analysis of the 'real' economy and for another senior economist to work with Christopher Dow on that side, and John Flemming was recruited in the mid 1970s. The arrival of Robin Leigh-Pemberton in 1983 then led to another structural reshuffle in 1984. Among the constituent elements in that reshuffle was the need to find a replacement for Christopher Dow, the retiring Executive Director with responsibility for Economics. The Governor chose John Flemming. This was a severe blow to me since it was the only step up the promotion ladder to which I could seriously aspire, and John was younger than me.

My personal hurt was lessened by the fact that John was (and remains) both a close friend and an excellent economist. Even so, it left the prospect of continuing with the same job that I had, in effect, been doing for the last 16 years for a further 13 years (till retirement). I could see myself becoming both bitter and stale. I learnt about the various promotions and reshuffles – in which I did not figure – almost accidentally, as those having been promoted discussed what was then to happen. Apart from a very brief and largely formal word with the Governor, a couple of weeks later ('Difficult choice', etc., etc.), no one spoke to me at all about my own future prospects. It struck me then, and strikes me still, as appalling man management not to talk as carefully, or even more so, with the big 'losers' as with the big 'winners' from any reorganisation. So, despite the fact that my job at the Bank had been satisfying and fulfilling (until 1984), I decided to return to academic life.

5. RETURN TO ACADEMIA (LSE); ANALYSIS OF (FOREIGN EXCHANGE) MARKETS; AND CENTRAL BANK AUTONOMY

5.1 LSE and the Financial Markets Group

Returning to academic life was easier decided than achieved. Although I had continued with research and publication at the Bank, I had been increasingly absorbed with the work of a senior official. My technical abilities, weak at best, had atrophied further. The preferred forms of analysis and teaching in the academic profession had moved on, and become more mathematical and formal. Some of my (LSE) colleagues had doubts whether I could still rank as a professional academic economist at all or, if so, whether my appointment, as a Professor, would not use up one of the rare Chairs that could go to someone younger and more proficient.

Fortunately for me Eric Sosnow[29] wanted to endow a Chair at LSE in honour of his son, Norman, who had tragically died in an air crash, in banking and finance. The special appointments Board for this named Chair contained non-academics, as well as academics, and my background was considered suitable; anyhow I was appointed, and remained the Norman Sosnow Professor of Banking and Finance ever since, until my retirement in 2002.

LSE is not a wealthy university with, by Oxbridge and US comparatives, minuscule endowments. Being sited in mid-London where space is expensive, it is extremely cramped and, having grown in size over time, is a rabbit warren of interconnecting buildings, whose geographical juxtaposition is somewhat random (you deserve an MSc in Geography for finding your way around). Apart from its superb Robbins Library, and good IT, its other support staff are similarly skimped, crammed in and penurious. It is a miracle that the LSE administration manages to keep the place afloat at all, a miracle largely achieved by a few really dedicated key personnel.

In this inner-city slum, however, lives a world-class set of social science faculties,[30] notably one of the very best economics faculties in the UK. When I arrived Richard Layard (now Lord Layard) was Departmental Convener (Head), shortly to be followed by Meghnad Desai (now Lord Desai). Other eminent figures were Tony Atkinson (now Master of Nuffield College, Oxford), Nick Stern (now at the World Bank) and Mervyn King (now Deputy Governor at the Bank of England). David Hendry and Steve Nickell (though he was to return later) had recently gone to Oxford. John Moore and Charlie Bean (now Chief Economist at the Bank of England), were prominent among the younger faculty.[31]

Given the heavy teaching and administrative load, academics in the UK nowadays have to use and protect their remaining time with fierce devotion if they are going to keep up with reading and research. The general perception is that academic life is comfortable and full of holidays compared with life in the public sector or the City. My own experience is that, so long as you want to continue making your mark in the academic profession, then the reverse is true.

Meanwhile the squeeze on resources for higher education meant that not only secretarial assistance was disappearing (becoming totally replaced by individual word processing on PCs), but also research assistance was not affordable for the universities. Moreover, research activity and methodology increasingly involved – often required – joint work. When I left academic life for the Bank in 1968, it was considered slightly disreputable to involve one's PhD research students in your own research. By 1985, and increasingly thereafter, it had become the norm!

Another culture shock, on returning to LSE, was that in the Bank nobody talked about the need to raise money for this, or that, project. At LSE it was a perennial focus for discussion. Apart from a few theoreticians, content to live alone with their thoughts and equations, research now meant groups of faculty with research officers and assistants, and that required raising external finance, because LSE had none to spare.

The main economics research centre at LSE then (the Suntory–Toyota International Centre for Economics and Related Disciplines – STICERD

– established by Michio Morishima) covered many aspects of the social sciences, but not money and finance. So, I was happy to join with Mervyn King who had the idea of trying to set up a research group, the Financial Markets Group, concentrating on such issues. Given our proximity to the City, and the focus of our research, we hoped that we could raise sufficient finance from the private sector, especially from City financial firms, to do the kind of basic research into such issues that should (in the longer run) help to support the City's development (and in the process train a few of its brightest recruits). But we were adamant that we would *not* do direct consultancy; moreover, we would do research in-house, rather than try to supplement, or compete with, Richard Portes' brilliantly successful Centre for Economic Policy Research (CEPR) role in networking economists doing research at separate establishments around Europe.

With the help of Sir David Walker, our first Chairman, and the blessing and assistance of the Bank of England, we did manage in 1986/87 to obtain sufficient financial support[32] to open our doors for business (with a party) on January 14, 1987.[33] Mervyn and I were joint Directors, but in reality the FMG was his creation, and he ran it with devotion (to every detail).

The FMG prospered greatly. We attracted excellent research students, good research officers, and we had sufficient funding to attract a flow of eminent visitors. It would be anomalous to pick out names, which are anyhow set out in the FMG's *Annual Reports*. Besides occasional conferences, the research output of the FMG usually first sees the light of day in the form of Discussion and Special Papers, though they subsequently often get published later in journal and book form. The Discussion Papers are more analytical/theoretical/econometric in content; the Special Papers are more institutional/policy/practical oriented. The main fields that the FMG covered were Corporate Finance and Governance, Market Structure, Asset Price Determination and Volatility, and Monetary Policy and Financial Regulation. Since 1987, until January 2002, the FMG has published 397 DPs and 133 SPs.

It was, of course, a serious blow for the FMG when Mervyn was picked by the Bank in 1991 as the new Executive Director in charge of Economics, following John Flemming's move to the EBRD (and thence to being Warden of Wadham College, Oxford). At that time, moreover, I was acting as Head of Department, and neither could, nor wanted to, take over as Director myself. We were fortunate to have David Webb, who was then moving from Economics to become a Professor in the Department of Accounting and Finance, to take on this (increasingly arduous) role. Since then David has greatly strengthened the Finance wing of that Department, and has succeeded in supplementing our private sector funds with a (largely matching) public sector contribution from the ESRC, for whom we have become (since 1993) a Research Centre. With the shift from Mervyn to David, the balance of our work has moved slightly from economics towards finance.

My own publications and research at the FMG have been primarily in two main areas. First, I have written a large number of papers on current issues in monetary policy, both on international matters such as ERM/EMU, and on domestic questions, for example relating to the role and functions of the Central Bank, and also on financial regulation, where I was fortunate to have been assisted first by Dirk Schoenmaker and then by Philipp Hartmann as Research Officers. Many of these papers have been gathered together in *The Central Bank and the Financial System* (1995a) and a further set in *The Emerging Framework of Financial Regulation* (1998). Most of these papers were policy oriented, so it is not surprising that the number of SPs of which I have been an author, 42, of which 8 were jointly authored (by January 2002), considerably outnumbers my contributions to the FMG DP series, 25, of which all but 3 were jointly authored. One subfield in which I have played a role more recently, with much of the work joint with Boris Hofmann, relates to the issue of how the monetary authorities might respond to sharp fluctuations in asset prices. On this see Bernanke and Gertler (1999/2000) and Cecchetti, et al. (2000). My own contributions include, Goodhart (1995b) and (2001b), and Goodhart and Hofmann (2000a and b, 2001a and b).

However, the majority of my DPs – and serious journal articles – related to my second main field of research, to which I turn next.

5.2 Analysis of Foreign Exchange Markets

The standard theory of asset price determination, the rational efficient markets hypothesis, proposes that all, publicly available, relevant information should be factored into existing prices, so that asset prices should move in future primarily[34] in response to unanticipated 'news'. Furthermore, if one subscribes to the (Dornbusch) overshooting hypothesis, some asset prices should jump beyond their eventual 'equilibrium' on the receipt of certain news, for example of monetary changes in the case of the foreign exchange (forex) market, and then slowly revert to equilibrium.

But when I was regularly watching markets at the Bank, this stylised picture seemed far from reality. With a few exceptions (such as, for example, the release of monetary announcements in the USA during the period of Volcker's adoption of non-borrowed reserve base control (1980–82)), the response of the forex market to identifiable economic (and political) 'news' seemed to account for only a small proportion of the market's gyrations – and a long way from the supposed 'jumps' that were supposed to occur.

Moreover, much of the movements and volatility in the forex market seemed largely unrelated to anything that could be identified as public 'news'. In the stock market, of course, one might relate fluctuations in individual shares to the release of 'private' news on each firm; but in the huge forex market, say in the enormous spot market for $/Dm, would one really expect private news, for example on customer orders for forex transactions at the many competing individual banks, to have much effect on rates? After all, it is conventional wisdom that (sterilised) intervention by Central Banks is too comparatively small to be successful. If their orders are too small to move markets, why should other customers' orders be any more effective?

What determines movements in forex prices seemed a mystery, far from fully explicable in terms of the advent of unanticipated (public) news.[35] Anyhow that mystery struck me as a worthwhile subject for academic research, one probably requiring sufficiently detailed and patient pursuit that only academics would be likely to resolve it.

Anyhow this question, the determination of the movement of forex rates, became a second focus of my research, and the basis for my inaugural lecture at LSE, on 'The foreign exchange market: A random walk with a dragging anchor', given in Autumn, 1987, and reprinted in *Economica*, (1988).

'News' is continuously occurring. It fills the pages of the newspapers, and television screens, every day. If one wants to isolate the effect of *individual* 'news' items on asset markets, it is necessary to go to very high frequency data (at a *minimum* hour by hour). But, it may be said that it may take quite a long time for news to be transmitted, assimilated and appreciated. This is *not* so in the case of economic news. The timing of most such announcements is known; the expected values for such variables are collected and reported in advance by institutions such as Money Market International Ltd.; bank traders are briefed at the outset of each day about what to expect, and on what response to take to an unexpected deviation (by the inhouse economists and technical analysts), and those same experts are on hand to give instant commentary and advice after the announcement.

Indeed my own (and others) research has shown that the full effect of any economic 'news' with a pre-announced release date is factored into forex prices within about five minutes (early research on economic news which arrives *unannounced* during market-open periods indicates that full assimilation takes significantly longer, around half an hour); moreover the associated spike in volatility subsides back to normality (for news with preset release times) in about twenty minutes. Thus, with the use of high frequency data, at hourly, or shorter, intervals, one can isolate, with a reasonable degree of (statistical) confidence, the market impact of individual 'news' items.

In any case, the higher the frequency, the closer one comes to the actual continuous operations of the market. It becomes possible to study the interaction between many (but not all, see further below) of the market variables of interest to an economist, for example the (absolute) size of price change, its volatility and the size of the bid–ask spread. This work was labour and data intensive, and I have worked with a succession of good PhD research students. I provided the data base and ideas; they provided their time, and often the latest econometric techniques. The series started with hourly data, with Marcelo Giugale as research assistant (1989, 1993); he later joined the World Bank; then minute by minute data, with Lorenzo Figliuoli (1991, 1992), who subsequently joined the IMF.

The basis of virtually all forex data at that time, that is the early 1990s, was the *indicative* price of bids and asks for bilateral spot rates put out by electronic screen vendors, such as Reuters, Telerate or Knight Ridder, on a continuous basis. End monthly, daily or hourly data are simply taken as snapshots from a continuous data stream. Why throw away all the intervening data? So with the kind help of Reuters PLC, and the IT assistance of Russell Lloyd, I installed a data feed direct from the FXFX, FXFY (and AAMM) pages of Reuters screens, and collected three months of continuous (9 April–3 July, 1989) data on forex bilateral spot rates (from the FXFX and FXFY pages) and associated news (from the AAMM page) (1989/1990).

Unbeknownst to me, a specialist consultancy/advisory/research firm in Zurich, Olsen and Associates, was currently doing even better on this front, collecting continuous forex and interest rate data from electronic screens from the mid 1980s to date; they have, I believe, the best library of such data in existence. We met subsequently, and I encouraged Richard Olsen to extend his, already widespread, links with the economic academic community by holding Conferences on the use of High Frequency Data in Finance (HFDF); the first was held, most successfully in Zurich in March 1995, the second in March 1998, connected with which Richard has, with characteristic generosity and enthusiasm, made freely available much of his own data base for academic research use.

Anyhow, with Antonis Demos (1990, 1991, 1996) and Riccardo Curcio (1991, 1992, 1993, 1997), I undertook research into this continuous data series, for example confirming the existence of first order negative autocorrelation between quotes at very high frequencies, for example at periodicities less than five minutes, which I had earlier discovered in my work with Figliuoli. With Riccardo, I also tried to explore – using similar high frequency data series – whether, and possibly how, Chartist (technical analysis) might work. There was also related work on the micro-structure of the forex market with Patrick McMahon, who sadly died early, and his research associate, Yerima Ngama (1992, 1993, 1997), with Mark Taylor (1992); Thomas Hesse (1993); Hall, Henry and Pesaran (1993), and a survey article with Maureen O'Hara (1997), initially prepared as the introductory paper presented at the Olsen HFDF (1995) Conference, already noted.

This field of study has continued, though after I joined the MPC in 1997 I did not have time to play such a hands-on role; most of the work at the FMG in this field since then has been directed by Richard Payne. Richard and I collected all our earlier work, up to about 1998, in a book on *The Foreign Exchange Market* (2000).

As often beforehand, recent research in this field at the FMG has revolved around attempts to obtain additional, and better, data bases to study. The Reuters FXFX page provided continuous data on indicative bid and ask quotes.[36] But the series has several shortcomings:

1. the data show the quotes of the latest bank to enter its quotes, *not* the best bid or ask available in the market;
2. the quotes are indicative of prices ruling, and *not* firm, and either better, or in some market conditions worse, terms can be obtained by direct (telephone) contact;
3. the spreads are conventional in size, and again *not* representative of the true market spread;
4. the data may be unreliable at times when the market is particularly busy and volatile (because dealers may be too busy to update entries);
5. there are no associated transaction data available at all.

Meanwhile Reuters, and its main competitor EBS (which merged with Minex, based primarily in Japan, in the late 1990s), have developed electronic broking systems; the Reuters system is called D-2002 (and they have another electronic system, D-2001, for facilitating communications between dealers). These can provide greater immediacy than telephone search, and are cheaper to use than inter-dealer brokers. On these (private) systems, the member banks can input firm offers to buy, or sell, for chosen quantities expressed in standardised units. The quantities available at the best firm bid, and ask, are shown on screen, and then another bank can 'hit' the best bid (or ask) for an amount up to that shown to be offered at that price. Although electronic broking initially only accounted for a fraction of the total market (though this fraction has been growing rapidly in recent years), this data set is clearly vastly superior in many ways to the FXFX series.

When I first approached Reuters, they were hesitant to make any of their D-2002 data available, for confidentiality reasons. However they had themselves made video-tapes of their own screen, for seven hours, on 16 June

1993, for promotional and presentational reasons, and they were prepared to pass these video-tapes on to me. With the assistance of Professor Taka Ito and Richard Payne, who passed rapidly from the stage of research assistant, to faculty colleague, to research director in this field, we exploited this (brief) data set in a series of papers (Goodhart, Ito and Payne, 1996; Goodhart and Payne, 1996; Payne, 1996a and b).

I persevered with requests to Reuters to release more D-2002 data for academic research. I next persuaded them to release, under my care, but for the use of all accredited academic research workers, one week of continuous data from D-2002 for the $/Dm spot market for the week October 6 to 10, 1997, and the exploitation of this data set has been, and continues to be, (partly) responsible for numerous papers, notably Danielsson and Payne (2001, 2002) and Payne (2001).

But we, at the FMG, were not the only economists seeking to obtain high-frequency micro-market data, either directly from market participants or from electronic sources. In particular, Martin Evans, who had been visiting FMG, persuaded the Bank of England to subscribe to, record, and allow him access to several months of continuous D-2001 data in 1996. These had the characteristic that the observer could directly tell whether a transaction was buyer, or seller initiated. This allowed the researcher to construct a series of directionally-signed (net) trades, that is buys less sales. What Evans and Lyons (1999/2002) then demonstrated was that such a net trade series could explain much more of the (relatively high frequency, at least up to weekly) variation in fx exchange rates, (often about 30 per cent), than, say, public economic news on interest rates (often about 3 per cent). Such findings were subsequently replicated, subject to a few qualifications, by Rime (2001) and by us at the FMG, in Danielsson, Payne and Luo (2002).

This finding ran counter to my earlier scepticism about the role of private news in this market. But in a sense it simply pushed back the mystery of the fx market one step. The problem was now to explain what were the factors that caused net trade imbalances and, perhaps, to predict them. At the time of writing (early 2002), this remains an intractable problem.

5.3 Central Bank Autonomy

I have been fortunate to have been quite closely involved in three occasions of major regime changes in Central Banks, in Hong Kong in 1983 (though the Hong Kong Monetary Authority was not then a fully-fledged Central Bank), in New Zealand in 1988/89 and now in the UK in 1997.

I was somewhat distantly aware of the monetary crisis in Hong Kong in September 1983. Prior negotiations between Chairman Deng and Mrs Thatcher on the future of Hong Kong had not gone well. Flight capital began to leave Hong Kong, driving down the exchange rate, which had no anchor. The fall in the exchange rate began to raise local prices sufficiently rapidly to cause domestic concern. The PRC attributed the developing panic to stratagems by the British to remove their money from Hong Kong in good time, which was untrue. But their sabre-rattling further heightened the panic. In turn, the panic caused property prices to drop, and that made the Hong Kong Association of Banks (HKAB) reluctant to raise interest rates sharply for fear of collapsing asset values.[37]

So, at the behest of the Chancellor,[38] two officials with some knowledge of monetary economics, David Peretz of HMT and I, were flown out to Hong Kong, to find that the Senior Monetary Adviser, Douglas Bly, had already publicly committed to achieving a monetary reform, but that there were no clear plans as to what it should be. There was, however, a blueprint for reform already on the table, in the shape of a currency board system linked to the US$, which had been proposed by John Greenwood, a senior economist at G.T. Management Plc. A problem was that Greenwood had made himself *persona non grata* with the then Chief Secretary by his prior, biting criticisms of the unanchored, flexible regime which Sir Philip Haddon-Cave had been personally responsible for putting in place. Sir John Bremridge, the Financial Secretary, and Bly were not monetary experts and too unsure of themselves in this field to accept a scheme from an outspoken local critic.

So, our job was to assess the proposed 'link' to the US$, decide if it was a good idea – which it was, and remains – and to work out both transitional details, and, with much help from the local commercial bank executives, especially from the Hong Kong and Shanghai Bank, the various technical details of applying a currency board system to the particularities of the Hong Kong financial system (this latter was not an easy task). Hong Kong was particularly well suited to the 'link' since its extraordinarily flexible markets enable it to adjust to monetary conditions, and interest rates, established by the Fed in the USA for domestic American objectives (that is which might not be conjuncturally best suited to current HK conditions). Equally HK's complex political position as a UK colony then shortly to change its status in 1997 to a Special Administrative Region of the People's Republic of China, with two economic systems in one country, made the establishment of a currency board linked to the US$ (and *not* to the currency of the previous colonial power) extremely helpful, simultaneously both a strong and calming influence.[39]

I remained since then in fairly close touch with HK monetary affairs, serving on the Exchange Fund Advisory Council, (an Advisory Board for HKMA) for the better part of a decade – which involved quite frequent lengthy plane trips – and also maintaining connections with the City

University of Hong Kong, where I had a position as external visiting Professor for a couple of years. More recently I completed a study on the speculative attack on the Hong Kong foreign exchange and equity markets, the 'double-play' challenge, in August 1998, with a co-author, Dai Lu, that I hope to have published soon (2003).

Let me turn next to my connection with the Reserve Bank of New Zealand. During my time at the Bank I had had the opportunity to meet, and become friends with, the senior economists and officials at the RBNZ, especially Rod Deane and Peter Nicholl. I was asked to give a public lecture in Wellington on the occasion of their 50th anniversary, and then, more important, to act as one of their external advisers (Geoff Wood of the City University Business School being another), when the Labour Government, (under Lange and Douglas), proposed an Act[40] to give the RBNZ autonomy to vary interest rates in pursuit of an inflation target agreed between Minister and Governor, and openly published and laid before Parliament.

I have argued in numerous papers that this framework, with the government determining the quantified inflation objective to be pursued and then giving the Central Bank autonomy to vary interest rates so as to achieve that target, is optimal. It is, for example, in my view much preferable to the procedure of the European System of Central Banks, whereby the ESCB decides on its own (inflation) objectives; this leaves an excessive democratic deficit. But the main framework of the RBNZ Act of 1989 was determined by themselves in Wellington, not by external advisers,[41] though I was delighted to have the opportunity to comment in writing and to appear publicly in support of the draft Bill before one of their Select Committees.

Indeed, my particular memory of this episode relates to one piece of advice that I pushed strongly, which was *not* accepted. I advised that the Governor's salary should be linked to his success in achieving the inflation target. I had advocated a Walsh contract in practice[42] (see Walsh, 1995), before it was shown to be optimal in some theoretical contexts. The reason why it was turned down, on Treasury advice, was primarily presentational. When inflation threatened, the Governor could be perceived as increasing his own income by raising interest rates that (in the short term) would lower the disposable income and employment of others. What this argument, which has some force, illustrated to me was that the short-term demand for higher employment, without proper concern for medium-term price stability or sustainable growth, emanated from the general public (and parts of the press) as much as, or rather than, from supposedly self-seeking politicians.[43]

While I have consistently supported Central Bank autonomy in setting interest rates, to achieve an inflation objective set by the political authorities, I have at the same time had doubts about the virtues of the main theoretical analysis paraded in support of that step, that is the time inconsistency argument. There is little compelling empirical evidence that governments have sought consciously to use expectational inertia to trick people into working harder, in pursuit of a short-run electoral feel-good factor, and, indeed, little evidence, given the long lags with which monetary policy works, that they could do so even if they wanted; this argument was formalised in Goodhart and Huang (1998). In my view, key, central elements in the conduct of monetary policy are the long lags in monetary policy and the wide range of uncertainty surrounding the effects of such policies over time on nominal incomes and prices. Yet in most time-inconsistency models, the monetary authorities can control prices instantly and perfectly! Absolute nonsense.

Yet this model not only survives, but is highly influential. This is partly because it combines technical, mathematical virtuosity with a fashionable cynicism about the motives and agenda of politicians. The reality in my view is rather more mundane. The future is always uncertain and debatable, so it is never easy to take a step that is currently painful in order to correct some uncertain future problem (that is increasing inflation or a 'bubble' in asset prices). The temptation is always (and admittedly especially so before elections) to defer raising interest rates until actual hard current data show undeniable proof of worsening inflation. Given the lags, however, it is then too late to stop the dynamic process easily or quickly. Politicians are clearly liable to vary interest rates 'too little, too late', but not, in my view, essentially out of a conscious desire to fool people into working harder.

Given the lags, the aim of monetary policy must be to control the level of the future (technically best constructed) forecast of inflation.[44] For the reasons stated above, this is best done by an autonomous Central Bank, working to an objective set out by the political authorities. It was, therefore, with great pleasure that I learnt in early May 1997 that the Chancellor of the Exchequer, Gordon Brown, of the incoming Labour Government had initiated a regime change in the UK more or less exactly along these lines, and an even more personal pleasure to find out a few weeks later that I was to be an external (that is non-Bank) member of the newly-created Monetary Policy Committee. It has been an unusual privilege for an economist to try to make work in practice what he has advocated in theory.

5.4 Decision-making in the Monetary Policy Committee

When the Chancellor outlined his plans for the new Monetary Policy Committee of the operationally independent Bank of England on 6 May, 1997, he announced that there would be four external members, in addition to five from within the Bank.[45]

I was, not surprisingly, hopeful that I would be appointed as one of the externals, but extremely uncertain, not least because my family had no ties to the Labour party, indeed the reverse with one elder brother by then an ex-Conservative MP and the other elder brother a senior figure in the Liberal-Democratic party, and soon to be a spokesman for them in the House of Lords. Nevertheless after a seemingly long wait for any announcement about the composition of the externals to be made, I was telephoned by Sir Alan Budd of the Treasury at the very end of May to say that I had been appointed. Alan was himself joining the Committee as an external, after retiring from the Treasury, and the other two external appointees were Willem Buiter, then teaching at Cambridge, and DeAnne Julius, then the chief economist at British Airways.[46]

Although there had been widespread general support for granting operational independence to the Bank of England, for example in the Roll Committee Report (1993), of which I was a member, and in the Treasury Select Committee Report (1993), prior to the 1997 general election, the then Shadow Chancellor Gordon Brown had implied that any such move would be a lengthy process, and dependent on evidence about the quality of Bank of England advice on policy. So, when he, with supporting advice from his personal assistant, Ed Balls (see HM Treasury, 2002), decided to take this step immediately, the timing came as a great surprise. Consequently there was little, or no, public discussion of the detailed modalities of the procedures to be followed.

However, the move towards operational independence had been evolutionary, and two main procedural arrangements were already in place in the Bank. The first was the Inflation Report, which was initially published in February 1993 (see Goodhart, 2001a). The second was the internal briefing meeting for the Governor in advance of his, and the Bank's team, monthly meetings with the Chancellor; the Governor's advice (on interest rate setting) had been published from 1994 onwards. These two arrangements, the monthly general briefing session (on the Friday preceding the MPC meetings) and the quarterly (published) Inflation Forecast were then carried seamlessly forward into the MPC's own procedures, thereafter supplemented by private MPC meetings on the Wednesday afternoon (to discuss the conjuncture, in the light of the preceding briefing meeting), and the Thursday morning (to reach a decision), usually the first Wednesday and Thursday of each month.[47]

These latter meetings were, of course, new, and their procedures remained to be established. At the first such Thursday meeting in June 1997, the Governor turned first to Mervyn King on his right, to set the scene and get us started, and then went round the large table, where we all had our allocated seats, until the final, and if necessary casting, vote lay with the Governor himself. After a few such repeat performances, I suggested to the Governor that a pre-set order of voting should be replaced by a randomised order. He agreed, and it was (roughly) randomised except that Mervyn King continued to set the scene (partly out of kindness to everyone else, who would not have to prepare to do so), and the Governor has kept the final word.

With decisions on the appointment of external members only taken at the end of May, Willem and I were pitchforked into this procedure within days of our appointment. I had no clear prior idea of what the role of an external member was meant to be (beyond participating in the process of deciding on the determination of short term interest rates); and there had been no general discussion of this at all. As usual, the press had been far more concerned about personalities, that is who the externals might be, than with what the externals were supposed to be doing.

There were, and are, many potential ways of incorporating externals into the process. One is to put them on an equivalent basis to the internals by giving them some line management responsibilities in the Bank, as is done in the Bank of Japan. This amounts to making 'externals' effectively into 'internals' after appointment. A second would be to encourage the externals to develop their own separate, alternative sources of briefing, forecasts, advice, and so on, perhaps in conjunction with an outside team of forecasters, for example the National Institute. This would have the effect of emphasising the separation of the externals from the internals; and if the externals should choose a common source of outside advice, forecasts, and so on, might tend to lead to an adversarial, 'them versus us', approach. The Governor was keen to avoid this latter, and wanted everyone to be in exactly the same position, with respect to briefing, forecasting, and so on; so that what we would bring to the table would be our individual judgments, not separate information sets.

This latter led to some difficulties, in part since absolute equality is impossible. For example the externals, without internal line management duties, had much more time on their hands,[48] and being highly-skilled professionals would want to use such time in testing, exploring and extending the forecasting and other processes involved in reaching the interest rate decision. But to do so would involve seeking help and assistance from the limited and stretched research staff of the Monetary Analysis division in the Bank. Meanwhile, like most other large organisations, the Bank's staff was organised hierarchically into Divisions and Groups, and the Monetary Analysis Division answered to the Chief Economist and thence to the responsible Deputy Director. So the externals, with both spare time and good ideas, would go to the staff of Monetary Analysis for research assistance, and the staff would become severely stretched between meeting their regular workload and the unpredictable, but often frequent, demands from the externals. Staff naturally tended to give priority to those who would assess them, promote them (or not), and otherwise determine their future. So, the externals became frustrated with the extent of research assistance actually available; there were also a few undertones and suggestions that some of the 'insiders' were using the staff to set the agenda in such a way as to support their own policy inclinations (though in so far as there were any such aspersions, they were in my view unwarranted). In any case the issue, which unfortunately surfaced publicly, was largely resolved by granting the externals some (limited) dedicated staff of their own (which matched the staff in the so-called private offices of the insiders, but were used in somewhat different ways); and also by formalising the process of setting priorities for internal research.

One of the features of the Bank's Inflation Forecast was that it was predicated on the basis of unchanged interest rates from the current level into the far horizon of the future. That assumption was inevitable pre-1997, so long as the Chancellor was responsible for setting interest rates. The Bank had no locus for appearing to tell the Chancellor what to do, only for predicting what might happen if interest rates were left unchanged. But that same assumption, of unchanged future interest rates, was also carried on once the Bank was granted operational independence. In practice I believe that this is a good working assumption since it effectively puts pressure on the MPC to adjust interest rates immediately on the occasion of the forecast, in order to be able to claim (and the number of participants in the forecasting exercise is large enough to ensure honesty, should there be outside doubters on this score) that they had already moved interest rates enough to meet their desired objective at the appropriate horizon[49] (subject of course to stochastic shocks, model uncertainties, and so on and so forth). In short, it tends to force the MPC to act pre-emptively; in so far as the main weakness of monetary policy is 'too little, too late', this is a good thing.

Nevertheless this procedure led to considerable outside criticism. The assumption of constant interest rates over the next two years was unlikely to be the path believed by the market, nor, except by chance, the probable optimal path, see the critique by Martijn and Samiei of the IMF (1999); also Meyer (2001) and Svensson (2002). While there is some force in such criticisms, I have defended the procedure at some length, partly because of the difficulties of agreeing any non-constant path, and partly, as already noted, because it tends to push the MPC into acting more aggressively and pre-emptively than it otherwise would (see Goodhart, 2001c).[50] Moreover, the concern that this assumption would only rarely be shared by the markets was addressed, at least in part, by doing a separate run of the forecast based on the markets' apparent prediction of interest rates, as implied and backed out from the money market yield curve, and publishing the result in the Inflation Forecast.

Anyhow I interpreted my remit, as an external member of the MPC, to adjust interest rates now, so that, if they were to be held constant thereafter, we would have the best possible chance of hitting our target (a 2½ per cent growth in our allotted index, RPIX), at an horizon of about 18–24 months. If this was what my colleagues were also doing (and the occasions of my dissenting from the majority decision were infrequent) then, in principle, interest rates should have followed a path close to a random walk.[51] The path of interest rates did not do so at all during the history so far of the MPC. Instead there has been just as much autocorrelation in interest rate changes, with continued small steps of rates in the same direction, interspersed with only occasional reversals of direction of change, as ever before. This was the theme of my 1998 Keynes Lecture at the British Academy (1999).

What explains such 'interest rate smoothing', as such behaviour is often termed? This was especially intriguing to me since I thought that I was taking decisions in a way that should have precluded its occurrence. I do not know the answer, and have not done the academic work necessary to test the hypothesis properly. Nevertheless my assessment of my experience of the period, and my interpretation of some work done by Rudebusch (2000) (in which he contrasts the *ex post* smoothing path of policy-determined short US rates with the lack of information in the US money market yield curve about future short rates), is that the smoothing does not arise from the decision-making process, but from the forecasting process. Auto-correlated errors in forecasts cause the forecast for a future year to be revised several times in the same direction, so that the policy-maker is always playing 'catch-up'.

Take the recent series of interest rate reductions in 2001, which was common to all the major Central Banks (except Japan). Did this occur because the FOMC appreciated at the start of the year that cuts of the order of 4 to 500 basis points might be needed, but instead agreed to phase them in a series of small, graduated steps, so as not 'to scare the horses'? That suggestion strikes me as self-evidently nonsense, though on a couple of occasions, perhaps, such cuts *may* have been reduced in scale, or briefly deferred for 'smoothing'-type reasons. Instead the major cause of the autocorrelation was that it only slowly dawned on forecasters generally how steep, and possibly severe and prolonged, was the slide into potential recession. This can be documented from successive IMF forecasts.

As a generality none of the really sharp shifts in economic conditions, for example the 1998/99 collapse in financial confidence (o.a. the Russian default and LTCM), the 1999/2000 IT-related boom, the 2001 slide, were, or probably could have been, forecast in advance. Hence policy-makers will usually be playing 'catch-up'; and 'smoothing' will appear an *ex post* stylised fact, even though no one may be trying to do so *ex ante*.

The above list of shocks indicates that the period since 1997 when the MPC was formed was not trouble-free; yet the measured deviations of inflation around its target, and of output around its sustainable trend (as far as we can now tell) have been remarkably and historically low. As of the date of writing, RPIX has *never* exceeded the 1 per cent margin around its 2½ per cent target that would trigger a required letter (partly of explanation) to the Chancellor, much to the initial surprise of most of us.

What explains this success, so far at least? I find it difficult to attribute it, more than in some useful part, to our decisions on the MPC. Our best estimates, as outlined in our booklet on 'The Transmission Mechanism of Monetary Policy' (1999), suggest that a 100 basis point (1 per cent) rise (fall) in interest rates only cuts (increases) output/inflation after the usual standard lags (as earlier) described, by about 25/33 basis points. We did not change interest rates by enough to have had a really sizeable effect. The overall conjuncture for the UK must, therefore, have remained quite stable. A more promising argument is that monetary policy worldwide, and especially so in the USA, helped to stabilise global trends (except in Japan) between 1997 and 2000.[52] It will be for the historians to reach a firmer conclusion.

5.5 Financial Regulation

Whereas the switch to inflation targeting by operationally independent Central Banks has seemed the single most important structural change in recent years in the field of monetary policy, there have at the same time been several major and far-reaching structural changes in the field of financial regulation and supervision. In the UK alone, the Bank of England was stripped of most of its supervisory (but not regulatory) role in 1997, which was transferred to the newly established Financial Services Authority; in Europe there were questions about the harmonisation of financial regulation, and the relevant roles of federal and national bodies (not least in banking about the parts to be played by the ESCB and NCBs respectively); internationally there are questions, exacerbated by the Asian crisis of 1997/98, about the role of the IMF, and how far it might act as a lender of last resort.

My position on the MPC did not preclude my taking part in the resulting discussions. Moreover, my continuing participation (as Deputy Director, though this was more honorific than executive) in the Financial Markets Group actively encouraged such a line of work. The FMG was sometimes perceived as being a bit narrowly theoretical and academic. Financial regulation issues, though they were being increasingly subject to rigorous theoretical analysis over the last decade, had the advantage of being policy relevant, inter-disciplinary (accounting, economics, finance and law), and of key interest to practitioners. So, my own work in the field played an important role in the FMG's becoming a funded ESRC centre, and in our communication with practitioners, officials, and so on. In particular, the FMG's Special Paper series, as contrasted with the more academic Discussion Paper series, largely consisted of papers relating to the subject. In the SP series, out of the 133 papers circulated up to the end of 2002, some 40 related to financial regulation, of which I was an author of 11 of these.

I was fortunate during these years in having a number of colleagues who were interested in this field, notably Dirk Schoenmaker. He, and I, completed a number of papers in this arena (notably 1995 and 2002). Much of the work on the lender of last resort function of central banks (and of the IMF) had been descriptive, historical and/or legal. When I wanted to see if the subject could be made more theoretical, mathematical and rigorous, I turned for help to my colleague Haizhou Huang, and we completed a couple of such papers in this field (2000, 2001).

With so much going on in this subject, not least in the last couple of years with the Basel II exercise, it was straightforward to arrange a series of conferences at the FMG in the last few years with my fellow organisers on the London Financial Regulatory Seminar. These tended to result either in books, or in Special Papers (see Goodhart, 1998, 2000a and b; Danielsson et al. 2001). In addition I helped Eilis Ferran to edit the proceedings of a conference in Cambridge (2001), and following a stimulating conference in Frankfurt in 1999, Gerhard Illing and I put together a set of Readings (famous papers and articles) on the subject of the lender of last resort (2002).

Just as the first version of this autobiographical note ended just at the time when my appointment to the MPC had occurred, so this revised version concludes with yet another return to the Bank, at the start of 2002, this time as Adviser to the Governor on Financial Stability. Let us hope that conditions remain so stable and secure that there is no pressing need for such advice! In any case I hope to continue work in the field for some time yet.

I wonder whether the fact that I have joined the Bank on three separate occasions represents some kind of record.

NOTES

1. This is an extended version of an earlier (December 1997) contribution to a series of recollections on the professional experience of distinguished economists published by the Banca Nazionale del Lavoro; this earlier version appeared in their *Quarterly Review*, No. 203, December 1997. The series opened with the September 1979 issue of this review. The editor is grateful for permission to reprint the revised version here.
2. The family figures prominently in Stephen Birmingham's *Our Crowd. The Great Jewish Families of New York*; also see Allan Nevins, *Herbert H. Lehman and his Era*; and Roland Flade, *The Lehmans: From Rimpar to the New World; A Family History*.
3. See *The Dictionary of National Biography*, 1986, pp. 350–51.
4. *Poland and the Minority Races*, 1920.
5. During this Service, I was tangentially involved in the events of 1956, the Hungarian uprising and the Suez crisis. My battalion was responsible for running barracks to house those Hungarians who fled to the UK. During the Suez Crisis, I was appointed Intelligence Officer in a Brigade to be formed to go into Suez in a second wave. That wave was cancelled. In the meantime the Brigadier had asked me to go through his private safe and burn all the secret papers that would not be needed. Out of several hundred, I burnt all but three, an early grounding for my subsequent conviction that people (*not* just bureaucrats, see Section 5), grossly over-classify papers as Confidential or Secret when there is no need for that.
6. Invisible to undergraduates. His great (1960) book, *Production of Commodities by Means of Commodities*, had, however, a major influence on the theoretical outlook of the Cambridge faculty at the time, but failed to make any significant breakthrough into the increasingly dominant school(s) of North American economists.
7. Apart from one lecturer on US economic history whose views I so disliked that I learnt a lot from trying to think up mental refutations as he proceeded.
8. By far the best lecturer of that period was not an economist. He was Noel Annan, who lectured on the great philosophers. He was the only social scientist who could fix his lecture hour at 9 a.m. and still command a sizeable, and sustained, audience.
9. There was a well-known quip about a foreigner who came to Trinity in search of the prototype English gentleman. Eventually he claimed to have found two, but one was Italian (Sraffa) and the other a communist (Dobb).
10. See for example Shackle (1949).
11. The same was *not* the case for Oxford graduates where the PPE (Politics, Philosophy and Economics) course put them on roughly the same level as their US counterparts.
12. Having entered monetary economics from the historical vantage point, I was largely unaware then (1962) of theoretical stirrings in Chicago. It was because of my historical expertise that Duesenberry showed me the manuscript (of Chapter 4) of Friedman and Schwartz's great book, *A Monetary History of the United States, 1867–1960*. And having been named in the preface as a (small) helper, I was later privileged to write one of the first reviews in the UK (in *Economica*) of that book (1964).
13. This paper, and most of the other key published papers issued by the Bank, have been gathered together in Bank of England (1984).
14. While most of the formal economic analysis was Radcliffe/Keynesian, there remained some residual monetarist-type gut feelings among the domestic monetary operators in the Bank. They *hated* the application of credit ceilings, which were, they believed intrusive, inefficient, cumbersome and ultimately ineffective; so they were more willing to give (sharper) fluctuations in interest rates a try as an instrument for domestic monetary control. Also, the concern of the domestic monetary operators in the Bank with trying to maintain confidence and good conditions in the gilts market was, I believe, *au fond* based on a worry about having to flood the country with additional money, or near-money assets, if the gilts market should go on strike.
15. I was the main author of Bank of England (1969b).
16. The importance of this niche to the Bank, and the interest and satisfaction of the work

to me, led me to move on from a position of temporary secondment to a full-time position, as an Adviser.

17. I was involved in most of the discussions, but the real work was done by the Home Finance side, primarily John Fforde, the Executive Director, and John Page, the Chief Cashier, with the assistance of Andrew Crockett. Andrew drafted the paper that went to the Treasury in 1971, following Fforde's internal paper to the Governor, Leslie O'Brien, at the end of 1970. *Competition and Credit Control* (Bank of England, 1971, and also 1984, Chapter 2), as titled and published, was mainly written by the Chief Cashier, John Page.
18. See Walters (1986), Chapter 6.
19. From the end of 1972 until the autumn of 1973, I had taken leave from the Bank to write my main textbook, *Money, Information and Uncertainty*. I reckoned that I was, by then, as well placed as I ever would be to combine theory with practical policy insights. Because prices of paper and wood-pulp were then rising so rapidly, my publishers, Macmillan, were uncertain how to price it. So they sat on it, not publishing it until 1975, and then with a tiny typeface. I was not best pleased.
20. His predecessor as Overseas Director, Jeremy Morse, left to take on the thankless task of trying to patch up the collapsing Bretton Woods international exchange rate system in the Committee of 20, taking the young Eddie George with him as his personal assistant.
21. The main debate, in 1977, was whether interest rates should be used primarily to control the exchange rate (that is to keep it at the low, competitive level established in 1976), or to control the domestic monetary aggregates (and hence inflation), or some combination of the two.
22. I have written on this several times subsequently, notably in 1994 and 1995b.
23. Lawson (1992), p. 72.
24. Select Committee evidence, see Treasury and Civil Service Committee (1981).
25. Thatcher (1993), p. 125; Walters (1986), Chapters 6 and 8.
26. Walters (1986), pp. 123–4 and 147.
27. I am not sure who first said this. Some attribute it to Montagu Norman; in any case it has been frequently repeated.
28. I was asked, once or twice, in my early years at the Bank, whether I wanted to move from an economic policy advisory to an operational post. Although it was implied, but unstated, that such broadening would be a prerequisite to eventual promotion to a really top job, I always felt that my comparative advantage lay in sticking to my academic last, and I refused.
29. Eric had escaped from Poland before World War II intending to go on to Israel, but had taken on a temporary job in London as a financial journalist – his prior occupation – and had stayed. After the war he moved on to financing trade with the Eastern bloc, and built up his own financial, import/export firm.
30. LSE is frequently perceived as a left-wing University. It is unclear why this reputation should linger on, being often attributed to the role and presence of Laski after World War II. It is true that, at the end of the 1960s and early 1970s, the Law Department was unusually left-leaning; but the Economics Department has Lionel Robbins as its great figure – and was home for a time to Hayek. So the Economics tradition at LSE has been more (neo) Classical than almost anywhere else in the UK. In particular, LSE economics never became infected with a quasi-Marxist sub-group, of the kind which embroiled certain other UK universities in the 1970s and 1980s. Of course, LSE economics, and other faculties, had the usual mixture of left, middle and right political supporters, but the economics faculty never split, or became seriously internally at odds, on ideological grounds.

    A greater division lay between those who had taken up applied specialties, for example transport, development, welfare, housing economics, and those who believed that the core of economics lay in theoretical analysis. The former group tended to feel treated as second-class citizens, and several of them, over time, migrated towards other faculties.
31. In recent years LSE has fallen slightly in academic ranking, as measured by publications in top journals, relative to its US comparators, though on most counts it has still

remained top in Europe. One reason why this may have been so is that, as the above account demonstrates, LSE has been the previous home of more (macro) economists in senior official positions than other UK universities, and comparatively more so than any individual US university (though I have not checked this latter claim).

32. Our main donors initially were Citibank, County NatWest, Investors in Industry (3i), Salomon Brothers and Nomura International Finance.
33. FMG Annual Report (1987).
34. Given the pattern of existing interest rate differentials, a small, anticipated, rate of change of foreign exchange prices is generally expected over the future. In very high frequency data, for example seconds, minutes, hours, even days, such expected changes approximate zero.
35. Whenever I used to ask the Bank forex dealers, perplexed, why some sharp surge in an exchange rate had occurred, I would usually receive the reply, 'more buyers than sellers'!
36. Though not *all* such quotes, since the FXFX technology can only handle one new quote every second, or so. That shortcoming was overcome with their new RICs pages, which shows all such quotes.
37. I have written a fuller account of this panic in my entry in Glasner, *Business Cycles and Depressions* (1997).
38. Lawson (1992), p. 523.
39. Also see Thatcher (1993), pp. 489–90.
40. I have argued for several years that Labour governments are more likely to give autonomy to Central Banks than Conservative governments. Their credibility gain (in reduced interest rates) is likely to be greater; moreover the Conservative opposition party can hardly object, given their ideological position. Hence such a Central Bank regime change, introduced by a Labour government, should receive all-party support, as indeed happened in New Zealand. That greatly enhances the credibility of the whole exercise.
41. The Governor, Don Brash, has been far too generous in his allocation of partial responsibility to me.
42. Rumours of this suggestion somehow leaked. Although it was not accepted, for some years there was a common misapprehension that it had been.
43. I have expressed these views more formally in a paper with Dr H. Huang (1996).
44. As has been advocated in a number of recent, excellent papers by Lars Svensson (for example, 1997a and b).
45. The Governor, the two Deputies, the Chief Economist and the Executive Director in charge of Financial Market Operations.
46. Since Alan and DeAnne were shifting jobs, they needed to take some time to do so; DeAnne arriving in September and Alan in December 1997.

    Although the switch to twin Deputy Governors was announced in May 1997, with one responsible for Monetary Policy and the other for Financial Stability, this could not be put into practice until the revised Bank of England Act was passed a year later. Moreover, the then Deputy Governor, Howard Davies, had been appointed, again in May 1997, as the first Chairman of the new mega-supervisory body, the Financial Services Authority. So the first meetings of the MPC in June 1997 took place with Howard Davies still the one Deputy Governor; the Governor; Mervyn King as Executive Director in charge of economic analysis; Ian Plenderleith as Executive Director in charge of home finance, Willem and me. Howard left after the July meeting, and David Clementi replaced him in September as the then sole Deputy Governor. After the Bank of England Act was passed next Spring, the final bits of the jigsaw were completed, with Mervyn joining David as joint Deputy Director, and John Vickers appointed as Chief Economist. So for the first year the number on the Committee varied between 5 (August 1997) and 8, rather than the statutory number, 9.
47. The previous meetings, with published Minutes, of Chancellor/Governor, the so-called Ken and Eddie show (after Chancellor Ken Clarke and Governor Eddie George) had been monthly. The requirement that the meetings of the MPC should be monthly too was likewise carried straight through from past practice and even incorporated into the Bank of England Act. There was again little, or no, public discussion of whether such a

monthly periodicity might be optimal. My own experience suggests that the FOMC's timetable in the USA is better. They have eight regular meetings. Four would then coincide with the four forecasts, and the other four would allow mid-term corrections to be made. Twelve meetings a year is too frequent to allow either for the accumulation of a sufficiency of new information, or for the efficient handling of internal support staff. But at least it was better than the fortnightly meetings of the Governing Council of the ESCB, before they sensibly switched to monthly towards the end of 2001.

48. This was the case for externals who were full-time at the Bank. It was not absolutely *necessary* to be full-time, since MPC duties only took up, from my own experience, about 5 working days a month during non-forecasting months, and about 15 days a month during the forecasting months. However, the range of (non-commercial) jobs that an MPC member could take on was limited; during forecasting months it was difficult to fit in *any* other job; and the large number of meetings, whose schedule would often be shifted, made it almost impossible to have a second job outside of London. Primarily for this latter reason, Willem gave up trying to remain on a part-time basis after the first year. Thereafter I was the only part-time member (on a two-fifths basis), until Steve Nickell came in on a (less punishing) (four-fifths) basis.
49. This term, 'the appropriate horizon', hides some complex issues about what this might be. The transmission mechanism of monetary policy involves lags; a useful rule of thumb is that it takes about one year for such policy to have its full effect on the real economy, and about two years to influence inflation strongly. So, aiming to control inflation at a much shorter horizon than about 1½ years, would either be impossible and/or lead to excessive, destabilizing fluctuations in interest rates and exchange rates. Similarly worrying about inflation more than say three years ahead ran into problems of growing uncertainty, whereas subsequent policy measures could be deployed more effectively. So the MPC tended, but did not set in concrete, to focus on controlling inflation at about a two-year horizon. As may be imagined this has been academically contentious with some, like Lars Svensson (2002), in this volume, arguing that the MPC *should* minimize a properly specified 'loss function' over an infinite horizon subject to some 'appropriate' time discount function. On all this, see also Batini and Haldane (1999), and Batini and Nelson (2000).
50. Whereas an (external) member of the MPC is obviously subject to certain constraints on what (s)he can say about current policy issues, there were fewer such bars to making public comments on procedural issues; and I found such issues increasingly interesting. In this context I was pleased to participate in the 3rd ICMB/CEPR (Geneva) Report (2001) on the subject of Central Bank communications (Blinder, Goodhart, et al.).
51. Not necessarily exactly a random walk because foreseen trend factors likely to affect the economy just beyond the 'horizon' could induce a trend in interest rates as time passed.
52. The main problem that remained in the UK was that, for some inexplicable reason, the euro was so weak that sterling became seriously overvalued. To maintain growth, and to avoid deflation, interest rates had to be kept at low enough levels to stimulate the consumer and the housing market towards somewhat excessive expansion. The two economies, of a depressed tradeable goods sector, and a booming domestic services sector, remained an uncomfortable reality.

REFERENCES

Bank of England (1969a), 'The Operation of Monetary Policy since the Radcliffe Report', *Bank of England Quarterly Bulletin*, 9 (4), 448–60.

Bank of England (1969b), 'Domestic Credit Expansion', *Bank of England Quarterly Bulletin*, 9 (3), 363–82.

Bank of England (1971), *Competition and Credit Control*, London: Bank of England, May.

Bank of England (1981), 'Monetary Control – Provisions', *Bank of England Quarterly Bulletin*, 21 (3), 347–50.
Bank of England (1984), *The Development and Operation of Monetary Policy, 1960–1983*, Oxford: Clarendon Press.
Batini, N. and A. Haldane (1999), 'Forward Looking Rules for Monetary Policy', Bank of England, Working Paper No. 91.
Batini, N. and E. Nelson (2000), 'Optimal Horizons for Inflation Targeting', Bank of England, Working Paper No. 119.
Bernanke, B. and M. Gertler (1999/2000), 'Monetary Policy and Asset Price Volatility', in Federal Reserve Bank of Kansas City *Economic Review*, Fourth Quarter, 1999, 17–51, and in *New Challenges for Monetary Policy*, proceedings of the 1999 Jackson Hole Conference (2000), Federal Reserve Bank of Kansas City.
Birmingham, S. (1968), *Our Crowd. The Great Jewish Families of New York*, London: Longmans.
Blinder, A., Goodhart, C., Hildebrand, P., Lipton, D. and C. Wyplosz (2001), *How do Central Banks Talk?*, Geneva: International Center for Monetary and Banking Studies; and London: Centre for Economic Policy Research.
Cairncross, A. (1996), *Managing the British Economy in the 1960s: A Treasury Perspective*, London: Macmillan.
Cecchetti, S., Genburg, H., Lipsky, J. and S. Wadhwani (2000), *Asset Prices and Central Bank Policy*, 2nd Geneva Report, Geneva: International Center for Monetary and Banking Studies; and London: Centre for Economic Policy Research.
Crockett, A.D. (1970), 'Timing Relationships between Movements of Monetary and National Income Variables', *Bank of England Quarterly Bulletin*, 10 (4), 459–72.
Curcio, R. and C.A.E. Goodhart (1992), 'When Support/Resistance Levels are Broken, Can Profits be Made?', Financial Markets Group Discussion Paper, No. 142, July; revised and reworked as Curcio, R., Goodhart, C., Guillaume, D. and R. Payne (1997), 'Do Technical Trading Rules Generate Profits? Conclusions from the Intra-Day Foreign Exchange Market', *International Journal of Finance and Economics*, 2 (4), October, 267–80.
Curcio, R. and C.A.E. Goodhart (1993), 'Chartism: A Controlled Experiment', *Journal of International Securities Markets*, 7 (Autumn), 173–86.
Danielsson, J., Embrechts, P., Goodhart, C., Keating, C., Shin, H., Renault, O. and F. Muennich (2001), 'An Academic Response to Basel II', Financial Markets Group, LSE, Special Paper No. 130 (May).
Danielsson, J. and R. Payne (2001), 'Measuring and Explaining Liquidity on an Electronic Limit Order Book: Evidence from Reuters D2000–2', FMG working paper (31 January), available at http://www.riskresearch.org and http://fmg.lse.ac.uk/rpayne.
Danielsson, J. and R. Payne (2002), 'Real Trading Patterns and Prices in Spot Foreign Exchange Markets', *Journal of International Money and Finance*, 21 (2), April, 203–22.
Danielsson, J., Payne, R. and J. Luo (2002), 'Exchange Rate Determination and Inter-Market Order Flow Effects', FMG working paper (August), available from http://www.riskresearch.org.
Demos, A.A. and C.A.E. Goodhart (1996), 'The Interaction between the Frequency of Market Quotations, Spread and Volatility in the Foreign Exchange Market', *Applied Economics*, 28, 377–86.

Dictionary of National Biography (1986), Oxford University Press.
Evans, M.D. and R.K. Lyons (1999), 'Order Flow and Exchange Rate Dynamics', NBER Working Paper No. 7317, *Journal of Political Economy* (2002), 101 (1), February, 170–80.
Ferran, E. and C.A.E. Goodhart (eds) (2001), *Regulating Financial Services and Markets in the 21st Century*, Oxford: Hart Publishing.
Fforde, J.S. (1954), *The Federal Reserve System, 1945–49*, Oxford: Clarendon Press.
Financial Markets Group (FMG) (1987 – to date), *Annual Report*, Financial Markets Group, London School of Economics.
Flade, R. (1996), *The Lehmans: From Rimpar to the New World*, Würzburg, Germany: Königshausen & Neuman.
Foot, M.D.K.W., Goodhart, C.A.E. and A.C. Hotson (1979), 'Monetary Base Control', *Bank of England Quarterly Bulletin*, 19 (2), 149–59.
Frankel, J.A., Galli, G. and A. Giovannini (1996), *The Microstructure of Foreign Exchange Markets*, for the NBER, University of Chicago Press.
Friedman, M. and A.J. Schwartz (1963), *A Monetary History of the United States, 1867–1960*, NBER, Princeton University Press.
Glasner, D. (ed.) (1997), *Business Cycles and Depressions: An Encyclopedia*, New York: Garland Publishing Inc.
Goldfeld, S.M. (1973), 'The Demand for Money Revisited', *Brookings Papers on Economic Activity*, 13, 577–638.
Goodhart, A.L. (1920), *Poland and the Minority Races*, London: George Allen & Unwin Ltd.
Goodhart, C.A.E. (1962), 'National Banking System Reactions to Seasonal Variations, 1900–1913', 2 vols, PhD Thesis, Harvard University, Cambridge, Mass.
Goodhart, C.A.E. (1964), Review of *A Monetary History of the United States, 1867–1960*, by M. Friedman and A. Schwartz, *Economica*, XXXI (123), 314–18.
Goodhart, C.A.E. (1965), 'Profit on National Bank Notes, 1900–1913', *Journal of Political Economy*, LXXIII (5), 516–22.
Goodhart, C.A.E. (1969), *The New York Money Market and the Finance of Trade, 1900–1913*, Harvard Economic Studies, Vol. 132, Cambridge, Mass.: Harvard University Press.
Goodhart, C.A.E. (1972), *The Business of Banking, 1891–1914*, London: Weidenfeld and Nicolson.
Goodhart, C.A.E. (1973), 'Monetary Policy in the United Kingdom', Chapter 12 in *Monetary Policy in Twelve Industrial Countries*, ed. K. Holbik, Federal Reserve Bank of Boston.
Goodhart, C.A.E. (1975), *Money, Information and Uncertainty*, revised 2nd edition 1989, London: Macmillan.
Goodhart, C.A.E. (1984), 'The Problems of Monetary Management: The UK Experience', Chapter III in *Monetary Theory and Practice* (same author), London: Macmillan.
Goodhart, C.A.E. (1988), 'The Foreign Exchange Market: A Random Walk with a Dragging Anchor', *Economica*, 55 (220), 437–60.
Goodhart, C.A.E. (1989a), '"News" and the Foreign Exchange Market', Manchester Statistical Society, Pamphlet, 17 October; reprinted as Financial Markets Group Discussion Paper, No. 71, January 1990.
Goodhart, C.A.E. (1989b), 'The Conduct of Monetary Policy', *Economic Journal*, 99 (396), 293–346.
Goodhart, C.A.E. (1994), 'What should Central Banks do? What should be their

Macroeconomic Objectives and Operations?', *Economic Journal*, 104 (427), 1424–36.

Goodhart, C.A.E. (1995a), *The Central Bank and the Financial System*, London: Macmillan.

Goodhart, C.A.E. (1995b), 'Price Stability and Financial Fragility' in K. Sawamoto, Z. Nakajima and H. Taguchi (eds), *Financial Stability in a Changing Environment*, Ch. 10, 439–510, London: Macmillan.

Goodhart, C.A.E. (1995c), 'Money Supply Control: Base or Interest Rates', Chapter 7 in *Monetarism and the Methodology of Economics*, eds K.D. Hoover and S.M. Sheffrin, Aldershot, England: Edward Elgar.

Goodhart, C.A.E. (1997), 'Hong Kong Financial Crisis (1983)', in *Business Cycles and Depressions: An Encyclopedia*, ed. D. Glasner, New York: Garland Publishing Inc.

Goodhart, C.A.E. (ed.) (1998), *The Emerging Framework of Financial Regulation*, London: Central Banking Publications.

Goodhart, C.A.E. (1999), 'Central Bankers and Uncertainty', *Bank of England Quarterly Bulletin*, 39 (1), 102–14, also in the *Proceedings of the British Academy: 1998 Lectures and Members* (1999), vol. 101, 229–71, Oxford University Press.

Goodhart, C.A.E. (ed.) (2000a), *Which Lender of Last Resort for Europe*, London: Central Banking Publications.

Goodhart, C.A.E. (2000b), 'The Organisational Structure of Banking Supervision', Financial Markets Group, LSE, Special Paper No. 127, October.

Goodhart, C.A.E. (2001a), 'The Inflation Forecast', *National Institute Economic Review*, No. 175, January, pp. 59–66.

Goodhart, C.A.E. (2001b), 'What Weight Should be Given to Asset Prices in the Measurement of Inflation?', *Economic Journal*, 111 (472), 335–56.

Goodhart, C.A.E. (2001c), 'Monetary Transmission Lags and the Formulation of the Policy Decision on Interest Rates', Federal Reserve Bank of St Louis *Review*, 83 (4), 165–81, July/August.

Goodhart, C.A.E. and R.J. Bhansali (1970), 'Political Economy', *Political Studies*, XVIII (1), 43–106.

Goodhart, C.A.E. and A.D. Crockett (1970), 'The Importance of Money', *Bank of England Quarterly Bulletin*, 10 (2), 159–98.

Goodhart, C.A.E. and R. Curcio (1991), 'The Clustering of Bid/Ask Prices and the Spread in the Foreign Exchange Market', Financial Markets Group Discussion Paper, No. 110, January.

Goodhart, C.A.E. and Dai Lu (2003), *Intervention to Save Hong Kong: The Authorities Counter-Speculation in Financial Markets*, Oxford University Press, forthcoming.

Goodhart, C.A.E. and A.A. Demos (1990), 'Reuters Screen Images of the Foreign Exchange Market; The Deutschemark/Dollar Spot Rate', *The Journal of International Securities Markets*, 4, 333–57.

Goodhart, C.A.E. and A.A. Demos (1991), 'Reuters Screen Images of the Foreign Exchange Markets: The Yen/Dollar and the Sterling/Dollar Spot Market', *The Journal of International Securities Markets*, 5, Spring, 35–64.

Goodhart, C.A.E. and L. Figliuoli (1991), 'Every Minute Counts in Financial Markets', *Journal of International Money and Finance*, 10, 23–52.

Goodhart, C.A.E. and L. Figliuoli (1992), 'The Geographical Location of the Foreign Exchange Market: A Test on an "Islands" Hypothesis', *Journal of International and Comparative Economics* (*JOICE*), 1 (1), 13–28.

Goodhart, C.A.E. and M. Giugale (1989), 'Some Evidence on Daily Trading in the London Foreign Exchange Market', *The Journal of International Securities Markets*, Summer, 137–46.

Goodhart, C.A.E. and M. Giugale (1993), 'From Hour to Hour in the Foreign Exchange Market', *Manchester School*, LXI (1), 1–34.

Goodhart, C.A.E., Hall, S.G., Henry, S.G.B. and B. Pesaran (1993), 'News Effects in a High Frequency Model of the Sterling-Dollar Exchange Rate', *Journal of Applied Econometrics*, 8 (1), 1–13.

Goodhart, C.A.E., Hartmann, P., Llewellyn, D.T., Rojas-Suarez, L. and S. Weisbrod (1998), *Financial Regulation: Why, How and Where Now?*, London: Routledge.

Goodhart, C.A.E. and T. Hesse (1993), 'Central Bank Forex Intervention Assessed in Continuous Time', *Journal of International Money and Finance*, 12 (9), 368–89.

Goodhart, C.A.E. and B. Hofmann (2000a), 'Do Asset Prices Help to Predict Consumer Price Inflation?', *The Manchester School Supplement*, 68, 122–40.

Goodhart, C.A.E. and B. Hofmann (2000b), 'Financial Variables and the Conduct of Monetary Policy', Sveriges (Sweden's) Riksbank Working Paper, No. 112.

Goodhart, C.A.E. and B. Hofmann (2001a), 'Asset Prices, Financial Conditions and the Transmission of Monetary Policy', paper presented at Conference on 'Asset Prices, Exchange Rates and Monetary Policy', Stanford University, 2/3 March, 2001.

Goodhart, C.A.E. and B. Hofmann (2001b), 'Deflation Credit and Asset Prices', Financial Markets Group, LSE, preliminary draft.

Goodhart, C.A.E. and H. Huang (1998), 'Time Inconsistency in a Model with Lags, Persistence, and Overlapping Wage Contracts', *Oxford Economic Papers*, 50, 378–96.

Goodhart, C.A.E. and H. Huang (2000), 'A Simple Model of International Lender of Last Resort', *Economic Notes*, 29 (1), 1–11.

Goodhart, C.A.E. and H. Huang (2001), 'A Model of the Lender of Last Resort', Working Paper revised 2001, Financial Markets Group, LSE, Discussion Paper no. 313, 1999.

Goodhart, C.A.E. and G. Illing (eds) (2002), *Financial Crises, Contagion and the Lender of Last Resort*, Oxford University Press.

Goodhart, C.A.E., Ito, T. and R. Payne (1996), 'One Day in June 1993: A Study of the Working of the Reuters 2000–2 Electronic Foreign Exchange Trading System', Chapter 4 in *The Microstructure of Foreign Exchange Markets*, eds J.A. Frankel, G. Galli and A. Giovannini, University of Chicago Press; also published as NBER Technical Working Paper, No. 179, April 1995.

Goodhart, C.A.E., McMahon, P.C. and Y.L. Ngama (1992), 'Does the Forward Premium/Discount Help to Predict the Future Change in the Exchange Rate?', *Scottish Journal of Political Economy*, 39 (2), 129–40.

Goodhart, C.A.E., McMahon, P.C. and Y.L. Ngama (1993), 'Testing for Unit Roots with Very High Frequency Spot Exchange Rate Data', *Journal of Macroeconomics*, 15 (3), 423–38.

Goodhart, C.A.E., McMahon, P.C. and Y.L. Ngama (1997), 'Why Does the Spot-Forward Discount Fail to Predict Changes in Future Spot Prices', *International Journal of Financial Economics*, 2 (2), 121–30.

Goodhart, C.A.E. and M. O'Hara (1997), 'High Frequency Data in Financial Markets: Issues and Applications', *Journal of Empirical Finance*, 4 (2/3), 73–114.

Goodhart, C.A.E. and R. Payne (1996), 'Microstructural Dynamics in a Foreign

Exchange Electronic Broking System', *Journal of International Money and Finance*, 15 (6), 829–52.
Goodhart, C.A.E. and R. Payne (2000), *The Foreign Exchange Market*, London: Macmillan.
Goodhart, C.A.E. and D. Schoenmaker (1995), 'Should the Functions of Monetary Policy and Banking Supervision be Separated?', *Oxford Economic Papers*, 47, 539–60.
Goodhart, C.A.E., Schoenmaker, D. and P. Dasgupta (2002), 'The Skill Profile of Central Bankers and Supervisors', Working Paper, also presented at European Finance Association Conference in Barcelona, August, 2001.
Goodhart, C.A.E. and M.P. Taylor (1992), 'Why Don't Individuals Speculate in Forward Foreign Exchange?', *Scottish Journal of Political Economy*, 39 (1), 1–13.
Harcourt, G.C. (1972), *Some Cambridge Controversies in the Theory of Capital*, Cambridge: Cambridge University Press.
Holbik, K. (1973), *Monetary Policy in Twelve Industrial Countries*, Federal Reserve Bank of Boston.
Lawson, N. (1981), 'Thatcherism in Practice. A Progress Report', Speech to the Zurich Society of Economics, 14th January, HM Treasury Press Release.
Lawson, N. (1992), *The View from No. 11, Memoirs of a Tory Radical*, London: Corgi Books.
Martijn, J.K. and H. Samiei (1999), 'Central Bank Independence and the Conduct of Monetary Policy in the United Kingdom', International Monetary Fund Working Paper 99/170.
Meyer, L. (2001), 'Commentary' [on Goodhart (2001)], Federal Reserve Bank of St Louis *Review*, 83 (4), 183–6, July/August.
Monetary Policy Committee, Bank of England (1999), *The Transmission Mechanism of Monetary Policy*, booklet, Bank of England.
Nevins, A. (1963), *Herbert H. Lehman and his Era*, New York: Scribner's.
Niehans, J. (1981), 'The Appreciation of Sterling – Causes, Effects, Policies', Money Study Group Discussion Paper, mimeo, February.
Payne, R. (1996a), 'Announcement Effects and Seasonality in the Intra-day Foreign Exchange Market', Discussion Paper 238, Financial Markets Group, London School of Economics.
Payne, R. (1996b), 'Information Transmission in Inter-Dealer Foreign Exchange Transactions', Working Paper, Financial Markets Group, London School of Economics.
Payne, R. (2001), 'Informed Trade in Spot Foreign Exchange Markets: An Empirical Investigation', FMG working paper.
Richardson, G. (1978), 'Reflections on the Conduct of Monetary Policy', *Bank of England Quarterly Bulletin*, 18 (1), 51–8.
Rime, D. (2001), 'US Exchange Rates and Currency Flows', Stockholm Institute for Financial Research working paper.
Roll, E., Chairman of an Independent Panel's Report (1993), *Independent and Accountable: A New Mandate for the Bank of England*, London: Centre for Economic Policy Research.
Rudebusch, G.D. (2000), 'Term Structure Evidence on Interest Rate Smoothing and Monetary Policy Inertia', Federal Reserve Bank of San Francisco, draft paper, September.
Shackle, G.L.S. (1949), *Expectations in Economics*, Cambridge: Cambridge University Press.

Sraffa, P. (1960), *Production of Commodities by Means of Commodities: Prelude to a Critique of Economic Theory*, Cambridge: Cambridge University Press.
Svensson, Lars (1997a), 'Optimal Inflation Targets, "Conservative" Central Banks, and Linear Inflation Contracts', *American Economic Review*, 87 (1), 98–114.
Svensson, Lars (1997b), 'Inflation Forecast Targeting: Implementing and Monitoring Inflation Targets', *European Economic Review*, 41, 1111–46.
Svensson, Lars (2002), 'The Inflation Forecast and the Loss Function', this volume, Chapter 4, pp. 135–52.
Thatcher, M. (1993), *The Downing Street Years*, London: Harper Collins.
Treasury, Her Majesty's (1980), *Financial Statement and Budget Report*, incorporating the Medium Term Financial Strategy, London: Her Majesty's Stationery Office (HMSO).
Treasury, HM (2002), *Reforming Britain's Economic and Financial Policy*, eds E. Balls and A. O'Donnell, Basingstoke, Hants: Palgrave.
Treasury and Civil Service Committee (1981), *Monetary Policy: Report*, London: HMSO.
Treasury Select Committee (1993), *The Role of the Bank of England*, 2 vols, London: HMSO.
Walsh, C.E. (1995), 'Optimal Contracts for Central Bankers', *American Economic Review*, 85 (1), 150–67.
Walters, A. (1986), *Britain's Economic Renaissance: Margaret Thatcher's Reforms, 1979–1984*, Oxford University Press.

1. No money, no inflation – the role of money in the economy

Mervyn King[1]

1. INTRODUCTION

Most people think economics is the study of money. But there is a paradox in the role of money in economic policy. It is this: that as price stability has become recognised as the central objective of central banks, the attention actually paid by central banks to money has declined.

It is no accident that during the 'Great Inflation' of the post-war period money, as a causal factor for inflation, was ignored by much of the economic establishment. In the late 1970s, the counter-revolution in economics – the idea that in the long run money affected the price level and not the level of output – returned money to centre stage in economic policy. As Milton Friedman put it, 'inflation is always and everywhere a monetary phenomenon'. If inflation was a monetary phenomenon, then controlling the supply of money was the route to low inflation. Monetary aggregates became central to the conduct of monetary policy. But the passage to low inflation proved painful. Nor did the monetary aggregates respond kindly to the attempts by central banks to control them. As the governor of the Bank of Canada at the time, Gerald Bouey, remarked, 'we didn't abandon the monetary aggregates, they abandoned us'.

So, as central banks became more and more focused on achieving price stability, less and less attention was paid to movements in money. Indeed, the decline of interest in money appeared to go hand in hand with success in maintaining low and stable inflation. How do we explain the apparent contradiction that the acceptance of the idea that inflation is a monetary phenomenon has been accompanied by the lack of any reference to money in the conduct of monetary policy during its most successful period? That paradox is the subject of this chapter.

Of course, some central banks, especially the Bundesbank and the Swiss National Bank, always paid a good deal of attention to monetary aggregates. But when the European Central Bank acquired responsibility for monetary policy it adopted a reference value for money growth as only one of its two pillars of monetary policy, with an assessment of the outlook for inflation as the other. And the Swiss National Bank recently replaced its target for the monetary aggregates with one for inflation. In the United States, the Federal Reserve, at its own request, has been relieved of the statutory requirement, imposed in 1978, to report twice a year on its target ranges for the growth of money and credit. As Larry Meyer, a Governor of the Federal Reserve Board explained earlier in 2001, 'money plays no explicit role in today's consensus macro model, and it plays virtually no role in the conduct of monetary policy'.

The decline and fall of money in policy formation is confirmed by a fall in the number of references to money in the speeches of central bank governors. So much so that over the past two years, Governor Sir Edward George has made one reference to money in 29 speeches, Chairman Greenspan one in 17, Governor Hayami one in 11, and Wim Duisenberg three in 30.

2. MONEY AND INFLATION: THE EVIDENCE

Let me begin by looking at some of the historical evidence. Figure 1.1, which extends the results of McCandless and Weber (1995), shows the correlation between the growth of the monetary base and inflation over different time horizons for a large sample of 116 countries. Countries with faster growth rates of money have experienced higher inflation. It is clear from Figure 1.1 that the correlation between money growth and inflation is greater the longer is the time horizon over which both are measured. In the short run, the correlation between monetary growth and inflation is much less apparent. Understanding why this is so is at the heart of monetary economics and still poses problems for economists trying to understand the impact of money on the economy. I shall return to this later.

Few empirical regularities in economics are so well documented as the co-movement of money and inflation. Figure 1.2 shows that this relationship is true for broad money as well as the monetary base. The other side of the coin to this close relationship between money and prices is the absence of a long-run relationship between money and output growth, shown in Figure 1.3. Over the thirty-year horizon 1968–98, the correlation coefficient between the growth rates of both narrow and broad money, on the one hand, and inflation, on the other, was 0.99. Correspondingly, the correlation between the growth of narrow money and real output growth was –0.09 and between broad money growth and output was –0.08.

Correlation, of course, is not causation. The essence of monetary theory is trying to understand the *structural* relationship between money growth,

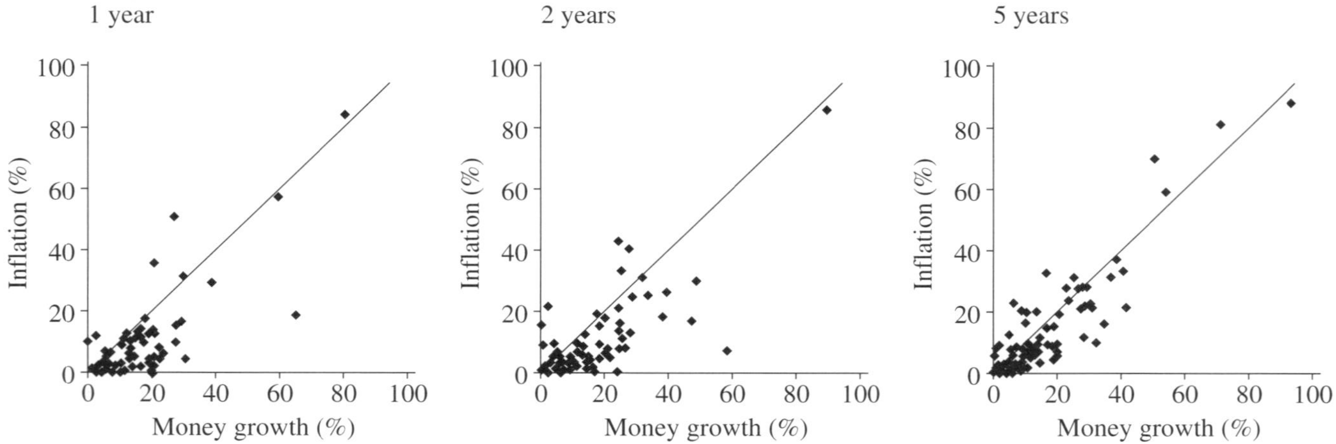
1 year
2 years
5 years
Inflation (%)
Money growth (%)
0
20
40
60
80
100

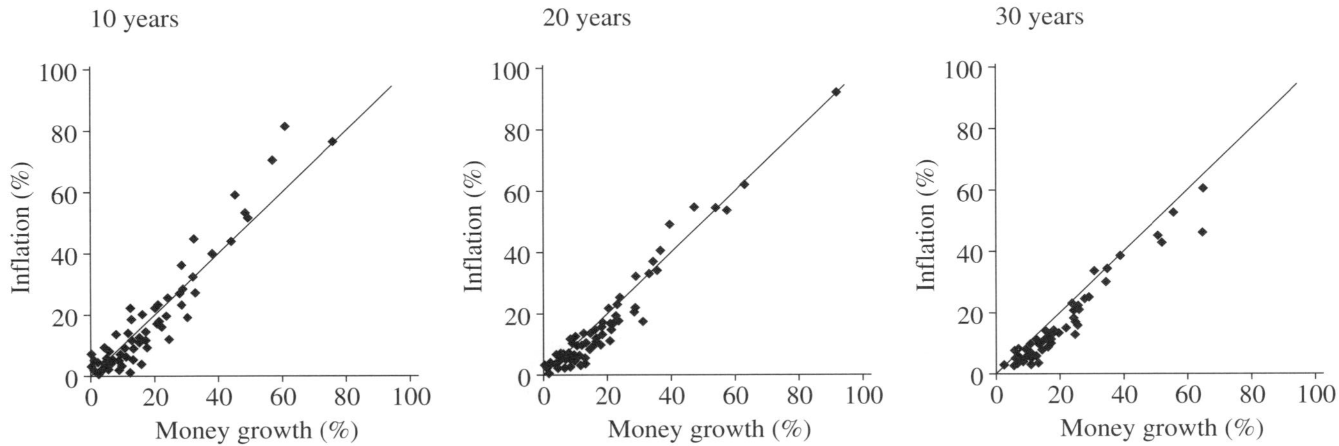

Notes:
Narrow money is Reserve Money, which includes currency in circulation (data item 14 in each IFS country table).
Inflation is the percentage increase in the consumer price index (item 64).
For presentation purposes, countries with average annual money growth or inflation exceeding 100% have not been included in the charts.

Source: International Financial Statistics (International Monetary Fund).

Figure 1.1 Annual inflation and growth of narrow money at different horizons across countries

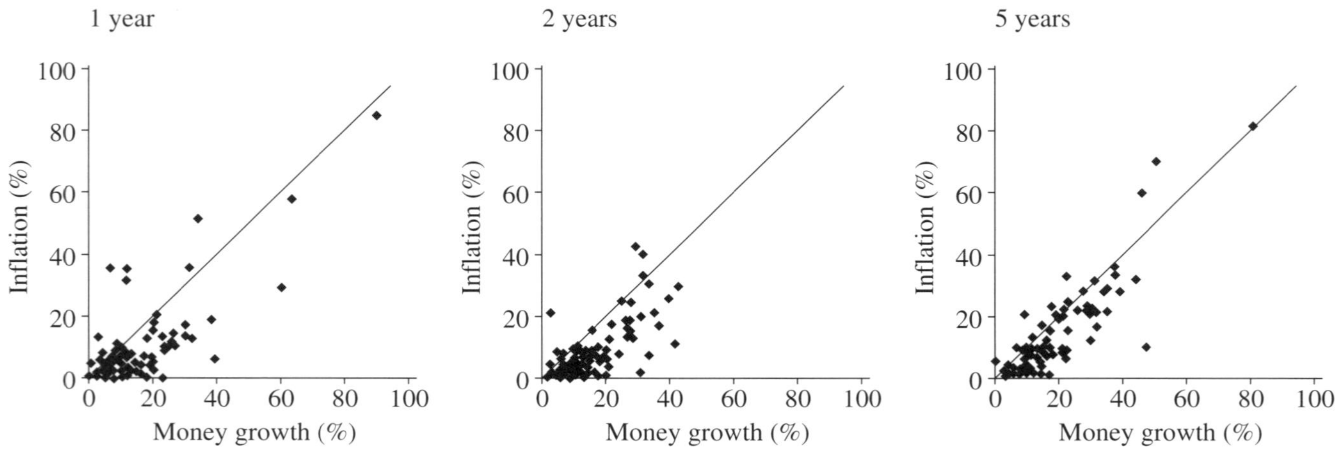
1 year
2 years
5 years
Inflation (%)
100
80
60
40
20
0
0
20
40
60
80
100
Money growth (%)

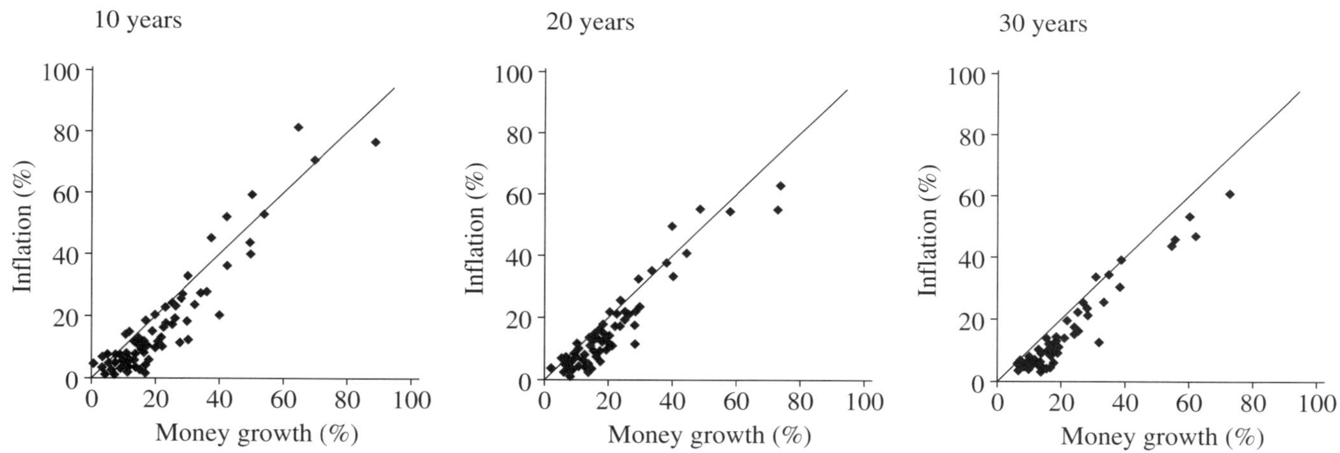

Notes:
Broad money includes demand deposits and time deposits (data items 34 and 35 in each IFS country table).
Inflation is the percentage increase in the consumer price index (item 64).
For presentation purposes, countries with average annual money growth or inflation exceeding 100% have not been included in the charts.

Source: International Financial Statistics (International Monetary Fund).

Figure 1.2 Annual inflation and growth of broad money at different horizons across countries

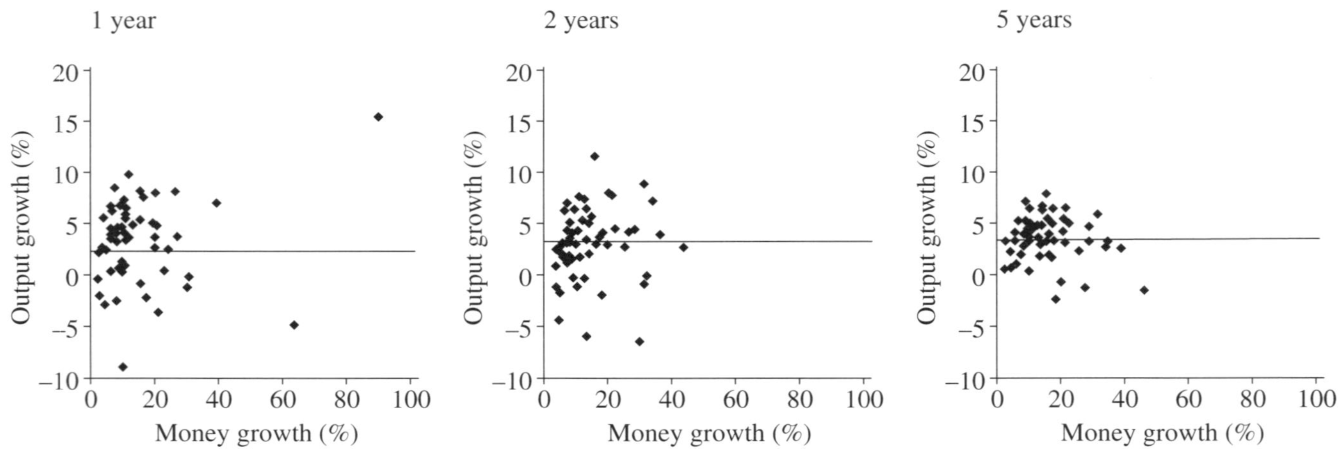
1 year
2 years
5 years
Output growth (%)
Money growth (%)
20
15
10
5
0
–5
–10
0
20
40
60
80
100

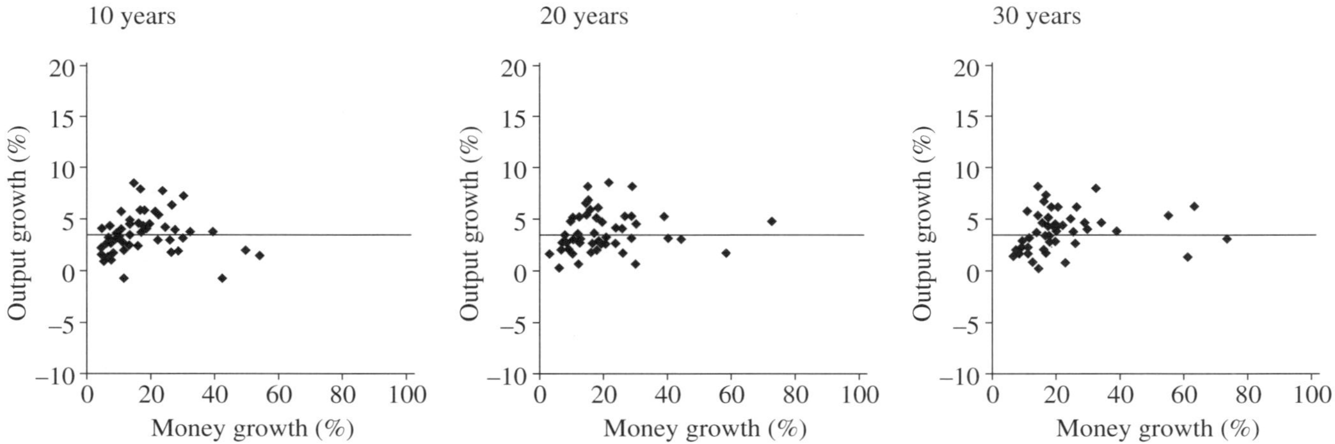

Notes:
Real output is nominal GDP (data item 99b in each IFS country table) deflated by the consumer price index (item 64). A GDP deflator was only available for a small sample of countries, and was therefore not used.
The horizontal line represents the average annual real output growth across countries for each time horizon.
For presentation purposes, countries with average annual money growth or inflation exceeding 100% have not been included in the charts.
There were 8 countries that had negative average real output growth over the 1978–98 period. These countries have not been included in the charts.

Source: International Financial Statistics (International Monetary Fund).

Figure 1.3 Annual growth of broad money and output at different horizons across countries

demand, output and price movements. Stable structural relationships can give rise to unstable short-run correlations between any of these variables. It is, therefore, somewhat surprising that some economists have argued that the instability of observed short-run correlations casts doubt on the long-run importance of money growth in the inflationary process. Figure 1.4 shows the behaviour of the price level in the UK and its relationship with the ratio of money to real income over the period from 1885 to 1998. Short-run movements in the velocity of money are apparent, as well as the long-run link between money and inflation.

The view that money does not matter has been encouraged by those who point to regressions of inflation and output growth on monetary growth, and find that the influence of money is either insignificant or unstable. But these results tell us little about the significance of money in the transmission mechanism of monetary policy. They are based on reduced-form equations, the coefficients of which will be complex functions of the true

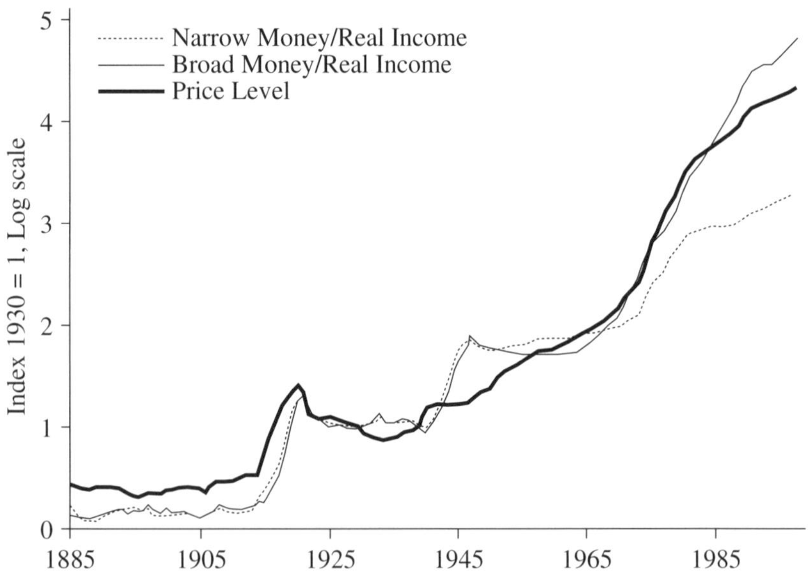

Sources: Capie, F. and Webber, A. (1985), 'A Monetary History of the United Kingdom', 1870–1982, Vol. 1: Data, Sources, Methods, London, Allen and Unwin; Feinstein, C.H. (1972), 'National Income Expenditure and Output of the United Kingdom', 1855–1965, Cambridge, Cambridge University Press; Bank of England (M0 from 1969, M4 from 1963) and ONS (GDP from 1948, RPIX from 1976).

Figure 1.4 Prices and money relative to real incomes in the UK: 1885–1998

structural parameters of the economy, as well as expectations of future policy responses by the monetary authorities. There is no reason to expect a simple relationship between inflation and output and money growth in reduced form estimates.

This last point was clearly grasped by Friedman in his 1963 volume on inflation. In the famous study of money in the United States Friedman, with Anna J. Schwartz, took great care to identify periods in which there was an exogenous shock to the money supply, such as moves on to and off the gold standard, and changes in reserve requirements imposed on banks. More recent studies, such as Estrella and Mishkin (1997), Hendry (2001), Gerlach and Svensson (2000) and Stock and Watson (1999) produce conflicting and unstable regression results for the influence of money growth on inflation.

To understand the true role of money, a clear theoretical model is required and that model must allow for the central role of expectations. The key role of expectations is best illustrated by considering extreme cases of high inflation, known as hyperinflations. In hyperinflations the effect of expectations on money and inflation is amplified relative to other influences, such as the business cycle.

Figure 1.5 shows the link between money and prices in four hyperinflations. Two of these are drawn from the inter-war period, namely the hyperinflations in Austria and Hungary, and two are post-war hyperinflations, in Argentina and Israel. At their peak, these hyperinflations involved annual inflation rates of 9,244 per cent, 4,300 per cent, 20,266 per cent, and 486 per cent respectively. All four hyperinflations illustrate the importance of expectations. In the case of the two inter-war hyperinflations, large government deficits were monetised, leading to rapid money growth and inflation. The public tried to economise on money holdings, and so real money demand fell. Announcements of credible fiscal stabilisations changed inflation expectations and led extremely quickly to a rapid fall in inflation. Lower inflation encouraged real money demand to rise again, and so nominal money growth continued to rise for some time after inflation had fallen. Inflation was, therefore, stabilised *ahead* of the slowdown in money growth, although the *causation* ran from the credible announcement of monetary contraction to lower inflation. The vertical lines in the charts indicate the announcement dates of stabilisation packages. In Argentina, inflation expectations were stabilised by the convertibility plan of 1991 which established a currency board to back the local currency in terms of the US dollar. Inflation expectations fell, and, as in the earlier cases, the fall in inflation preceded the slowdown in money growth. The case of Israel is somewhat different in that the absence of any delay between the announcement and the implementation of the stabilisation programme in 1985

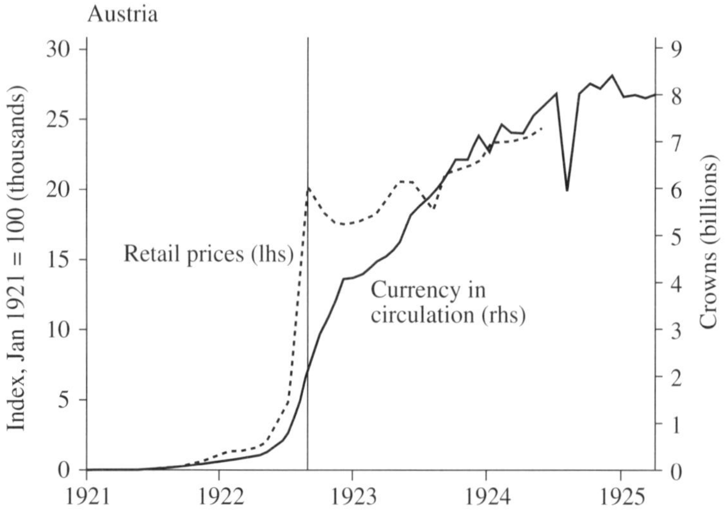

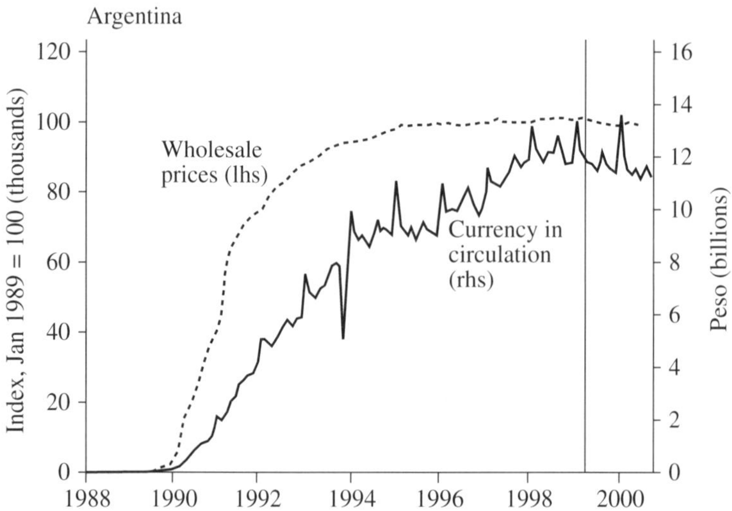

Note: Vertical lines indicate the date at which a stabilisation plan involving fiscal and monetary reforms was announced.

Sources: Austria and Hungary: Sargent, T. (1993), *Rational Expectations and Inflation*, New York: Harper Collins College Publishers, pp. 80–92. Argentina and Israel: International Financial Statistics (International Monetary Fund).

Figure 1.5 Money and prices during four hyperinflations

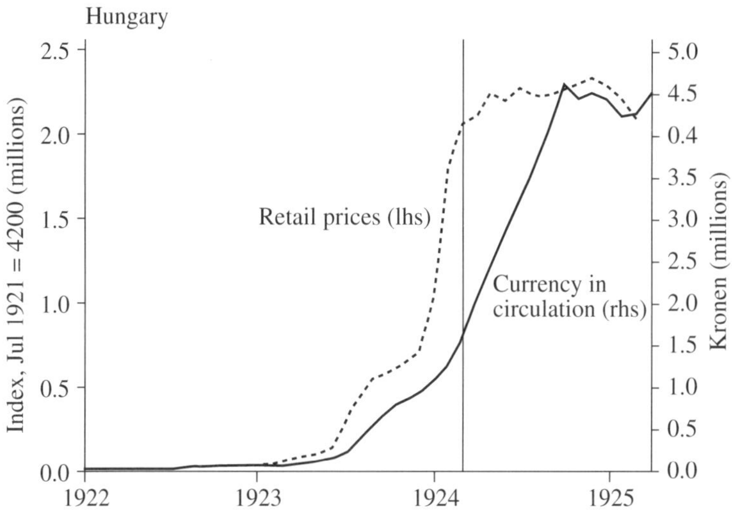

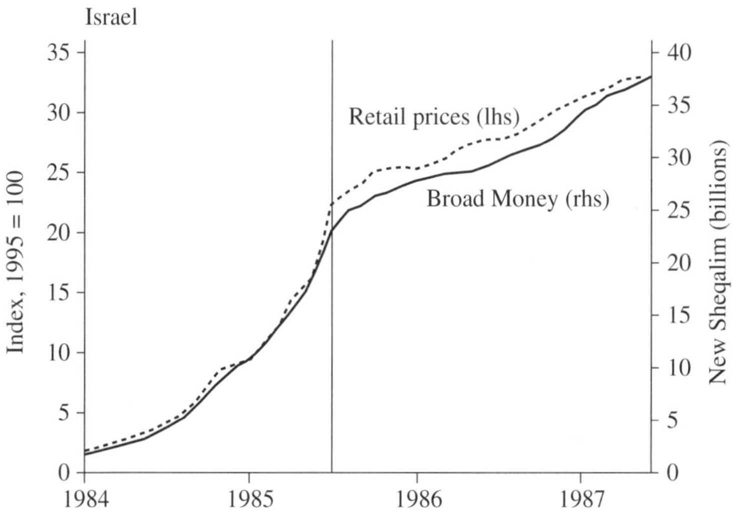

Figure 1.5 *(continued)*

meant that the gap between the fall in inflation and the contraction of monetary growth was shorter than in the other cases shown in Figure 1.5. Although hyperinflations are extreme examples, they do illustrate the fact that, even when monetary contraction is evidently the cause of a fall in inflation, the rapid response of expectations means that inflation may fall before signs of a slowing of monetary growth appear.

To make progress, a more complete account is required of the role of money in the transmission mechanism, and it is to this that I now turn.

3. UNDERSTANDING THE ROLE OF MONEY

There is an old joke to the effect that economists spend their time trying to work out how something that works in practice can work in theory. The role of money in the economy offers an excellent example. In modelling the monetary transmission mechanism, economists have tended to rely on two types of 'rigidities' which introduce time lags into the process by which changes in money lead to changes in prices. These are lags in the adjustment of prices and wages to changes in demand – so-called 'nominal rigidities' – and lags in the adjustment of expectations to changes in the monetary policy regime – so-called 'expectational rigidities'. These rigidities mean that money affects real variables in the short run and prices in the long run.

But we have no good theories to explain either type of rigidity, nor a clear idea of when the short run turns into the long run. Hence Milton Friedman's dictum that there are 'long and variable' time lags between changes in monetary policy and their impact on inflation. To understand these theoretical shortcomings, it is helpful to consider an abbreviated history of the models used by economists to analyse the impact of money. The standard or consensus model comprises four basic equations (see Figure 1.6). First, there is an equation for aggregate demand which relates total demand to either money or interest rates and to expected inflation. The aggregate demand function is sometimes known as the 'IS' curve. Second, there is an equation describing the supply side of the economy in which total output is related to differences between expected and actual inflation; this is the 'Phillips–Lucas supply curve'. Third, there is an equation for the demand for money relating broad money holdings to total expenditures and the interest rate; the 'LM' curve. Fourth, there is an equation describing monetary policy in which the supply of broad money is determined by the actions of the central bank in controlling base money (bank reserves plus notes and coin in circulation) which in turn influences broad money provided by the banking system through the 'money multi-

$$(1)\quad Y_D = f_1(M, i, E(\pi))$$

$$(2)\quad Y_S = f_2(\pi - E(\pi))$$

$$(3)\quad M_D = f_3(Y_D, i)$$

$$(4)\quad M_S = f_4(Y_D, i, \pi)$$

Given (i) a model for $E(\pi)$
(ii) equilibrium, i.e. $Y_D = Y_s = Y$; $M_D = M_S = M$
then the four equations determine $\{Y, M, i, \pi\}$

Figure 1.6 Standard monetary model

plier'. This equation represents the monetary policy reaction function of the central bank. The model determines the values of output, inflation, the interest rate, and money growth. Most models used to analyse monetary policy are based on a variant of this four-equation system, with increasing importance over time given to the role of expectations in the Phillips curve.

In this framework, the standard theoretical view of the transmission mechanism of monetary policy works as follows. An unexpected increase in the money supply reduces the nominal interest rate in order to persuade households to hold larger money balances. If inflation expectations are slow to adjust to the increase in the money supply – because of expectational rigidities – then the fall in the nominal interest rate also implies a fall in the real rate of interest. This raises expenditures on items such as investment and consumer durables which are sensitive to interest rates. If prices and wages are slow to adjust to higher demand – because of nominal rigidities – then in the short run firms are induced to supply more output. As the pressure on capacity in the economy rises, employees demand higher wages to reflect increased demand and both wages and prices rise. In the long run output is determined solely by real factors, and the increase in money supply is reflected in a rise in the price level.

More recently, the equation for money supply has been replaced by an explicit feedback rule for interest rates. The money demand equation plays no explicit role in determining output, inflation and interest rates. Money, it would appear, has been eased out of the picture. In these new models, a loosening of monetary policy – characterised by an unexpected reduction in the nominal interest rate – raises demand, output and, ultimately, inflation. In the long run the inflation rate is determined by monetary policy, in the sense that the monetary policy reaction function determining interest rates contains an explicit inflation target. Money growth is higher, the higher is the inflation rate, but, if the model were an accurate description of the economy, the interest rate would be a sufficient statistic of monetary policy. Models of this type in which interest rates are the policy instrument are widely used both in theoretical analysis and in the design of empirical policy rules, such as the well-known Taylor rule. Given this prominent role for interest rates rather than money in the theoretical analysis of policy, it is, perhaps, not surprising that econometric forecasting models in most major central banks include interest rates, but not the quantity of money.

Despite appearances, however, these new models give no less weight to money than the older versions. Irrespective of whether the central bank uses base money or interest rates as the policy instrument, the quantity theory of money still applies. In the new models, monetary quantities play no independent role in the transmission mechanism over and above that summarised in interest rates. But, equally, in the old models too, monetary policy impacted on the economy through its effects on interest rates. The key question is not whether the central bank uses the monetary base or interest rates as its policy instrument. It is whether the equations which are embedded in both the old and new models of monetary policy exclude important channels through which monetary policy works.

Before attempting to answer this question, the consensus model can be used to illustrate a key point made earlier, namely that there is no reason to expect a stable relationship between money and inflation in the short run. Using a linearised model of the type described in Figure 1.6, the exact details of which are given in the technical appendix, simulated data can be generated for long time periods corresponding to realisations of the various shocks to the economy. In particular, a quarterly model was constructed using calibrated parameters and processes for the stochastic shocks in each equation. Several variants of the model were then created, keeping the main model parameters constant, but altering the variance and persistence of the stochastic shocks. By simulating the shock processes 10,000 times for each variant, several datasets spanning 2,500 years were created. Reduced form regressions were then run on the variants of the model to estimate the dependence of inflation on lagged values of output, money growth and inflation itself. Note that, *by construction*, money has a stable causal effect on inflation. The regression results obtained from different sample periods produce a wide variation of estimated coefficients on money in determining inflation (see Table 1.1). In fact, these coefficients can be either positive, negative or insignificantly different from zero, depending on the constellation of shocks hitting the economy. Moreover, the reduced form relationships change with the length of the horizon (see Table 1.2). Money appears to contain little information about very short-term inflationary pressures, but it becomes much more significant in the long run. In contrast, the impact of output growth on inflation falls as the horizon lengthens. The

Table 1.1 What can we learn from this model about simplistic econometrics?

Consider two reduced-form regressions, specified as:

$$\pi_t = \sum_{s=1}^{i} \gamma_s \pi_{t-s} + \sum_{s=0}^{j} \delta_s (y_{t-s} - \bar{y}_{t-s}) + \sum_{s=0}^{k} \mu_{t-s}(\Delta m_{t-s}) \quad (1)$$

$$\pi_t = \sum_{s=1}^{i} \gamma_s \pi_{t-s} + \sum_{s=0}^{j} \delta_s (\Delta y_{t-s}) + \sum_{s=0}^{k} \mu_{t-s}(\Delta m_{t-s}) \quad (2)$$

Long-run coefficient on money growth (1)	(2)	Changes to the sources or magnitudes of shocks from the baseline
−0.14	0.05	Case 1: None.
−0.50	−0.08	Case 2: Increase in the autocorrelation of demand shocks to 0.5.
−2.51	−1.4	Case 3: Increase in the standard deviation of mark up shocks to 0.01.
0.65	0.78	Case 4: Increase in the standard deviation of mark up shocks to 0.01, the autocorrelation of cost push shocks to 0.8 and the standard deviation of policy shocks to 0.04.

Notes and sources: Precise details are provided in the technical appendix. Under the baseline, demand (ε_1 from the technical appendix), mark-up (ε_2), monetary policy (ε_3) and supply (ε_4) shocks are generated with standard deviations of 0.01, 0, 0.0082 and 0.0072, respectively, and with first-order autocorrelation of 0.33, 0, 0.3 and 0.95 respectively. These values are consistent with Nelson (2000) and Neiss and Nelson (2001). Each regression uses 10,000 observations.

Table 1.2 What can we learn about money from simplistic econometrics?

The correlations between the simulated data depend on their frequency, as they do in the historical data.

	$corr(y-\bar{y},\Delta p)$	$corr(\Delta m,\Delta p)$
Short run	0.79	0.23
Long run	0.05	0.68

Note: Short-run means a contemporaneous correlation between the variables and long-run means a correlation between the output gap today and average inflation over the following twenty-five years, or average money growth and inflation both over a twenty-five-year period.

conclusion is straightforward. Simplistic reduced-form econometrics is no substitute for a clear theoretical structural model of how money-output and inflation are related (a point also made by Nelson (2001)). Thinking on this point needs to be liberated from the 'tyranny of regressions'.

Both old and new models of the monetary transmission mechanism have important limitations. Crucially, there is only a single financial asset. But in the traditional monetarist account (Friedman and Schwartz, 1963) money is an imperfect substitute for a wide range of financial and real assets, including bonds, equity, physical capital and durable goods. A monetary policy change induces a re-balancing of portfolios in general, affecting nominal demand both directly (through wealth and substitution effects on real assets), and indirectly (through adjustments in a wide range of financial yields relevant to expenditure decisions). Hence both old and new models may ignore an important part of the transmission mechanism of monetary policy.

The practical relevance of this consideration is extremely topical. The conventional model suggests that monetary policy is ineffective if interest rates have reached their natural floor of zero and a further reduction of real interest rates is required to stimulate demand. Japan appears to be in exactly that situation at present. Figure 1.7 shows the recent experience of monetary policy in Japan. Inflation has been very low; indeed, it has been negative in recent years. The Bank of Japan has lowered interest rates to the point where they have now hit their lower bound of zero. Interest rates have been extremely low for five years, and have been almost exactly zero since February 1999. The question of whether monetary policy is impotent when interest rates are zero has remained open since the possibility of a 'liquidity trap' was suggested by Keynes in the *General Theory* and revived recently by Paul Krugman.

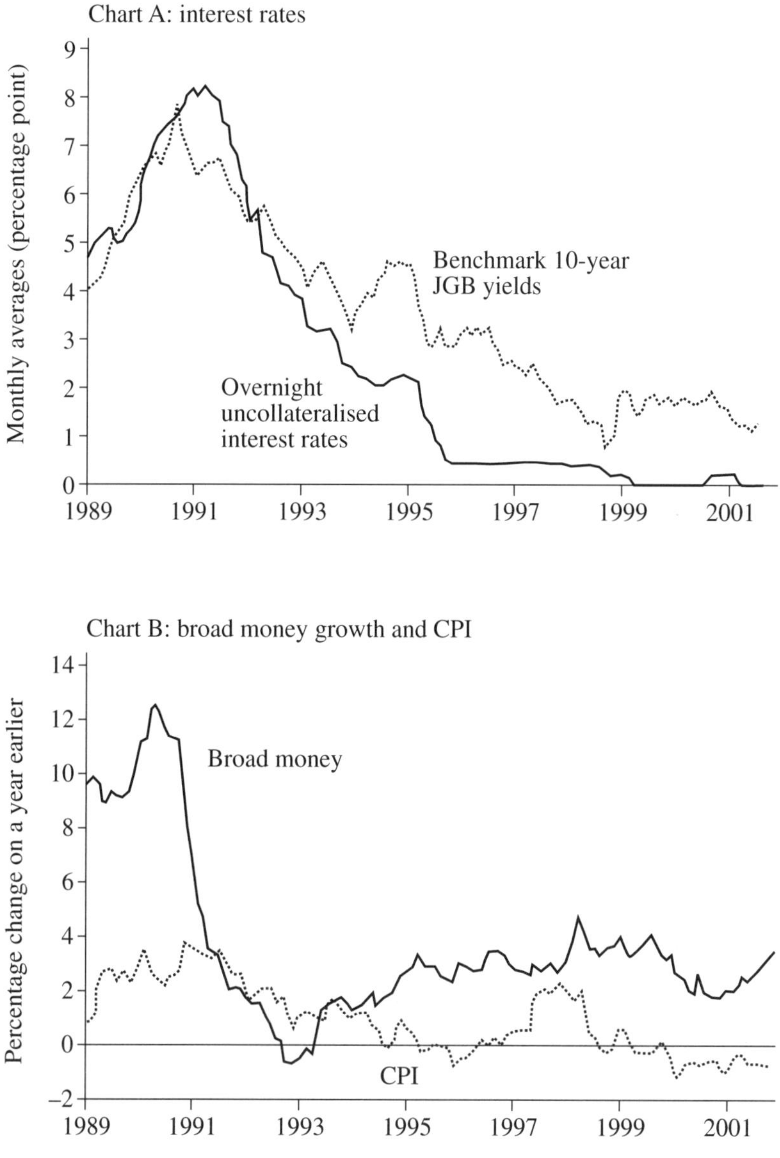

Note: Broad money is M2 and CDs.

Source: (A) Bank of Japan; (B) Bank of Japan (broad money); Ministry of Public Management, Home Affairs, Post and Telecommunications (CPI).

Figure 1.7 Interest rates, money and inflation in Japan: 1989–2001

Broadly speaking there are two answers to this question. The first is that monetary policy is indeed impotent when interest rates are zero. At this point, households and firms have an infinitely elastic demand for money balances, and so any increase in money supply is absorbed passively in higher balances. An increase in money supply has no implications for spending or output. In such circumstances, the only way to affect the economy is by an expansionary fiscal policy. The second answer is that, at some point, households and firms become satiated with money balances at the current level of income, and any attempt to increase the money supply leads them to adjust portfolios in order to limit their holding of money balances. These changes in household portfolios lead to changes in relative yields on different financial and real assets, and hence on asset prices and, in turn, real spending. Despite interest rates remaining at zero, monetary policy, in this world, can influence nominal spending and incomes.

Which view is the more attractive theoretically and empirically? It is clear that, in part, the answer depends on the response of the demand for money as interest rates tend to zero. If the demand for money tended to infinity, as the interest rate tended to zero, then an expansion in the money supply would have no real effect on demand and output because any additional money created would simply be absorbed passively in money holdings. But if the demand for money is satiated at a finite level as interest rates tend to zero, then the creation of money beyond that point would be translated into a demand for other assets and higher incomes. Since observations on interest rates close to zero are rare in practice, there is little evidence to enable us to distinguish between these two hypotheses.

A recent study by economists in the Bank of England (Bakhshi, Martin and Yates, 2002) finds some evidence of a satiation point in the demand for narrow money in the UK, although Bental and Eckstein (1997) and Lucas (2000) find evidence for an asymptote. The empirical evidence is not, therefore, decisive. There are very considerable uncertainties surrounding these estimates. But they are at least consistent with the possibility that monetary policy may have potency even at zero interest rates.

What, therefore, has economic theory to say about how changes in money might affect nominal demand, over and above any influence via interest rates? This is a question that is relevant to all economies, not just those, such as Japan, facing zero interest rates. One view, associated with Pigou (1943) and Patinkin (1965) is that a monetary expansion will, in the presence of sticky prices ('nominal rigidities') lead to a rise in the real value of the money stock which will, in turn, raise household net wealth, and lead to higher expenditures. There are two objections to this view. The first is that the only part of the money supply which constitutes net wealth for the economy as a whole is 'outside' money, namely the monetary base. And this accounts for only a very small fraction of financial wealth – a little over 1 per cent in the UK – so the quantitative impact of the real balance effect is inevitably small. Second, even this effect is subject to households failing to take into account the impact on future generations of the use of monetary financing. Nevertheless, models by which money changes real balances have become more fashionable recently. Building on the work of Sidrauski (1967), a number of economists have examined the impact of higher money holdings on the size of transactions costs. An unexpected monetary expansion lowers transactions costs, according to this view, and increases the attractions of consumption. Effects of varying size have been claimed by authors such as Ireland (2001a, 2001b), Koenig (1990), McCallum (2001) and Woodford (2002). Such transmission mechanisms, however, do not appear to be empirically significant nor do they correspond to the main channels of policy as seen by earlier generations of economists.

The main difference between the models described above and earlier writings on money is the absence in those models of financial yields other than the short-term interest rate. In principle, many more asset yields could enter the demand for money. In his own writings, Keynes placed emphasis on the yield on long-term government bonds. In this view, expansionary monetary policy can take the form of open market operations in which the central bank purchases a wide variety of assets, not just short-term government securities. Yields on a wide variety of financial assets respond, and in turn so does demand. One of these financial prices is the exchange rate. That is why some economists see the salvation for Japan in terms of the exchange rate. They recommend strategies such as expanding the monetary base in order to produce a fall in the market exchange rate which would lead to an upturn driven by net trade. Alternatively, economists such as Svensson (2001) have recommended pegging the yen at a much lower exchange rate against the dollar. This, it is argued, would lead to expectations of higher inflation which, given zero nominal interest rates, would produce a negative real interest rate that would generate an expansionary impact on the economy.

The major question, however, is how an expansion of the money supply operates through indirect effects on the yields of other assets which are excluded from conventional models of the transmission mechanism. If future interest rates are incorporated into optimal consumption behaviour, then the only channel by which monetary policy can operate, other than via interest rates, is through changes in risk premia.

How might we try to integrate monetary theory and portfolio theory? Little help will come from traditional finance theory. The reason is extremely simple. Most finance theory is based on the assumption that equilibrium yields on assets, including risk premia, are independent of the quantities of the supplies of different assets. Hence the search for a better model of the monetary transmission mechanism is, in part, a search for evidence of supply effects on financial asset yields. That is why the view that money matters, over and above interest rates, is intimately bound up with a question of whether the supplies of different assets affect yields, and hence whether the composition of government debt affects both money and real economic behaviour. In the UK, Tim Congdon has emphasised the importance of 'funding policy' in the determination of the broad money supply, a subject which has been analysed in detail by Goodhart (1999). The broad weight of opinion, to date, is that supply effects are hard to find. Many years ago, for example, the US tried to change the slope of the yield curve on its government debt by 'Operation Twist' in which the composition of government debt was altered in an attempt to change relative yields. This experiment was widely regarded as a failure. Intriguingly, however, there is renewed interest among finance theorists in the impact of supply effects on yields. More and more puzzles in the theory of finance appear to be related to the existence of supply effects.

There seems to be a gap between modern finance theory and the traditional monetarist account in which a monetary expansion causes a rebalancing of portfolios putting direct upward pressure on a range of asset prices, which in turn stimulates higher nominal demand. To bridge this gap requires a more careful analysis of exactly what is special about money. Much of the traditional monetarist account relies on the imperfect substitutability between various marketable assets, including money. But there is often a weak theoretical rationale for the mechanisms discussed. Thus, while it is clear that financial markets have a much richer structure than is conventionally assumed by the models described earlier, the monetarist argument that this is sufficient to imply a significant role for money remains unproven. What are the promising avenues for future research? The solution, I conjecture, will be based on two observations:

1. Transaction costs are important in determining asset prices – many of the puzzles in the behaviour of asset prices, such as the equity risk premium, can be resolved by taking the effects of transaction costs seriously.
2. Money reduces transaction costs.

Rather than rely on a barter economy, goods (or labour) can be exchanged for money, and money for goods. But there is no reason to suppose that the same argument cannot be used in asset markets.

If the quantity of money can affect the size of transaction costs in financial markets, then it will have an effect on expenditures and inflation, over and above any change via the transmission from changes in risk-free interest rates. Over the past decade, economists have made strides in setting out a more coherent theoretical story of the way in which money reduces trading frictions in markets for goods and services. Traditional models of exchange economies make strong demands on the institutional arrangements that underlie transactions. Money can help reduce these transactions costs. And it is possible that money might have a similar role in alleviating frictions in financial markets, thus expanding the scope of the transmission mechanism of monetary policy. It is striking that nearly a quarter of the money stock in the UK is held by non-bank financial firms. The frictions which money helps to overcome in financial markets are related to its role in providing liquidity services. Money enables individuals, both households and firms, to avoid borrowing should they hit a cashflow constraint. Since the probability of experiencing such a constraint falls as the stock of money rises, changes in money could affect relative asset returns. Introducing financial frictions into models of asset prices, and recognising the role of money in reducing those frictions, provides, in my view, a potentially more significant role for money in the transmission mechanism than has been examined hitherto in a rigorous way. The theoretical support for, and empirical relevance of, such an approach is still unclear. So there is a substantial agenda for future research.

The link between money and the provision of financial services more generally is clear in the historical evolution of 'inside money', such as checking accounts and credit cards, which now constitute the bulk of broad money. Credit services can displace the use of 'outside money' in transactions, but only where their cost is sufficiently low, and that may depend upon the individual characteristics of the agents undertaking the transactions. As a result, the parameters of the money demand function are dominated by the technology of transaction services, and can be unstable over time (as for example, in the model of Aiyagari, Braun and Eckstein, 1998). This instability derives not from the irrelevance of money, but from changes to technology.

4. MONEY AND MONETARY POLICY

What does this debate about the transmission mechanism of monetary policy mean for the conduct of monetary policy today? The role of money in determining the price level, and its embodiment in the quantity theory of money, evolved over several hundred years. The broad shape of this theory was accepted by most economists. It is certainly evident in the writings of both John Maynard Keynes and Irving Fisher. As the theory of monetary economics developed, so too did the practice of monetary policy. In Britain, the beginning of the theory and practice of monetary policy as we know it today started with the Bank Charter Act of 1844. Keynes wrote that prior to the 1844 Act, 'the principles and methods of currency management were but ill understood by those responsible for its management, namely, the Governors and Court of the Bank of England' (*Treatise on Money*, pp. 14–15). He went on to conclude, 'The efficiency of bank-rate for the management of a managed money was a great discovery and also a most novel one – a few years earlier the Bank of England had not had the slightest understanding of any connection between bank-rate policy and the maintenance of the standard' (op. cit. p. 15). I hope that the Bank of England today has at least some understanding of the relationship between interest rates and inflation!

Thinking of monetary policy in terms of interest rates has become the norm in central banks today. Frequent and volatile shifts in the demand for money led central banks to change their focus from monetary aggregates towards the control of short-term interest rates. Few major central banks now place the monetary aggregates at the centre of their targeting regime. Instabilities in the demand for money are not new. In the early years of the Bank of England, there were unexpected shifts in the demand for money and credit resulting from uncertain arrival times in the Port of London of ships laden with commodities from all over the world. The uncertainty derived from changes in the direction and speed of the wind carrying ships up the Thames to the Port of London. Hence the Court Room of the Bank of England contained a weather vane which provided an accurate guide to these shifts in money demand – the weather vane is there to this day, and it still works. If only monetary policy could be as scientific today! Financial liberalisation and changes in the technology of payments and settlements have led to large volatilities in money demand. No one has yet worked out how to translate such shifts into a simple reading on the financial equivalent of a weather vane. So central banks have paid decreasing attention to the monetary aggregates as an intermediate indicator of their policy stance.

Although there is no mechanical link from the monetary aggregates to inflation, the underlying relationships, in quantitative form, still hold. Hence it is important for a central bank to understand changes in money. One of the features of Bank of England analysis of monetary developments is the attempt to understand the implications of the entire range of monetary quantities and prices facing agents in the economy. Each month the Monetary Analysis and Strategy Division of the Bank of England produces a *Quarterly Monetary Assessment* in order to provide the Monetary Policy Committee with as much information as possible about monetary developments. Part of this includes an analysis of equilibrium interest rates and the stance of monetary policy. Rules, such as the Taylor rule, provide a useful benchmark against which to judge whether interest rates are too high or too low. But the analysis provided by the Bank of England is not restricted to interest rates. It is crucial to look at developments in quantities in the monetary area and credit conditions, as well as prices. Using historical relationships estimated from the data, developments in money and credit, and their sectoral patterns, can be used as indicator variables for near-term activity and inflation. The short-term outlook for consumption, for example, can be related to movements in Divisia Money, and the outlook for investment is related to the financial position of the corporate sector.

5. CONCLUSIONS

I return to the paradox with which I began. Most people believe that economics is about money. Yet most economists hold conversations in which the word 'money' appears hardly at all. Surprisingly, that appears true even of central bankers. The resolution of this apparent puzzle, is, I believe, the following. There has been no change in the underlying theory of inflation. Evidence of the differences in inflation across countries, and changes in inflation over time, reveal the intimate link between money and prices. Economists and central bankers understand this link, but conduct their conversations in terms of interest rates and not the quantity of money. In large part, this is because unpredictable shifts in the demand for money mean that central banks choose to set interest rates and allow the public to determine the quantity of money which is supplied elastically at the given interest rate.

The disappearance of money from the models used by economists is, as I have argued, more apparent than real. Official short-term interest rates play the leading role as the instrument of policy, with money in the wings off-stage. But the models retain the classical property that, in the long run, monetary policy, and hence money, affect prices rather than real activity. Nevertheless, there are real dangers in relegating money to this behind-the-scenes role. Three dangers seem to me particularly relevant to present circumstances. First, there is a danger of neglecting parts of the monetary transmission mechanism that operate through the impact of quantities on risk and term premia of various kinds. The current debate about the appropriate monetary policy in Japan illustrates this point. Second, by denying an explicit role for money there is the danger of misleading people into thinking that there is a permanent trade-off between inflation, on the one hand, and output and employment, on the other. Third, by discussing monetary policy in terms of real rather than monetary variables, there is the danger of giving the impression that monetary policy can be used to fine tune short run movements in output and employment, and to offset each and every shock to the economy. These dangers all derive from the habit of discussing monetary policy in terms of a conceptual model in which money plays only a hidden role.

Habits of speech not only reflect habits of thinking, they influence them too as Ben Friedman reminds us later in this volume. So the way in which central banks talk about money is important. There is no inconsistency between the consensus models we use to analyse policy in terms of interest rates and the proposition that monetary growth is the driving force behind higher inflation. But it would be unfortunate if the change in the way we talk led to the erroneous belief that we could turn Milton Friedman on his head, and think that 'Inflation is always and everywhere a real phenomenon'.

My own belief is that the absence of money in the standard models which economists use will cause problems in future, and that there will be profitable developments from future research into the way in which money affects risk premia and economic behaviour more generally. Money, I conjecture, will regain an important place in the conversation of economists. As Hilaire Belloc wrote,

> I'm tired of Love: I'm still more tired of Rhyme.
> But Money gives me pleasure all the time.

NOTE

1. An earlier version of this paper was given at the Maxwell Fry Global Finance Lecture, University of Birmingham, Wednesday 24 October 2001. I would especially like to thank Andrew Hauser, James Proudman and Jan Vlieghe for their help in preparing this paper. I have also benefited from useful comments from Peter Andrews, Kosuke Aoki, Zvi Eckstein and John Power. Richard Geare, Alex Golledge and Amit Sohal provided help with the data.

REFERENCES

Aiyagari, S.R., Braun, R.A. and Eckstein, Z. (1998), 'Transaction Services, Inflation, and Welfare', *Federal Reserve Bank of Minneapolis Staff Report*, vol. 241, p. 35.

Bakhshi, H., Martin, B. and Yates, T. (2002), 'How Uncertain are the Welfare Costs of Inflation?', Bank of England Working Paper, no. 152.

Bental, B. and Eckstein, Z. (1997), 'On the Fit of a Neoclassical Monetary Model in High Inflation: Israel 1972–1990', *Journal of Money, Credit, and Banking*, vol. 29, no. 4, Part 2, 725–52.

Estrella, A. and Mishkin, F.S. (1997), 'Is There a Role for Monetary Aggregates in the Conduct of Monetary Policy?', *Journal of Monetary Economics*, vol. 4, no. 2, 279–304, October.

Friedman, M. (1961), 'The Lag in Effect of Monetary Policy', *Journal of Political Economy*, vol. 69, 447–66, October.

Friedman, M. (1963), *Inflation: Causes and Consequences*, New York: Asia Publishing House.

Friedman, M. and Schwartz, A.J. (1963), *A Monetary History of the United States, 1967–1960*, Princeton, NJ: Princeton University Press.

Gerlach, S. and Svensson, L.E.O. (2000), 'Money and Inflation in the Euro Area: A Case for Monetary Indicators?', NBER Working Paper No. 8025.

Goodhart, C. (1999), 'Monetary Policy and Debt Management in the United Kingdom: Some Historical Viewpoints', in *Government Debt Structure and Monetary Conditions*, edited by K. Alec Chrystal, Bank of England.

Hendry, D.F. (2001), 'Modelling UK Inflation, 1875–1991', *Journal of Applied Econometrics*, vol. 16, no. 3, 255–75.

Ireland, P.N. (2001a), 'Money's Role in the Monetary Business Cycle', NBER Working Paper No. 8115.

Ireland, P.N. (2001b), 'The Real Balance Effect', NBER Working Paper No. 8136.

Keynes, J.M. (1930), *Treatise on Money, Volume 1: The Pure Theory of Money*, London: Macmillan and Co. Limited.

Keynes, J.M. (1936), *The General Theory of Employment, Interest and Money*, London: Macmillan.

King, R. and Watson, M. (1995), 'The Solution of Singular Linear Difference Systems under National Expectations', *International Economic Review*, vol. 39, no. 4, 1015–26.

Koenig, E.F. (1990), 'Real Money Balances and the Timing of Consumption: An Empirical Investigation', *Quarterly Journal of Economics*, vol. 105, no. 2, 399–425.

Krugman, P. (2000), 'Thinking about the Liquidity Trap', *Journal of the Japanese and International Economies*, vol. 14, no. 4, 221–37.

Lucas, R.E. Jr (2000), 'Inflation and Welfare', *Econometrica*, vol. 68, no. 2, 247–74.

McCallum, B.T. (2001), 'Monetary Policy Analysis in Models Without Money', NBER Working Paper No. 8174.

McCandless, G.T. Jr and Weber, W.E. (1995), 'Some Monetary Facts', *Federal Reserve Bank of Minneapolis Quarterly-Review*, vol. 19, no. 3, 2–11, Summer.

Meyer, L.H. (2001), 'Does Money Matter?', *Federal Reserve Bank of St. Louis Review*, vol. 83, no. 5, 1–15, Sept.–Oct.

Neiss, K. and Nelson, E. (2001), 'The real interest rate gap as an inflation indicator', Bank of England Working Paper No. 130.

Neiss, K. and Pappa, E. (2002), 'A monetary model of factor utilisation', Bank of England Working Paper No. 154.

Nelson, E. (2000), 'UK monetary policy, 1972–97: a guide using Taylor rules', Bank of England Working Paper No. 120.

Nelson, E. (2001) 'What does the UK's monetary policy and inflation experience tell us about the transmission mechanism', CEPR Discussion Paper No. 3047.

Patinkin, D. (1965), *Money, Interest and Prices*, 2nd edn, New York: Harper and Row.

Pigou, A.C. (1943), 'The Classical Stationary State', *Economic Journal*, vol. 53, 343–51.

Sargent, T. (1993), *Rational Expectations and Inflation*, 2nd edn, New York: Harper and Row.

Sidrauski, M. (1967), 'Rational Choice and Patterns of Growth in a Monetary Economy', *American Economic Review*, vol. 57, no. 2, 534–44.
Stock, J.H. and Watson, M.W. (1999), 'Forecasting Inflation' NBER Working Paper No. 7023.
Svensson, L.E.O. (2001), 'The Zero Bound in an Open Economy: A Foolproof Way of Escaping from a Liquidity Trap', *Monetary and Economic Studies*, vol. 19, no. 5-1, Special Edition, 277–312.
Woodford, M. (2003), *Interest and Prices: Foundations of a Theory of Monetary Policy*, forthcoming for Princeton University Press.

TECHNICAL APPENDIX

The Generation of the Simulation Results

The model used here is a linearised version of that shown in Figure 1.6, similar to that given in McCallum (2001), where the interest rate reaction function below replaces the money supply equation.

1 Model

$$y_t = E_t y_{t+1} - (i_t - E_t \pi_{t+1}) + \varepsilon_1$$

$$\pi_t = 0.99 E_t \pi_{t+1} + 0.1(y_t - \bar{y}_t) + \varepsilon_2$$

$$m_t - p_t = y_t - 7i_t$$

$$i_t = (1.5)(1 - 0.3)(\pi_t - \pi^*) + (0.5)(1 - 0.3)(y_t - \bar{y}_t) + 0.3 i_{t-1} + \varepsilon_3$$

$$\bar{y}_t = \varepsilon_4$$

where y is the natural log of output, i is the nominal interest rate, π is the inflation rate, $\bar{y}$ the natural log of potential output, m the natural log of money, π^* the inflation target. The parameter values are based on Nelson (2000), Neiss and Nelson (2001), and Neiss and Pappa (2002).

2 Calibration of the stochastic shocks

Each of the shocks is independently normally distributed with mean zero, and standard deviations and autocorrelations shown below for the benchmark case.

ε_1 *(demand):*	standard deviation 0.01, autocorrelation coefficient 0.33
ε_2 *(mark up):*	standard deviation 0
ε_3 *(monetary policy):*	standard deviation 0.0082, autocorrelation coefficient 0.3
ε_4 *(supply):*	standard deviation 0.0072, autocorrelation coefficient 0.95

These values are consistent with Nelson (2000), Neiss and Nelson (2001), Neiss and Pappa (2002). In case 1, the baseline parameters shown above are chosen. In case 2, we use the benchmark parameters, but increase the autocorrelation of demand shocks to 0.5. Case 3 is the benchmark, with the standard deviation of mark-up shocks raised to 0.01. Case 4 is the benchmark, with an increase in the standard deviation of mark-up shocks to 0.01, the autocorrelation of mark-up shocks to 0.8 and the standard deviation of policy shocks to 0.04.

3 The experiment

Simulated data were created by taking 10,000 random draws from a standard normal distribution for each shock, and scaling and transforming as appropriate for each of the shocks to create autocorrelated series where required. Using the realisations for the shocks, we can solve for the model variables using the solution algorithm of King and Watson (1995). This gives a time series of 10,000 simulated observations for each model variable. Correlation coefficients and ordinary least squares regression coefficients were then calculated using standard statistical techniques on the simulated data.

2. Central bank independence

Charles Freedman[1]

1. INTRODUCTION

It is an honour and a privilege for me to be participating in this festschrift for Professor Charles Goodhart. I have known Charles as a senior member of the staff of the Bank of England, as an academic, and as a member of the Monetary Policy Committee of the Bank. And in all three guises he has been the consummate professional, addressing real issues with technical proficiency and presenting his ideas in a way that is accessible to less technical readers. Indeed, one of Charles's great virtues has been his ability to bridge the gap (sometimes a chasm) between academics and policy-makers, drawing the attention of the academics to policy issues that need to be addressed, and interpreting and assessing the value of new ideas coming from academia for the benefit of policy-makers. And all this with a wonderful sense of humour and excellent writing and speaking styles.

Two of the most interesting and striking developments in central banking over the latter part of the twentieth century have been the spread of central bank independence (CBI) and the increased focus on the importance of an explicit objective or mandate for central banks (the latter leading in many countries to the use of inflation targets). The period of high inflation that began in the mid-1960s and has come to be called the Great Inflation was probably the key factor in motivating both of these developments. In addition, the theoretical and empirical literature on CBI, linked mainly to the inflation bias in the time-inconsistency model, played an important role in influencing governments to grant independence to their central banks. The goal of this chapter is to examine both of these developments and their relationship with each other. More specifically, I re-examine and assess the time-inconsistency model, offer an alternative explanation to inflation bias for the Great Inflation, propose a somewhat different justification for CBI, and explore the relationship between CBI and the mandate of the central bank.

I would like to begin my discussion of central bank independence by relating an anecdote about Charles that illustrates the lack of independence of the Bank of England some twenty years ago. It took place during a meeting at the OECD of the Committee of High-Level Monetary Experts, when Charles was the staff member representing the Bank of England. This was the only OECD Committee at which central bank representatives spoke ahead of their Treasury counterparts. The exception to this practice was the United Kingdom, where the delegate from the Treasury spoke first, since he represented the institution responsible for conducting monetary policy. On the second round of interventions, Charles stood up, put his arm around the shoulders of his Treasury colleague, and began his comments by saying 'My keeper has kindly allowed me to make the following remarks.'

As a follow up, I will note that at the 1998 meeting of this group, following the granting of independence to the Bank of England, the Bank of England representative spoke ahead of the Treasury representative for the first time. A fitting symbolic change reflecting the important substantive change that had occurred a few months earlier.

The next section of this chapter sets out the standard or canonical time-inconsistency model on which much of the literature on central bank independence is based. This is followed by a critique of that model. The subsequent section offers an alternative explanation to time inconsistency for the widespread increase in inflation in the second half of the 1960s and again in the 1970s. The following two sections examine aspects of CBI in the context of an environment in which the time-inconsistency framework does not hold. Thus, the fifth section sets out the arguments for CBI in the absence of time inconsistency while the sixth section discusses the relationship between CBI and the central bank's mandate. The last section contains brief concluding remarks.

2. THE STANDARD TIME-INCONSISTENCY MODEL[2]

The high rates of inflation through much of the industrialized and developing world in the period between the mid-1960s and the early 1980s, the 'Great Inflation', resulted in the development of a literature that aimed at explaining what was perceived to be an inflationary bias in the economy. A simple model, due to Kydland and Prescott (1977) and Barro and Gordon (1983), turned out to be capable of generating a systematic inflationary outcome even when inflation was perceived to be costly.

Only two equations were needed.

$$L = (\dot{p} - \dot{p}^*)^2 + \beta(Q - Q^*)^2 \qquad (2.1)$$

$$Q - Q^N = \gamma(\dot{p} - \dot{p}^e) + \varepsilon \qquad (2.2)$$

The first equation, the loss function of the authorities (or public), is a quadratic function of the deviation between the actual rate of inflation, $\dot{p}$, and the desired rate of inflation, $\dot{p}^*$ (typically set at zero in the literature), and of the deviation between the actual level of output, Q, and its desired level, Q^*. The second equation is an aggregate supply function linking the difference between output and its natural or capacity level, Q^N, to surprise inflation, the difference between actual inflation and expected inflation, $\dot{p} - \dot{p}^e$. There is often also a shock, ε, which is usually interpreted as a supply shock, in the supply function.[3]

The timing set-up in some versions of the model is as follows. The public first decides on its expectations of inflation. Then, given inflation expectations, the central bank sets the rate of inflation. Finally, the shock, ε, takes place. The inflation surprise and the shock together determine the level of output. Other versions of the model have the central bank acting to set the rate of inflation subsequent to the shock or in a set-up without a shock.[4]

Now suppose $Q^* > Q^N$, that is, the authorities wish to achieve a higher level of output than is consistent with capacity. This desire to achieve a higher level of output than capacity can be motivated by an inefficiency in the system, such as distortionary taxes or unemployment benefits or union power. If policy is set on a discretionary basis, if the public knows the structure of the model, and if the public sets its expectations rationally, this simple model yields an inflationary outcome $\dot{p} > \dot{p}^*$ with output at capacity. And this is the case in spite of the fact that the same level of output and inflation at its desired rate, $\dot{p}^*$, would clearly be a better outcome.

The intuition behind the outcome is as follows. Once the public decides on its inflation expectations, the central bank can try to surprise it by setting a higher rate of inflation than it had expected, with the intent of moving output above Q^N to Q^*. However, since the public is aware of the incentives that the authorities face to create inflation surprises, it take these into account in rationally setting its inflation expectations. The outcome is a rate of inflation that is high enough to remove all incentives for the authorities to create surprises, with the cost of additional inflation offsetting on the margin any benefit from higher output. That is, $\dot{p} > \dot{p}^*$ and $Q = Q^N < Q^*$.[5]

In part because of its analytic tractability, variants of the simple model have been used to explore a wide variety of situations. (See Cukierman (1992) and the survey articles cited in Note 2.) For example, with asymmetric information about the objectives of the central bank (the desired rate of inflation, $\dot{p}^*$, and the value of β), the public must draw inferences about the objective of the central bank on the basis of imperfect information (because of imperfect control of money growth or imperfect links between money growth and inflation).

Given the unsatisfactory outcome resulting from the inflation bias, why do the authorities not simply aim at $\dot{p}^*$, since they cannot in any case achieve output greater than capacity? The typical response in the literature is that the authorities lack a precommitment technology that would enable them to credibly commit to inflation at $\dot{p}^*$. As Persson and Tabellini (1994) put it, in a second best world (that is, in a world without a precommitment technology), an attempt to achieve a first best outcome, $Q = Q^*$, under discretion leads to a third best outcome, $Q = Q^N$, $\dot{p} > \dot{p}^*$.

A number of solutions have been proposed to deal with the inflation bias problem. The first, and simplest, is for the authorities to commit to a rule that would avoid inflation. While some argue that the authorities have no credible way of committing to such a rule (since there is no precommitment technology), others, most notably McCallum (1995, 1997) have argued, convincingly in my view, that by simply aiming consistently at the desired rate of inflation, the authorities would develop a reputation of being committed to low inflation, their policy would gain credibility, and hence they would be able to eliminate the inflation bias.[6]

The second proposed solution involves the appointment of a conservative central banker (Rogoff, 1985), who has a smaller β than that of the public or government. This results in a lower rate of inflation than in the basic model but in a less-than-optimal response to supply shocks. That is, this solution involves a trade-off between the achievement of a lower rate of inflation and the capacity to counteract shocks, the so-called credibility-flexibility trade-off. A variant of this approach (Lohmann, 1992) shows that the Rogoff solution can be improved by providing the government with a potential override over central bank actions in exceptional circumstances. Under such arrangements, the conservative central banker would be able to act to offset large shocks to a greater extent than otherwise, without harming his credibility.

The third proposed solution (Persson and Tabellini, 1993 and Walsh, 1995) relies on a contract between the government and the central bank that offsets the incentives giving rise to the inflation bias. The contract can involve pecuniary penalties directly related to the rate of inflation or the potential for dismissal of the central bank governor if the desired rate of inflation is not achieved. McCallum (1995, 1997) is sceptical of the usefulness of this way of dealing with the problem since he questions the credibility of the commitment of the government to enforce the contract.

In the second and third proposed solutions, central bank independence plays an important role in lessening or eliminating the problem of inflation bias. Thus, in the second solution, the conservative central banker is given the independence to act on the basis of a smaller β than appears in the loss function of the public or government, with or without an override provision by the government. And in the third solution, a contract is agreed by the principal (government) and the agent (central bank), following which the central bank acts independently. However, the first solution does not necessarily involve CBI since the authority responsible for monetary policy can be either the government or the central bank (with or without independence)[7] and it simply aims at consistently achieving the desired rate of inflation (à la McCallum).[8]

3. CRITIQUE OF THE STANDARD MODEL

It is of interest that a number of academics who have spent time at very senior levels in the central banking community have been very sceptical of the standard model. A few quotes will give the flavour of this scepticism:

> As an academic, I found this analysis [Barro–Gordon] unpersuasive. And what I learned as a central banker strongly reinforced this view.
>
> Blinder (1998, p. 40).

> There is a large literature on inflation bias, but it is simply not applicable to the MPC. We have no desire to spring inflation surprises to try to bump output above its natural rate (wherever that may be).
>
> Vickers (1998, p. 369)

> I have never found the literature on time inconsistency particularly relevant to central banks.
>
> Meyer (2000, p. 3)

Goodhart's own views on the time-inconsistency model were set out in his very interesting review (1994) of Cukierman's (1992) book on CBI. While basically sympathetic to the approach taken by Cukierman, Goodhart raises a number of objections to the standard model, which tend to reflect his experience as a central banker. While he is 'deeply skeptical about some of the basic building blocks of the formal time-inconsistency model' (as employed in the Cukierman volume), he believes that 'these exercises can still be justified on the basis of weaker, heuristic assumptions' (p. 103). In particular, he is concerned about the justification for the preference of the authorities for a level of employment higher than the natural rate, the factors that might affect the ability of the authorities to precommit, the problem of lags and the role of political factors. In the end, he concludes that while some of the detailed architecture of the time-inconsistency model is dubious, its 'more roughhewn foundations are strong, because they can rely on an appeal to stylized real-life facts' (p. 105). He concludes that the model (as developed in Cukierman) 'may, indeed, be oversimplified in some respects and leaves out (abstracts from) much relevant practical detail; nevertheless, the model is *not* silly, and the results are important and relevant' (p. 114).

My own long-standing scepticism about the standard model relates to its inability to explain the onset of the period of high inflation (Freedman, 1993) and to concerns about the validity (or relevance) of the two key assumptions of the model.

Let me begin with the former point. The model as presented is ahistoric. As such, it suggests that the inflation bias is inherent in the economic system under the institutional arrangements prevalent for most of the post-war period. But through the 1950s and the first half of the 1960s rates of inflation were very low throughout the industrialized world (and in a considerable part of the developing world). Admittedly, most countries were on a fixed exchange rate vis-à-vis the US dollar. But this simply pushes the question back one level. How was the United States (or the Federal Reserve) able to achieve low inflation outcomes over this period without falling prey to the inflation bias? The time-inconsistency model does not provide an answer to this question unless one puts inordinate weight on the residual link to gold during this period. I offer an alternative explanation for the onset of high inflation in the next section.

Turning to the model itself, I would begin by noting that an economic model uses a series of simplifying assumptions to represent an economic reality. The issue is how good a representation of the key facets of reality any model is able to deliver. In the case of the standard time-inconsistency model, I would argue that there are important disconnects between the model and the reality faced by those responsible for the conduct of monetary policy.

As discussed earlier, a key motivating factor for the inflation bias is the desire of the authorities to achieve a level of output greater than that consistent with a constant rate of inflation. In fact, there has been widespread acceptance since the 1970s of the view that there is no long-run trade-off between the level of output (or the unemployment rate) and the rate of inflation because of the way that inflation expectations adjust. This has brought in its wake the recognition that monetary policy should avoid creating a situation of excess demand at a time when inflation is at or above its desired level because of the implications for the future rate of inflation.[9] Hence, monetary policy has not aimed at persistently achieving a level of output greater than capacity (or a level of unemployment below the natural rate).[10]

In my view, a focus on the seigniorage motive rather than on a deviation between desired output and natural output provides a more convincing argument for inflation bias in those countries that rely heavily on seigniorage (as discussed in Cukierman, 1992). Indeed, the historical argument for CBI was based on the view that it is important to separate the power to spend from the power to print money. But this framework does little to explain developments in industrialized countries.

My second concern with the standard model is its reliance on the flex-price aggregate supply function in which inflation surprises are the principal source of output movements. In the mainstream models based in part on price or wage stickiness that are typically used by central banks in making policy,[11] the timing set-up and the causal sequence are completely different. In these models, central bank changes in the policy interest rate lead to a variety of changes in other interest rates and the exchange rate. These affect output with a lag, and movements in output relative to capacity affect inflation with a further lag. In the case of Canada, for example, the effect of a change in the policy interest rate on output cumulates over three to four quarters, and the effect of a change in the policy interest rate on inflation cumulates over a period of six to eight quarters. There are similar lags in the transmission mechanism in other countries.

From a causal perspective, I would argue that most central banks think of the economy in terms of some variant of an expectations-augmented Phillips curve, with the output gap and expected inflation (often a mix of forward- and backward-looking expectations) driving inflation,[12] rather than an aggregate supply curve in which inflation surprises drive the output gap. Of course, in practice central banks use a variety of models to explain and forecast inflation, including models that use monetary aggregates as an important explanatory variable.[13] But, typically in such models, movements in output precede the movements in inflation, rather than follow them.

Goodhart and Huang (1998) recognized the problem of timing in the standard model and introduced lags into the model by means of overlapping wage contracts. Using the standard loss function they were able to get similar qualitative conclusions to the typical time-inconsistency model by assuming that the fixed wage contract was about twice as long as the lag between monetary policy actions and inflation. In their conclusion, the authors 'doubt whether the standard model of time inconsistency provides a satisfactory explanation to rationalize the inflationary proclivities of the industrialized world in the last half century. Our more realistic model, with both the lags and persistence effects accompanied by an overlapping wage contracts setting, predicts a picture of a rather small incentive on average towards inflation, combined with a time-varying incentive to shift policy in a deflationary or inflationary direction that depends on the state of the economy and on previous forecast errors' (p. 393).

The Goodhart–Huang model is considerably more realistic than the standard model because of its use of overlapping wage contracts. Nonetheless, there are difficulties with the specification of their model, in particular with the assumption that the length of the contract is twice that of the policy lag. While the typical union contract may be longer than the lag between policy action and inflation, in Canada and the United Kingdom the proportion of the labour force that is unionized is less than one-third and in the United States it is less than one-sixth. And for non-unionized workers, the bulk of the labour force, wage arrangements are typically made for a shorter period, often for a year, while the lag from policy actions to inflation is closer to two years.

To sum up this section, the standard model does not explain why inflation picked up in the mid-1960s (or, more accurately, why it was quiescent until the mid-1960s) and the assumptions underlying both of its key equations do not seem to me to be firmly based in reality. The next section develops an alternative explanation for the Great Inflation and the subsequent section examines the arguments for CBI in the absence of time inconsistency.

4. WHAT WAS THE CAUSE OF THE 'GREAT INFLATION'?

An alternative explanation to that provided by the time-inconsistency model for the step-up of inflation in the mid-1960s and its acceleration in the 1970s is based on the interaction of economic shocks and policy errors. The shocks included the increase in aggregate demand related to the Vietnam War in the latter part of the 1960s, and shifts in the natural rate of unemployment and/or the capacity rate of growth of output in the 1970s. The policy errors that led to the accommodation of the shock-induced inflation pressures resulted from an incorrect framework of analysis and insufficient regard for the costs of inflation. Together, these factors resulted in what might otherwise have been a transitory bout of inflation pressures turning into an ongoing period of high and pervasive inflation.

Recall that the prevailing view among economists (if not among all central bankers) in the 1950s and 1960s was that there was a long-run trade-off between output (or unemployment) and inflation, and that the role of the authorities in this framework was to choose the optimal point on the trade-off curve. The appearance of a trade-off was a reflection of an environment in which inflation expectations were low and stable, and there was a lack of attention to the potential role of inflation expectations in the inflation process.[14] The firmly-held expectations of continuing low inflation at the time were likely the result of a long period of low peace-time inflation outcomes, buttressed by the fairly conservative economic policies of the 1950s.

Moreover, at the time, the economics profession underestimated the costs of inflation, since economists had difficulty in quantifying those costs. The empirical relationship between high rates of inflation and unpredictable rates of inflation was not widely recognized. Nor was there much awareness at the time of many of the links between even a predictable or expected rate of inflation and unfavourable economic outcomes.[15]

Thus, in the United States in the 1960s, the prevailing wisdom seemed to support the view that the authorities responsible for fiscal and monetary policies should tend to be broadly stimulative in their policy actions, since even an overly expansionary situation was seen as leading only to a once-and-for-all rise in the rate of inflation and not to a continuing acceleration of inflation, and since higher inflation was deemed to be not all that costly.

The Vietnam War expenditures and the political decision to have both 'guns and butter' was the direct cause of a period of excess demand in the second half of the 1960s, while the synchronized expansion of the major world economies was the key factor in creating global excess demand in the early 1970s. And the supply shocks in the 1970s, which were facilitated by the environment of global excess demand, exacerbated the inflationary pressures. Although policy-makers responded to the situation of strong demand and supply shocks by taking tightening actions, these actions proved to be far from sufficient to offset the upward pressures on inflation, especially in the 1970s.

In part, the overly weak response to the demand and inflation pressures reflected a less-than-complete realization of the implications of unhinging the low level of inflation expectations that had provided an anchor for low inflation in earlier years. In addition, in the early 1970s there was a worldwide decline in the rate of growth of productivity and, in some countries, a rise in the natural rate of unemployment, both of which the authorities became aware of only gradually. Thus, policy-makers were focusing on indicators of labour market and product market pressures that were very misleading. On the basis of these indicators they believed that they were tightening policy sufficiently to offset the inflationary pressures. It was also likely the case that insufficient attention was paid to the distinction between nominal and real interest rates. In the event, with the decline in the rate of growth of capacity, demand remained at unduly high levels relative to capacity, and the actions that policy-makers took were insufficient to offset the inflation pressures.[16]

The experience of high inflation and the increased understanding by economists and central banks of the inflationary process and the costs of inflation led to a stronger commitment to move the rate of inflation down and to keep it at low levels. However, the persistently high inflation rates of the 1970s had unhinged inflation expectations, thereby rendering the process of returning inflation to a lower path much more difficult. Once the genie of inflation was out of the bottle it proved very difficult to get it back in. Indeed, the rate of inflation only returned to low levels following a major worldwide recession in the early 1980s and another, in some countries, in the early 1990s.

To sum up, the combination of an overly-optimistic estimate of capacity, an underestimate of the costs of inflation and insufficient attention to inflation expectations meant that policy-makers were not aware at the time that they were taking serious risks of overheating the economy and they did not act sufficiently vigorously to offset the inflationary pressures that developed.[17] And once inflation expectations became entrenched at a high level, it became much more difficult to get the rate of inflation down than would have been the case in an environment in which the public expected that inflation shocks would be temporary and rapidly reversed.

5. THE CASE FOR CENTRAL BANK INDEPENDENCE IN THE ABSENCE OF TIME INCONSISTENCY

Historically, as I noted earlier, the argument for CBI was based on the tendency of the authorities to debauch the value of the currency in order to finance spending. This argument for CBI was encapsulated in the maxim that it was important to separate the power to print money from the power to spend it. And this rationale for CBI still holds true in those developing countries that rely on seigniorage for a significant portion of their revenues.

But what is the basis of the argument for CBI in industrialized economies, in which seigniorage plays a small or insignificant role in government revenues, if one does not accept the time-inconsistency framework for inflation bias? In my view, the argument for CBI hinges on the interaction of three factors – the nature of the lags in the monetary policy transmission mechanism, uncertainties surrounding the decision process for monetary policy, and the tendency of governments to have a shorter horizon than central banks. Together, these factors would lead governments to be willing to take more risks in the direction of stimulating the economy than would be the case for central banks, even when there is no systematic attempt to achieve a level of output in excess of capacity. In the wake of the experience with high inflation, it has been the desire to avoid this tendency to be overly stimulative that has caused governments to give central banks increased independence in the conduct of monetary policy.

The timing of the output and inflation outcomes in the monetary policy transmission process, with the effects of monetary policy actions on output preceding the effects on inflation, is central to this analysis. Thus, in the case of a disinflation, the costs in terms of slower growth come before the benefits in terms of lower inflation. Similarly, in the case of an overly-expansionary monetary policy (including the setting of interest rates that are not high enough to offset positive aggregate demand shocks), the perceived benefits in terms of higher output precede the costs in terms of higher inflation. It is also the case that the time horizon before the full effects of monetary policy actions on inflation is quite long (six to eight quarters), requiring considerable patience on the part of the policy-maker before the benefits are realized.

A second element central to the analysis is that policy is always made under uncertainty of various kinds. There is uncertainty about the forward momentum of the economy deriving from both domestic and external developments (including the stimulative or depressive effects of past interest rate changes still in the pipeline), there is uncertainty about the level and/or the rate of growth of capacity, there is related uncertainty about the natural rate of unemployment, there is uncertainty about the links between the policy interest rate and other interest rates and the exchange rate, and there is uncertainty about the model of the transmission mechanism. With all these uncertainties, it is not surprising that reasonable people can differ on the appropriate action that the authorities responsible for monetary policy should take in various circumstances. This is especially the case at or around turning points in the economic cycle when decision making is particularly difficult.

Finally, governments and central banks have tended to focus on different horizons, with governments putting more weight in their thinking on the shorter-run consequences of policy actions and central banks putting more weight in their thinking on the longer-term outcomes.[18] Given the timing of the effects of monetary policy actions on output and inflation, this means that governments tend to emphasize the shorter-run effects on output while central banks keep a close eye on the longer-term effects on inflation. Thus, governments may well have a tendency to want lower interest rates than those preferred by central banks.

The framework that I am putting forward implies that governments would be particularly averse to the possibility that policy errors in an environment of uncertainty would lead to slower-than-desired output growth in the short run, and that central banks would be particularly averse to the possibility that policy errors in such an environment would lead to excessive inflation in the medium to longer run. In effect, while the central bank and the government would each take account of both the output and inflation developments arising from a monetary policy action or, for that matter, inaction (such as a failure to raise rates when needed to counter demand pressures), the government, in practice, would place more weight on the earlier output effects and less weight on the longer-term inflationary consequences than would the central bank.

Let me be somewhat more concrete. In the context of the various types of uncertainty listed earlier, policy-makers, in deciding on interest rates, take into account both a base case scenario and the balance of risks surrounding that scenario. For example, suppose that the base case scenario at a time of weak activity indicated a future pick-up of demand such that the prevailing level of interest rates was consistent with the medium-term desired outcome for inflation. Suppose further that the balance of risks was on the downside because of concerns about the weakness of the world economy and its impact on domestic exports. Those wanting to increase the likelihood that economic activity would be sustained even at some risk of higher inflation would opt for lower interest rates, while those wanting to put more weight on having inflation at its desired level would opt for no change in interest rates. Put otherwise, even if they had the same view about the level of capacity output and no desire to achieve a higher level, policy-makers can have different views on which direction they are prepared to take risks. The tendency of governments in these circumstances would be to take the risk on the upside for inflation in order to lessen the downside risk for economic activity while central banks would typically focus more on the base case to avoid the upside risk for inflation.

The experience of high inflation in the second half of the 1960s, the 1970s, and the 1980s convinced many governments and legislatures that, empirically, taking risks in the direction of higher economic activity in spite of possible inflationary outcomes was likely to yield less good outcomes than taking risks in the direction of less inflation. This was an important factor contributing to the widespread delegation of responsibility to independent central banks, since independent central banks would tend to focus more on the longer-term inflationary consequences of policy actions.[19] This argument for independent central banks is sometimes phrased in terms of the need for CBI to remove monetary policy from day-to-day political pressures. As Alan Blinder (1998, pp. 55–6) has aptly put it, because of the long lags in monetary policy, with the output effects coming before the inflation effects, 'if politicians made monetary policy on a day-to-day basis, the temptation to reach for short-term gains at the expense of the future (that is, to inflate too much) would be hard to resist. Knowing this, many governments wisely try to depoliticize monetary policy by, e.g., putting it in the hands of unelected technocrats with long terms of office and insulation from the hurly-burly of politics'.

But what about the possibility that the central bank will do the reverse of government and put too much weight on getting inflation to its desired level overly quickly and not enough weight on avoiding the volatility of output? Or, to put it in its starkest form, how does one ensure that the central bank is not an 'inflation nutter', in King's (1997) terms? This brings us to the relationship between CBI and the mandate or objectives under which the independent central bank conducts policy, to which I turn in the next section.

Before leaving this section, however, I want to note two recent articles by Alex Cukierman (1999, 2000), in which he developed a model to explain inflation bias that resembles the view of the nature of the inflation process that I have just set out.

Cukierman's new model functions with either an aggregate supply curve driven by inflation surprises or a new-Keynesian transmission mechanism. It incorporates uncertainty about the future state of the economy and asymmetries in the output gap segment of the central bank loss function (with more output always preferred to less output, rather than the quadratic function in the standard literature). Cukierman shows that in this model there is an inflation bias even if the authorities target the natural level of output.

To quote Cukierman (2000, p. 22),[20] 'intuitively, this bias arises because the [authority] is more sensitive to policy errors in which monetary policy is too tight than to policy errors in which it is too expansionary in conjunction with the fact that it does not have perfect information about the state of the economy. The upshot is that an inflationary bias arises even when the [authority] targets potential output. This bias arises whenever the [authority] is more averse to negative than to positive output gaps in conjunction with the fact that it is uncertain about the state of the economy. The second condition is obviously highly realistic and the first one appears to be satisfied for at least some [authorities]'.

While Cukierman's new model is clearly an improvement over the standard model, it still does not account for the timing of the Great Inflation, as opposed to the explanation based on policy errors. Also, his model does not distinguish between the government and the central bank and hence does not give an explicit rationale for CBI.

6. CBI AND THE POLICY MANDATE FOR THE CENTRAL BANK

I now turn to the relationship between CBI and the mandate of the central bank. Recall that, as discussed earlier, three principal solutions to the inflation bias result have been proposed in the context of the standard model. The first is to set an objective or rule for policy, although many authors argue that this cannot be done effectively without a precommitment mechanism. In any case, this is an argument for setting an objective or mandate for the authority responsible for monetary policy rather than for CBI. The second solution, Rogoff's conservative central banker, clearly does imply independence for the central bank since the policy actions either cannot be overridden by the government or can only be overridden in extreme circumstances, but it does not require a mandate for the central bank. The third solution, involving a contract between the government and the central bank, involves both CBI and a policy mandate for the central bank since the key element is to hold the central bank accountable for achieving its low inflation goal.

In the context of the first two proposed solutions to inflation bias in the standard model, therefore, the objective of policy (or mandate) and CBI are effectively substitutes, with one or the other used to deal with the problem of time inconsistency. In contrast, most central bankers (and the third proposed solution) see CBI and the policy mandate as complements, with the two together leading to the desired outcome in low inflation or price stability over the medium term and reasonably low volatility of output and inflation.

In terms of the approach put forward in the previous section, CBI allows the individual or committee responsible for taking monetary policy actions (that is, setting the path for the policy rate of interest) to take a longer-term perspective, with appropriate weight on the inflation consequences of policy actions. At the same time, an explicit mandate contributes to the enhancement of the credibility of the policy framework, helps to avoid the perception (or reality) of an overly conservative central bank, facilitates the central bank response to supply and demand shocks (that is, allows for flexibility), and contributes importantly to the accountability of the central bank.

In analysing the role of CBI in the conduct of policy, the distinction developed in Debelle and Fischer (1995) and Fischer (1995) between instrument independence and goal independence for the central bank is often used. A central bank that is instrument independent is provided with a goal for inflation by the government and is given virtually complete freedom to take whatever monetary policy actions are needed to achieve that goal. A goal independent central bank, in contrast, sets the goal for policy. In practice, a goal independent central bank typically also has instrument independence.

Ideally, the mandate in its broadest sense, say price stability, should be set in legislation. Meyer (2001) notes that there are two ways in which this is typically done. A hierarchical mandate makes price stability the primary goal of monetary policy and typically adds a secondary goal of support for the government's policy, provided that this does not interfere with the achievement of the primary goal. A dual mandate sets two objectives, typically price stability and full employment, and gives them equal status. In practice, I would argue that there is little difference today between the two types of arrangements, since central banks under both kinds of mandate behave as if they have a loss function with both output variability and inflation variability as arguments, and hence aim at achieving the inflation goal over time and limiting the fluctuations in output and inflation.

With price stability or low inflation as *a* or *the* legally mandated objective, the next issue is what entity should have the responsibility for operationalizing it, that is, deciding what it means in practice. In England, the Chancellor of the Exchequer annually announces the objective of policy (currently 2½ per cent) and the Bank of England is therefore seen as an example of a central bank with instrument independence but without goal independence. In the case of the European Central Bank, often used as the example of a goal independent central bank, it was the Governing Council of the Bank that decided that price stability should be defined as below 2 per cent inflation. In between these polar cases, there are the cases of New Zealand and Canada where the decision about the target is jointly agreed by the government and the central bank.

In one sense, the perceived distinction between central banks with goal independence and those with instrument independence tends to be overstated. As long as the broad objective of policy is set in legislation or treaty, even those central banks with the responsibility for operationalizing that goal are limited in the scope of their choices. For example, it is hard to conceive of a circumstance in which a goal independent central bank would operationalize a mandate of price stability to be, say, a 5 per cent rate of inflation or a 3 per cent rate of deflation. Thus, by setting the broad mandate in legislation or treaty, governments do play a role in setting the target even for so-called goal independent central banks.

I would go one step further and argue that it is appropriate for governments to be directly involved in operationalizing the objective of monetary policy. Such an involvement is useful from a credibility point of view since it makes clear to the public and to the financial markets that the government is explicitly committed to the announced quantitative target. But I would also argue that there are clear advantages to arrangements, such as those in place in Canada and New Zealand, in which the central bank is also involved in the operationalization of the quantitative goal of policy.

The decision on the operational goal for policy involves judgments on a number of technical matters where the central bank has considerable expertise. These include such issues as the statistical bias in the measure of inflation being used as the target, the importance in the economy of downward rigidity in prices or wages, the implications of the zero lower bound in interest rates, the likelihood and potential costs of going through periods of deflation, and the relative benefits of, say, a 1 per cent target for inflation as opposed to a 2 per cent target.[21] Typically, the staff of the central bank will have done considerable research on these issues.[22] Thus the central bank will be able to contribute importantly to the discussion and decision making on what, in the end, is an issue that requires judgment based on a blend of both theoretical and empirical analysis.

In arrangements of joint decision-making, what would happen if there were a fundamental disagreement on the operational goal for policy between the government and the central bank? In my view, in a democratic society the government should in the limit be able to insist on its views. But the mechanisms should be such that the public is informed of significant differences in views. In New Zealand, the Governor would not take office or would resign if he could not reach a Policy Targets Agreement with the Finance Minister. And, in Canada, while the government could use its directive power to impose its views regarding the policy goal, this would almost certainly lead to the resignation of the Governor.[23]

An interesting aspect of the combination of CBI and a price stability or low inflation mandate is that it typically involves an 'incomplete contract' (Bean, 1998). That is, in all cases that I know of, it is the central bank and not the government that decides on the point on the Taylor trade-off curve between the variance of inflation and the variance of output. It does this in effect by choosing the time period for the return of the rate of inflation to its target following a shock that pushes it away from target. For example, in the first half of the 1990s the Reserve Bank of New Zealand chose to try to return inflation to its target over a relatively short time period, resulting in tight inflation control but a relatively volatile path for output (and for financial variables). In the latter part of the decade, in contrast, it moved to a longer horizon for returning inflation to the target, consistent with less variability in output and financial variables and a willingness to accept more variability in inflation. The Bank of Canada, throughout its first decade of inflation targeting, used a six to eight quarter horizon.[24]

Vickers (1998) argues that it is almost impossible to specify precisely a policy committee's loss function or choice of a point on the trade-off curve. Or, to put it slightly differently, writing a contract dealing with all potential contingencies is not possible, and a contract with a subset of potential contingencies may lead to less good policy than allowing some discretion on the part of the central bank. Hence, governments seem to be prepared to give central banks the discretion to decide on their policy horizon or speed of return to target and to allow them to deal with different kinds of shocks differently.[25]

Inflation-targeting arrangements are typically structured in a way that reduces the concern of government that the central bank will be overly conservative and will respond more vigorously to positive demand shocks than to negative demand shocks or will maintain an excessively pessimistic view of the level of potential output. As long as the targeting framework is symmetric, one would expect equally strong responses to movements of inflation away from the target in both directions (that is, toward the top and bottom of the range for those central banks that have a formal range), and, on average over longer time periods, inflation should be close to the target.[26] Overly conservative behaviour by the central bank would, in contrast, lead to a tendency for inflation outcomes to be lower on average than the targeted rate.[27] And such a result would be highlighted by the accountability mechanisms typically associated with inflation targeting regimes and independent central banks.

7. CONCLUDING REMARKS

The time-inconsistency literature and the empirical work that flowed from it played an important role in promoting the spread of central bank independence. Reframing this analysis on the basis of more realistic assumptions regarding the objectives of policy, the transmission mechanism between central bank actions and economic activity and inflation, and the uncertainty facing policy-makers should provide useful additional insights about institutional arrangements for the conduct of monetary policy.

NOTES

1. The views expressed in this paper are those of the author and are not to be attributed to the Bank of Canada. Errors of interpretation remain those of the author. I would like to thank Robert Amano, John Chant, Paul Jenkins, Michael King, David Longworth, John Murray, Jack Selody, and Gabriel Srour for comments on earlier drafts of this paper.
2. A very large literature has developed around the time-inconsistency framework. The seminal articles originating the discussion were Kydland and Prescott (1977) and Barro and Gordon (1983). Cukierman (1992) contains a detailed exegesis of many variants of the basic model. Useful summaries of the literature can be found in the introduction to Persson and Tabellini (1994), Eijffinger and de Haan (1996), and Berger, de Haan and Eijffinger (2000). Collections of some of the main articles can be found in Persson and Tabellini (1994) and Eijffinger (1997). The analysis in this chapter focuses on a relatively limited part of the burgeoning literature. In particular, I do not discuss the empirical literature, the models closely tied to political factors, or the recent literature relating to wage bargaining, references to all of which can be found in the summaries cited above.
3. See McCallum (1997) for a discussion of other ways to interpret ε.

4. This simple model can be complicated in many ways. For example, there can be uncertainty about Q^N, control errors with respect to the determination of $\dot{p}$, or uncertainty about the size of β.
5. A similar incentive for monetary expansion on the part of the authorities can be motivated by seigniorage benefits or the desire to improve the balance of payments. See Cukierman (1992).
6. After a period of high inflation, however, it might take quite some time for a central bank to gain credibility.
7. Indeed, Kydland and Prescott (1977) and Barro and Gordon (1983) do not have a central bank separate from government in their models.
8. As discussed in detail in the penultimate section of this chapter, an explicit mandate for the central bank can play an important role in the achievement of the desired rate of inflation.
9. Put somewhat differently, it became clear that only structural policies that aimed at reducing or eliminating the inefficiencies in the system could increase capacity output or reduce the natural rate of unemployment, and that macroeconomic actions could not keep output above capacity persistently without giving rise to an acceleration of the rate of inflation.
10. Nonetheless, in the discussion below of the argument for independence in the absence of a systemic inflation bias of the sort portrayed in the standard model, I do recognize a kernel of truth in the approach taken in the standard model. It is based on the various uncertainties faced by policy-makers, the relative timing of the effects of monetary policy actions on output and inflation, and the possibly different horizons of the central bank and the government in their approach to policy.
11. For Canada, see Black et al. (1994) and Coletti et al. (1996); for England, see Bank of England (1999); for the United States, see Brayton and Tinsley (1996); and for the ECB, see Fagan et al. (2001).
12. In such a model, both predicted and unpredicted monetary policy actions affect aggregate demand and output.
13. See, for example, Adam and Hendry (2000).
14. Friedman (1968) emphasized the role of inflation expectations in challenging the prevailing view.
15. See Fischer (1981) and Feldstein (1997) for a discussion of such links.
16. See Orphanides (2001) for a detailed discussion of the views of the Fed on the capacity of the economy during this period, including a comparison of the output gap as it was perceived at the time and as it is now viewed in retrospect.
17. See DeLong (1998) for a similar multi-faceted explanation of the acceleration of inflation. Ireland (1999), in contrast, argues that the acceleration of inflation in the 1960s and 1970s can be explained by the time-inconsistency model in the context of an upward trend in the natural rate of unemployment over the period.
18. This approach is, of course, similar to that of the political business cycle literature.
19. Posen (1993), in contrast, argues that the apparent causal linkage between CBI and low inflation is illusory and that the basis for the apparent association can be found in the political domain.
20. I have taken the liberty of replacing the term central bank with the term authority in this quotation to avoid confusion with the argument I put forward earlier in this section.
21. See Bank of Canada (2001) for an assessment of these issues from a central bank perspective at the time that the Bank and the government jointly agreed to extend until 2006 the 2 per cent inflation target and the 1 to 3 per cent target range.
22. See Bank of Canada (2000, 2001) for an example of such research.
23. As Thiessen (1998–99, p. 98) put it, 'if there were a fundamental disagreement on the targets when they came up for renewal, the Minister could impose his will via a directive. That would likely lead to the Governor's resignation and a new Governor, who was prepared to accept the desired targets, would have to be chosen.'
24. The difference in behaviour between the two central banks in the first half of the decade may have reflected the fact that the inflation target range in New Zealand was perceived

to be hard-edged while that in Canada was soft-edged. The Reserve Bank of New Zealand therefore actively adjusted interest rates to bring about movements of the exchange rate, in order to take advantage of the pass-through from the exchange rate to prices, a mechanism that operates more quickly than the mechanism operating through aggregate demand to prices.

25. To the extent that it helps to anchor inflation expectations, a credible inflation targeting policy may even prevent some of the deleterious effects of supply shocks because it reduces pass-through to inflation from the shock. See Freedman (1996).
26. See Crawford (2001) for a discussion of the decline in the variance of the average rate of inflation as the time period over which the average is taken is increased.
27. A tendency for inflation to fall below the target on average may also be associated with a series of unpredictable negative shocks or the difficulty a central bank may have in easing monetary conditions before its credibility is established. See Freedman (2001).

REFERENCES

Adam, Charleen and Scott Hendry (2000), 'The M1 Vector-Error-Correction Model: Some Extensions and Applications', in *Money, Monetary Policy, and Transmission Mechanisms*, Ottawa, Canada: Bank of Canada, pp. 151–80.

Bank of Canada (2000), *Price Stability and the Long-Run Target for Monetary Policy*, Ottawa, Canada: Bank of Canada.

Bank of Canada (2001), 'Renewal of the Inflation-Control Target: Background Information', *Bank of Canada Review*, Summer, 59–67.

Bank of England (1999), *Economic Models at the Bank of England*, London: Bank of England.

Barro, Robert J. and David B. Gordon (1983), 'A Positive Theory of Monetary Policy in a Natural Rate Model', *Journal of Political Economy*, 91(4), 589–610.

Bean, Charles (1998), 'The New UK Monetary Arrangements: A View From the Literature', *Economic Journal*, 108(451), 1795–1809.

Berger, Helge, Jakob de Haan and Sylvester C.W. Eijffinger (2000), *Central Bank Independence: An Update of Theory and Evidence*, Discussion Paper Series No. 2353, London: Centre for Economic Policy Research.

Black, Richard, Douglas Laxton, David Rose and Robert Tetlow (1994), *The Bank of Canada's New Quarterly Projection Model, Part 1, The Steady State Model: SSQPM*, Ottawa, Canada: Bank of Canada, Technical Report No. 72.

Blinder, Alan S. (1998), *Central Banking in Theory and Practice*, Cambridge, Mass.: MIT Press.

Brayton, F. and P. Tinsley (eds) (1996), *A Guide to FRB/US: A Macroeconomic Model of the United States*, Washington: Federal Reserve Board, Finance and Economics Discussion Series, 1996–42.

Coletti, Donald, Benjamin Hunt, David Rose and Robert Tetlow (1996), *The Bank of Canada's New Quarterly Projection Model, Part 3, The Dynamic Model: QPM*, Ottawa, Canada: Bank of Canada, Technical Report No. 75.

Crawford, Allan (2001), 'Predictability of Average Inflation over Long Time Horizons', *Bank of Canada Review*, Autumn, 13–20.

Cukierman, Alex (1992), *Central Bank Strategy, Credibility, and Independence*, Cambridge, Mass.: MIT Press.

Cukierman, Alex (1999), *The Inflation Bias Result Revisited*, Tel Aviv, Israel: Tel Aviv University, Foerder Institute for Economic Research, Working Paper No. 38–99.

Cukierman, Alex (2000), 'Are Contemporary Central Banks Transparent about Economic Models and Objectives and What Difference Does it Make?', paper presented at Bundesbank/CFS Conference on 'Transparency in Monetary Policy', Frankfurt am Main.
Debelle, Guy and Stanley Fischer (1995), 'How Independent Should a Central Bank Be?', in Jeffrey C. Fuhrer (ed.), *Goals, Guidelines and Constraints Facing Monetary Policymakers*, Boston: Federal Reserve Bank of Boston, Conference Series No. 38, pp. 195–221.
DeLong, J. Bradford (1998), 'The Shadow of the Great Depression and the Inflation of the 1970s', *Economic Letter*, Federal Reserve Bank of San Francisco, May 1.
Eijffinger, Sylvester C.W. (ed.) (1997), *Independent Central Banks and Economic Performance*, Cheltenham, UK and Brookfield, US: Edward Elgar.
Eijffinger, Sylvester C.W. and Jakob de Haan (1996), *The Political Economy of Central-Bank Independence*, Princeton, NJ: Princeton Special Papers in International Economics, No. 19.
Fagan, Gabriel, Jerome Henry and Ricardo Mestre (2001), *An Area-Wide Model (AWM) for the Euro Area*, Frankfurt am Main: European Central Bank, ECB Working Paper, No. 42.
Feldstein, Martin (1997), 'The Costs and Benefits of Going from Low Inflation to Price Stability', in Christina D. Romer and David H. Romer (eds), *Reducing Inflation: Motivation and Strategy*, Chicago: University of Chicago Press, pp. 123–56.
Fischer, Stanley (1981), 'Towards an Understanding of the Costs of Inflation: II', *Carnegie-Rochester Conference Series on Public Policy*, 15, 5–41.
Fischer, Stanley (1995), 'Central Bank Independence Revisited', *American Economic Review, Papers and Proceedings*, 85(2), 201–6.
Freedman, Charles (1993), 'Designing Institutions for Monetary Stability: A Comment', *Carnegie-Rochester Conference Series on Public Policy*, 39, 85–94.
Freedman, Charles (1996), 'What Operating Procedures Should be Adopted to Maintain Price Stability? – Practical Issues', in *Achieving Price Stability*, Kansas City: Federal Reserve Bank of Kansas City, pp. 241–85.
Freedman, Charles (2001), 'Inflation Targeting and the Economy: Lessons from Canada's First Decade', *Contemporary Economic Policy*, 19(1), 2–19.
Friedman, Milton (1968), 'The Role of Monetary Policy', *American Economic Review*, 58(1), 1–17.
Goodhart, Charles A.E. (1994), 'Game Theory for Central Bankers: A Report to the Governor of the Bank of England', *Journal of Economic Literature*, 32(1), 101–14.
Goodhart, Charles A.E. and Haizhou Huang (1998), 'Time Inconsistency in a Model with Lags, Persistence, and Overlapping Wage Contracts', *Oxford Economic Papers*, 50(3), 378–96.
Ireland, Peter N. (1999), 'Does the Time-Consistency Problem Explain the Behavior of Inflation in the United States?', *Journal of Monetary Economics*, 44(2), 279–91.
King, Mervyn (1997), 'Changes in U.K. Monetary Policy: Rules and Discretion in Practice', *Journal of Monetary Economics*, 39(1), 81–97.
Kydland, Finn E. and Edward C. Prescott (1977), 'Rules Rather than Discretion: The Inconsistency of Optimal Plans', *Journal of Political Economy*, 85(3), 473–91.

Lohmann, Susanne (1992), 'Optimal Commitment in Monetary Policy: Credibility versus Flexibility', *American Economic Review*, 82(1), 273–86.
McCallum, Bennett T. (1995), 'Two Fallacies Concerning Central-Bank Independence', *American Economic Review*, Papers and Proceedings, 85(2), 207–11.
McCallum, Bennett T. (1997), 'Crucial Issues Concerning Central Bank Independence', *Journal of Monetary Economics*, 39(1), 99–112.
Meyer, Laurence H. (2000), *The Politics of Monetary Policy: Balancing Independence and Accountability*, Remarks Delivered at the University of Wisconsin, LaCrosse, Wisconsin, 24 October.
Meyer, Laurence H. (2001), *Inflation Targets and Inflation Targeting*, Remarks Delivered at the University of California at San Diego Economics Roundtable, San Diego, California, 17 July.
Orphanides, Athanasios (2001), 'Monetary Policy Rules Based on Real-Time Data', *American Economic Review*, 91(4), 964–85.
Persson, Torsten and Guido Tabellini (1993), 'Designing Institutions for Monetary Stability', *Carnegie-Rochester Conference Series on Public Policy*, 39, 53–84.
Persson, Torsten and Guido Tabellini (eds) (1994), *Monetary and Fiscal Policy*, Volume 1, *Credibility*, Cambridge Mass.: MIT Press.
Posen, Adam S. (1993), 'Why Central Bank Independence Does Not Cause Low Inflation: There Is No Institutional Fix For Politics', in Richard O'Brien (ed.), *Finance and the International Economy*: 7, Oxford: Oxford University Press, pp. 41–65.
Rogoff, Kenneth (1985), 'The Optimal Degree of Commitment to an Intermediate Monetary Target', *Quarterly Journal of Economics*, 100(4), 1169–90.
Thiessen, Gordon G. (1998–99), 'The Canadian Experience with Targets for Inflation Control', *Bank of Canada Review*, Winter, 89–107.
Vickers, John (1998), 'Inflation Targeting in Practice: The UK Experience', *Bank of England Quarterly Bulletin*, 38(4), 368–75.
Walsh, Carl E. (1995), 'Optimal Contracts for Central Bankers', *American Economic Review*, 85(1), 150–67.

3. The use and meaning of words in central banking: inflation targeting, credibility and transparency

Benjamin M. Friedman*

1. INTRODUCTION

Charles Goodhart is the Samuel Johnson of monetary policy. Few people in the field have written more. Few have written in more genres: in Goodhart's case, scholarly research papers expanding the frontier of the subject; practical analyses illuminating the policy problems of the day; memoranda, including many never published, for circulation within the central bank; even textbooks for educating future generations of economists and central bankers. Few people have written works of greater quality, or with greater effect on how one's readers think and act. And like Johnson (or so the historical accounts tell us), Charles Goodhart exhibits – how to put the matter delicately? – a plethora of personal eccentricities that are as endearing to his countless friends as they must be baffling to anyone who merely observes him at a distance.

Goodhart's career spans an extraordinary period of development in both the thinking and the practice of monetary policy. Notwithstanding the many false starts in both thinking and practice – and there have been many – few informed persons would doubt that both are in far better condition today than they were four decades ago. Especially with respect to the making of actual monetary policy, and especially in a volume like this one, a certain amount of self-congratulation would certainly be in order. But problems remain nonetheless, including problems stemming directly from the most recent series of advances. As the late Christopher Lasch (1991) observed, 'The advance of the intellect is highly desirable, but it will not go very far if it looks constantly backward to admire the distance already traveled'. The object of this chapter is therefore to point to a part of the monetary policy-making glass that yet remains empty, and to speculate about what central bankers might do to fill it.

Perhaps oddly for an aspect of economic policy that involves actually *doing* something – buying or selling securities in the open market, making advances to banks, and so on – many of the problems at the centre of monetary policy-making today concern the use of words. Samuel Johnson was sufficiently taken with the importance of using words correctly that he spent seven years producing the first modern dictionary of the English language. Two centuries later another Englishman, Eric Blair (a.k.a. George Orwell), highlighted the threat to democratic society posed by governmental institutions that use words to mean whatever it suits their purposes to have them mean. Neither evidently thought much in particular about monetary policy. But as so much of the new research in the field during the last few decades has rightly emphasized, monetary policy too is partly a matter of communication. And here too, it is important to use words to mean what they are properly supposed to mean, even if it might suit the convenience of the central bank to have them mean something else.

2. WHAT DOES INFLATION TARGETING MEAN?

One of the most significant developments in the theory and practice of monetary policy in recent years has been inflation targeting. The Bank of England is but one of an increasing number of central banks that have adopted explicit inflation targeting as the conceptual framework within which they formulate their monetary policy decisions and communicate those decisions to financial market participants, firms and households more generally, other government decision makers, and ultimately the world at large. But what exactly does inflation targeting mean?

As Mervyn King (1997) among others has usefully emphasized, inflation targeting need not mean that the sole objective guiding monetary policy is to achieve a specified rate of price inflation. (King colourfully described advocates of such a policy 'inflation nutters'.) In principle, an inflation-targeting regime is consistent not only with directing monetary policy toward real objectives like output and employment but, indeed, with giving priority (although not absolute priority) to such matters over concerns about the rise or fall of prices and wages. But in that case, why put the matter in terms of an inflation target?

The rationale for inflation targeting emerges as the joint consequence of two familiar lines of thought within the economics of monetary policy. First, because the central bank in effect has only one instrument at its disposal – it can be either open market operations or the interest rate the bank charges on advances – the standard Tinbergen–Theil logic implies that it is possible to express the policy chosen at any time in terms of the intended outcome (or, in a dynamic setting, the intended trajectory) of *any* single economic magnitude that monetary policy affects: inflation, output, employment, the economy's foreign balance, even some magnitude of no intrinsic importance whatsoever (the obvious example is the level or growth rate of some measure of 'money').

But, then, why choose inflation? The second line of thought within the field that underlies the concept of inflation targeting is the Phelps–Friedman 'natural rate' model of aggregate supply in the market for goods and services. Under most familiar versions of the natural rate model, a trade-off exists between real outcomes like output and employment and nominal outcomes like prices and inflation – and, moreover, a trade-off that the central bank can exploit – but only over some finite (and presumably fairly short) horizon. By contrast, in the long run there is no such trade-off, or at least not one subject to exploitation by monetary policy. Long-run real outcomes depend on such real factors as endowments, preferences and technologies. In the long run only nominal magnitudes are subject to monetary influences. The conceptual appeal of inflation targeting, therefore, is to express the objective of monetary policy not in terms of the intended trajectory for just any randomly selected variable, as the Tinbergen-Theil logic would permit, but in terms of the trajectory for a variable that monetary policy can presumably affect in the long as well as the short run.

In fact, the evidence for the natural rate model has never been as strong as the prevailing consensus within the economics profession (not to mention the case for inflation targeting) has let on. As Robert Solow has argued, the natural rate model seems a good description of the US experience in the post World War II period, but only that – and in particular, not of the European post-war experience, nor of either the US or the European experience before the war. Theoretical work (by Blanchard and Summers (1986), for example) has shown numerous ways in which some part of what the natural rate model takes to be purely temporary departures of output, employment or unemployment from the equilibrium level induce permanent, or at least very long-lasting, changes in the equilibrium itself. Empirical work based on fairly long time periods indicates that the evidence for a negatively sloped Phillips curve (King and Watson, 1994), or for a positive link between inflation and the economy's investment rate (Ahmed and Rogers, 2000), is at least as strong as the evidence for long-run neutrality. But the evidence is hardly conclusive on either side, and for the moment the logic of the natural rate model underlies much of the structure of modern macroeconomics. The logic behind inflation targeting is consistent with that whole.

Even so, as King has emphasized, the important point about inflation targeting is that expressing the intended policy outcome in terms of the trajectory for any one variable does not imply that the central bank is indifferent with respect to outcomes for all other variables. The point is most explicit in the inflation targeting framework suggested by Lars Svensson (1997), in which the central bank targets its own forecast of future inflation as if that forecast were a classical intermediate target variable such as money.[1]

In Svensson's formulation, the central bank at each point in time seeks to make its forecast of future inflation follow a specific trajectory. If some economic disturbance or policy error has resulted in an inflation rate different from whatever rate the central bank is seeking to achieve, and if inflation is the only variable about which the central bank is not indifferent, then the optimal trajectory simply involves returning to the desired inflation rate instantly – or more practically, in the presence of lags, as soon as is at all possible. If other variables like output or employment (or even the level or change of interest rates) matter too, the optimal trajectory following a disturbance or a policy error then involves bringing the forecast of future inflation into line with the unconditionally desired inflation rate only over some longer period of time.

Not surprisingly, the length of the interval over which the forecast of future inflation optimally returns to the unconditionally desired rate in this formulation – or, equivalently, the optimal speed of convergence if it is conceived as asymptotic – depends on the strength of the central bank's preferences with respect to inflation vis-à-vis its other objectives. For a given short-run cost of disinflation in terms of output and employment, the stronger is the preference for being at the unconditionally desired inflation rate, the faster the optimal inflation forecast trajectory returns to it. Conversely, the stronger is the preference for being at equilibrium output and employment, the more slowly the optimal inflation forecast trajectory returns to the unconditionally desired rate. (Similarly, for given preferences, the smaller is the short-run cost of disinflation, the faster the optimal trajectory returns to the unconditionally desired inflation rate, and vice versa.) Hence not only does inflation forecast targeting not necessarily mean that the central bank is an 'inflation nutter', but there is an explicit way in which its preferences with respect to real outcomes can enter the inflation targeting framework.

3. DO CENTRAL BANKS TARGET REAL OUTCOMES? SHOULD THEY?

It is a familiar characteristic of policy debate, and probably of intellectual discourse more generally, that the language in which that debate takes place exerts a powerful influence over the substance of what the participants say, and eventually even over what they think. As David Hume remarked about one of the central political debates of his day, 'The Tories have been obliged for so long to talk in the republican stile, that they . . . have at length embraced the sentiments, as well as the language of their adversaries'. Notwithstanding the compatibility in principle of inflation targeting as a conceptual framework for implementing a monetary policy in which real outcomes matter as well as inflation, an observer who has paid attention to the last quarter century of debate about monetary policy is entitled to suspect that a powerful motivation for adopting this framework, at least in some quarters, is the hope that if the explicit discussion of the central bank's policy is carried out entirely in terms of an optimal inflation trajectory, concerns for real outcomes may somehow atrophy or even disappear from consideration altogether.

One of the most striking developments in monetary economics during this last quarter century has been the renewed attempt to banish from the purview of monetary policy-making any sense of responsibility for real outcomes. This is in fact an old debate, with familiar antecedents in central banks' response to the depression of the 1930s and well before that. Although there is no necessary link, there is ground for thinking that inflation targeting may in practice be yet the latest incarnation of this effort.

One reason for suspecting that this is so is the reluctance, within today's central banking community, to acknowledge openly an interest in or concern for real outcomes. For example, the charter of the European Central Bank either does or does not charge the bank to be responsible for such matters depending upon how one reads the relationship of Article 103 to Article 102a, and of Article 102a and Article 105 to Article 2, in the Maastricht Treaty. Because few people either have read or ever will read these formal statements – and, even more so, because their language obscures plain meaning for anyone who tries – the issue defies resolution. The ECB, of course, has not adopted inflation targeting (at least not formally). But among central banks that have done so, often the articulation of what that inflation targeting strategy means is typically devoid of any explicit reference to real outcomes.

One frequently stated rationale for eschewing concern for real outcomes is the proposition that there is nothing the central bank can usefully do to affect them anyway: in effect, the neutrality of the natural rate model holds in the short as well as the long run.[2] As Ernst Welteke, president of the Deutsche Bundesbank and therefore a member of the ECB's governing council, recently stated the argument, 'The ECB doesn't have the job of steering the economy. The best contribution monetary policy can make to growth and employment is to keep prices stable'. Today this idea is familiar from many sources, including central banks (and central bankers) other than the ECB: Maintaining price stability fosters greater output and employment in the long run. And in the short run there is nothing monetary policy can do about either output or employment anyway.[3]

The most immediate problem with such a point of view is that even if inflation were the only aspect of economic activity that the central bank sought to affect, it is unclear how it would go about doing so without in the first instance deliberately influencing the pace of real activity. In an earlier era some economists believed that simply keeping the quantity of money, however measured, in step with some predetermined growth path would lead to a corresponding inflation path for prices. But the collapse of empirical relationships between money and prices in many countries roughly twenty years ago has mostly removed this idea from the realm of practical monetary policy-making (although money certainly can be, and often still is, used as an information variable to help predict future inflation and so on). Instead, the conceptual route to keeping inflation on target lies through the short-term aggregate supply curve. For practical purposes, targeting inflation means in the first instance targeting output – not because output necessarily matters for its own sake, but because output in relation to some capacity benchmark is what matters for inflation.[4]

But once the point is accepted that monetary policy does systematically affect real outcomes in the short run – indeed, so much so that this is the key to its influence over price inflation – the rationale that the central bank should not seek to affect real outcomes because it cannot becomes vacuous. It is then necessary to address the issue on its merits. The monetary economics literature provides no such argument, however. The most familiar line of thinking on the issue in the literature of the past two decades has been the argument, based on time inconsistency, that the wrong kind of concern for real outcomes can lead in the long run (and, depending on expectations, perhaps in the short run as well) to an undesirable rate of inflation with little (in the limit, no) gain in real terms anyway. But the fact that the wrong kind of concern for real outcomes can have these undesirable consequences does not constitute a generic case against treating output or employment as proper objectives of monetary policy at all.

Nonetheless, the call for monetary policy to adopt an exclusive focus on prices to the exclusion of real outcomes has been widespread throughout this period. In Japan, for example, Yasuo Matsushita, at the time Governor of the Bank of Japan, argued that 'Most people agree that the objective of monetary policy is the maintenance of price stability. . . . The maintenance of price stability does not conflict with the achievement of stable economic growth and employment conditions. For example, measures to prevent overheating (or recession) of the economy can at the same time contain inflation (or avoid deflation), and provide medium- to long-run price stability; and this price stability in turn, is a prerequisite for achieving sustainable growth of the economy'.[5]

In the United States, a few years ago the chairman of the Joint Economic Committee of the Congress introduced legislation to repeal the reference to 'maximum employment' in the Federal Reserve System's existing mandate, and to charge US monetary policy-makers, except for an initial transition period, simply to 'maintain a monetary policy that effectively promotes price stability'. Although in the end Congress did not pass the bill, numerous senators co-sponsored it including the then-majority leader, Bob Dole (and his successor, Trent Lott). Another US example is the unfortunate experience of the then-vice chairman of the Federal Reserve, Alan Blinder, who found himself subject to overwhelming criticism from both central banking and private financial circles for saying explicitly that US monetary policy should focus on both inflation and employment – as, indeed, the law requires. (Prevailing legislation charges the Federal Reserve to conduct monetary policy 'so as to promote effectively the goals of maximum employment [and] stable prices', among other objectives.)

Not surprisingly, outside academic circles most of the talk of banishing real outcomes from the purview of monetary policy took place during an era of sustained economic growth.[6] When business is expanding and profits are strong and jobs are plentiful (even in chronically high-unemployment European countries), it is easy to say that inflation is all that should matter. More recently, now that economies are slowing, talk of ignoring real outcomes in favor of a sole focus on price stability has begun to disappear.

Here again the US experience can serve as a useful example: No one pretended that the five rounds of easing that the Federal Reserve instituted in 2001 before the atrocities of 11 September were necessary to prevent inflation from falling too low. Consumer prices in 2000 rose by 3.4 per cent, up from a 2.7 per cent increase the year before and just 1.6 per cent the year before that. Excluding food and energy, US consumer prices rose by 2.6 per cent in 2000, compared to 1.9 per cent the year before. As of August 2001, the twelve-month increase was 2.7 per cent. No one argued in public discourse that this was too little. (Other inflation measures, including most measures of wage inflation, had likewise either moved higher or at best remained unchanged.) Instead, everyone recognized that the purpose of the Federal Reserve's easier policy was to spur nonfinancial economic activity, or at least to prevent further slowing. Yet in central banking circles, open acknowledgment of responsibility for preventing an economic slowdown – except when too low a rate of output might threaten too low a rate of inflation – remains mostly unacceptable.

4. WHAT DOES TRANSPARENCY MEAN?

The meaning attached to ordinary words in any specific context often depends on the prior evolution of how that word has been used in that context. As a result, a listener or reader not sufficiently sensitive to this prior evolution may wonder why the word is now used as it is, or may even fail to understand the current meaning altogether. Monetary economics is no exception.

One familiar example is the theory of 'real business cycles'. One might suppose from the label that the idea is to emphasize the role of any of a variety of real phenomena, as opposed to monetary influences (including monetary policy in particular), in accounting for observed business fluctuations. But in the literature of monetary economics today, 'real business cycle theory' means something even more specific – namely, a focus on factors affecting aggregate supply (technologies, willingness to work, and so on), as opposed to factors affecting aggregate demand (consumer sentiments, 'animal spirits of entrepreneurs', and so on), in causing business fluctuations. The explanation is that real business cycle theory came into the field in the wake of a long-standing debate that, at least at the time, seemed to point to the primacy of monetary factors over real aggregate demand factors as the source of aggregate fluctuations. With real demand-side factors thus out of consideration, arguing that business fluctuations were due to real rather than monetary factors then implicitly made them a supply-driven phenomenon.

An example that moves closer to monetary policy is central bank independence. In much of the literature of this subject, 'independence' means largely what an ordinary speaker of the language might well suppose: the ability, on institutional as well as practical grounds, of central bank policy-makers to take the decisions they think best, without either prior or subsequent interference from other authority.[7] But in parts of the literature, 'independence' instead refers to the strength of the central bank's preferences with respect to inflation vis-à-vis real outcomes. For example, the widely read paper by Guy Debelle and Stanley Fisher, 'How Independent Should a Central Bank Be?', primarily addresses the question of how much weight a central bank should place on its inflation objective compared to its objectives for real outcomes. In the formal model that represents the core of the paper's analysis, 'central bank independence' is simply 'defined as the central bank's aversion to inflation'. As a result, 'the inflation rate is clearly zero when the central bank is fully independent'.

How did this usage arise? Again the answer lies in the prior evolution of context. The literature of central bank independence developed in the wake of the literature of time inconsistency, according to which the explanation for the high and chronic inflation that then plagued so many industrialized economies around the world was a systematic attempt by central bankers to 'trick' private-sector decision makers into producing more by bringing about a higher inflation rate than they were expecting. But why would central bankers do such a foolish (and, according to the literature, ultimately unsuccessful) thing? Surely, left to their own devices they would not. Only the pressure of higher political authority to which they were subject could explain such blatant folly. Hence a central bank that was completely independent in the conventional sense would presumably exhibit no concern for real outcomes whatever – which is the meaning then attached to 'independence' in this strand of the literature.

Today a major theme in the discussion and practice of monetary policy, closely connected to the strategy of inflation targeting, is 'transparency'. Again quoting Mervyn King (2000), 'It is truly remarkable how much has changed over the past decade. The mystery and mystique has given way to transparency and openness. . . . It is difficult to listen to a speech on domestic or international financial policy these days, without hearing about transparency. . . . The communication of policy-makers' intentions with a view to enhancing their credibility has come to play a central role in monetary policy'.

As ample discussion in the literature also makes clear, considerations of communication, including in particular the quest for credibility and transparency, have also been a central motivation for inflation targeting. Congressional attempts at clarification notwithstanding, it is difficult for the public to know what 'maximum employment' and 'price stability' mean in the Federal Reserve's official mandate, much less to figure out how US central bankers weight these two objectives over the short and medium run. By contrast, saying that the Bank of England's objective is to achieve inflation of 2½ per cent per annum, with departures above and below to be treated as equally undesirable, has a certain ready clarity. Nor is the matter limited to conveying in advance the central bank's intentions. In the absence of sharp definitions of the Federal Reserve's objectives, or of the relative weighting between them, neither the Congress (which under the US Constitution has direct responsibility for monetary policy) nor any other element of the body politic can readily evaluate the central bank's performance after the fact. By contrast, judging how closely the Bank of England has met its inflation target is straightforward (although assessing blame is not).

But the emphasis on transparency and credibility did not emerge in a vacuum either, and the context in which these concepts came to the fore of the discussion of monetary policy in recent decades suggests that these words too may not bear entirely conventional meanings. In both cases the relevant context was in the first instance the time inconsistency literature, and more broadly the theory of the forward-looking aggregate supply curve.

The standard forward-looking aggregate supply curve that is the workhorse of so much of today's monetary economics literature expresses current inflation as a positive function of (1) the level of output supplied in relation to some benchmark equilibrium, (2) a shock to production costs or sellers' mark-ups, and (3) price-setters' expectations of future inflation.[8] All else equal, therefore, lower inflation expected for the future means lower inflation today. Similarly, the lower is expected future inflation, the higher today's output can be in relation to equilibrium output without resulting in higher inflation today. On both counts (which are really just two ways of expressing the same relationship), as long as the central bank has preferences with respect to real output as well as inflation, it is beneficial to have private-sector decision makers expect that inflation will be low in the future.

But as the experience of the 1970s harshly demonstrated, merely claiming that inflation will be low in the future is not sufficient to induce the public to expect that this will be so. Indeed, the original point of the time inconsistency argument was that even if policy-makers are entirely sincere in their intentions to deliver on such a pledge – and even in the absence of surprise shocks – under some circumstances there is good reason for private-sector decision makers to believe that inflation will be high anyway: the low-inflation pledge will not be 'credible'.

In the wake of the evolution of this literature, a 'credible' central bank therefore means something more than just a central bank that can be believed to follow through on its declared policy, whatever that policy may be. Specifically, in today's context a 'credible' central bank is one that is believed to be firmly committed to low inflation. And in parallel, a 'transparent' policy means one that the public understands to be 'credibly' committed to low inflation.

Seen in this light, the connection to inflation targeting becomes (in the dictionary sense) transparent. Inflation targeting is a way of manipulating private-sector decision makers' expectations about future inflation. It puts before them the central bank's long-run objective of achieving inflation equal to such-and-such a rate. It removes from explicit discussion whatever objectives the central bank may hold for output, employment, or other real outcomes, over less than the long run. It likewise removes from discussion the trade-off that monetary policy-makers perceive between inflation and real outcomes over less than the long run. It achieves 'credibility', in the specific sense of making a commitment to low inflation believable, by keeping out of the discussion those considerations that would reveal that commitment to be qualified, and hence not completely credible in the usual sense.[9] It is 'transparent' in that it holds a part of what the central bank is doing before clear glass while obscuring other parts behind a logical partition.

The point is perhaps easiest to see in Svensson's (1997) framework of inflation forecast targeting. Few if any central banks that have adopted an inflation targeting strategy seek, or even say they seek, to return inflation to the unconditionally desired rate immediately (or, in the presence of lags, as immediately as is possible) after a supply shock or a policy error has resulted in some different rate. The reason is that doing so would unduly push real economic activity away from equilibrium.

To recall, the optimal speed of return is a direct expression of the relative weight placed on inflation vis-à-vis real outcomes. But while it is not uncommon for inflation targeting central banks to be open about the time horizon for returning to the unconditionally desired inflation rate (typically two years or more), few are explicit about the underpinnings from which, as Svennson shows, this optimal horizon arises: the level of output or employment that policymakers regard as desirable over this horizon, or, even more so, the weight, compared to that on inflation, that they place on such objectives. 'Transparency' is one-dimensional. It is so in order to achieve 'credibility'.

An analogous reluctance also appears in contexts other than strict inflation targeting. The ECB, for example, consistently defines the price stability that its charter enjoins it to achieve as 'a rate of price increase less than 2½ per cent per annum'. But does, say, an inflation of minus 1 per cent (in other words, deflation) qualify as less than 2½ per cent? No, when pressed ECB officials explain that the phrase 'a rate of price increase' implicitly rules out negative inflation. But for formal purposes the Bank does not use language that makes explicit the idea that any rate of inflation can be too low. In this example, 'transparency' is not one-dimensional but one-sided. But here as well, the point of the asymmetry is to foster 'credibility'.

5. CONCLUDING REMARKS

The theory and practice of monetary policy have advanced enormously over the past few decades, and as of the beginning of the twenty-first century inflation targeting has emerged as one of the most salient new developments on both the theoretical and the practical fronts. Taken at face value, this framework holds out the prospect of resolving some of the internal contradictions that have thwarted central banks' efforts to achieve widely recognized macroeconomic goals in the past. It also offers the promise of introducing a logic and consistency that some central banks' deliberations sorely missed in the past. (Whether inflation targeting actually played a role in the achievement of more stable prices, as has occurred in many of the countries that have adopted this framework – but also in others that have not – is an empirical issue that lies beyond the scope of this paper.)

But inflation targeting – at least in today's inherited monetary policymaking context – also serves two further objectives that are of more questionable import, and while seemingly contradictory, the two are ultimately related: By forcing participants in the monetary policy debate to conduct the discussion in a vocabulary pertaining solely to inflation, inflation targeting fosters over time the atrophication of concerns for real outcomes. In the meanwhile, inflation targeting hides from public view whatever concerns for real outcomes policy-makers do maintain. Both objectives are understandable. Whether either is desirable on economic grounds is an open question. Neither is very consistent with the role of monetary policy in a democracy.

Hence there is work remaining to do, and it is serious work at that. Charles Goodhart would be disappointed if it were otherwise.

NOTES

* This paper was written for the Conference in Honour of Charles Goodhart, Bank of England, London, 15–16 November, 2001. I am grateful for research support from the Harvard Program for Financial Research.

1. Because of the relation between a future outcome and its expectation, however, this particular form of intermediate targeting is not subject to the standard criticisms of the use of money or other such variables as intermediate targets. Moreover, by targeting its own forecast, rather than that of private-sector forecasters, the central bank can avoid potential dynamic instabilities of the kind identified by Woodford (1994), although there is an obvious sacrifice of the efficacy of external monitoring of policy performance.
2. Alternatively, even if monetary policy is not neutral with respect to real outcomes in the short run, the familiar problems of uncertainty and lagged impact are sufficiently severe that attempting to exploit this short-run nonneutrality is as likely to do harm as good.
3. Similar views are familiar in the US as well. For example, as Alfred Broaddus, president of the Federal Reserve Bank of Richmond, recently argued, 'both theory and evidence indicate that the Fed cannot control real variables directly with monetary policy, and in my view there are reasonable grounds to presume that the Fed will optimize its contribution to the economy's overall performance by maintaining credibility for low inflation (here Mr. Broaddus cites Goodfriend and King, 2001). A unitary goal focused on low inflation would strengthen credibility by making the Fed's commitment to this objective definite and unambiguous'.
4. For example, the fact that a central bank's monetary policy actions approximately follow a 'Taylor rule', with a significant role for the usual output or unemployment term in determining its chosen short-term interest rate, need not imply that the central bank is concerned with real outcomes for their own sake. Output or unemployment may be present in the central bank's reaction function merely as a source of information about future inflation.

5. Governor Matsushita's remarks clearly admit only the possibility of disturbances to aggregate demand, which influence output and prices in the same direction. As much of the academic literature of optimal monetary policy has emphasized, the more interesting problem arises in the case of disturbances to aggregate supply, which normally influence output and prices in opposite directions. (For a concise review, see Clarida et al., 1999.)
6. Even the remarks by Governor Matsushita quoted above date from 1996, when the Japanese economy was enjoying a recovery (which in retrospect turned out to be short-lived). Earlier in the same speech, Mr. Matsushita stated that 'the risk of a deflationary spiral, which was an issue of concern last year, has been practically eliminated'.
7. The literature has also usefully distinguished between such independence with respect to 'goals' versus 'instruments' of monetary policy.
8. As Roberts (1995) has conveniently shown, a relationship of this generic kind can emerge as a result of random timing of price increases as in Calvo's (1983) model, nominal wage contracts as in Taylor's (1979) model, or convex costs of price adjustment as in Rotemberg's (1982) model.
9. The opportunity for the central bank to affect the credibility of its policy in this way – via its communications strategy – is absent in the standard literature of time consistency. The reason is that this line of analysis usually assigns to private-sector decision makers full knowledge of the relevant parameters (including parameters describing policy-makers' preferences, the slope of the short-run aggregate supply curve, and so on), so that a policy either is or is not 'credible' depending upon whether it is or is not time consistent. But when the public lacks this knowledge, it is possible that communications by the central bank may affect private-sector perceptions, including perceptions about these key parameters, and hence may affect whether or not the public sees any given policy as time consistent and therefore 'credible'.

REFERENCES

Ahmed, Shaghil and John H. Rogers (2000), 'Inflation and the Great Ratios: Long Run Evidence from the US', *Journal of Monetary Economics*, 45 (February), 3–35.

Blanchard, Olivier J. and Lawrence H. Summers (1986), 'Hysteresis and European Unemployment', *NBER Macroeconomics Annual*, 1, 15–78.

Broaddus, J. Alfred, Jr (2001), 'Transparency in the Practice of Monetary Policy', Federal Reserve Bank of Richmond, *Economic Quarterly*, 87 (Summer), 1–9.

Calvo, Guillermo A. (1983), 'Staggered Contracts in a Utility-Maximizing Framework', *Journal of Monetary Economics*, 12 (September), 383–98.

Clarida, Richard, Jordi Gali and Mark Gertler (1999), 'The Science of Monetary Policy: A New Keynesian Perspective'. *Journal of Economic Literature*, 37 (December), 1661–707.

Debelle, Guy and Stanley Fischer (1994), 'How Independent Should a Central Bank Be?', in Fuhrer (ed.), *Goals, Guidelines, and Constraints Facing Monetary Policy*, Boston: Federal Reserve Bank of Boston.

Goodfriend, Marvin and Robert King (2001), 'The Case for Price Stability', *The First ECB Central Banking Conference, Why Price Stability?*, Frankfurt: European Central Bank.

Hume, David (1741 [1985]), 'Of the Parties of Great Britain', *Essays: Moral, Political, and Literary* (Miller, ed.), Indianapolis: Liberty Fund.

King, Mervyn (1997), 'Changes in UK Monetary Policy: Rules and Discretion in Practice', *Journal of Monetary Economics*, 39 (June), 81–97.

King, Mervyn (2000), 'Address to the Joint Luncheon of the American Economic Association and the American Finance Association', unpublished: Bank of England.
King, Robert G. and Mark W. Watson (1994), 'The Post-War U.S. Phillips Curve: A Revisionist Econometric History', *Carnegie-Rochester Conference Series on Public Policy*, 41 (December), 157–219.
Lasch, Christopher (1991), *The True and Only Heaven: Progress and Its Critics*, New York: Norton.
Matsushita, Yasuo (1996), 'The Role of Monetary Policy', Speech to the Research Institute of Japan (6 November), Bank of Japan website: www.boj.or.jp/en/press/koen004.htm.
Roberts, John M. (1995), 'New Keynesian Economics and the Phillips Curve', *Journal of Money, Credit and Banking*, 27 (November), 975–84.
Rotemberg, Julio J. (1982), 'Sticky Prices in the United States', *Journal of Political Economy*, 60 (November), 1187–211.
Solow, Robert M. (1998), 'How Cautious Must the Fed Be?', in Solow and Taylor, *Inflation, Unemployment and Monetary Policy*, Cambridge, Mass.: MIT Press.
Svensson, Lars E.O. (1997), 'Inflation Forecast Targeting: Implementing and Monitoring Inflation Targets', *European Economic Review*, 41 (June), 1111–46.
Taylor, John B. (1979), 'Staggered Contracts in a Macro Model', *American Economic Review*, 69 (May), 108–13.
Welteke, Ernst (2001), remarks quoted in *The New York Times*, 30 August, W1.
Woodford, Michael (1994), 'Nonstandard Indicators for Monetary Policy: Can Their Usefulness Be Judged from Forecasting Regressions?', in Mankiw (ed.), *Monetary Policy*, Chicago: University of Chicago Press.

Discussion of 'No money, no inflation', 'Central bank independence' and 'The use and meaning of words in central banking'

John S. Flemming

It is an honour for me, as others have said of themselves, to pay tribute to Charles Goodhart, my colleague here at the Bank for most of the 1980s and a friend for much longer. When I briefly taught Monetary Economics at the LSE, while Alan Walters was on leave, it was Charles's book *Money Information and Uncertainty* on which I relied almost exclusively. Happily I had been in the Bank of England temporarily in 1976 when the publication party was held there.

I am also honoured to have been invited to discuss such distinguished contributors as we have just heard. With two Charles's, two Deputy Governors, a Freedman and a Friedman (both pronounced the same) they have to be Ben (Friedman), Charles (Goodhart), Chuck (Freedman) and Mervyn (King) from now on, but I shall take them in order of their presentations.

Mervyn King cited telling and incontrovertible data on correlations between money, prices and output in the long run and the short run – and of effects of expected inflation on velocity in hyper-inflation and subsequent stabilisations. Introducing a third Friedman in the discussion, Milton Friedman's famous dictum cited by Mervyn could be supported by Mervyn's correlations – but that is all they are. The issue of causation depends on how the central bank actually behaves, which might change from time to time. Mervyn says that 'recently the equation for the supply of money has been replaced by an explicit feedback rule for interest rates'.

In Mervyn's history the unnamed theorists are each consistent; Keynes was not (see pages 245 and 246 of the *General Theory*) – as I argued at greater length at the similar conference to mark Don Patinkin's 70th birthday (c.f. Flemming, 1993). I have long preferred the exogenous (policy determined) interest rate version for three reasons:

1. it is more realistic;
2. it makes the standard macro-model recursive rather than strictly simultaneous – and therefore easier to teach;
3. it alone makes any sense of Keynes' speculative demand for money, private agents speculating 'against' the central bank as suggested by Mervyn's own account of their power to manipulate expectations about future interest rates.

I would dispute his claim that 'the new (Taylor rule) models give no less weight to (quantities of) money than do the older (exogenous, policy determined, money) versions'. Likewise, in the absence of model specifications, it is hard to assess the inference from his simulations that they are generated by the reduced form of models in which 'by construction, money has a stable causal effect on inflation'. Money is driven by nominal income and interest but, itself – typically – drives nothing. It normally has no causal role though it will be stably correlated with the price level – after a suitable interval.

Mervyn has given us an interesting discussion of the Japanese problem and the proposition that even when the interest rate is virtually zero government purchases of its own bonds, foreign bonds, or of foreign currencies will probably have some effects. I agree: indeed I am not sure that one has to go to such extremes to find such portfolio effects – despite the reported failure of the US 'operation twist' of long ago – I have never understood how over-funding in the UK in the 1980s contained monetary growth, at the expense of that of credit, unless its effects on the composition of private portfolios also affected relative yields (at a given level of the short-term interest rate). I am sympathetic to Mervyn's speculations as to how monetary theory might advance through analysis of money's role in the transaction costs of adjusting private portfolios.

In his conclusion he says 'the models retain the classical property that, in the long run, monetary policy [yes] and hence money [no] affect prices rather than real activity'. What is preserved is the long-run correlation of money and prices, not the causal role of a now fully endogenised variable. Mervyn goes on to express fears that downplaying money's role, despite the continuing key role of monetary policy, will resuscitate the unaugmented persistent Phillips curve trade-off. I do not share this fear: the message of experience is that we need a nominal anchor. There are at least three possibilities:

1. the exchange rate;
2. the money supply;
3. or last year's price level – as augmented under inflation targeting.

Ben and Chuck traverse related ground – neither having much time for time inconsistency models of monetary policy. Chuck stresses that whatever their theoretical coherence they cannot explain the time-path of inflation.

If it represents an eternal truth inflation should occur whenever commitment mechanisms fail or are absent. No attempts, he says, have been made to explain the historical path of inflation in these terms – although independent central banks have recently become fashionable partly on the basis of credibility and commitment arguments.

Chuck also challenges the realism of the assumption underlying the Barro–Gordon model, notably the implications of the Lucas supply curve for the link between prices and output, and offers a plausible account of the dangers of political proximity to the instruments of monetary policy from its initial impact on quantities – also stressed by Mervyn. Chuck's conclusion that 1970s inflation was caused by shocks and mistakes is one I find very plausible.

In the UK policy-makers misunderstood the implications of floating the exchange rate in 1971. Advantages were seen in abandoning an irksome constraint while overlooking the need for another nominal anchor. I also find his explanation of the virtues of central bank independence, in terms of its effects on output preceding those on inflation, convincing. Indeed I agree with so much of Chuck's argument that I shall now turn to Ben's discussion of inflation targeting. His discussion also has a verbal theme and a reference to George Orwell that is very apt to the works (and words) of Tony (not Eric) Blair and Gordon Brown – not to mention their spin-doctors. But is it true of monetary policy? Ben has a point in Stan Fischer's apparent identification of the degree of central bank independence with the degree of exclusivity of its concern for inflation rather than output. I take the view that it is inappropriate to delegate anything other than pursuit of a politically assigned trajectory for prices to an unaccountable central bank – but that is a political/economic judgement, not a claim to semantic identity. As Ben says the problematic cases for inflation targeting arise when it is off its appointed course.

I know of no central banker who would say that one should get inflation back on course as fast as possible whatever the cost in terms of other variables. Nor do I know any central banker who would believe it constitutionally appropriate for the central bank to determine the target path unilaterally – though many might be willing to fill the gap if no-one else would.

We in Britain have not had to face the question in four years of inflation targeting as we were close to the chosen 2½ per cent rate when that target was set – and the obligation for the Governor to write to the Chancellor if we moved more than 1 per cent away (on either side) would ensure that a dialogue was opened on the return trajectory in good time. Situations such as those Ben writes of, in which the central bank's own preferences in these matters are decisive, should never arise.

A more interesting and relevant case is that of the last year or so. To what extent should the monetary authorities anticipate the effects of recessionary forces? One orthodox answer would be 'to the extent they affect its inflation forecast'. Clearly this would not satisfy Ben – nor is it how Alan Greenspan has behaved. The Fed, of course, has a double-barrelled statutory objective dating from the Keynesian post-war era.

Thus the question can be reformulated as follows: should we change our target to be more inclusive as is the Fed's? Or can we rationalise Greenspan-type behaviour with an inflation-only target without doing violence to the language?

I would be reluctant to follow the Fed's formulation – it is too vague. In fact, once it has secured its inflation target (and only then) the Bank of England is enjoined to support government policies for full employment and growth – but in unspecified ways – and similar formulae apply elsewhere.

I think one could justify an anticipatory policy in either of two ways – at least one of which I believe to be unacceptable to Charles – he shot me down in draft when I tried one in a Clare Group article.

Throughout the period of the asset price bubble sensible forecasters identified downside risks making for negatively skewed or even bi-modal forecasts. Giving some weight to the typically suppressed lower mode (or negative tail) in an inflation forecast would have justified a modest relaxation of monetary policy even while the bubble was intact. This, I think was Charles's objection. But if one had for that reason been exercising restraint while the bubble was intact one might have moved quite decisively when it ruptured.

I admit that this is not without its dangers – it may have been thinking like this that led to the perception expressed by Marcus Miller of a 'Greenspan put' underpinning the still expanding bubble. Martin Wolf's continuing asset price bearishness might induce him to pursue or to justify an expansionary monetary policy without having to invoke a direct concern for output as such. Charles has argued, and in this I have followed him, for the inclusion of asset prices in an inflation measure which might warrant a more restrictive monetary policy in the earlier phase of a bubble.

Thus I am less critical of inflation targeting regimes than is Ben, just as I do not yet accept that either the word 'credible' or the word 'transparent' – both of which apply I hope to these remarks – has yet been debased by Tony Blair's spinners to Eric Blairite 'newspeak'.

REFERENCE

John S. Flemming (1993), 'Money, Interest and Consumption in the General Theory', in *Monetary Theory and Thought*, Haim Barkai, Stanley Fischer and Nissan Liviatan (eds), Basingstoke: Macmillan, pp. 74–86.

Discussion of 'No money, no inflation', 'Central bank independence' and 'The use and meaning of words in central banking'

Stanley Fischer

I am grateful for the opportunity to contribute, even in a small way, to this Festschrift tribute to Charles Goodhart. Charles has been both a policy-maker and a major contributor to many of the key debates on monetary policy. His contributions are distinctive, reflecting his own way of thinking, not for the sake of being different, but because Charles is not content to accept ideas without thinking them through and putting them into a coherent overall framework.

We have all learned much from his many contributions over the years, in areas highlighted in the chapters in this volume. Recently I have benefited particularly from his work on the role of the lender of last resort, some of it together with Haizhou Huang. And we have all on some occasion referred to Goodhart's Law – a combination of the Lucas Policy Evaluation Critique and Murphy's Law – that an empirical relationship will hold up until it is relied on for policy purposes.

The chapters by Charles Freedman, Benjamin Friedman, and Mervyn King cover two broad issues on which I would like to comment: inflation targeting as a monetary policy framework, discussed by both Charles Freedman and Ben Friedman; and the role of money in monetary policy as currently practised, discussed by Mervyn King.

1. INFLATION TARGETING

As Deputy Governor of one of the first central banks to adopt a formal inflation targeting regime successfully, Charles Freedman accepts the framework for policy purposes. But he questions its analytic basis. In particular, he asks why, if there was always an inflationary bias to monetary policy-making, as implied by the original Kydland–Prescott and Barro–

Gordon models, global inflation was low in the 1950s and only increased in the late 1960s and the 1970s.

Freedman's explanation is that in the early post-World War II period most policy-makers believed their task was to choose the optimal point on a downward-sloping long-run Phillips curve, and that the choice was for a relatively low inflation rate. With stable aggregate demand and supply conditions, that choice would produce a low inflation rate, even though the long-run Phillips curve is vertical. But then in the mid-1960s, an aggregate demand shock resulting from the Vietnam War led to an increase in the inflation rate, which was exacerbated by the supply shocks of the early 1970s. In the face of these shocks, policymakers 'did not act sufficiently vigorously to offset the inflationary pressures that developed'.

This explanation accords with my recollections of what happened at the time. But it makes sense only if there is a serious trade-off between inflation and unemployment within a period relevant to policy choices. That is the topic of the chapter by Ben Friedman, to be discussed below.

Freedman also points out that the Barro–Gordon inflationary bias approach to monetary policy does not directly imply that an inflation targeting regime is the best policy choice, nor that central bank independence is the best institutional framework for monetary policy. His more subtle explanation is that monetary policy – even a fully anticipated monetary policy – operates with lags, and typically affects output more rapidly than inflation. And further, that since there are always uncertainties about the outcome of policy choices, no-one can be sure at the time a policy is set what its output and inflation effects will be. These factors, he argues, imply 'that governments would be particularly averse to the possibility that policy errors . . . would lead to slower-than-desired output growth in the short run, and that central banks would be particularly averse to the possibility that policy errors . . . would lead to excessive inflation in the medium to longer run. In effect, . . ., the government, in practice, would place more weight on the earlier output effects and less weight on the longer-term inflationary consequences than would the central bank'.

Freedman then argues that during the 1980s, having observed the adverse consequences of not taking account of the longer-term effects of monetary policy, governments began to realize that they should give central banks the independence to pursue monetary policy goals set by the government.

I find the Freedman argument convincing, and a richer description of the monetary policy issues than implied in the Barro–Gordon model. But it does not appear to be fundamentally different from the Barro–Gordon explanation. For in the Barro–Gordon model, monetary policy *can* affect output in the current period, and the government does want to exploit that trade-off, at the expense of higher inflation. Rogoff's conservative central banker is less willing to exploit that temporary trade-off to attain a higher output. If uncertainty, in the form of supply and demand shocks, is added to the deterministic Barro–Gordon model, then the stochastic model behaves in essentially the way implied by Charles Freedman's more complex and more convincing description of reality – which means that the Barro–Gordon model does what a good model should: it captures the essence of an important problem, even if not all its details, in tractable form.

Ben Friedman casts his critique of inflation targeting and central bank independence as one about semantics. It is also substantive, in particular, a complaint that inflation targeting regimes do not in practice make explicit the short and medium term output–inflation trade-offs they want the central bank to pursue. That is a valid complaint, for monetary policy does have to take account of the short- and medium-term trade-off between inflation and output. The proof is simple: faced with a significant inflationary shock, no central bank will aim to eliminate it within the next month, for fear that the output effects would be too great.

The Friedman complaint is valid, but it is not clear from the chapter what to do about it. Central banks have to resolve the issue in practice. The British monetary policy framework does that by targeting the expectation of inflation two years out, implying that monetary policy is free to take output effects of monetary policy into account provided the impacts of such actions on inflation are absorbed within two years. And any reader of the Bank of England's *Inflation Report* understands that output–inflation trade-offs are explicit in the Monetary Policy Committee's decision-making processes. Other central banks using an inflation targeting approach also include short-term output prospects in their accounts of their policy choices. Similar issues arise with regard to the effects of monetary policy on the real exchange rate.

Why not give inflation and output equal billing in setting out the central bank's policy mandate? Because there is an inherent asymmetry in the central bank's ability to affect inflation and output in the long run, and there is no simple way of taking that asymmetry into account in describing the central bank's mandate. Given what we now know or believe about the non-existence of a long-run trade-off between inflation and output, it is essential that legislation specify that the central bank be held responsible for the long-term behaviour of inflation. But it is not clear how to do that, if the central bank is also being held responsible for the short-term behaviour of inflation and output – for the legislature to which the central bank has to report is far more likely to want to focus on the current situation than on the long-term behaviour of inflation.

Under these circumstances, the Bank of England compromise seems a sensible one. So are policy mandates that specify that the central bank's primary responsibility is to maintain inflation close to the target level, and that it should also try to influence output to the extent that does not conflict with its primary responsibility. Neither of these compromises is fully satisfactory, and neither is likely to be the last word. And like Ben Friedman, I disagree with statements by central bankers that they cannot influence the behaviour of output, and wonder whether those who make them believe what they are saying.

So, I expect we will continue to work on refining the mandate that should be given to the the central bank. If I have a difference on this issue with Ben Friedman, it is implicit: I believe the inflation targeting framework is better than earlier approaches, including vague mandates such as that given to the Fed. I believe that although the Fed has managed monetary policy well in the last twenty years, it would be better in the long run for the United States to institute a formal inflation targeting framework – for the key point about any policy-making framework is not how well it works when headed by exceptional people, like Paul Volcker and Alan Greenspan, but how it performs when headed by a person closer to the expected level.

2. MONEY AND MODERN CENTRAL BANKING

Mervyn King's chapter seeks to explain the disappearance of the money stock from econometric models and monetary policy discourse. His explanation is summarized in the superb quote from former Governor of the Bank of Canada, Gerald Bouey, 'we didn't abandon the monetary aggregates, they abandoned us'. King argues that even so we should not overlook the role of money as an indicator of monetary conditions, pointing to the discussions of monetary and credit quantities in the Bank of England's *Inflation Report*. And he forecasts that, given the role of money in reducing transaction costs, we will one day find the quantity of money making its re-entry into useful empirical models and assessments of monetary policy.

The turnaround in the centrality of the money stock in monetary policy discussions that Mervyn King points to is based on the breakdown of an empirical relationship. In some economies, in which a workably stable money demand function can be identified, it remains useful to specify quantity rules for money stock magnitudes, and this remains the practice in the bulk of IMF programs. More recently, though, the IMF has had to begin adapting its programs to take account of the adoption of an inflation targeting approach by several program countries.

The last comment I would like to make on Mervyn's chapter is that it is hard now to recall the passion and vehemence that went into the debate on interest rates versus the quantity of money in monetary policy. Milton Friedman's 1968 presidential address is now famous for its introduction of the expectational Phillips curve. But it also included an explanation of why a monetary policy based on interest rates rather than the quantity of money would lead to ever-increasing inflation. Subsequently, with the introduction of the rational expectations approach to macroeconomics, it was proved that an interest rate rule could leave the price level indeterminate. And there were many who argued that a constant growth rate rule for money was in practice the best that monetary policy could do.

What happened to those arguments? In the first instance, the theoretical arguments omitted the result that the price level or the inflation rate would be determinate if an interest rate rule reacted appropriately to some nominal magnitude. And in the second, Goodhart's Law intervened on the empirical side. For those engaged in the debate twenty years ago, it is an astonishing reversal, albeit not one often acknowledged by most monetarists.

4. The inflation forecast and the loss function

Lars E.O. Svensson*

1. INTRODUCTION

In Goodhart (2001), Charles defends the current use by the Bank of England's Monetary Policy Committee (MPC) of inflation forecasts conditional on a constant interest rate. He also expresses misgivings about the appropriateness and feasibility of the MPC specifying an explicit loss function for monetary policy. This chapter criticizes Charles's views and argues the opposite: that the MPC can and should specify an explicit loss function, and that it should abandon the constant-interest-rate forecasts for those conditional on time-varying interest-rate paths.

Announcing an explicit loss function improves the transparency of inflation targeting and eliminates some common misunderstandings of the meaning of 'flexible' inflation targeting. Using time-varying instrument-rate paths avoids a number of inconsistencies and other problems inherently associated with constant-interest-rate forecasts.

Since I end up criticizing some of Charles's views, I am afraid that this chapter may to some readers not correctly convey how deeply I admire Charles as a scholar, policy-maker and person, and how much I appreciate the opportunity (over many years in the past and hopefully many years in the future) to learn from his deep knowledge and vast experience, both by reading his work and by many discussions with him. Although I do not always agree with Charles, I always learn from him.

Section 2 deals with specifying the loss function. Section 3 deals with forecasts conditional on constant or time-varying interest rate paths. Section 4 presents some conclusions on how I believe practical inflation targeting should be further developed.

2. THE LOSS FUNCTION

There is by now widespread agreement among central bankers and academics that inflation targeting in practice is 'flexible' inflation targeting, as is apparent in, for instance, several contributions in Federal Reserve Bank of Kansas City (1996, 1999): The objective is to stabilize inflation around the inflation target, but also to put some weight on stabilizing the real economy, for instance, as represented by the output gap, the difference between actual output and the 'natural' output level, that is, potential output (the level of output that would result with flexible prices).

However, without further specification, the precise monetary-policy objectives under inflation targeting are still open to interpretation and suffer from a lack of transparency. For instance, how much weight is put on stabilizing the real economy relative to stabilizing inflation around the inflation target? Indeed, the objectives can be misunderstood. For instance, Meyer (2001b), although arguing strongly in favour of a numerical inflation target, interprets the inflation-targeting regimes in New Zealand, Canada and the United Kingdom as having a 'hierarchical' mandate for price stability and contrasts this with a 'dual' mandate (which he favours) in Australia and the United States. Although, as explained below, I believe this distinction between a hierarchical and dual mandate is a misunderstanding of the nature of flexible inflation targeting (and I argue in Svensson (2001a) that New Zealand is currently a prime example of flexible inflation targeting), as long as inflation targeting central banks do not announce a precise loss function for monetary policy, misunderstandings of the precise objectives are invited.

However, the objectives corresponding to flexible inflation targeting can be described precisely by a quadratic intertemporal loss function in period t,

$$\mathcal{L}_t = (1-\delta)\mathrm{E}_t \sum_{\tau=0}^{\infty} \delta^\tau L_{t+\tau} \tag{4.1}$$

where δ $(0<\delta<1)$ is a discount factor, E_t denotes expectations conditional on information available in period t, and L_t denotes the 'period' loss function. The period loss function is quadratic and given by

$$L_t = \frac{1}{2}[(\pi_t - \pi^*)^2 + \lambda x_t^2] \tag{4.2}$$

where π_t and x_t denote inflation and the output gap in period t, respectively, π^* is the inflation target, and $\lambda > 0$ is the relative weight on output-gap stabilization. Thus, inflation and the output gap are the 'target variables,' that is, the variables that enter the loss function. The corresponding 'target levels' are π^* and zero.

The zero target level for the output gap corresponds to an output target equal to potential output. There is general agreement that inflation-targeting central banks do normally not have overambitious output targets, that is, exceeding potential output. Thus, discretionary optimization does not result in average inflation bias, counter to the case in the standard Kydland–Prescott–Barro–Gordon setup. Since the inflation target is subject to choice but not the output target, there is an asymmetry between the inflation and output target, consistent with the inflation target being the 'primary objective.' In this sense, flexible inflation targeting can be interpreted as a 'hierarchical' mandate. On the other hand, given the inflation target, the objective is to minimize an expected weighted sum of squared inflation deviations from the inflation target *and* squared output deviations from potential output. In this sense, flexible inflation targeting can be interpreted as a 'dual' mandate. Thus, flexible inflation targeting can be interpreted as having *both* a hierarchical and a dual mandate, and no conflict need arise between them.

Regarding the two parameters, the discount factor and the relative weight, δ and λ, the discount factor is for all practical purposes likely to be very close to one, especially when the period is a quarter. Interestingly, when the discount factor approaches one (and the intertemporal loss function is scaled by $1-\delta$ as in (4.1)), the intertemporal loss function approaches the weighted sum of the unconditional variances of inflation and the output gap,

$$\lim_{\delta \to 1} \mathcal{L}_t = \frac{1}{2}(\mathrm{Var}[\pi_t] + \lambda \mathrm{Var}[x_t]) \tag{4.3}$$

(when the unconditional means of inflation and the output gap equal the inflation target and zero, respectively: $\mathrm{E}[\pi_t] = \pi^*$ and $\mathrm{E}[x_t] = 0$).[1] As mentioned, flexible inflation targeting corresponds to $\lambda > 0$. 'Strict' inflation targeting would be the unrealistic case of $\lambda = 0$.

Goodhart (2001, p. 173) states that there is a variety of problems with both establishing and minimizing a loss function. 'First, formally establishing such a loss function, unless it was agreed by the Chancellor, might be seen as the MPC abrogating the right to select its own (short-term) goals; it could be thought of to involve a "democratic deficit."' On the other hand, Charles implies that the Chancellor's letter '... does provide some tightly limited room for discretion, recognizing that "the actual inflation rate will on occasions depart from its target as a result of shocks and disturbances. Attempts to keep inflation at the inflation target in these circumstances may cause undesirable volatility in output."' My own view is that the Chancellor's words are completely consistent with a loss function of the form (4.1) and (4.2), and that the MPC definitely has the right to give an operational interpretation to the Chancellor's letter in the form of an explicit loss function. Therefore, I think that the MPC should go ahead and make the loss function explicit. Then, the Chancellor also gets the chance to voice any objection to the interpretation.[2]

'Second, it might be difficult for a committee to agree on any formal functional representation. The coefficients in the function would be somewhat arbitrary (and what would be done about the standard central bank practice of interest rate smoothing?). Moreover, membership of the committee is time-varying, and existing members may find that their views about the (short-run) loss function shift as the context changes.'

I find the quadratic loss function above very attractive and intuitive. In particular, the marginal loss of deviating from the target, $\partial L_t/\partial|\pi_t - \pi^*| = |\pi_t - \pi^*|$ and $\partial L_t/\partial|x_t| = \lambda|x_t|$, is rising in the distance from the target and close to zero when the distance is close to zero. Thus, it is more important, to return to the target the further away from it, and inflation and the output gap close to their targets is almost as good as them being on target. The quadratic form makes the marginal loss linear, the simplest functional form for an increasing function. Therefore, I believe that the MPC members would easily see its advantages and agree to this form.[3]

It remains for the MPC to decide on the parameters δ and λ, as well as the estimate of potential output that is used in constructing the output gap. Regarding the inflation target, π^*, the Chancellor has already specified that inflation should be measured as 12-month increases in the RPIX and that the inflation target is 2.5 per cent.[4] As for the discount factor δ, as noted above, it can uncontroversially be approximated by one. The main sticking point is the relative weight, λ. For the MPC, voting is a natural mechanism for aggregating decisions and preferences. Then the MPC's λ would be the *median* of the MPC members' individual λs.[5] Of course, the MPC members may need some introspection and assistance in deciding what their individually favoured λ is, for instance, by ranking a few potential outcomes. As a revealed-preference exercise, this is relatively trivial. Regarding the estimate of potential output, voting on it would result in the MPC's estimate of potential output being the median of the MPC members' individual estimates.

Indeed, this aggregation procedure into an MPC loss function is quite simple, compared to many other real-world committee decisions. After the MPC's loss function has been specified, the members should agree to apply that loss function rather than their individual ones. The loss function can be interpreted as reflecting the interpretation of the majority of the MPC of the Chancellor's letter. Any (minority) MPC member who does not want to comply with the majority loss function can of course explicitly dissent and note his/her own loss function as a better interpretation of the Chancellor's letter.

Regarding additional objectives, like interest-rate stabilization and/or smoothing (corresponding to additional terms $\lambda_i(i_t - i^*)^2 + \lambda_{\Delta i}(i_t - i_{t-1})^2$), my own view is that there is no good reason why they should enter a loss function corresponding to inflation targeting (this is discussed in some detail in Svensson (2003, section 5.6)). I believe the observed serial correlation in actual instrument-rate settings can be explained by other circumstances (gradual updating of unobservable state of the economy, implicit history-dependence corresponding to a commitment to 'continuity and predictability' or optimal policy in a timeless perspective, and so on). However, if MPC members interpret the Chancellor's letter as implying such additional objectives, they should vote on how to specify them and make the corresponding terms in the loss function explicit. Furthermore, I believe that additional objectives like financial stability and a functioning payment system are best handled as constraints that do not bind under normal circumstances. In exceptional circumstances, when they do bind, this should be explicitly announced and entered into the motivation for policy decisions. Under normal circumstances, the constraints can be disregarded and do not affect policy.

The period loss function (4.2) is a symmetric loss function (the value for $\pi_t - \pi^*$ is the same as the value for $-(\pi_t - \pi^*)$, and so on). Some researchers have argued that asymmetric preferences are relevant in monetary policy and also examined their implications. This would require a more complex loss function. Put differently, a second order approximation is not enough, and higher order terms are needed. I find a symmetric loss function for monetary policy very intuitive, especially since these days not only too high inflation but also too low inflation is considered undesirable, due to the risk of falling into liquidity traps and deflationary spirals. Furthermore, more complex loss functions and more complicated tradeoffs may be too sophisticated to be both operational and sufficiently verifiable for reasonable accountability.[6]

3. FORECASTS

3.1 Forecast Targeting

Monetary policy affects the economy with considerable lags. Current inflation and output are, to a large extent, determined by previous decisions of firms and households. Normally, current monetary-policy actions can only affect the future levels of inflation and the output gap, in practice with substantial lags and with the total effects spread out over several quarters. This makes forecasts of the target variables crucial in practical monetary policy. By 'forecast targeting', I mean using forecasts of the target variables effectively as intermediate target variables, as in King's (1994) early characterization of inflation targeting. This means minimizing a loss function where forecasts enter as arguments.

Let us assume that the transmission mechanism is approximately linear, in the sense that the future target variables depend linearly on the current state of the economy and the instrument rate. Furthermore, assume that any uncertainty and any deviation from the simple models enter additively. Finally, let the intertemporal loss function be quadratic, as above in (4.2). It is then a standard result in optimal-control theory that so-called certainty-equivalence applies, and that optimal policy need only focus on conditional *mean* forecasts of the future target variables, that is, mean forecasts conditional on the central bank's current information and a particular future path for the instrument rate.[7] Since this means treating the forecasts as (intermediate) target variables (that is, putting forecasts of the target variables in the loss function), the procedure can be called 'forecast targeting'.[8]

Let me be more specific. Let $i^t = \{i_{t+\tau,t}\}_{\tau=0}^{\infty}$ denote an instrument-rate plan in period t. Conditional on the central bank's information in period t, I_t (including its view of the transmission mechanism, and so on), and its 'judgment', z^t (to be discussed further below), and conditional on alternative instrument-rate plans i^t, consider alternative (mean) forecasts for inflation, $\pi^t = \{\pi_{t+\tau,t}\}_{\tau=0}^{\infty}$, and the output gap, $x^t = \{x_{t+\tau,t}\}_{\tau=0}^{\infty}$ (consisting of the difference between y^t, the (mean) output forecast, and y^{*t}, the (mean) potential-output forecast). That is, $\pi_{t+\tau,t} = \mathrm{E}[\pi_{t+\tau} | i^t, I_t, z^t]$, and so on.[9] Furthermore, consider the intertemporal loss function in period t applied to the *forecasts* of the target variables, that is, when the forecasts are substituted into the intertemporal loss function (4.1) with (4.2),

$$\mathcal{L}_t = (1-\delta)\sum_{\tau=0}^{\infty} \delta^{\tau}\frac{1}{2}\left[(\pi_{t+\tau,t} - \pi^*)^2 + \lambda x_{t+\tau,t}^2\right] \tag{4.4}$$

Each period t, conditional on the central bank's forecasting model, information I_t and judgment z^t, the bank should then find the combination of forecasts π^t and x^t and instrument-rate plan i^t that minimizes (4.4) and then makes the current instrument-rate decision according to the current optimal instrument-rate plan. The process will result in an endogenous reaction function for the current instrument-rate decision, a function $F(I_t, z^t)$ of the central bank's information and judgment in period t. This reaction function need not be specified explicitly, however, and it need not be followed mechanically.[10]

Forecast targeting requires that the central bank has a view of what the policy multipliers are, that is, how instrument-rate adjustments affect the conditional inflation and output-gap forecasts. But it does not imply that forecasts must be exclusively model-based. Instead, it allows for extra-model information and judgmental adjustments, as well as very partial information about the current state of the economy. It basically allows for any information that is relevant for the inflation and output-gap forecasts.

How would the central bank find the optimal forecasts and instrument-rate plan? One possibility is that, conditional on the information I_t and the judgment z^t, the central-bank staff generates a set of alternative forecasts for a set of alternative instrument-rate plans. This way, the staff constructs the 'feasible set' of forecasts and instrument-rate plans. The MPC would then select the combination of forecasts that 'looks best', in the sense of achieving the best compromise between stabilizing the inflation gap and stabilizing the output gap, that is, implicitly minimizes (4.4). This can be done informally with visual inspection of the forecasts. It can also be done more formally with an explicit loss function, since then the loss for each combination of inflation and output-gap forecasts can easily be calculated numerically. (To do the latter is one of my suggestions to the Reserve Bank of New Zealand in Svensson (2001a).)

Another possibility is that the MPC determines a 'specific targeting rule,' a condition that the forecasts of the target variables must fulfil. Conditional on the information and the judgment, the staff then has to generate a combination of forecasts and instrument-rate plan that fulfils the specific targeting rule. The Bank of England and the Riksbank have formulated a simple specific targeting rule to guide policy, which can be expressed approximately as 'set the instrument-rate so a constant-interest-rate inflation forecast about two years ahead is on target' (Goodhart, 2001 and Heikensten, 1999). As Charles puts it (Goodhart, 2001, p. 177): 'When I was a member of the MPC I thought that I was trying, at each forecast round, to set the level of interest rates so that, without the need for future rate changes, prospective (forecast) inflation would on average equal the target at the policy horizon. This was, I thought, what the exercises was supposed to be.' With the period being a quarter, this targeting rule can be written

$$\pi_{t+8,t} = \pi^* \tag{4.5}$$

with the understanding that the inflation forecast is constructed under the assumption of a constant interest rate. Although this specific targeting rule is both simple and operational, it is not likely to be optimal.[11] As is discussed in Svensson (2003), an *optimal* specific targeting rule instead expresses the *equality of the marginal rates of transformation and substitution* between the target variables in an operational way.

As an example (the details are explained in Svensson (2003)), consider a variant of the popular New Keynesian model, where inflation and the output gap are predetermined one period (a small concession to realism relative to the standard variant when both inflation and the output gap are treated as forward-looking variables, a.k.a. jump variables) and, in particular, 'judgment' matters. The aggregate-supply/Phillips curve is

$$\pi_{t+1} = \pi_{t+2|t} + \alpha_x x_{t+1|t} + \alpha_z z_{t+1} \tag{4.6}$$

where $\pi_{t+2|t}$ denotes expectations in period t of inflation in period $t+2$, and so on, α_x is a positive constant, α_z is a row vector, and z_{t+1} is a column vector, the 'deviation', to be explained below. Thus, inflation in period $t+1$ is determined by expectations in period t of inflation in period $t+2$ and of the output gap in period $t+1$ and by the deviation in period $t+1$. The aggregate-demand/IS curve is

$$x_{t+1} = x_{t+2|t} - \beta_x(i_{t+1|t} - \pi_{t+2|t}) + \beta_z z_{t+1} \tag{4.7}$$

where β_x is a positive constant, $i_{t+1|t}$ is the expectation in period t of the nominal interest rate in period $t+1$ and β_z is a row vector. Thus, the output gap in period $t+1$ is determined by expectations in period t of the output gap in period $t+2$ of the output gap in period $t+2$ and of the real interest rate in period $t+1$ and by the deviation in period $t+1$.

The deviation represents the difference between the true model and this simplified New Keynesian model and includes all other determinants of inflation and the output gap. For simplicity it is treated as an exogenous variable. The central bank's 'judgment', $z^t \equiv \{z_{t+\tau,t}\}_{\tau=0}^{\infty}$, is the central bank's best forecast of the deviation. This is a way to represent the importance and inevitability of judgment in monetary policy. Conditional on the central bank's judgment, the bank's forecasting model in period t is then given by

$$\pi_{t+\tau,t} = \pi_{t+\tau+1,t} + \alpha_x x_{t+\tau,t} + \alpha_z z_{t+\tau,t} \tag{4.8}$$

$$x_{t+\tau,t} = x_{t+\tau+1,t} - \beta_x (i_{t+\tau,t} - \pi_{t+\tau+1,t}) + \beta_z z_{t+\tau,t} \tag{4.9}$$

for forecast horizons $\tau \geq 1$ (where $\pi_{t+\tau,t}$ refers to the central bank's τ-period-ahead forecast of inflation in period t, and so on).

The optimal specific targeting rule for the loss function (4.4) and the model (4.8) and (4.9) can then be found by finding the marginal rate of transformation (MRT) and substitution (MRS) between (the forecasts of) the target variables (inflation and the output gap), and setting these equal.[12] A marginal increase in inflation two periods ahead only, $d\pi_{t+2,t} > 0$, $d\pi_{t+j,t} = 0, j \neq 2$, by the aggregate-supply relation (4.8) requires a fall in the output gap one period ahead, $dx_{t+1,t} = -d\pi_{t+2,t}/\alpha_x < 0$, and an equal increase in the output gap two periods ahead, $dx_{t+2,t} = -dx_{t+1,t} > 0$. We can then define the marginal rate of transformation of the linear combination $\tilde{x}_{t+1,t} \equiv (x_{t+1,t}, x_{t+2,t}) \equiv (1, -1)x_{t+1,t}$ into $\pi_{t+2,t}$, $\text{MRT}(\pi_{t+2,t}, \tilde{x}_{t+1,t})$, which will equal

$$\text{MRT}(\pi_{t+2,t}, \tilde{x}_{t+1,t}) \equiv \left.\frac{d\pi_{t+2,t}}{dx_{t+1,t}}\right|_{dx_{t+2,t}=-dx_{t+1,t}} = -\alpha_x \tag{4.10}$$

From the loss function (4.4) follows that the marginal rate of substitution of $\pi_{t+2,t}$ for $x_{t+j,t}$ is given by $\text{MRS}(\pi_{t+2,t}, x_{t+j,t}) \equiv d\pi_{t+2,t}/dx_{t+j,t}|d\mathcal{L}_t=0 = -\lambda x_{t+j,t}/(\pi_{t+2,t} - \pi^*)$ (in the limit when $\delta \to 1$, for simplicity). From this it is easy to show that the marginal rate of substitution of $\pi_{t+2,t}$ for the above linear combination $\tilde{x}_{t+1,t}$, MRS $(\pi_{t+2,t}, \tilde{x}_{t+1,t})$, will be given by

$$\text{MRS}(\pi_{t+2,t}, \tilde{x}_{t+1,t}) \equiv \left.\frac{d\pi_{t+2,t}}{dx_{t+1,t}}\right|_{d\mathcal{L}_t=0, dx_{t+2,t}=-dx_{t+1,t}} = \frac{\lambda(x_{t+2,t} - x_{t+1,t})}{\pi_{t+2,t} - \pi^*} \tag{4.11}$$

Redoing this for $\pi_{t+\tau,t}$ for all $\tau \geq 1$ and setting the marginal rates of transformation equal to the marginal rates of substitution leads to the optimal specific targeting rule,

$$\pi_{t+\tau,t} - \pi^* = -\frac{\lambda}{\alpha_x}(x_{t+\tau,t} - x_{t+\tau-1,t}) \tag{4.12}$$

where $x_{t,t}$ for $\tau = 1$ is understood to be $x_{t,t-1}$, the one-period-ahead forecast of the output gap in period $t-1$. Thus, the optimal targeting rule in this example can be expressed as 'find an instrument-rate path so the inflation-gap forecast is $-\lambda/\alpha_x$ times the change in the output-gap forecast'.[13]

As discussed more thoroughly in Svensson (2003), the optimal specific targeting rule has the attractive properties that it only depends on the marginal tradeoffs between the target variables. Therefore, it only depends on the loss function (via the relative weight λ) and the form of the aggregate supply/Phillips curve (via the slope of the short-run Phillips curve, α_x). In particular, judgment does not enter explicitly in the optimal targeting rule. Still, judgment will be incorporated in the construction of the forecasts. Furthermore, the targeting rule solves the time-consistency problem, so that it corresponds to the full commitment equilibrium 'in a time-less perspective' (Woodford, 1999a and Svensson and Woodford, 2003).

In this example, inflation-forecast targeting can then be described as:

1. Conditional on the judgment $z^t \equiv \{z_{t+\tau,t}\}_{\tau=0}^{\infty}$ and the aggregate-supply relation (4.8), find inflation and output gap forecasts that fulfil the specific targeting rule (4.12).
2. Substitute these forecasts into the aggregate-demand relation (4.9) so as to find the corresponding instrument-rate plan.

3. Announce these forecasts and the instrument-rate plan, and set the current instrument rate accordingly.

This results in the optimal/appropriate instrument-rate setting, conditional on the judgment, z^t, without having to specify the optimal reaction function.[14]

We note that the optimal specific targeting rule (4.12) refers to the whole future path of the inflation and output-gap forecasts. It does not refer to a specific horizon, like the two-year horizon emphasized by the Bank of England and the Riksbank at which the inflation forecast shall be on target. Indeed, the focus on a specific horizon is not supported by this approach.

Furthermore, as discussed in Svensson (1999) and (2001c), inflation-forecast targeting, either in the general form of minimizing a loss function over forecasts or in the specific form of fulfilling a specific targeting rule is generally *not* the same thing as implementing a 'forecast-based' instrument rule, as

$$i_t = \gamma(\pi_{t+T,t} - \pi^*) \tag{4.13}$$

where the instrument rate responds to a T-period-ahead inflation forecast, or the variants thereof that originated in Bank of Canada's Quarterly Projection Model and are examined by, for instance, Batini and Haldane (1999), McCallum and Nelson (1999) and Batini and Nelson (2001).[15]

3.2 Optimal Time-varying Instrument-rate Paths instead of Constant Ones

The above decision-making process centres on finding the optimal combination of inflation and output-gap forecasts and instrument-rate plan, the (π^t, x^t, i^t) that minimizes the intertemporal loss function or fulfils the specific targeting rule, conditional on current information, including the view of the transmission mechanism, and current judgement. There is no reference to the forecasts conditional on unchanged instrument rates used by the Bank of England and the Riksbank (and by the Eurosystem as well). Thus, the process involves the MPC agreeing on forecasts and instrument-rate plans that normally are time-varying.

Using forecasts conditional on constant-interest-rate forecasts leads to a variety of problems and inconsistencies. Goodhart (2001, p. 171) lists most of them:

1. Such instrument-rate paths are normally not optimal.
2. In backward-looking models they lead to Wicksellian instability, in

that inflation eventually veers off its target level, rather than approaches this asymptotically as optimal paths tend to do. In models with forward-looking models, they imply indeterminacy of the forecasts. A frequent remedy is to apply a stabilizing interest-rate reaction function from a period beyond the 8-quarter forecast horizon, at which point the interest rate frequently jumps substantially. This is 'spatchcocked', as Charles put it.

3. Market expectations of interest rates normally correspond to a time-varying path. One alternative is then to use market expectations and exchange rates and other asset price as inputs in the forecasts that are inconsistent and hence systematically falsified by the interest-rate path used and inflation and forecast paths constructed. The other alternative (which I favour, see footnote 9) is to use hypothetical market expectations and asset prices consistent with the constant interest-rate path assumed, as if the private sector actually believe that the interest-rate path would be constant. This allows internal consistency (which I favour) but implies using inputs in the forecasts that are normally quite different from observed market prices.
4. Since the constant interest rate is not the best forecast for the actual interest rate, the corresponding inflation and output-gap forecasts are not the best forecasts of actual outcomes. This makes it more difficult and less relevant to compare actual outcomes to central bank forecasts.[16]

In spite of all these problems, and to the surprise of Charles's discussant of that paper (Meyer 2001a) (and to my own surprise), Charles ends up defending constant-interest-rate forecasts, on the ground that there are no feasible better alternatives. Charles (2001, pp. 172–3) argues that 'it is hard to see how a committee could ever reach a majority for any particular time path. A great advantage of restricting the choice to what to do now, this month, is that it makes the decision relatively simple, even stark. Given the difficulties involved already in achieving majority agreement in the MPC on this simple decision, the idea of trying to choose a complete time path by discretionary choice seems entirely fanciful and counter-productive.'

I am afraid that I don't buy this argument. The MPC is already agreeing on time-varying inflation and output forecasts, so agreeing on a time-path does not seem to be impossible at all. It is true that there are general problems aggregating preferences in a MPC and that it is easiest to vote about a one-dimensional issue, like an instrument-rate level (or the parameter λ as discussed above). In particular, majority voting will lead to the median-voter outcome, in which the median of the MPC members' individually favoured levels of the instrument rate will be chosen.

Along these lines, I have a simple proposal for agreeing on an instrument-rate plan: Let each MPC member plot his/her preferred instrument-rate plan in the same graph with the future periods (quarters) on the horizontal axis and the instrument rate on the vertical axis (the resulting set of curves might cross each other at several future dates). Form the MPC's aggregate instrument-rate plan by taking the median of the instrument rates for each future quarter.[17] This median instrument-rate plan can be seen as the result of a majority vote in a particular voting procedure.[18] Conditional on this instrument-rate plan, agree on the inflation and output-gap forecasts. If necessary, let each MPC plot his/her conditional inflation and output-gap forecast, and pick the median outcome of these. If these do not look good, let each MPC member consider new individual instrument-rate plans, and then take the median of these. I would be surprised if this procedure does not converge very quickly.

The observant reader will realize that a median instrument-rate plan and inflation and output-gap forecasts picked this way need not be entirely consistent, in the sense that the median inflation forecast may include segments that correspond to instrument-rate plans differing from the median instrument-rate plan. Still, I believe any such inconsistency must be a minor problem, and a final round of adjustments in the MPC's decision may explicitly aim to reduce or eliminate any such inconsistency.

The resulting instrument-rate plan and inflation and output-gap forecast should then be seen as reflecting the majority view of the MPC. Dissenters then have the option to explicitly dissent in the minutes of the meeting. The general setup with the MPC's decision reflecting the majority view and the possibility of dissent is already used by the Riksbank's Executive Board. I think it is more logical and easy to understand than the idea of 'the best collective judgment' used by the Bank of England's MPC.

As an alternative to agreeing on a time-varying interest-rate path, Charles considers 'optimal control procedures'. After dismissing the idea of specifying a loss function, which I have dealt with above, he states:

'Third, it is not clear that optimal control procedures could be applied in practice to larger, messy forecasting models incorporating a wide variety of subjective assumptions, residual adjustments, and such other discretionary adjustments as the MPC adjusts to its own forecast.'

'Fourth, if such optimal control [OC] procedures were applied to the forecast, the resulting outcome of time paths for interest rates, inflation, etc., would become a hideously complex interaction of forecast and OC procedure ... [Introducing such OC procedures] might lead MPC members to regard the whole exercise as a mysterious 'black box' whose entrails are only comprehensible to a tiny number of staff academic specialists.'

'Fifth, if the MPC should find it more difficult to understand how the resultant outcome for the relevant variables had been determined, how would it be possible to explain it to the public, or to justify the decisions that would hang in part from it? To say that we have done what our model told us was best to do is not very convincing, especially given the track record of fancy economic models.'

I cannot help interpreting this as a misunderstanding of 'optimal control procedures', or at least of the procedures that I have in mind and have discussed above. Indeed, the only thing required is that the staff and the MPC generate a few alternative combinations of inflation and output-gap forecasts and instrument-rate plans, conditional on the information available and the MPC's judgment, and that the MPC then picks the combination that minimizes the loss function, or finds a combination that fulfils the 'specific targeting rule', as discussed above.

The advantages in using the optimal inflation and output gap forecasts and instrument plans seem overwhelming to me:

1. This combination of forecasts and instrument plan are the best forecasts of inflation, the output gap and the instrument rate conditional on the information available and the central bank's judgment. This means that it makes sense to compare these to private-sector forecasts, and to actual outcomes.
2. When policy is credible, there would be little difference between the central-bank forecasts and market expectations for inflation, the output gap and interest rates. This means that market values of exchange rates and asset prices can without inconsistency be used as inputs in the forecasts.

Charles (Goodhart, 2001, p. 175) presents an additional argument in favour of unchanged-interest-rate forecasts, namely that a time-variable path would imply some degree of undesirable commitment to future policy actions, and that such commitments would be burdensome and unhappy. I am afraid that I don't buy that argument either. Observers of inflation-targeting central banks are already used to seeing published graphs of time-varying inflation and output-gap forecasts, and they have already learned that new information may warrant revisions of previously announced forecasts. There is no difference between revising a forecast of optimal time-varying interest rates due to new information and revising other forecasts. Furthermore, the Reserve Bank of New Zealand already publishes time- varying interest-rate forecasts that are revised when new information arrives, and during my review (Svensson, 2001a) of its policy I did not notice that this created any problems or misunderstanding by observers of the Bank.

In addition, to the extent that published instrument-rate paths would be understood as some degree of commitment, this may actually be a good thing. It is a well-known result that optimal policy with forward-looking variables require a degree of history-dependence and inertia (Oudiz and Sachs, 1985; Backus and Driffil, 1986; Currie and Levine, 1983; Woodford, 1999a and 1999b; Svensson and Woodford, 2003).

4. CONCLUSIONS

Finally, let me summarize the conclusions I draw for practical inflation-targeting monetary policy from the above discussion:

- Inflation-targeting central banks should specify explicit loss functions. Without putting a specific relative weight on output-gap stabilization relative to inflation stabilization, the objectives under inflation targeting remain somewhat nontransparent and invite misunderstanding. The MPC should simply vote on the form of the loss function and the value of its parameters, and then make the result public.
- If the MPC chooses a quadratic loss function, the advantage of which I have explained above, consistency requires that it should let the 'central tendency' of the forecasts be the mean rather than the mode (that is, the most likely) forecasts.
- The use of the problematic constant-interest-rate paths should be discontinued. Inflation and output-gap forecasts should be constructed conditional on time-varying instrument-rate paths. The MPC should in each decision period decide on its optimal instrument-rate path and the corresponding inflation and output-gap forecasts and make those public. Such decisions are feasible with the aggregation and voting procedures I suggest.
- The use of the simple specific targeting rule (a constant-interest-rate inflation forecast two-years ahead on target) applied by Bank of England and the Riksbank should be discontinued. The two-year horizon should be deemphasized, and the emphasis should be on finding inflation and output-gap forecast paths that minimize the loss function.
- More generally, and as argued in more detail in Svensson (2003), I believe that inflation-targeting, neither from a descriptive nor prescriptive perspective, should be described or interpreted as a commitment to a simple instrument rule, like a Taylor rule or a forecast-based instrument rule. Instead, inflation-targeting central

banks should formulate operational and approximately optimal specific targeting rules, which can be derived from their loss functions and their estimated aggregate supply relations/Phillips curves.[19]

NOTES

* This paper was presented at the Goodhart Festschrift, Bank of England, 15–16 November, 2001. I thank Charles Bean, Charles Goodhart, Lawrence Meyer, Edward Nelson, Marianne Nessén, Torsten Persson and participants in the Festschrift and in a seminar at Sveriges Bank for comments, and Kathleen DeGennaro for editorial and secretarial assistance.

1. However, a fine point to remember is that, since (4.3) does not allow derivatives with respect to inflation and output gap in a particular (future) period, when such derivatives are needed, they must be computed before the limit is calculated.
2. Indeed, my guess is that the Chancellor's eminent advisors had exactly such a quadratic loss function in mind, when they proposed the precise wording in the Chancellor's letter.
3. Charles (Goodhart, 2001, p. 179) states that his loss function is not quadratic but corresponds to the absolute deviation from the target level. Consequently, he did not focus on the mean forecast (which becomes the relevant focus with a quadratic loss function and a linear model) but the median forecast (which becomes the focus with an absolute-deviation loss function and a linear model). This would here correspond to $L_t = |\pi_t - \pi^*| + \lambda |x_t|$. But this loss function has the counter-intuitive property that it is as important to reduce inflation 0.1 percentage point when it is 0.1 percentage point away from the target as when it is 2 percentage points away from the target (since $\partial L_t / \partial |\pi_t - \pi^*| = 1$ and $\partial L_t / \partial |x_t| = \lambda$). Put differently, the derivative of the loss function with respect to one of its arguments is discontinuous at the target level, $\partial L_t / \partial \pi_t = 1$ for $\pi_t > \pi^*$ and $= -1$ for $\pi_t < \pi^*$. I find this awkward and counter-intuitive and am convinced the majority of any MPC would rather settle for a quadratic loss function.
4. In the inflation-targeting countries like Sweden, where the government does not determine the inflation target and the objective for monetary policy is more generally specified as 'price stability,' the central bank also has to specify both the price index and the level of the inflation target that it deems consistent with price stability.
5. Let median(v) denote the median of the elements of the vector v. For an MPC with J members, let λ_j denote the individually preferred relative weight of member j, $j = 1, \ldots, J$. Then the MPC's aggregate relative weight, $\bar{\lambda}$, will simply be given by $\bar{\lambda} = \text{median}(\lambda_1, \lambda_2, \ldots, \lambda_J)$.
6. Nobay and Peel (1998), ali-Nowaihi and Stracca (2001) and Ruge-Mercia (1999) examine alternative asymmetric monetary-policy loss functions. Asymmetric loss functions are frequently motivated from a descriptive rather than prescriptive point of view, for instance, corresponding to observed deviations from rational behaviour. I believe an informed and competent MPC deciding on the appropriate loss function should approach the issue from a prescriptive point of view and select the most appropriate and rational loss function.
7. Wallis (1999) and Vickers (1998) have examined symmetric alternatives to the quadratic loss function, relating the form of the loss function to the 'central tendency' of the forecast. Thus (under the assumption of a linear model of the transmission mechanism), a quadratic loss function corresponds to a mean forecast, an 'absolute deviation' loss function (Charles's favourite, cf. footnote 3) corresponds to a median forecast, an 'all or nothing' loss function (a so-called Dirac delta function) corresponds to a mode forecast, and a 'zone of indifference' loss function corresponds a condition of equality of the probability densities of the forecast at the edges of the zone. Again, I believe a majority of an informed and competent MPC would quickly see the advantages of a quadratic loss function and the corresponding mean forecast.
8. In cases when the assumptions of a linear model and quadratic loss function are not

fulfilled, as discussed in Svensson (2001b), one can still apply 'distribution forecast targeting,' where the forecasts are explicit probability distributions and the intertemporal loss function is the explicit or implicit integral over those distributions.

9. Constructing conditional forecasts in a model without forward-looking variables is straightforward. Constructing such forecasts in a model with forward-looking variables raises some specific difficulties, which are explained and resolved in the appendix of the working-paper version of Svensson (1999). The conditional forecasts for an arbitrary interest-rate path derived there assume that the interest-rate paths are 'credible', that is, anticipated and allowed to influence the forward-looking variables. Leeper and Zha (1999) present an alternative way of constructing forecasts for arbitrary interest-rate paths, by assuming that these interest-rate paths result from unanticipated deviations from a normal reaction function.
10. For simplicity I here abstract from a time-consistency problem that arises with models with forward-looking variables. Even in the absence of an average inflation bias, this time-consistency problem results in 'stabilization bias' (non-optimal coefficients in the implicit reaction function) and a lack of history-dependence. The magnitude of the problem may be small in realistic models with relatively strong backward-looking elements. The nature of the problem and possible solutions, including 'a commitment to continuity and predictability' and a commitment to an optimal specific targeting rule are discussed in Svensson and Woodford (2003) and Svensson (2003).
11. Bank of England (2000, p. 67) actually states that '[h]owever, there is no mechanical link between the projected level of inflation in two years time based on constant interest rates and the appropriate current setting of monetary policy.'
12. For simplicity, inflation π_t in (4.4) is then taken to refer to quarterly inflation, as in (4.8) and (4.9), and not 4-quarter inflation. Nessén (2001) and Nessén and Vestin (2000) examine the consequences of explicit multi-period averages of inflation in the loss function.
13. As is explained in Svensson (2003), (4.12) also applies for $\tau = 1$, when $x_{t,t}$ is interpreted to be $x_{t,t-1}$. Formulating the targeting rule this way leads to 'optimality in a time-less perspective,' corresponding to a situation of commitment to optimal policy far in the past, as discussed in Woodford (1999a) and Svensson and Woodford (2003).
14. As is shown in Svensson (2003), even for this relatively simple model, the optimal reaction function is overwhelmingly complex, especially since it must specify how to respond optimally to judgment, making verifiability and commitment directly to the optimal reaction function completely unrealistic.
15. Batini and Nelson (2001) discuss these two very different definitions of the policy horizon in monetary policy, calling them the 'optimal policy horizon' and the 'optimal feedback horizon'. The former refers to the horizon at which inflation reaches the target after a shock away from the target; the latter refers to the optimal horizon T for a forecast in a forecast-based instrument rule. In general, there is no specific relation between the leads of inflation that appear in the optimal specific targeting rule and the leads that correspond to these optimal-horizon definitions. Put differently, there is no specific 'optimal horizon'.
16. Leitemo (2001) provides additional analysis and criticism of constant-interest-rate forecasts.
17. Let each member j, $j = 1, \ldots, J$, of the MPC individually prefer the instrument-rate plan $i^{tj} \equiv \{i^j_{t+\tau,t}\}^{\infty}_{\tau=0}$ in period t. Then the MPC's aggregate instrument-rate plan, $\bar{\imath}^t \equiv \{\bar{\imath}_{t+\tau,t}\}^{\infty}_{\tau=0}$, fulfills $\bar{\imath}_{t+\tau,t} = \text{median}\,(i^1_{t+\tau,t}, i^2_{t+\tau,t}, \ldots, i^J_{t+\tau,t},)$ for all $\tau \geq 0$.
18. The proposal can be seen as a mechanism for aggregating preferences that avoids the so-called Condorcet paradox, that with multiple policy alternatives there may not be a policy that commands a majority vote against all alternatives (see, for instance, Persson and Tabellini (2000)). The proposal means that the MPC members vote *simultaneously* on the instrument rate for all future periods, by each member first writing down his/her preferred instrument rate for each period. The aggregate instrument rate for each period, the median rate for that period, can then be seen as the result of voting on the instrument rate in that period, *independently* of the outcome of the voting for other periods.

19. Optimal specific targeting rules are the Euler conditions corresponding to optimizing monetary policy. I believe it is much better to describe and prescribe inflation targeting as goal-directed, optimizing policy than as following a mechanical instrument rule. Monetary policy by the world's more advanced central banks these days is at least as optimizing and forward-looking as the behaviour of the most rational private agents. I find it strange that a large part of the literature on monetary policy still prefers to represent central-bank behaviour with the help of mechanical instrument rules, like a Taylor rule or a forecast-based instrument rule. The literature long ago ceased representing optimizing households and firms as following mechanical consumption and investment functions, and instead represents their behaviour by Euler conditions, optimal first-order conditions. The concept of general and specific targeting rules is designed to provide a discussion of monetary policy rules that is fully consistent with the optimizing and forward-looking nature of modern monetary policy. From this point of view, general targeting rules essentially specify operational objectives for monetary policy, and specific targeting rules essentially specify operational Euler conditions for monetary policy. In particular, an optimal targeting rule expresses the equality of the marginal rates of transformation and the marginal rates of substitution between the target variables in an operational way. I hope there will be more research along these lines in the future.

REFERENCES

al-Nowaihi, Ali and Livio Stracca (2001), 'Non-Standard Central Bank Loss Functions, Skewed Risks, and the Certainty-Equivalence Principle', working paper.

Backus, David and John Driffill (1986), 'The Consistency of Optimal Policy in Stochastic Rational Expectations Models', *CEPR Discussion Paper No. 124*.

Bank of England (2000), *Inflation Report, November 2000*, Bank of England.

Batini, Nicoletta and Andrew G. Haldane (1999), 'Forward-Looking Rules for Monetary Policy', in John B. Taylor (ed.), *Monetary Policy Rules*, Chicago University Press, pp. 157–92.

Batini, Nicoletta and Edward Nelson, (2001), 'Optimal Horizons for Inflation Targeting', *Journal of Economic Dynamics and Control*, 25, 891–910.

Currie, David and Paul Levine (1993), *Rules, Reputation and Macroeconomic Policy Coordination*, Cambridge: Cambridge University Press.

Federal Reserve Bank of Kansas City (1996), *Achieving Price Stability*, Kansas City: Federal Reserve Bank of Kansas City.

Federal Reserve Bank of Kansas City (1999), *New Challenges for Monetary Policy*, Kansas City: Federal Reserve Bank of Kansas City.

Goodhart, Charles A.E. (2001), 'Monetary Transmission Lags and the Formulation of the Policy Decision on Interest Rates', *Federal Reserve Bank of St. Louis Review*, July/August 2001, 165–81.

Heikensten, Lars (1999), 'The Riksbank's Inflation Target – Clarification and Evaluation', *Sveriges Riksbank Quarterly Review*, 1/1999, 5–17.

King, Mervyn A. (1994), 'Monetary Policy in the UK', *Fiscal Studies*, 15, No. 3, 109–28.

Leeper, Eric M. and Tao Zha (1999), 'Identification and Forecasting: Joint Inputs to Policy Analysis', working paper.

Leitemo, Kai (2001), 'Targeting Inflation by Constant-Interest-Rate Forecasts', *Journal of Money, Credit, and Banking*, forthcoming.

McCallum, Bennett T. and Edward Nelson (1999), 'Performance of Operational

Policy Rules in an Estimated Semi-Classical Structural Model', in John B. Taylor (ed.), *Monetary Policy Rules*, Chicago University Press, pp. 1–45.
Meyer, Laurence H. (2001a), 'Comment', *Federal Reserve Bank of St. Louis Review*, July/August 2001, 183–86.
Meyer, Laurence H. (2001b), 'Inflation Targets and Inflation Targeting', Speech at University of California at San Diego Economics Roundtable, San Diego, July 17, 2001.
Nessén, Marianne (2001), 'Targeting Inflation over the Short, Medium and Long Term', *Journal of Macroeconomics*, forthcoming.
Nessén, Marianne and David Vestin (2000), 'Average Inflation Targeting', working paper.
Nobay, Robert P. and David A. Peel (1998), 'Optimal Monetary Policy in a Model of Asymmetric Central Bank Preference', FMG Discussion Paper No. 306.
Oudiz, Gilles and Jeffrey Sachs (1985), 'International Policy Coordination in Dynamic Macroeconomic Models', in William H. Buiter and Richard C. Marston (eds), *International Economic Policy Coordination*, Cambridge: Cambridge University Press.
Persson, Torsten and Guido Tabellini (2000), *Political Economics: Explaining Economic Policy*, Cambridge, Mass.: MIT Press.
Ruge-Murcia, Francisco J. (1999), 'Inflation Targeting under Asymmetric Preferences', working paper.
Svensson, Lars E.O. (1999), 'Inflation Targeting as a Monetary Policy Rule', *Journal of Monetary Economics* 43, 607–54. Working-paper version with unabridged appendix available at www.princeton.edu/~svensson/.
Svensson, Lars E.O. (2001a), 'Independent Review of the Operation of Monetary Policy in New Zealand: Report to the Minister of Finance', www.princeton.edu/~svensson/.
Svensson, Lars E.O. (2001b), 'Price Stability as a Target for Monetary Policy: Defining and Maintaining Price Stability', in Deutsche Bundesbank (ed.), *The Monetary Transmission Process: Recent Developments and Lessons for Europe*, New York: Palgrave, pp. 60–102. (Also available as CEPR Discussion Paper No. 2196.)
Svensson, Lars E.O. (2001c), 'Requiem for Forecast-Based Instrument Rules', working paper.
Svensson, Lars E.O. (2003), 'What is Wrong with Taylor Rules? Using Judgment in Monetary Policy through Targeting Rules', working paper.
Svensson, Lars E.O. and Michael Woodford (2003), 'Implementing Optimal Policy through Inflation-Forecast Targeting', working paper.
Vickers, John (1998), 'Inflation Targeting in Practice: the UK Experience', *Bank of England Quarterly Bulletin*, 38, 368–75.
Wallis, Kenneth F. (1999), 'Asymmetric Density Forecasts of Inflation and the Bank of England's Fan Chart', *National Institute Economic Review*, 167 (January), 106–12.
Woodford, Michael (1999a), 'Commentary: How Should Monetary Policy Be Conducted in an Era of Price Stability?', in Federal Reserve Bank of Kansas City (1999), pp. 277–316.
Woodford, Michael (1999b), 'Optimal Monetary Policy Inertia', working paper.

5. Six practical views of central bank transparency

Adam S. Posen

1. INTRODUCTION

In the span of fifteen years, central bank transparency has gone from being highly controversial to motherhood and apple pie (or knighthood and fish and chips for a British audience). It is now an accepted broad goal to which all central banks pay at least lip service. Both the Bank of England and Charles Goodhart personally have been at the forefront of this trend, in research and in practice. Yet, like many other broad concepts in economic policy, such as 'fiscal discipline' or 'price stability', what central bank transparency actually means remains rather open to debate. As we celebrate the work of Professor Charles A.E. Goodhart, work notable for its clarity and its relevance, it is worthwhile to try to apply a similar standard to this central banking concept *du jour*.

Recent monetary theory has been unsuccessful in providing this clarity. The bulk of today's theoretical models applied to central bank transparency – including in the formal analysis of inflation targeting – have cast the issue as whether or not a representative agent of the public can discern the central bank's 'type', wet or dry, that is soft or hard on inflation, and therefore whether it is more or less 'credible'.[1] This is simply the wrong question to frame, especially in the developed economies: no one really has any doubts about the commitment of any current central banks to low inflation, and any reasons for doubt that arise there would quickly become self-evident.[2] Discerning runaway fiscal positions, overt political pressures upon central bank governors, or economic world views at odds with today's consensus on a vertical long-run Phillips curve is rather easy. Moreover, the all-or-nothing trigger strategy in these models implies that once a central bank type is revealed, all is determined. This unrealistically reduces the conversation between central banks and the private sector to a simple long-lasting thumbs up-or-down.

In practice, central bank transparency has implications for a number of narrower but more relevant day-to-day issues. These include the persistence of inflation, the response of financial markets to central bank announcements, and the treatment of intermediate monetary targets – that is, central bank transparency influences the short-run dynamics of private-sector expectations. The evidence, in fact, is that the effect of greater transparency on these dynamics is beneficial. A number of other interpretations of central bank transparency, grounded in the formal type-and-credibility literature, however, are unsupported by the evidence. In particular, the belief coming out of several recent models that more credible central banks will find excessive transparency unduly constraining, leading to sub-optimal results, is without empirical foundation.[3] The setting of central banks' basic goals, and the public's evaluation of those goals (rather than of the implementation of them), appears to be unaffected by transparency.

The apparent disjunction between central bank transparency and accountability in reality is doubly disturbing. For purposes of even applied research, the failure of these widely-used models' predictions raises further questions[4] about much of the theoretical time-inconsistency framework that has been the work horse of monetary economics in the last twenty years.[5] For purposes of practical policy and of this chapter, the issue is more pressing. Recent developments in Japan and, to a lesser degree, in the United States and the Eurozone have amply demonstrated that central bank independence can expand in harmful ways even as transparency increases. It is time to discard two misleading claims: first, that increased transparency inhibits central bank independence; and second, that transparency provides sufficient accountability for central banks in democratic societies. Instead, we should increase both transparency and formal accountability structures. In particular, we should remove the goal independence of all central banks which retain it, including those of the Bank of Japan, the Federal Reserve, and the European Central Bank.

2. THE GOODHART RIPENESS INDICATOR

Before considering the six practical views of central bank transparency, I want to invoke authority for why this is the topic to tackle at this time. The answer is simple: Goodhart is writing about it these days.[6] In the field of monetary economics, there is no surer sign that a subject is ripe than that Charles is engaged with it. By ripe, I mean like a fruit on the vine at the peak of flavour and nutritional value, that is, full of intellectual interest and policy relevance for central bankers. That is not to say that Charles has not been ahead of his time on some topics, nor that he has not had the final word on some others (leaving little that would be original and reasonable for remaining economists to say) – but that on the big questions of monetary economics, Charles' engagement is the contemporaneous indicator that a matter is reaching maximum salience.

My contention that work by Charles Goodhart has been the indicator of where the juiciest issue in the field of applied monetary economics would be is borne out by my personal experience. First, as an undergraduate at Harvard in the mid-1980s, I caught the empirical work being done on the failure of monetary aggregates as useful intermediate targets for monetary policy, all coming on the heels of the proclamation of Goodhart's Law. Then, in graduate school, I was lucky enough to have my dissertation topic critiquing central bank independence validated by the release of the Roll report, *Independent and Accountable*, and Goodhart's *Journal of Economic Literature* article, 'Game Theory for Central Bankers'.[7] As I took up a job at the Federal Reserve Bank of New York in the mid-1990s, it turned out that inflation targeting was the rising monetary framework to be assessed, and Charles' MPC service and writing under the exemplary Bank of England regime was an important component to be considered in that assessment.[8] In the last few years, he has made several contributions to debates over the role of lender(s) of last resort in financial crises, and the viability of monetary policy in a world of e-money, which have indeed been the hot button issues.[9]

And now, in the CEPR's *How Do Central Banks Talk?* (2001), Goodhart joins several other distinguished economists with senior policy experience in taking up the issue of transparency in monetary policy. In so doing, Charles makes me feel timely in directing some of my own research to the topic, and therefore justified in bringing the results of that work to this Festschrift.[10] But not every ripe fruit offers the same juice, and so my views on central bank transparency differ in some ways from those of Charles and some others in the field. I will leave it to the ongoing harvest of research to determine which particular variant proves sweetest.

3. THE CELLPHONE-LIKE USES OF CENTRAL BANK TRANSPARENCY

Think of the relationship between a central bank and the attentive public as analogous to the relationship between a married couple. Good communication is key if the relationship is to cope well with the bumps and bruises of everyday life. While familiarity removes the need for too much explicitness in communication, changing surroundings and personal needs over time make it dangerous to take too much previous understanding for granted. Presumably, the relationship is for the long term, and day-to-day misunderstandings do not imperil the relationship, but they can make it less pleasant or mutually beneficial.

My wife already has a (subjective) estimate of how considerate a husband I am, that is, my 'type' on a scale of wet to dry. While she may update it if I were to do something extraordinarily bad or good repeatedly, she is unlikely to do so as a result of our quotidian existence. In fact, small variations in the day-to-day signals she gets from me are likely to be ignored, while any big changes will be easily noticed, whatever the day-to-day signals. Communication between us therefore is not about her judging my type or my commitment – instead, it is about the smaller, practical, issues of co-ordination.

This fall, in response to the more worrisome world in which we find ourselves, my wife had me get a cellphone. This cellphone increases the transparency with which I live my life: I can be reached at any time that we are apart, and similarly I can reach her; in an emergency (God forbid), I can make a call; and, most concretely, we can use it to update each other on our schedules, such as who is likely to get home first from work, or whose plane is more delayed. I can be more or less considerate about updating her using the cellphone (probably well within one standard deviation of how considerate I was prior to having this transparency mechanism). Yet, her primary concern is to know where I am for practical reasons, and not to have a means of monitoring of my commitment.

Being a bit more explicit, there are six conceivable channels through which my use of the cellphone could affect her:

- She could be more relaxed in general if updates via cellphone about my comings and goings reduce her worry;
- She could find life a little easier if this device makes it simpler for us to adjust our schedules;
- She could find that after all she really does not care about what I say on the cellphone, just that I am no less prompt or responsive than I was before;
- She could herself become more cognizant of my activities, and use this to demand greater responsiveness, perhaps interfering with my normal habits;
- She could become annoyed if I were to say that I would call at a specified time and am late in doing so; or
- She could be more rather than less worried if she came to count on my calls, and events beyond my control, even innocuous ones, prevented me from calling.

It is ultimately an empirical matter which of these various, occasionally contradictory, but all theoretically plausible, effects will turn out to be of practical import to the day-to-day functioning of our relationship. To repeat, none of this, however, should change her basic estimate of what type of husband I am, and therefore of my level of commitment.

Now, consider the analogous situation of a central bank (even an Old Lady) communicating with her public (including financial markets) as part of an ongoing relationship based on a fundamental assumption of trust and good will. The addition of various recent measures of transparency to monetary policy-making – announced inflation targets, disclosure of votes, timely publication of minutes, explicit forecasts, and so on – in hopes of showing sensitivity to markets and the public's concerns are the equivalent of my acquisition and use of the cellphone in response to my wife's concerns. Being a bit more explicit, there are six conceivable channels through which central banks' enhanced transparency could influence the public's and markets' reaction to monetary policy (see Table 5.1):

- The public could be *reassured* in general if updates via regular releases about policy decisions reduce worry about what is going on in the short term;
- The public and particularly markets could find it a little easier to plan if transparency about the *details* of the economy makes the world more predictable;
- The public could find that, after all, what central banks say is *irrelevant, so* long as the central banks are no less responsive to shocks than before;
- The public, and particularly markets, could become more cognizant of central bank activities, and use this to demand greater responsiveness *contingent* on specific targets, perhaps interfering with central banks' normal habits;
- The public could become *annoyed,* adding political pressures, if central banks were to announce a specific target or forecast, and fail to meet it; or
- The public could be more rather than less worried in general, if it demanded adherence to announced targets, *diverting* central banks from responding optimally to shocks.

As Table 5.1 summarizes, each of these six practical views of central bank transparency (reassuring, details, irrelevance, contingent, annoyance, and diverting) focuses on a specific set of information releases, with a specific hypothesis for the impact of those releases upon expectations and central bank behaviour, and for the mechanism by which this impact is transmitted. None of these hypotheses can be ruled out *a priori* on theoretical grounds, and these multiple options show the diversity of implications possible from (and proposed in) the current literature on central bank transparency. All are subject to empirical examination, however, and the rest of this chapter summarizes the relevant variables to observe and evidence to date on each account. Examination of central bank transparency is largely a matter of examining the effects of inflation targeting, since that is where today's practical debate over what central banks should disclose comes to the fore, and where most of the empirical work has been done.

Table 5.1 Practical views of central bank transparency

View of Transparency	Information Released	Hypothesized Impact	Cause of Impact	Testable Impact	Result
Reassuring	Regime, speeches	Greater flexibility	Greater trust	Inflation persistence	Supported by evidence
Details	Forecasts, models	Greater predictability	Greater disclosure	Market response	Supported by evidence
Irrelevance	Whatever	None	Only actions matter	Inflation level	Exact opposite – lower inflation
Contingent	Mandate, votes	Stronger reputation	Greater credibility	Inflation volatility	Unsupported by evidence
Annoyance	Minutes, targets	Greater confusion	Increased politicization	Effect of target misses	Unsupported by evidence
Diverting	Targets, goals	Less discretion	Increased oversight	Output volatility	Unsupported by evidence

4. THE REASSURING VIEW OF CENTRAL BANK TRANSPARENCY

The first view of central bank transparency to consider is what I will term 'the reassuring view', which is the view that the central bank engenders greater good will in the public sphere and the markets simply by the fact of communicating its general intentions. The key information released by the central bank in operational terms are statements about the nature of the monetary regime (Is there an inflation target? Does that target require a strict rule?), and about the goals of the regime (What is the inflation target? What factors recently caused the bank to allow a temporary overshooting of the target?). These are conveyed in the release of general information about the central bank and of speeches by senior officials, usually voting board members, about the purposes of the central bank. The actual specific content of the speeches are less important than that the effort to communicate is made and that it conveys the basic intent of the regime.

The theoretical framework or underlying model for such a view of central bank transparency is the 'optimal state contingent rule' (OSCR), as described by King (1997). In this framework, communication by the central bank about its long-term inflation goal allows the bank to be more flexible in response to (supply) shocks in the short run. The greater flexibility is the result of greater trust in the central bank that deviations from the target do not indicate a lack of commitment to the long-term target – the central bank which responds to shocks is not punished with the stabilization bias (see Svensson, 1997). As extended in Kuttner and Posen (1999), the testable hypothesis of the OSCR or reassuring view of central bank transparency is that inflation persistence will decrease as the central bank approaches the OSCR (builds greater trust). This is because one-time shocks will not have pass-through effects on inflation expectations since the belief is strong that long-run inflation will return to target level.

Empirical evidence is quite strong in support of this view. Kuttner and Posen (1999) looks at the shift in bond market responses (proxying for inflation expectations) in Canada, New Zealand, and the United Kingdom before and after adopting inflation targeting for whether there is no change in inflation dynamics, a greater proclivity to an increase in interest rates following shocks (consistent with there being an increase in counter-inflationary conservatism), or a greater proclivity to a decrease in interest rates (consistent with there being less persistence of inflation), and finds strong evidence that adoption of inflation targeting increases flexibility.[11] Kuttner and Posen (2001) and Vinhas de Souza (2001) examine the same hypothesis in a quasi-panel format, constructing datasets of monetary frameworks – observations on countries' central bank independence, announced domestic targets, and exchange rate arrangements – for a broad range of countries; both find statistically (and economically) significant effects of inflation targeting to reduce inflation persistence, but no such effects from any other element of the monetary framework. Nothing reassures like transparency about goals apparently.

This seemingly 'touchy-feely' matter of trust in the central bank's long-term intent turns out to be a matter of high stakes. As Walsh (1998, Chapter 10) summarizes the literature, most of the welfare costs of disinflation and of monetary policy response to shocks arise as a result of inflation persistence. Thus, if transparency in the form of inflation targeting does reduce inflation persistence, it has a major impact on welfare. It is important to recognize that the definition of inflation targeting made operational in Kuttner and Posen (1999, 2001), consistent with Bernanke et al. (1999), is a central bank which publicly announces a quantitative target for the inflation rate, no more and no less. Therefore one policy implication of this view is that general talk about long-term goals in a world of shocks confers benefits that 'implicit inflation targeting', as many characterize the US Federal Reserve approach, does not. Another implication is that there is no reason to unduly fear missing intermediate targets, such as those for monetary growth or inflation, in the short run when shocks arise, because trusting expectations will revert back to a reasonable central bank's long-term goal.[12]

5. THE DETAILS-ORIENTED VIEW OF CENTRAL BANK TRANSPARENCY

What I will term the 'details-oriented view' of central bank transparency is much narrower than that of the reassuring view, and much more focused on the response of financial markets to central bank behaviour. The information released by central banks important to this view is that of forecasts, economic models, and the accompanying explanations of specific central bank decisions (for example instrument interest rate movements). As discussed in Blinder (1998) and Blinder et al. (2001), the Federal Reserve has taken steps in this direction, for example, by cleaning up inter-meeting directives, spelling out the Federal Funds Rate target, and so on. The hypothesized impact is that greater disclosure will allow the (bond) markets to see (or enforce) greater predictability in central bank actions. This goes to the general idea that communication removes noise from financial markets. Some European central bankers in the 1970s and 1980s demonstrated their belief in this principle by looking to surprise markets with their exchange rate and other interventions so as to intentionally cause greater uncertainty in markets.

The testable hypothesis of this view is that shifts in disclosure policy about policy board meeting-to-meeting decisions affect the market response to announcements. For this, recent work (for example Kuttner, 2001; Poole, Rasche and Thornton, 2001) has shown that the evidence is clear in the US Treasuries market that the changes in Federal Reserve disclosure policies of the last 15 years (particularly since 1994) have reduced market volatility and increased predictablity. There is less clear evidence regarding foreign exchange markets and very short-term movements in financial (including bond) markets (Bomfim and Reinhart, 1999), with some indications that openly contentious discussion among central bank board members (as on the Bank of England Monetary Policy Committee at times) can make for strange intra-day announcement effects (Clare and

Courtenay, 2001). Note that this effect is independent of and acts through different channels (and over a shorter time-frame) than the effect examined under the reassurance view: the independent variable of disclosure associated with instrument interest rate movements in the details view versus the explanation of long-term targets in the reassurance view; the dependent variable of market volatility and predictability versus inflation persistence. This has the policy implication that these transparency enhancements can have their effect (and presumable benefits) without any change in fundamental regime, to or from inflation targeting. This also stresses why it is necessary to break down the examination of central bank transparency into separate practical views.

6. THE IRRELEVANCE VIEW OF CENTRAL BANK TRANSPARENCY

This listing of practical views of central bank transparency must include the commonly expressed view of some (particularly US-based) practitioners, that central bank transparency is a lot of fuss over nothing. This 'irrelevance view' asserts that talk is very cheap, and that credibility of a central bank is built up only through actions.[13] Expectations, both in the markets and in general, are largely adaptive if not skeptical. It is possible to link this view to the theoretical literature, following Cukierman and Meltzer (1986), about the establishment of reputation (see, for example Garfinkle and Oh, 1995). Transparency here is at most the absence of interference with the markets seeing what the central bank actually does – given the usual assumption, however, that the only private information the central bank has is about its own preferences, the focus of markets and the public is on inflation and output outcomes which potentially reveal that information. Claims by a central banker to have a specific goal could just be attempts by a wet to mimic a dry, and will be discounted.

The empirical implication of this irrelevance view is that changes in policy announcements alone should be ineffective in changing inflation expectations. If anything, those central banks who cannot do are the ones that talk, so the average inflation level should either be unchanged or increase (if after a shock a dovish central bank tries to cover its preferences). Explicit inflation targeting should be indistinguishable from implicit inflation targeting in its effects, so long as both are in pursuit of the same goal for inflation, holding real economy structures constant. This view, however, is resoundingly rejected by the data. The classification of monetary frameworks in Kuttner and Posen (2001) directly separates implicit from explicit inflation targeters and finds that explicit inflation targeters have lower inflation (as well as lower inflation persistence) than implicit targeters.[14]

Consider as well the experience of the ECB adopting the Bundesbank's mantle: a tighter pursuit of low inflation, and lower short-term inflation results, on the part of the ECB have not resulted in lower long-term inflation expectations nor reduced volatility or inflation persistence versus its predecessor. Given the institutional mimicry of the Bundesbank by the ECB, and the lack of structural change in Europe over the period, this would seem to be attributable to the reduced transparency of the ECB versus the Bundesbank due to its multinational consensus committee practices and its use of a 'monetary masquerade' in far more confusing fashion than the Bundesbank ever did.[15] It does not make sense to attribute these results to the ECB's newness (as some ECB board members seem to do), under this irrelevance interpretation, because the inflation has been kept low enough under the ECB to clearly demonstrate its (conservative) type under these models. In short, explicit inflation targeting does seem to matter, whereas the irrelevancy view would suggest that it would not. This has an important policy implication for some of the major central banks around the world which claim that there is no need for the public announcement of an internal inflation target (arguments by some that explicit inflation targeting also does harm is tackled in the next three views).

7. THE CONTINGENT VIEW OF CENTRAL BANK TRANSPARENCY

The view of central bank transparency based on the most sophisticated theoretical framework, and attracting the most research attention at present, is what I will term the contingent view. Exemplified by Cukierman (2002) and Faust and Svensson's (2001, 2002) recent work, this class of models builds directly on the earlier work about discerning central bank types: the optimal degree of transparency for a central bank depends upon the degree of counter-inflationary conservatism of a central bank. Since more credibly conservative central banks are thought to induce more flexibility in price- and wage-setting (and a more vertical short-run Phillips curve), their policy instruments are thought to have less traction over the real economy. Accordingly, there is a U-shaped curve for the amount of desirable transparency, with most and least credible central banks disclosing less than central banks of intermediate credibility, reflecting the trade-off between showing one's type and exerting monetary control.[16]

Thus, the key information released by central banks in this view is about their mandates and about the votes of policy board members, as these (combined with easily discerned inflation outcomes) will give the greatest information to the public and markets about central bank preferences. The practical impact is assumed to be that increasing counter-inflationary credibility produces a stronger reputation, but only over some intermediate range will this be associated with greater disclosure (since of course these are optimizing models, the most credible central banks will realize that they should not disclose as much as their less credible comrades do). The empirically testable impact is that there should be a trade-off of inflation volatility for output volatility.[17] This is closely related to some earlier arguments made about central bank independence, which also derived from the underlying Kydland–Prescott/Barro–Gordon framework.[18]

For all of the theoretical might behind it, the empirical evidence in favour of this view of central bank transparency is very limited. Chortareas et al. (2001) is the only study to date to offer some results directly in support of the argument that disclosures about votes, mandates, and forecasts reduce inflation volatility at the expense of a rise in output volatility, but the measures of transparency they use and their methodology has severe limitations (see the discussion in Posen, 2002). The broader mechanism assumed to be driving these models – that increases in counter-inflationary credibility steepen the Phillips curve and/or are accompanied by less attention to output stabilization – has been, however, rather decisively rejected by the available cross-sectional evidence on the relationship between central bank regimes and either sacrifice ratios or stabilization of real outcomes.[19] Of course, more complex theoretical models, with unobservable variables (credibility) and U-shaped relationships, are difficult to operationalize for empirical work. It may well be that new evidence will be discovered in support of the contingent view.[20]

The practical danger that arises from premature acceptance of this contingent view of transparency without adequate empirical support is threefold: first, it may encourage some 'fine-tuning' of transparency for the optimal level of disclosure and thus lose the benefits seen in the reassuring and details views; second, and relatedly, it may put an undue emphasis on mandates and votes to the detriment of other important information disclosures available to central banks; and third, it may contribute to a climate opposed to output stabilization by monetary policymakers without much basis for so doing. Given that there are strong empirical cases to be made for the effects of long-run goal disclosures on inflation persistence, of short-term policy decision disclosures on bond market volatility, and of countercyclical monetary policy on the real economy (even when undertaken by highly credible central banks like the Federal Reserve or the Bundesbank), we should await equally strong empirical confirmation of the contingent view, whatever its attractions as an object of formal research.

8. THE ANNOYANCE VIEW OF CENTRAL BANK TRANSPARENCY

The next issue is how transparency might do harm, rather than being a good strategy when appropriate (as in the contingency view) or a normal good where more is better (as in the reassurance or details views). The weaker version of how central bank transparency might cause harm to policy-making and economic outcomes is what I will term 'the annoyance view'. In this view, if the central bank discloses too much information about how policy gets set in the short term – releasing minutes and votes that induce perceptions of personalization of policy; announcing explicit intermediate targets only to miss them – there will be confusion in the public. This confusion will give an opening for opportunistic politicians to criticize or scapegoat the central bank (even well-intentioned but misinformed politicians might call a central bank to task for missing its rightfully ignored but institutionalized monetary growth targets). So disclosure leads to confusion which leads to politicization, which in turn annoys optimizing central bankers into overreacting to short-term pressures and targets. Though this empirical prediction is of course very different from that of the irrelevance view of transparency, it is similar in its world-weary, let the central bankers do their job, practitioners' spirit of thinking about disclosure.

Anecdotal support for this view seems to be easy to come by, at least as far as avoiding annoyance seems to have played a role in central bank decision-making. The Federal Reserve under Paul Volcker in the first half of the 1980s used announced monetary targets as a 'heat shield' to divert Congressional and public attention from its real aim of disinflation (Blinder, 1998); the Bank of Japan has opposed calls for an inflation targeting regime to counter deflation in recent years in part due to fear that they would miss an announced target, bringing in political pressure (Posen, 2000b); concern about personalization (or national identification) of policy leading to popular disapproval of tough choices has made the European Central Bank reluctant to release voting or detailed minutes of its discussions (Gersbach and Hahn, 2001a, 2001b).

More rigorous empirical examination of this view, however, remains to be done. One way of tackling it would be to consider the effect of intermediate or short-term target misses on inflation expectations or on measurable political pressures (perhaps proxied by newspaper reports of criticism of the central bank by legislators) in a time-series or event study context. Laubach and Posen (1998) go a certain length in this direction with the Bundesbank and Swiss National Bank experience, noting that the greater than 50 per cent of the time misses of the respective central banks' monetary targets seemed to enhance credibility, when accompanied by explanations, but it is unclear how much relevance these cases have for other countries. Anecdotally, it would appear that the Federal Reserve only gained in credibility and stature when it officially announced its abandonment of monetary targets it had long since stopped following, but separating that from the accumulating stature of the Greenspan Federal Reserve over the 1990s would also be difficult. On the broader cross-sectional evidence on inflation targeting, however, to the degree that inflation targets represent disclosure and short-term commitments occasionally foregone, the evidence is that increasing transparency is associated with lower average inflation rates – which is the opposite what would be expected if the annoyance view that disclosure gives openings for political pressure were to hold.

9. THE DIVERTING VIEW OF CENTRAL BANK TRANSPARENCY

The stronger and, I would argue, more serious view of how central bank transparency might cause harm to policy-making and economic outcomes is the one that announced targets and other disclosures force the central bank into more rule-like behaviour. I term this 'the diverting view' because the inflexibility of uni-dimensional (inflation) targets diverts the central bank's attention from responding appropriately to shocks. This is the exact mirror image of the reassurance view discussed first – the key information for the central bank to release is again about its medium-term targets and goals, but by releasing that information the central bank occasions increased oversight (rather than increased public trust), resulting in less discretion (rather than more flexibility) in responding to economic events. The theoretical case for the sub-optimality of strict rule-based inflation targeting (with zero weight on output goals) is relatively straightforward to make, and can be seen in King's (1997) discussion of the 'inflation nutter' or Ball (1999) and Svensson's (1999) treatments of 'inflation-only targeting'; Friedman and Kuttner (1996) make an extended empirical analogy between 'a price target for US monetary policy' and an assessment of the damage that could potentially be done by an overly rigid adherence to a fixed nominal anchor in the face of supply shocks.

The theoretical prospect that central banks might be unduly constrained by explicit inflation targets or other forms of disclosure, however, does not mean that they inherently must be or that they in fact are so constrained. Ball (1999), King (1997), and Svensson (1999) issue their warnings against inflation-only targeting from the point of view of inflation targeting advocates who are seeking to avoid an unnecessary diversion of a potentially welfare-enhancing regime. In terms of operational design, Bernanke et al. (1999) and Svensson's (2001) analyses of the Reserve Bank of New Zealand's inflation-targeting framework make a parallel case that specific structures of the inflation-targeting regime – beyond the public announcement of a quantitative inflation target – can influence the degree to which that regime looks like a rules-based system.

The empirical assessment of the diverting view comes down to the mirror image of the assessment of the reassuring view of transparency: do central banks who adopt inflation targets behave in a more conservative counter-inflationary fashion, putting more relative weight on inflation over output goals, thereby inducing greater output volatility? As indicated in the discussion of the reassuring view, the evidence appears to go solidly in the opposite direction. Kuttner and Posen (1999, 2000, 2001) undertake a variety of exercises – time-series evidence on before and after target adoption behaviour of central banks in response to economic shocks; checking for structural breaks in the estimated Taylor (1993) rules for disclosure changing central banks' relative coefficients on inflation and output;[21] and panel data across monetary frameworks on the effects of inflation targeting controlling for other monetary and exchange rate commitments – and find that inflation targeting central banks increase their flexibility in responding to shocks, and show no decline in their relative weight on output volatility. The key issue for policy is to invest in a communications framework that allows central bankers to respond gradually to the inflationary effects of supply shocks, as Posen (2000a) outlines and advocates based on the experience of the Bundesbank. Cellphones are best used for sufficient conversations rather than instant messaging if the goal of communication is avoiding misunderstandings; so, too, with central bank transparency, replacing the yes-no of whether targets are hit or not with ongoing conversations with the public and markets about the nature of shocks.

10. INDEPENDENT AND TRANSPARENT: THE NEXT QUESTION

To summarize, there are present in the literature and policy discussions six coherent views of central bank transparency that I have identified, but only two of them – the reassurance and the details-oriented views – have clear empirical support. Central bank announcements of medium-term inflation (or arguably other domestic nominal) targets increase flexibility in response to shocks and decrease inflation persistence, with presumably important welfare benefits; central bank disclosure of information regarding specific interest rate moves does reduce volatility in bond markets (except at the very short time-horizon). There are open empirical issues about whether the most credible central banks can be too open, meaning that the uses of transparency are contingent upon reputation (but the associated evidence on the effects of central bank credibility on the real economy seems to indicate this should not be taken too seriously), and about whether missed short-term targets lead to political pressures (some central bankers believe strongly they do; experience of various central banks seems to indicate they do not). There is no empirical support, however, for the strong version of the view that increased central bank transparency causes harm by diverting monetary policy from real stabilization into rule-like inflation nutter behaviour.

So in practice central bank transparency seems to be a good thing, with the current form of inflation targeting (as exemplified by the Bank of England) offering important benefits, and for the most part more transparency being better. But transparency should not be seen as good for whatever ails central banks. In particular, one word which has not appeared in this discussion is 'accountability', because transparency does not seem to have much effect on it. On the surface this seems implausible – Bernanke et al. (1999), Blinder et al. (2001), and even ahead of fashion the Charles Goodhart co-authored Roll et al. (1993) assert that greater transparency, among other things, will make it more difficult for central banks to behave incompetently or to diverge from public desires in an extended fashion.

These authors, however, failed to consider the interaction between central bank independence and transparency, or rather the lack of interaction.[22] The worldwide trend towards central bank independence has shown no signs of abating over recent years, and seems itself to be independent of whether or not countries adopt inflation targeting or other monetary transparency measures (Berger et al., 2001; Kuttner and Posen, 2001). Independent central banks have gained in stature around the globe as they have delivered low inflation, been perceived as necessary (in the EU and the accession countries, the Maastricht Treaty makes that necessity a fact, as do some instances of INF conditionality), and benefitted from erosion of support for elected officials. Few legislative powers have been enacted to keep up with this trend, and transparency alone has not acted as a check for exercise of central bank discretion beyond what accountability would ideally bear.

Recent developments in Japan and, to a (much) lesser degree, in the United States and the Eurozone have amply demonstrated that central bank independence can expand in harmful ways even as transparency increases. The Bank of Japan has become markedly more transparent since gaining independence in April 1998, publishing board votes and minutes and, more recently, an official forecast, as well as taking on a great campaign of speechifying by top officials. Yet, the Bank of Japan has pursued a disastrous deflationary policy, pointedly rejected entreaties by elected officials, and explicitly taken on policy issues (inducing bank and economic restructuring) not covered in its legal mandate. In fact, the transparency has shown the Bank ignoring the contradiction between its mandate to maintain price stability and its published forecast of ongoing deflation. The US Federal Reserve has taken advantage of the personalization of monetary policy in the form of widespread Greenspan admiration to chart its own course on what is an acceptable level of inflation and output (and some would say of the stock market) without much regard for Congress. The European Central Bank has from the start had excessive insulation from political oversight due to the structure of the Maastricht Treaty and the weakness of the European Parliament, but the democratic deficit of European monetary policy has been compounded by the ECB's switching back and forth between its two pillars of policy as explanations for behaviour and maintaining a 'less than 2 per cent' (rather than symmetrical) inflation target in the face of clear criticism of this visible behaviour.

This independence of central bank independence creates an apparent disjunction between central bank transparency and accountability in reality, which is disturbing. It is time to discard two misleading claims: first, that increased transparency inhibits central bank independence; and second, that transparency provides sufficient accountability for central banks in democratic societies. Instead, we should increase both transparency and formal accountability structures. Though it is not justified by the analysis in this chapter, I would ask consideration of the suggestion that we should remove the goal independence of all central banks which retain it, including that of the Bank of Japan, the Federal Reserve, and the European Central Bank. When Charles Goodhart advocated an 'independent and accountable Bank of England', he was right, and through the actions of him and the other founding members of the Bank's Monetary Policy Committee, the Bank has demonstrated the ample benefits of what transparent monetary policy and instrument independence can achieve under an inflation target set by elected officials – certainly, none of the valid practical views of the benefits of central bank transparency would be overturned by the removal of goal independence from those central banks which still have it.

NOTES

1. The seminal article starting this approach is Cukierman and Meltzer (1986).
2. Despite the constant invocation of the word 'credibility,' it remains unclear that this concept does any meaningful work, except as a circular validation of successful central banks' success. See Posen (1998).

3. See Faust and Svensson (2002) and Geraats (2001) among others.
4. Broader problems with this framework, such as the observation that removal of the inflation premium proved rather easy once central banks chose to remove it, have been noted previously by Blinder (1998), Friedman and Kuttner (1996), McCallum (1997) and others.
5. The critical papers being Kydland and Prescott (1977), Calvo (1978), and Barro and Gordon (1983), with the aforementioned Cukierman and Meltzer (1986) setting up a new sub-field in this area. In the spirit of transparency, I should acknowledge my own reliance on such models in, for example, Kuttner and Posen (1999), despite earlier published misgivings.
6. Blinder et al. (2001).
7. Roll et al. (1993); Goodhart (1994). Thanks to Charles' usual generosity to graduate students, the validation was more directly personal than that. While a visitor at Harvard in fall of 1993, Charles read, on referral from my advisor Benjamin Friedman, the job-market paper draft that became Posen (1993), my first published article. I was in the process of moving to Washington, and he tracked me down, via my mother's home, to ask me to come talk to him about my paper. This was one of the most encouraging things that could be done for an insecure graduate student.
8. See Bernanke et al. (1999), chapter 7.
9. See Goodhart (1999, 2000), both in *International Finance* – which journal would not have been founded had it not been for Charles' referral of Blackwell Publishers to Benn Steil and myself, but that's another (non-monetary) story.
10. Kuttner and Posen (1999, 2000, 2001), Laubach and Posen (1998), and Posen (1999, 2000a).
11. A recent revision and extension of this chapter extends the data to 2001, and adds in two non-inflation targeters (France and Germany) as control countries, and the evidence proves robust to these extensions of the sample, with only inflation target adoption – an increase in transparency – increasing flexibility. New results are available from the authors upon request.
12. These two implications are the ones that arise out of the narrative interpretation of post-Bretton Woods monetary targeting in Germany and Switzerland given in Laubach and Posen (1998) and Posen (2000a).
13. Even though this was a commonly heard view at monetary economic conferences in the second half of the 1990s, it is difficult to find an example of a central banker expressing this view on the written record, presumably for the obvious political reason that disparaging transparency could be seen as abuse of power. For an academic view in support of the deeds-not-words take on central bank transparency, see the paper by Benjamin Friedman in this volume.
14. Several papers presented at the 2001 Federal Reserve Bank of St. Louis Monetary Conference also provided evidence indicating positive effects of inflation targeting on economic outcomes.
15. See Posen (1999) for a discussion of the monetary masquerade. Kuttner and Posen (2000) makes a similar argument having to do with the link between transparency and exchange rate volatility.
16. Other papers developing this point include Gersbach and Hahn (2001a, 2001b), Jensen (2001), and with a slightly different approach Geraats (2001).
17. See Ball (1999) and Svensson (1999) for theoretical discussions of this tradeoff in the context of inflation targeting.
18. See Rogoff (1985) for the first statement, and Alesina and Summers (1992), Posen (1995), and Eijffinger and de Haan (1996) for critical empirical examinations of this point.
19. See Debelle and Fischer (1995), Blinder (1998), Posen (1998), Kuttner and Posen (1999), and Blinder et al. (2001), as well as the studies cited in the preceding footnote. Hutchison and Walsh (1996) offers some time-series evidence that over a long-span of time there is some decline in the New Zealand sacrifice ratio, but disentangling this from broader reforms in that economy is difficult.

20. Unreleased work by Chortareas, Stasavage, and Sterne usefully examines the relationship between their measures of central bank transparency and sacrifice ratios, but the unpublished results must be treated as preliminary.
21. It should be noted that Lars Svensson has raised questions about whether such relative reduced form coefficients in Taylor rules actually represent central bank preferences.
22. Which admittedly included myself circa 1997–98 in Bernanke et al. (1999).

REFERENCES

Alesina, A. and L.H. Summers (1993), 'Central Bank Independence and Macroeconomic Performance: Some Comparative Evidence', *Journal of Money, Credit, and Banking*, 25(2), 151–62.

Ball, L. (1999), 'Efficient Rules for Monetary Policy', *International Finance*, 2(1), 63–83.

Barro, R.J. and D.B. Gordon (1983), 'Rules, Discretion and Reputation in a Model of Monetary Policy', *Journal of Monetary Economics*, 12(1), 101–21.

Berger, H., J. de Haan and S. Eijffinger (2001), 'Central Bank Independence: an Update of Theory and Evidence', *Journal of Economic Surveys*, 15(1), 3–40.

Bernanke, B.S., T. Laubach, F.S. Mishkin and A.S. Posen (1999), *Inflation Targeting: Lessons from the International Experience*, Princeton, NJ: Princeton University Press.

Blinder, A.S. (1998), *Central Banking in Theory and Monetary Policy Regimes*, Cambridge, Mass.: MIT Press.

Blinder, A., C. Goodhart, P. Hildebrand, D. Lipton and C. Wyplosz (2001), *How Do Central Banks Talk? Geneva Reports on the World Economy 3*, CEPR.

Bomfim, A.N. and V.R. Reinhart (2000), 'Making News: Financial Market Effects of Federal Reserve Disclosure Practices', Federal Reserve Board Finance & Economics Discussion Series, no. 2000–14.

Calvo, G. (1978), 'On the Time Consistency of Optimal Policy in the Monetary Economy', *Econometrica*, 46(6), 1411–28.

Chortareas, G., D. Stasavage and G. Sterne (2001), 'Does it Pay to be Transparent? International Evidence from Central Banks', paper presented at the 26th Annual Economic Policy Conference of the Federal Reserve Bank of St. Louis, October.

Clare, A. and R. Courtenay (2001), 'Assessing the Impact of Macroeconomic News Announcements on Securities Prices Under Different Monetary Policy Regimes', Bank of England Working Paper, no. 125.

Cukierman, A. (2002), 'Are Contemporary Central Banks Transparent about Economic Models and Objectives and What Difference Does it Make?', *Federal Reserve Bank of St. Louis Review*, July, 15–36.

Cukierman, A. and A. Meltzer (1986), 'A Theory of Ambiguity, Credibility, and Inflation Under Discretion and Asymmetric Information', *Econometrica*, 54, 1099–128.

Debelle, G. and S. Fischer (1994), 'How Independent Should a Central Bank Be?', in J.C. Fuhrer (ed.), *Goals, Guidelines, and Constraints Facing Monetary Policymakers*, Federal Reserve Bank of Boston Conference Series 38, pp. 195–221.

Eijffinger, S. and J. de Haan (1996), 'The Political Economy of Central Bank Independence', *Princeton Special Papers in International Economics*, No. 19.

Faust, J. and L.E.O. Svensson (2001), 'Transparency and Credibility: Monetary Policy with Unobservable Goals', *International Economic Review*, 42, 369–97.

Faust, J. and L.E.O. Svensson (2002), 'The Equilibrium Degree of Transparency and Control in Monetary Policy', *Journal of Money, Credit and Banking*, 34, 520–39.

Friedman, B. and K. Kuttner (1996), 'A Price Target for U.S. Monetary Policy? Lessons from the Experience with Money Growth Targets', *Brookings Papers on Economic Activity*, 1, 77–146.

Garfinkle, M.R. and S. Oh (1995), 'When and How Much to Talk: Credibility and Flexibility in Monetary Policy with Private Information', *Journal of Monetary Economics*, 35(2), 341–57.

Geraats, P. (2001), 'Why Adopt Transparency? "The Publication of Central Bank Forecasts"', ECB Working Paper No. 41.

Gersbach, H. and V. Hahn (2001a), 'Should the Individual Voting Records of Central Bankers be Published?', Deutsche Bundesbank, Economic Research Centre, Discussion Paper 02/01, January.

Gersbach, H. and V. Hahn (2001b), 'Voting Transparency and Conflicting Interests in Central Bank Councils', Deutsche Bundesbank, Economic Research Centre, Discussion Paper 03/01, January.

Goodhart, C.A.E. (1994), 'Game Theory for Central Bankers: A Report to the Governor of the Bank of England', *Journal of Economic Literature*, 32(1), 101–14.

Goodhart, C.A.E. (1999), 'Myths about the Lender of Last Resort', *International Finance*, 2(3), 339–60.

Goodhart, C.A.E. (2000), 'Can Central Banking Survive the IT Revolution?', *International Finance*, 3(2), 189–209.

Hutchison, M.M. and C.E. Walsh (1996), 'Central Bank Institutional Design and the Output Cost of Disinflation: Did the 1989 New Zealand Reserve Bank Act Affect the Inflation–Output Tradeoff?', Reserve Bank of New Zealand Research Paper G96/6.

Jensen, H. (2001), 'Optimal Degrees of Transparency in Monetary Policymaking', CEPR Discussion Paper No. 2689.

King, M. (1997), 'Changes in UK Monetary Policy: Rules and Discretion in Practice', *Journal of Monetary Economics*, 39(1), 81–97.

Kuttner, K.N. (2001), 'Monetary Policy Surprises and Interest Rates: Evidence from the Fed Funds Futures Market', *Journal of Monetary Economics*, 47(3), 523–44.

Kuttner, K.N. and A.S. Posen (1999), 'Does Talk Matter after all? Inflation Targeting and Central Bank Behavior', Institute for International Economics Working Paper No. 99–10.

Kuttner, K.N. and A.S. Posen (2000), 'Inflation, Monetary Transparency, and G-3 Exchange Rate Volatility', in E. Hochreiter (ed.), *Adapting to Financial Globalization*, London: Routledge.

Kuttner, K.N. and A.S. Posen (2001), 'Beyond Bipolar: A Three-Dimensional Assessment of Monetary Frameworks', *International Journal of Finance and Economics*.

Kydland, F.E. and E.C. Prescott (1977), 'Rules Rather Than Discretion: The Inconsistency of Optimal Plans', *Journal of Political Economy*, 85, 473–90.

Laubach, T. and A.S. Posen (1998), 'Disciplined Discretion: Monetary Targeting in Germany and Switzerland', *Princeton Essays in International Finance*, No. 206, December.

Mahadeva, L. and G. Sterne (eds) (2000), *Monetary Policy Frameworks in a Global Context*, Routledge: London.

McCallum, B. (1997), 'Crucial Issues Concerning Central Bank Independence', *Journal of Monetary Economics*, 39, 99–112.

Poole, W., R.H. Rasche and D.L. Thornton (2001), 'Market Anticipations of Monetary Policy Actions', paper presented at the 26th Annual Economic Policy Conference of the Federal Reserve Bank of St. Louis, October.

Posen, A.S. (1993), 'Why Central Bank Independence Does Not Cause Low Inflation: There is No Institutional Fix to Politics', in *Finance and the International Economy*, 7, The Amex Bank Review Price Essays, pp. 40–65.

Posen, A.S. (1995), 'Declarations are not Enough: Financial Sector Sources of Central Bank Independence', in B. Bernanke and J. Rotemberg (eds), *NBER Macroeconomics Annual 1995*, Cambridge, Mass.: MIT Press.

Posen, A.S. (1998), 'Central Bank Independence and Disinflationary Credibility: A Missing Link?', *Oxford Economic Papers*, 50, July, 335–59.

Posen, A.S. (1999), 'No Monetary Masquerades for the ECB', in E. Meade (ed.), *The European Central Bank: How Accountable? How Decentralized?*, American Institute for Contemporary German Studies.

Posen, A.S. (2000a), 'Lessons from the Bundesbank on the Occasion of its Early Retirement', in L. Mahadeva and G. Sterne (eds), *Monetary Policy Frameworks in a Global Context*, London: Routledge.

Posen, A.S. (2000b), 'The Political Economy of Deflationary Monetary Policy', in Ryoichi Mikitani and Adam Posen (eds), *Japan's Financial Crisis and Its Parallels to U.S. Experience*, Washington, DC: Institute for International Economics, pp. 149–66.

Posen, A.S. (2002), 'Commentary on "Does it Pay to be Transparent?"', *Federal Reserve Bank of St. Louis Review*, July/August, 84(4), 119–26.

Rogoff, K. (1985), 'The Optimal Degree of Commitment to an Intermediate Target', *Quarterly Journal of Economics*, 100(4), 1169–89.

Roll, E. et al. (1993), *Independent and Accountable: A New Mandate for the Bank of England*, London: Centre for Economic Policy Research.

Svensson, L.E.O. (1997), 'Inflation Forecast Targeting: Implementing and Monitoring Inflation Targets', *European Economic Review*, 41, 1111–46.

Svensson, L.E.O. (1999), 'Inflation Targeting as a Monetary Policy Rule', *Journal of Monetary Economics*, 43(3), 607–54.

Svensson, L.E.O. (2001), *Independent Review of the Operation of Monetary Policy in New Zealand: report to the Minister of Finance*, http://www.iies.su.se/leosven/.

Taylor, J. (1993), 'Discretion Versus Policy Rules in Practice', *Carnegie-Rochester Conference Series on Public Policy*, 39, 195–214.

Vinhas de Souza, L. (2002), 'Integrated Monetary and Exchange Rate Frameworks: Are There Empirical Differences?', Working Papers of Eesti Pank, No. 2.

Walsh, C.E. (1998), *Monetary Theory and Policy*, Cambridge, Mass.: MIT Press.

6. The phases of US monetary policy: 1987–2001

Marvin Goodfriend[1]

1. INTRODUCTION

Inflation was relatively well-behaved in the 1990s in comparison with preceding decades, yet Federal Reserve monetary policy was no less challenging. The Fed took painful actions in the late 1970s and early 1980s to reverse rising inflation and bring it down, and inflation fell from over 10 per cent to around 4 per cent by the mid-1980s. The worst economic ills stemming from high and unstable inflation were put behind us. Yet central bankers and monetary economists recognized that more disinflation was needed to achieve price stability. Completing the transition to price stability was expected to be comparatively straightforward. Monetary policy promised to become more routine. Although the 1990s saw the longest cyclical expansion in US history, the promised tranquility did not materialize. In many ways the period to be chronicled here proved to be about as difficult for monetary policy as the preceding inflationary period.

My account of Fed monetary policy divides the period since 1987 into six distinct phases. This division is a natural one because in each phase the Fed was confronted with a different policy problem. Phase 1 begins with rising inflation in the aftermath of the October 1987 stock market crash and ends with the start of the Gulf War in August 1990. Phase 2 covers the 1990–91 recession, the slow recovery, and the disinflation to the end of 1993. Phase 3 tells the story of the Fed's preemptive tightening against inflation in 1994–95. Phase 4 deals with the long boom to 1999, the near full credibility for low inflation, and the rising productivity growth that made it possible. Phase 5 addresses the tightening of monetary policy to slow the growth of aggregate demand in 1999 and 2000. The 6th phase chronicles the collapse of investment in late 2000 and the recession in 2001.

This chapter presents a relatively compact account of the interaction between interest rate policy and the economy since 1987. It provides a minimum of descriptive detail needed to understand monetary policy during the period. The situations that confronted the Fed were remarkably varied. Nevertheless, the Fed's policy actions can be understood and interpreted as supporting the primary objectives of monetary policy which were the same throughout. First of all, the Fed aimed to achieve and maintain credibility for low inflation. Second, the Fed managed interest rate policy so that the economy could attain the full benefits of rising productivity growth. Third, the alleviation of financial market distress dictated interest rate policy actions on occasion. Fourth, the Fed steered real short-term interest rates sharply lower when economic stimulus was needed. The story of how monetary policy pursued these objectives follows.

2. OCTOBER 1987–JULY 1990: RISING INFLATION AND THE STOCK MARKET CRASH

From Wednesday, 14 October 1987 through the close of trading on Monday, 19 October the Dow Jones Industrial Average lost about 30 per cent of its value. That Monday alone, the Dow lost 23 per cent. Not since October 1929, when the Dow lost around 25 per cent in two consecutive days, had a sudden collapse of equity values been so great.[2]

The Fed responded to the October 1987 stock market crash in a number of ways. Most important for our purposes were these: the Fed accommodated the increased demand for currency and bank reserves with extensive open market purchases, and the Fed dropped its federal funds rate target from around 7.5 per cent to about 6.75 per cent.

Central bankers now know that sufficiently stimulative monetary policy might well have averted the deflation and depression of the 1930s. The Fed made sure that monetary policy was sufficiently stimulative to avert another catastrophe. Nevertheless, the Fed was concerned about the risks to price stability noting that its actions should not be seen as inflationary.[3]

As it turned out, inflation rose in 1988, 1989, and 1990 in spite of the fact that the Fed had put the economy through a severe recession in the early 1980s to restore price stability. Core CPI inflation rose from around 3.8 per cent in 1986 to 5.3 per cent in 1990. Employment cost inflation rose from around 3 per cent in 1986 to over 5 per cent in 1989, even as productivity growth averaged less than 1 per cent from 1986 to 1990. The unemployment rate fell from around 7 per cent in 1986 to 5.3 per cent in 1989. Annual average unemployment below 5.5 per cent had not been seen since 1973.

Part of the problem was that inflationary pressures began to build well before October 1987. Rising inflation expectations were already evident in the 30-year bond rate, which rose by 2 full percentage points from around 7.5 per cent to 9.6 per cent between March and October.[4] The Fed had responded aggressively to the previous inflation scare, when the bond rate rose from about 10.5 per cent to 13.5 per cent from mid-1983 to mid-1984. Then, the Fed raised the funds rate by 3 percentage points over roughly the same period. The aggressive response in 1983–84 helped precipitate a 6 percentage point fall in the bond rate, from 13.5 per cent in mid-1984 to 7.5 per cent by mid-1986, reflecting the largest reduction of inflation expectations on record.

In sharp contrast, the Fed reacted relatively little to the 1987 inflation scare. The Fed's failure to respond created doubts that it would hold the line on inflation, much less push on to price stability. The bond rate did not fall back to the 7.5 per cent range until late 1992, reflecting the slow restoration of credibility for low inflation that was lost in the second half of the 1980s.

In short, by mid-1987 there was sufficient reason for the Fed to tighten policy preemptively against inflation. The Fed raised the discount rate from 5.5 per cent to 6 per cent in September soon after Alan Greenspan replaced Paul Volcker as Fed Chairman.[5] But the October stock market crash intervened before policy could be tightened further.

All in all, it seems fair to say that monetary policy restraint was delayed by a couple of years due to the Fed's reluctance to act against inflation either before or after the crash of October 1987. By the time the Fed felt it was safe to tighten monetary policy further, it needed to counteract inflationary forces that were already well entrenched. As had been the case in the inflationary go/stop era, the restoration of credibility for low inflation after it was compromised required the Fed to raise real short rates higher than otherwise, with a greater risk of recession.

Beginning in the spring of 1988, the Fed began to raise the funds rate from the 6 to 7 per cent range to nearly 10 per cent in March 1989. With core CPI inflation then running at about 4.5 per cent that sequence of policy actions increased real short rates by over 3 percentage points to more than 5 per cent. Real GDP growth slowed from about 4 per cent in 1988 to 2.5 per cent in 1989. In response the Fed dropped the funds rate to around 7 per cent by late 1990. However, by then core CPI inflation was running at 5.3 per cent, well above its average in the mid-1980s.

3. AUGUST 1990–JANUARY 1994: WAR, RECESSION AND DISINFLATION

The August 1990 Gulf War dealt a severe blow to the US economy. It would take until March 1991 for US ground forces to eject Iraq from Kuwait and stabilize the region. The ground war went as well as could have been expected, lasting only 100 hours. But the outcome was in doubt until a few hours before the war was won. Consequently, uncertainty greatly affected the economy for nearly eight months. In August 1990 oil prices quickly spiked up from about $15 per barrel to over $35 falling back only gradually by early 1991. Households and businesses showed an inclination to postpone spending until the outcome of the war became clear. These supply and demand shocks caused economic activity to contract in the fall of 1990 through the first quarter of 1991. The National Bureau of Economic Research dates the 1990 recession from July 1990 to the trough in March 1991.

Monetary policy could do little to avert a recession during the Gulf War. Policy actions take time to act on the economy. Moreover, the Fed was caught with its credibility for low inflation having been compromised. Inflation was rising, and the Fed risked an inflation scare in bond markets if it cut the federal funds rate too sharply. Even so, the Fed brought the Federal Funds rate down from just above 8 per cent at the start of the Gulf War to just under 6 per cent at its close in the spring of 1991.

As a result of the restrictive policy actions undertaken prior to the Gulf War and the war-related recession itself, inflation began to recede. Core CPI inflation moved down to 4.4 per cent in 1991. The recovery from the recession trough in March 1991 proved to be slow in part because the recession itself was mild. The unemployment rate rose only a little more than 1 percentage point during the recession itself, from 5.5 per cent in July 1990 to 6.8 per cent in March 1991. Even though real GDP growth snapped back to 4 per cent in 1992 from the 0.8 per cent growth in 1991 the unemployment rate continued to climb, peaking at 7.8 per cent in June 1992. This was known as the 'jobless recovery'.

For its part, the Fed responded by steadily reducing the Federal Funds rate from 6 per cent in mid-1991, to 4 per cent by the end of 1991, to 3 per cent by October 1992, where it stayed until February 1994. Inflation fell as well, to around 3 per cent by 1992. The nominal Federal Funds rate cut partly reflected the 1½ percentage point fall in inflation, and partly represented a 1½ percentage point cut in the real Federal Funds rate, bringing the real rate approximately to zero.

Four factors account for the highly stimulative policy stance. First, the high and rising unemployment rate was a concern. Second, the banking system was undercapitalized in many areas of the country. Bank loans were expensive and somewhat more restricted than usual. Third, inflation had been brought down to around 3 per cent, 2 percentage points below where it was in 1990, and about 1 percentage point below where it had been in the mid-1980s. Fourth, the gains against inflation restored the Fed's credibility enough to risk moving to a zero real Federal Funds rate to stimulate aggregate demand and job growth.

The zero real short rate remained in place for about a year and a half until February 1994. During that time the unemployment rate fell from 7.8 per cent to 6.6 per cent. The inflation rate fell slightly. The long bond rate fell from around 7.5 per cent in October 1992 to around 6 per cent at the end of 1993. The lower bond rate may have been the result of a weak economic expansion and progress against the Federal budget deficit made at the time. The bond rate also probably reflected the acquisition of credibility for low inflation won by the Fed as a consequence of disinflationary policy actions taken since 1988.

4. FEBRUARY 1994–FEBRUARY 1995: PRE-EMPTING RISING INFLATION

The expansion gathered strength in late 1993. The zero real Federal Funds rate was no longer needed and would become inflationary if left in place. The Fed began to raise the Federal Funds rate in February 1994, taking it in seven steps from 3 per cent to 6 per cent by February 1995. Inflation showed little tendency to accelerate and remained between 2.5 per cent and 3 per cent. Thus, the Fed's policy actions took the real Federal Funds rate from zero to a little more than 3 per cent. The move raised real short-term interest rates to a range that could be considered neutral to mildly restrictive. In spite of the policy tightening, real GDP grew by 4 per cent in 1994, up from 2.6 per cent in 1993, and the unemployment rate fell from 6.6 per cent to 5.6 per cent from January to December 1994.

The policy tightening in 1994 succeeded in its main purpose: to hold the line on inflation without creating unemployment. The unemployment rate moved up only slightly to 5.8 per cent in April 1995 and then began to fall again. The 1994 tightening demonstrated that a well-timed preemptive increase in real short-term interest rates is nothing to be feared. Rather, it was needed to slow the growth of aggregate demand relative to aggregate supply to avert a build up of inflationary pressures. By holding the line on inflation in 1994 the preemptive policy actions laid the foundation for the boom that followed.

Pre-emptive policy in 1994 was in part motivated by the large increase in the bond rate beginning in October 1993. Starting from a low of 5.9 per cent, the 30-year bond rate rose through 1994 to peak at 8.2 per cent just before election day in November. The nearly 2½ percentage point increase in the bond rate indicated that the Fed's credibility for low inflation was far from secure in 1994. By January 1996 the bond rate had returned to around 6 per cent and journalists were talking about the 'death of inflation'.[6]

The 'death of inflation' talk was reassuring. It indicated that the Fed's pre-emptive actions had anchored inflation and inflation expectations more securely than ever before. This helps to explain why later in the decade the unemployment rate could fall to 4 per cent with little inflationary wage and price pressure. However, the 'death of inflation' talk was also disappointing because it tended to undervalue the role played by the Fed in 'killing' inflation. The actions taken in 1994 were a textbook example of a successful pre-emptive campaign against inflation. It is discouraging that even then, the public should misunderstand the crucial role played by the central bank in containing inflation. If inflation is to be contained permanently, the idea that inflation doesn't just 'die' but must be periodically vanquished by pro-active interest rate policy is one that the public must appreciate more fully.

Despite the relatively clear technical case for the pre-emptive tightening in 1994, the tightening was a difficult one for the Fed in another respect. For the first time the Fed began to announce its current intended Federal Funds rate target immediately after each FOMC meeting. Fed policy was more visible than ever. Starting with the 25 basis point increase in the Federal Funds rate at the February 1994 FOMC meeting, every increase in the Federal Funds rate target thereafter attracted considerable attention.

Transparency of the Fed's interest rate target is a good thing because it improves the public's understanding of monetary policy. However, since 1994 the Fed has operated with a transparent Federal Funds rate target and somewhat opaque medium- and longer-term goals.[7] The Federal Reserve Act does not specify how the Fed is to balance medium or longer-term objectives for inflation, economic growth, and employment. And the Fed does not clarify its medium- or long-term objectives as well as it could. The Fed's interest rate policy actions are scrutinized more than they would need to be if the Fed were more forthcoming about its objectives.

Part of the problem is that the Fed is naturally unwilling to specify its objectives more clearly without direction from Congress. And Congress has been unable to agree on a mandate for the Fed that would clarify them. The Fed has been operating without a clear mandate from Congress since the collapse of the gold standard and the Bretton Woods fixed exchange rate system in 1973. Under these circumstances, announcing the Federal Funds rate target increases the potential for counterproductive disputes between the Congress and the Fed.

A dispute broke into the open in 1994 when the Congress objected to the Fed's pre-emptive increase in interest rates and took the unprecedented step of inviting all twelve Reserve Bank presidents to explain their views before the House and Senate banking committees. Legislation that would remove the presidents from the FOMC was considered at the time on the grounds that the presidents were thought to favour excessively tight monetary policy. The net effect of this very public dispute was to create doubt about the Fed's ability and willingness to take the tightening actions necessary to hold the line on inflation. The public dispute between the Fed and the Congress probably contributed to the severity of the 1994 inflation scare in the bond market.

5. JANUARY 1996–MAY 1999: THE LONG BOOM

In many ways managing interest rate policy in the last half of the 1990s was more difficult than it was in the first half. Two major factors complicated interest rate policy in the period from 1996 to 1999. First, the Fed had to learn to operate with near full credibility for low inflation, credibility it had secured with its successful preemptive policy actions in 1994. Second, the Fed had to deal with rising productivity growth. Both complications benefited the economy greatly. The Fed has worked for almost two decades to achieve price stability. Economists had long hoped that advances in computer and information technology would bring an end to the productivity slowdown dating from the mid-1970s. Nevertheless, both developments challenged monetary policy in ways that were not anticipated. This section reviews the developments themselves and points out the complications for monetary policy. It concludes with an assessment of interest rate policy actions taken by the Fed during the period.

Near Full Credibility for Low Inflation

When near full credibility for low inflation is newly won, there is a tendency for both the central bank and the public to overestimate the economy's non-inflationary potential output. In other words, there is an inclination to be fooled by the central bank's credibility for low inflation in a way that restrains interest rate policy actions that may be necessary to sustain that very credibility. Even if inflation and inflation expectations remain firmly anchored, there is a risk that interest rate policy actions will be insufficient to head off an unsustainable *real* boom followed by a painful period of adjustment.[8] The nature of this risk is detailed below with reference to the long boom from 1996 to 1999.

When credibility for low inflation is secure, labour markets can get surprisingly tight without triggering inflationary wage pressures. Workers are less inclined to demand inflationary nominal wage increases because they have confidence that firms will not push product prices up. And firms are more inclined to hold the line on product price increases even if labour costs begin to rise. Firms and workers have confidence that any excess of aggregate demand over potential output will be temporary, reversed by sufficiently restrictive subsequent interest rate policy actions. Confidence in the central bank could enable the economy to operate above potential output for a while with little or no increase in inflation.

With inflation and inflation expectations firmly anchored, a central bank would be more inclined to delay monetary tightening when the economy moves above its presumed non-inflationary potential level of output. The central bank could take more time to discern whether an excess of aggregate demand is temporary or persistent before it responds with tighter monetary policy. When there is evidence of a rising trend in productivity growth, a central bank could explore the possibility that faster growth of aggregate demand might be accommodated without inflation.

The Fed's very success in anchoring inflation and inflation expectations meant that traditional indicators of excessive monetary stimulus became less reliable.[9] Inflation as measured by the core CPI ranged between 2 per cent and 3 per cent for the remainder of the decade. Price stability was maintained even though real GDP grew at around 4.4 per cent per year from 1996 through 1999, and the unemployment rate fell from 5.6 per cent in January 1996 to 4 per cent, a rate not seen since 1970.

Clearly, near full credibility for low inflation helped the economy to operate well beyond what would have created concerns about inflation in the past. Real indicators of incipient inflation such as the unemployment rate became less useful as guides for interest rate policy. Moreover, the bond market was less inclined to exhibit inflation scares. After having peaked at 8.2 per cent in late 1994, the 30-year bond rate returned to levels below 7 per cent and moved in a range between 5 per cent and 6 per cent in the last two years of the decade. This development recalled the bond market of the late 1960s which was confident that inflation would remain low even after economic activity moved above what was then considered its non-inflationary potential.

Nominal money growth also became less reliable as an indicator of inflation. Growth temporarily in excess of historical standards might be needed to accommodate an increased demand for money due to lower nominal interest rates and growing confidence in the stability of the purchasing power of money. Even truly excessive money growth might not cause inflation if the public believed that the Fed would tighten policy to reverse inflationary money creation before too long.[10]

If the public comes to think that the economy has become 'structurally' less prone to inflation, that is, that 'inflation is dead', then the risk of an unsustainable boom increases. Excessive optimism encourages households and firms to expect unrealistically high future real income prospects, triggering an unsustainable spending binge. Spending is encouraged further if the central bank appears to 'buy into' the optimism by not raising interest rates as aggregate demand accelerates. Excessively optimistic expectations of the economy's productive potential would be reflected in a run up in equity prices, real estate values, and asset prices in general. The risk of precipitating a collapse of asset prices, in turn, would make a central bank more cautious than otherwise in tightening interest rate policy.

Rising Productivity Growth

From 1986 Q1 until 1990 Q4 non-farm business productivity growth averaged only 0.8 per cent per year, reflecting the ongoing slowdown in productivity growth that began in the mid-1970s. In the next five years productivity growth rose to 1.7 per cent per year, and from 1996 Q1 to 2000 Q4 productivity grew on average by 2.4 per cent per year. In other words, productivity growth tripled over this 15-year period. In the late 1990s it was possible to argue that the burst of productivity growth was only temporary and would soon fall back to 2 per cent or less. But it was just as reasonable to argue that productivity growth would move even higher for a while as the economy continued to find new ways to employ advances in communications and information technology.

The trend productivity growth rate has enormous implications for standards of living, for perceived lifetime income prospects, and thus for current spending. When productivity grows at 1 per cent a year, national per capita product doubles roughly every 70 years. If productivity grows at 2 per cent per year, then per capita product doubles in 35 years and quadruples every 70 years. Sustained 3 per cent productivity growth would double per capita income in 23 years, quadruple it in 46 years, and result in an eight-fold increase in around 70 years. This last possibility seems unlikely; but sustained productivity growth between 2 per cent and 2.5 per cent per year well into the 21st century would match the 2.3 per cent average productivity growth rate that the US sustained between 1890 and 1970.[11] These figures indicate the tremendous long-term potential that many saw in the US economy in the last half of the 1990s – and still see in spite of the 2001 recession.

Real wages began to rise during the 1990s after stagnating during the productivity slowdown period. Households could count on the fact that throughout US economic history per capita productivity growth was transmitted to real wage growth as firms competed for evermore productive labor. Firm profits and equity values would benefit initially from the installation of more productive technology. But as the installation of that technology became widespread, firms would be forced to pay up for the more productive labour. Thus, the profit share of national income rose during the 1990s; but it could be expected to return to historic norms once real wages caught up. Whether it took the form of rising profits or wages, the underlying source of the increase in income and wealth was the rising trend in productivity growth.

In short, the period from 1996 to 1999 was characterized by an optimism about future income prospects that gave rise to an expansion in investment and productive capacity by firms matched by an increasing willingness of households to absorb the output that the growth of productive potential made possible.

Rising productivity growth had two critical implications for monetary policy. First, rising productivity growth reinforced the perception that the economy was inflation-proof, and provided an argument against more restrictive monetary policy. For a while, rising productivity growth more than offset the rising nominal wage growth associated with tight labour markets. The problem for monetary policy was that trend productivity growth was not likely to rise much above 2.5 per cent or 3 per cent per year. And productivity was already growing in that range by 1998. There was less reason to think that nominal wage growth would stop rising if labour markets remained as tight as they became during the period. Rising productivity growth might hold unit labour costs and inflation down for a while. But at some point unit labour costs would begin to rise, necessitating tighter monetary policy.

Second, although *rising* productivity growth made the economy more inflation-proof in the short run, *higher* trend productivity growth would require higher real interest rates in the long run. The reason being that at initial real interest rates, households are inclined to borrow against their improved future income prospects to spend some of the proceeds today, and firms are inclined to invest more in plant and equipment to profit from improved productivity. In the aggregate, however, households and firms cannot bring goods and services from the future into the present because the future productivity growth has not yet arrived.[12] In such circumstances, firms accommodate the growth in aggregate demand in excess of current productivity growth by hiring more labour to meet the demand.[13] Labour markets become increasingly tight, and the economy overshoots even its faster sustainable growth path.

To enable the economy to grow faster without inflation, the central bank would have to maintain higher short-term real rates on average over time to make households and firms sufficiently patient to defer their spending to the future. Higher short- and long-term real rates bring aggregate demand down to potential output so that both can grow together and the employment rate is neither expanding nor contracting over time. In short, when an economy enjoys an increase in the rate at which productivity can grow over the long run, it requires permanently higher real interest rates on average to offset the inclination of the public to spend the proceeds prematurely.[14]

The problem for US monetary policy was to ascertain the timing and magnitude of the increase in real interest rates necessary to allow the economy to make the transition to a higher growth path without imbalances in labour utilization that could lead to an outbreak of inflation or an unsustainable expansion of real activity. This policy problem was particularly formidable, as it had to be surmounted even as near full credibility for low inflation and rising productivity growth made the economy appear to be more inflation-proof than ever.

Interest Rate Policy, 1996–99

The Fed changed its Federal Funds rate target relatively little from January 1996 through June 1999. The rate was held at 5.25 per cent for over a year from January 1996 until March 1997 when it was raised to 5.5 per cent. The rate was then held constant for another year and a half at 5.5 per cent until the fall of 1998, when it was cut in three twenty-five basis-point steps in September, October, and November in the aftermath of the Russian debt default. Core CPI inflation averaged between 2 per cent and 2.5 per cent during the entire period, so the real short-rate was around 3 per cent, except when it was lowered by 75 basis points in the fall of 1998.

The single 25 basis point adjustment in March 1997 was taken as the economic expansion gathered momentum. By moving only once in March 1997, the Fed signaled that it was poised to act if necessary to restrain inflationary growth. However, the Fed declined to raise interest rates further for two years. Two world financial crises intervened: the 1997 financial crisis in East Asia and the 1998 financial crisis following the Russian default. Alleviating financial market distress became a primary focus of monetary policy in each case.

The Fed did not actually cut its Funds rate target in the second half of 1997 in response to the East Asian crisis, but it probably deferred tightening policy. The 75 basis point cut in the rate following the Russian default moved short-term interest rates in the opposite direction from what would ultimately be needed to stabilize the US economy. As was the case in the aftermath of the October 1987 stock market crash, the two financial crises in 1997 and 1998 helped to delay a necessary policy tightening by as much as two years.

Even without the two financial crises, policy-makers and the public would have been reluctant to tighten monetary policy between 1996 and 1999. Not only was inflation under control, but there was great uncertainty about the magnitude and timing of the interest rate policy actions needed to enable the economy to make the transition to a higher growth path without inflation. Under the circumstances, the Fed chose to wait before tightening very much until the need for restrictive policy became more obvious.[15]

6. JUNE 1999–DECEMBER 2000: RESTRAINING THE GROWTH OF DEMAND

Real GDP grew by 4.1 per cent, 6.7 per cent, 3.1 per cent, and 1.7 per cent from 1998 3Q to 1999 2Q. And it gradually became clear that the 75 basis point cut in the funds rate undertaken in the aftermath of the Russian default was no longer needed to stabilize financial markets and guard against the downside risk to the economy.

By the second half of 1999 the pool of available workers – unemployed plus discouraged workers – looked to be approaching an irreducible minimum. And the growth of aggregate demand in excess of plausible potential GDP tightened labour markets further. If real interest rates were kept too low, then the expansion would end in one of two ways. The Fed would lose its credibility for low inflation and the expansion would end as it had so often in previous decades, with rising inflation, an inflation scare in bond markets, and a policy tightening sufficient to restore credibility for low inflation. Alternatively, if the Fed's near full credibility for low inflation held fast, then rising unit labour costs would result in a profit squeeze, lower equity values, a collapse in investment, and slower growth of consumer spending.

Real GDP grew by a spectacular 4.7 per cent and 8.3 per cent in Q3 and Q4 of 1999, and the unemployment rate drifted down from 4.3 per cent in early 1999 to 4 per cent by the end of the year. The extraordinary growth of aggregate demand outstripped even the high accompanying productivity growth rates of 3 per cent and 7.4 per cent, respectively.

Clearly, real short rates needed to move up further. The Fed reversed the 75 basis point policy easing it had undertaken the previous autumn with three 25 basis point steps in June, August, and November of 1999. And the Fed raised its Federal Funds rate target by another 1 percentage point between November 1999 and May 2000 to 6.5 per cent where it was held until January 2001.

With core CPI inflation running at about 2.5 per cent, real short rates were then roughly 4 per cent. By comparison with other occasions of concerted monetary tightening, the real interest rate was not then particularly high. In part, this was due to the fact that the Fed had not yet lost credibility for low inflation and so did not need higher real rates to bring inflation down. The 4 per cent real rate seemed to be enough as real GDP growth in 2000 Q1 slowed by 6 percentage points to 2.3 per cent from the previous quarter. However, real growth accelerated again to 5.7 per cent in 2000 Q2 and the Fed maintained its 6.5 per cent funds rate target. Real GDP growth in Q3 again slowed, to 1.3 per cent, but the Fed needed another quarter of evidence that the slowdown would be sustained. That confirmation was received in late 2000 and early 2001, when it became clear that real GDP grew by around 2 per cent in 2000 4Q.

7. JANUARY 2001–PRESENT: THE COLLAPSE OF INVESTMENT AND THE 2001 RECESSION

The problem for monetary policy in 2001 was that real GDP growth failed to find a bottom and continued to fall, from 1.3 per cent in Q1, to 0.3 per cent in Q2, to −1.3 per cent in Q3. Personal consumption expenditure growth held up better, slowing from 3 per cent, to 2.5 per cent, and to 1 per cent, respectively, in the first three quarters of 2001. In part, consumer spending held up reasonably well because the unemployment rate rose relatively slowly from a very low 4 per cent at the end of 2000 to 4.6 per cent by July 2001. The relatively tight labour market continued to provide a sense of job security and robust real wage growth that supported consumer confidence.

The primary drag on growth in 2001 came from non-residential fixed investment and inventory liquidation. Investment in equipment and software grew much faster than GDP during the boom years. Advances in information processing and communication technologies led investment in equipment and software to rise from about 6 per cent of real GDP in 1990 to peak at around 12 per cent of real GDP in mid-2000. Real non-residential (business) fixed investment, which includes non-residential structures as well as equipment and software, grew at around 10 per cent per year from 1995 until 2000. Growth in business investment collapsed to near zero in 2000 Q4 and 2001 Q1 and then contracted at more than a 10 per cent annual rate in Q2 and Q3 of 2001.

The swing in inventory accumulation compounded the growth slowdown in 2001. After accumulating at an annual rate of $79 billion, $52 billion, and $43 billion dollars in Q2, Q3, and Q4 of 2000, inventories were liquidated at an annual rate of $27 billion, $38 billion, and $62 billion in the first three quarters of 2001, respectively.[16]

The developments outlined above reflected the fact that the economy overshot its sustainable growth rate in the late 1990s. Much capacity put in place during the boom began to look excessive in light of the slower growth rate. Higher trend productivity growth would eventually enable the economy to absorb that capacity, but not as soon as had been believed. Moreover, rising unemployment in the manufacturing sector caused a secondary collapse of demand that threatened to spill over to the services sector. The rising unemployment rate caused consumers throughout the economy to become more cautious, further weakening aggregate demand. This, in turn, gave businesses an additional reason to put investment plans on hold.

Financial factors significantly amplified the overshooting in investment and the painful adjustment thereafter. Excessive equity values cheapened equity finance during the boom years; the collapse of equity values raised the cost of equity finance during the slowdown. Likewise, high net worth facilitated external debt finance during the boom; and the loss of net worth raised the cost of external debt finance thereafter. Moreover, investment could be financed readily with internally generated funds during the boom, but the decline of profits during the slowdown increased the reliance on external finance even as it became more costly.

Recognizing the contractionary forces described above, the Fed cut its Federal Funds rate target in eleven steps from 6.5 per cent at the beginning of 2001 to 1.75 per cent in December 2001. Core CPI inflation did not change much during the year, translating the policy actions into a 4¾ percentage point cut in real short-term interest rates. This was a relatively large reduction in the real federal funds rate in so short a time by historical standards, though not when one considers that real GDP grew at around 5.2 per cent in the year through 2000 Q2 and grew at less than 1 per cent in 2001. Real short rates were then negative according to the core CPI inflation rate, which was running at about 2.5 per cent. The Fed was able to cut the real Federal Funds rate so far without an inflation scare because of the near full credibility for low inflation.

The 11 September 2001 destruction of the World Trade Center in New York made matters worse. Data for October indicated a sharp drop in consumer confidence, and a further contraction in the manufacturing sector. Most striking, roughly 800,000 jobs were lost in October and November combined. The rise in the unemployment rate in September, October and November was the fastest three-month increase since 1982, bringing the cumulative rise since January to about 1¾ percentage points. In November 2001 the National Bureau of Economic Research officially declared that the US had been in a recession since March.

The big jump in the unemployment rate has the potential to undermine consumer confidence. The unemployment rate in the US rose sharply by at least 2 percentage points on five occasions since 1960 during and following the recessions of 1960–61, 1969–70, 1973–75, 1981–82, and 1990–91. The cumulative rise during the 1980 recession was just 1.5 percentage points.[17] The unemployment rate rose by 4.2 percentage points in 1973–75, and by 3.6 percentage points in 1981–82.

That is only part of the downside risk. Historically, sharply rising unemployment has been associated with falling inflation. For instance, when the unemployment rate rose by 3.6 percentage points in 1981–82, the inflation rate fell by around 6 percentage points. In the past, disinflation has been a good thing because inflation was too high. The Fed then had the leeway to cut its nominal Federal Funds rate target to keep the real Federal Funds rate from rising as the disinflation ran its course. Today, the Fed has only 1¾ percentage points of leeway before the nominal Federal Funds rate hits the zero bound.

That said, there are three reasons to think that disinflation, if it occurs at all, will be relatively mild this time. First, the unemployment rate may not rise much more since the Fed has already cut the real Funds rate by 4¾ percentage points. Second, slower wage growth due to slack in the labour market may be matched by slower productivity growth this time. If that is the case, then unit labour costs would not fall much and there would be little downward pressure on prices. Third, the earlier recessions were set off in large part by tighter monetary policy aimed at controlling inflation. The Fed is not trying to bring the inflation rate down this time.

No one can say how the latest situation confronting US monetary policy will turn out. The zero bound may indeed become a problem. Hopefully, aggressive interest rate actions already undertaken will lay the foundation for a recovery in 2002. In that regard, it is worth noting that the Federal Funds rate futures market believes that the Funds rate has hit bottom and that the Fed will raise interest rates as the economy recovers in 2002.

8. CONCLUSION

The challenges facing monetary policy since 1987 have been surprisingly varied. Rising inflation was a problem for the Fed only briefly during the period. Restrictive monetary policy in the late 1980s and early 1990s reversed the rising inflation trend, and preemptive policy actions in 1994 secured near full credibility for low inflation in the late 1990s. The Fed dealt with three major financial crises: the October 1987 crash, the 1997 East Asian crisis, and the consequences of the Russian debt default in 1998. Monetary policy reacted to two wars: the 1990–91 Gulf War and the 2001 War on Terrorism. The Fed became more transparent – announcing its current Federal Funds rate target since 1994. Most importantly, monetary policy adapted to an environment in which the Fed acquired near full credibility for low inflation, and the Fed navigated a difficult transition toward higher trend productivity growth. Because the problems were so varied, it is difficult to draw overall lessons from the period. One thing is clear. The challenges are likely to be encountered again and the experience gained in surmounting them should help improve monetary policy in the future.

NOTES

1. This chapter was prepared for the Charles Goodhart Festschrift, Bank of England, November 2001. I would like to thank my discussant Charles Bean for excellent comments and Sandra Baker for excellent research assistance. The views expressed are mine alone and do not necessarily reflect those of the Federal Reserve Bank of Richmond or the Federal Reserve System.
2. This paragraph is heavily paraphrased from the Brady Report (1988), page 1.
3. Greenspan (1988), page 218.
4. Ireland (1996) shows quantitatively why a significant change in the long bond rate is likely to represent a change in inflation expectations rather than a change in the expected real rate. Goodfriend (1993) gives an account of inflation scares in the bond market during the 1980s.
5. The 1987 inflation scare may have reflected doubts about the credibility of Volcker's unknown successor.
6. See, for instance, Bootle (1996).
7. See Broaddus (2001).
8. Goodfriend (2001) and Taylor (2000) explore this sort of logic.
9. These informational problems add to the real-time data problems analysed in Orphanides (2001).
10. Taylor (2000) emphasizes this possibility.
11. See Romer (1989), p. 56.
12. In part, the US satisfied its demand for goods and services in excess of current output by importing capital from abroad (where growth prospects were not as bright) and running a current account deficit.
13. See Goodfriend and King (1997) for a discussion of the macromodel underlying the analysis in this chapter.
14. For log utility, the real interest rate must rise by the increase in the productivity growth rate.
15. A new literature considers whether asset prices should help guide interest rate policy. See Bernanke and Gertler (1999), Borio and Lowe (2001), Cecchetti et al. (2000), Gertler et al. (1998), and Goodhart (1995).
16. Annual GDP is around $10 trillion, so $100 billion is about 1 per cent of US GDP.
17. The 1980 recession was associated with the brief imposition of credit controls. See Schreft (1990).

REFERENCES

Bernanke, Ben and Mark Gertler (1999), 'Monetary Policy and Asset Price Volatility', in *New Challenges for Monetary Policy*, US: Federal Reserve Bank of Kansas City, pp. 77–128.

Bootle, Roger (1996), *The Death of Inflation*, London: Nicholas Brealey Publishing.

Borio, Caudio and Philip Lowe (2001), 'Asset Prices, Financial and Monetary Stability: Exploring the Nexus', Bank for International Settlements.

Brady Report (1988), *Report of the Presidential Task Force on Market Mechanisms*, Washington, DC: Government Printing Office.

Broaddus, Jr., J. Alfred (2001), 'Transparency in the Practice of Monetary Policy', Federal Reserve Bank of Richmond *Economic Quarterly*, 87 (3) (Summer), 1–10, and in 26th Annual Economic Policy Conference, US, *Federal Reserve Bank of St. Louis Review*, 84 (4), July/August 2002, 161–6.

Cecchetti, Stephen, Hans Genberg, John Lipsky and Sushil Wadhwani (2000), *Asset Prices and Central Bank Policy*, The Geneva Report on the World Economy No. 2.

Gertler, Mark, Marvin Goodfriend, Otmar Issing and Luigi Spaventa (1998), *Asset Prices and Monetary Policy*, London: Centre for Economic Policy Research.

Goodfriend, Marvin (1993), 'Interest Rate Policy and the Inflation Scare Problem: 1979–1992', Federal Reserve Bank of Richmond *Economic Quarterly* (Winter), 1–24.

Goodfriend, Marvin (2001), 'Financial Stability, Deflation, and Monetary Policy', *Monetary and Economic Studies* (Special Edition), Japan: Bank of Japan, pp. 143–66.

Goodfriend, Marvin and Robert King (1997), 'The New Neoclassical Synthesis and the Role of Monetary Policy', in Ben Bernanke and Julio Rotemberg (eds), *NBER Macroeconomics Annual 1997*, Cambridge, Mass.: MIT Press, pp. 231–82.

Goodhart, C.A.E. (1995), 'Price Stability and Financial Fragility', in Kuniho Sawamoto, Zenta Nakajima and Hiroo Taguchi (eds), *Financial Stability in a Changing Environment*, Japan: The Bank of Japan, pp. 439–97.

Greenspan, Alan (1988), 'Federal Reserve Response to the October Crisis', *Federal Reserve Bulletin* (April), 217–25.

Ireland, Peter (1996), 'Long-Term Interest Rates and Inflation: A Fisherian Approach', Federal Reserve Bank of Richmond *Economic Quarterly* (Winter), 21–35.

Orphanides, Athanasios (2001), 'Monetary Policy Rules Based on Real-Time Data', *American Economic Review* (September), 964–85.

Romer, Paul (1989), 'Capital Accumulation in the Theory of Long-Run Growth', in Robert Barro (ed.), *Modern Business Cycle Theory*, Cambridge, Mass.: Harvard University Press, pp. 51–127.

Schreft, Stacey L. (1990), 'Credit Controls: 1980', Federal Reserve Bank of Richmond *Economic Review* (November/December), 25–55.

Taylor, John (2000), 'Low Inflation, Pass Through, and the Pricing Power of Firms', *European Economic Review*, 44, 1389–408.

Discussion of 'The inflation forecast and the loss function', 'Six practical views of central bank transparency' and 'The phases of US monetary policy'

Charles Bean

First let me say what a very great pleasure it is to be present at this celebration of Charles's distinguished career. Others before me have lauded his contribution to economic thought and to central banking, so I would like to the opportunity to praise his contribution to the life of the economics department at the London School of Economics where Charles and I were colleagues for getting on for two decades. Academics can be a pretty self-centred bunch, but when I was a junior member of the department he always went out of his way to ask me how I was getting on and how my research was progressing. Such generosity of spirit is rare in life, and even rarer in academia.

Marvin Goodfriend has provided an excellent and compact survey of the events and challenges facing US monetary policymakers in the Greenspan era. The two most interesting periods and observations relate to the period of pre-emptive action against inflation (February 1994 to February 1995) and the 'Long Boom' (January 1996 to May 1999).

The earlier period saw official rates raised as the US economy recovered from recession, while the long bond rate stabilised at around 6 per cent. Talk of the 'Death of Inflation' might have been comforting from the perspective of keeping inflation expectations down and wage demands in check. But the tendency to neglect the role of the monetary authorities in this and to overplay the importance of proximate influences such as increased global competition was not. As monetary economists are only too aware, inflation (or deflation) cannot be killed once and for all – the maintainance of price stability requires eternal vigilance on the part of the policy-maker. And underestimation by politicians and the public of the role of central banks in achieving and maintaining price stability is the first step to demanding that they seek to achieve other, contradictory, objectives. An interesting question is whether an explicit inflation target, together with an associated published forecast, would have helped the Fed to explain its strategy to critical politicians during this period.

This raises the question of whether policy can be *too* successful? Perfect pre-emptive stabilisation of inflation (or output) paradoxically can make it look as if policy is impotent or irrelevant. For instance suppose that we on the MPC managed to hit our target inflation rate of 2.5 per cent continuously. Then regressions of inflation on just a constant and interest rates would find the latter statistically insignificant; this is but another example of James Tobin's (1970) venerable, but still valid, critique of the use of reduced form regressions to infer the effectiveness of policy. This suggests that while it is certainly sensible to move rates in the right direction, being too successful could actually harm the credibility of the central bank!

Turning to the 'Long Boom', New Keynesian models of price setting imply the short-run output–inflation trade-off becomes flatter as mean inflation drops (see for instance Ball, Mankiw and Romer, 1988). This flattening of the Phillips curve will be reinforced by forward-looking behaviour in wage and price-setting if monetary policy is credible and inflation expectations are firmly anchored. But a by-product is that the signal–noise ratio in inflation outturns is reduced, and this can lead policy-makers (and the public) to mistakenly think that the sustainable rate of activity is higher than it is. On top of that we saw an increase in trend productivity growth associated with rapid productivity growth in the high-tech sector, that is an increase in the future level of productivity. This raises demand relative to supply as households respond to the increase in permanent income by increasing spending and businesses respond to the increase in the marginal product of capital by raising investment. Consequently there is an increase in the equilibrium, or natural, real rate of interest, although this can be alleviated in an open economy where the excess demand can be (and in the US was) met through a deterioration in the current account. So a further pre-emptive tightening of monetary policy is required, but this may be difficult to implement if inflationary pressures appear dormant. Again all this may be easier to explain in the context of an articulated inflation-targeting framework.

Lars Svensson's latest contribution to the literature on inflation targeting makes two suggestions. First, that the MPC should announce the weights in its (majority) quadratic loss function. Second, that it should eschew constant interest rate (CIR) inflation forecast targeting.

With respect to announcing the relative weight on activity vis-à-vis inflation in the loss function, in principle this ought to be a job for the Chancellor of the Exchequer rather than the MPC, since it is society's loss function that we are really supposed to be minimising. However, there are difficulties in writing an algebraic objective function into legislation. The wording of the 1998 Bank of England Act – 'To maintain price stability, and subject to that, to support the economic policy of Her Majesty's Government, including its objectives for growth and employment' – in my view represents a practical compromise.

But this wording does not explicitly state what weight we are supposed to place on growth and employment. The question then is, would revealing the MPC's 'majority λ' enhance transparency in communicating with outside world? Whilst it might do so for an academic audience, I am less convinced that it would help us communicate with the broader public. Fortunately, I think this is also a largely irrelevant issue because empirical evidence tends to suggest the efficient policy frontier that depicts the minimum achievable output variability for a given inflation variability is in practice quite rectangular (see Bean, 1998). As a consequence the optimal policy is relatively insensitive to the choice of λ and most 'reasonable' objective functions should lead to similar interest rate decisions.

With respect to the use of CIR inflation projections, these are indeed subject to a number of criticisms – some of which I even noted myself in my former incarnation as an adviser to the Treasury Committee! First, the optimal policy is generally not to plan to keep rates constant, so targeting the CIR forecast is time inconsistent. Second, the inflation path under the CIR forecast will usually diverge (Wicksellian instability). Third, it is inconsistently constructed because current asset prices will usually be inconsistent with the assumed interest rate path. Finally, because they are conditioned on a hypothetical path for interest rates, CIR projections are difficult to use for *ex post* evaluation of forecast performance.

I should begin by pointing out that the CIR projections should be seen primarily as a pedagogical device to help explain the context for the MPC's policy decision to the public. But they are not the only vehicle, and we also provide projections based on market-based forward interest rates in the *Inflation Report* which avoid some of the above criticisms. These are two natural, neutral, benchmarks. Projections based on optimal conditional plans or even some sort of simple rule such as the Taylor rule are understandable to academics, but there is a real danger that they could be interpreted by the financial markets as a commitment to a future interest rate path.

Lars, along with a number of other observers, seem to believe that policy in the UK is now set so as to put the central projection for the CIR forecast equal to target at the two-year horizon, an impression that I confess appears to be validated by the quotation from one of Charles's papers. However, the MPC has repeatedly stated that there is *no mechanical link* between the central projection at the two-year horizon and the policy decision. Indeed the November 2000 *Inflation Report* contained a box on page 67 that explained this and gave three reasons why this was so. First, one needs to take account of the balance of risks, that is the skew in the distribution. Second, the prospects for inflation before and after the two-year horizon are relevant. And, third, that the trajectory for inflation and interest rates will depend upon the current and prospective levels of activity.

In the light of this it may seem surprising that the published projections have usually been so close to target. The reason for this is simply that, during the life of the MPC, inflation has been close to target and output close to potential, so that the choice between alternative inflation trajectories has not really been much of an issue. This would no longer be the case if inflation were no longer close to target (in which case we would also be in Open-Letter-writing territory). In that case the Committee would almost certainly want to explicitly consider a range of possible output, inflation and interest rate paths.

Adam Posen presents six contrasting views of what central bank transparency achieves, at least some of which strike a chord with my experience. Thus the 'reassuring' view suggests that communication facilitates flexibility in policy-making, and I would suggest that the aggressive pre-emptive policy actions here and in the US during the last year have been facilitated by clear communication over objectives and strategy.

The 'details' view appears to suggest that, by removing noise, more disclosure is better. There may be limits to how far one should go, however, as the disclosure of ever more peripheral details can lead to marginalia being over-emphasised by commentators and the markets. Essentially too much detail can lead to information overload, and some censoring out of marginal details by the central bank may be helpful to achieving overall clarity of the message. This argument is relevant, for instance, to the question of whether central banks should publish minutes that merely summarise the discussion of policy meetings, or full-blown transcripts.

The 'contingent' view wherein the optimal degree of disclosure is related to the type of the central banker seems to me rather less convincing, as it relies on the policy-maker wanting to be able to 'surprise' private agents. But while the canonical Kydland–Prescott/Barro–Gordon monetary policy game seems to me to be an insightful description of policy-making by politicians, I have always thought it a less convincing description of an independent central bank. This is because the latter has no obvious incentive to 'surprise' people in order to engineer a level of output above the natural rate (see Bean, 1998, for further discussion).

The 'irrelevance' view holds that talk is cheap and only actions matter. Transparency is thus irrelevant. Needless to say, I also find this unconvincing. Indeed if it were true, why would commentators read the minutes of the MPC and the *Inflation Report* so eagerly? However, at least one commentator has somewhat cynically likened our published projections to a

Victorian novel in which the reader knows how it will end, but not the route the plot will take to get there, so maybe this view holds sway in some quarters!

The 'annoyance' view suggests that a high level of transparency from pre-announced targets offers scope for politicians and the public to use the central bank as a scapegoat whenever the targets are missed. Now in the UK the targeted measure of inflation has generally been running just a little below the 2.5 per cent target for the last couple of years. The present regime requires the Governor to write an Open Letter to the Chancellor whenever inflation deviates more than 1 percentage point from target. At the inception of the new regime, outside commentators suggested that on the basis of past experience such Open Letters could be expected about 40 per cent of the time. Yet the Governor has not even been close to getting his pen out since the MPC was born, indicating that the inflation performance since 1997 has been about as close to a bull's eye as a policy-maker could hope for. Yet this has not prevented the Committee from being criticised by some politicians and journalists as being excessively hawkish and cautious.

Finally the 'diverting' or 'sad' view holds that clarity over a unidimensional target is likely to make policy too inflexible in the face of shocks. In practice, however, all inflation-targeting central banks, including the Bank of England, practice 'flexible' targeting in which supply shocks are (partially) accommodated and inflation is gradually, rather than sharply, returned to target. Communication of the weight placed on output then becomes an issue, but as already explained above one that I think is of limited practical importance.

REFERENCES

Ball, Larry, Greg Mankiw and David Romer (1988), 'The New Keynesian Economics and the Output-Inflation Tradeoff', *Brookings Papers on Economic Activity*, 1, 1–65.

Bean, Charles (1998), 'The New UK Monetary Arrangements: A View From the Literature', *Economic Journal*, 1705–809.

Tobin, James (1970), 'Money and Business Cycles: Post Hoc Ergo Propter Hoc?', *Quarterly Journal of Economics*, 301–27.

7. UK monetary policy, 1972–97: a guide using Taylor rules

Edward Nelson*

1. INTRODUCTION

In the period from the floating of the exchange rate in June 1972 to the granting of operational independence to the Bank of England in May 1997, UK monetary policy went through several regimes. These included the period in the 1970s when monetary policy was considered subordinate to incomes policy as the government's primary weapon against inflation; an emphasis on monetary targeting in the late 1970s and early 1980s; moves from 1987 toward greater management of the exchange rate, culminating in the UK's membership of the Exchange Rate Mechanism (ERM) from 1990 to 1992; and inflation targeting from October 1992.[1]

For the United States it has been shown by Taylor (1993) that Federal Reserve policy behaviour is well described by a simple rule relating the short-term nominal interest rate to inflation and the gap between actual and potential output. There has subsequently been an explosion of theoretical and empirical work on Taylor rules, including econometric estimates of rule coefficients for the US by Clarida, Galí, and Gertler (2000) and Judd and Rudebusch (1998).

This paper provides estimates of the Taylor rule for the UK over several different monetary policy regimes over 1972–97. It is not claimed that policy-makers actually adhered to a Taylor rule during any part of this period; rather, the Taylor rule estimates provided here can be regarded as a simple (two or three parameter) characterisation of developments in UK monetary policy. Under this interpretation, changes in the estimated Taylor rule coefficients across regimes reflect different policy responses over time to inflation or to output relative to potential.

Estimates of Taylor-style monetary policy reaction functions on quarterly UK data include those of Broadbent (1996), Clarida, Galí, and Gertler (CGG) (1998), and Adam, Cobham, and Girardin (2001). The present work departs from these studies in several ways. The estimation period is split into six distinct policy regimes, with interest rate reaction functions for each regime except the ERM period. By contrast, previous studies have estimated rules over samples (for example 1981–95 for Broadbent, 1979–90 for CGG), which, I argue, do not correspond to valid estimation periods because they include more than one policy regime.[2] Additionally, my longer sample allows a detailed examination of monetary policy behaviour both during the 'Great Inflation' of the 1970s, and under-inflation targeting (1992 onward). Finally, I estimate both backward-looking and forward-looking Taylor rules, and compare them as descriptions of UK policy behaviour.

Charles Goodhart's career and research are intertwined with the subject matter of this chapter in three respects. First, for half of the overall period considered here – namely, the period up to 1985 – Goodhart was involved in UK monetary policy in his capacity as Chief Monetary Adviser to the Bank of England. Secondly, as discussed in Section 2 below, the Taylor rule literature can be regarded as a response, both theoretical and empirical, by the monetary economics profession to criticisms that Goodhart made in the 1970s and 1980s of the state of monetary analysis. Thirdly, the period described here, 1972–97, witnessed an evolution of UK monetary policy that culminated in the creation of the Monetary Policy Committee (MPC), on which Goodhart served as an External member, and thus one of the nine individuals who made decisions on monetary policy in the United Kingdom. The years 1997–2000, during which Goodhart served as an MPC member, are outside the period I study,[3] but the estimates I provide of pre-1997 reaction functions can be compared with the type of interest rate rule that Goodhart laid out as desirable (see Goodhart, 1992, and Section 2 below).

For the sample periods covering the 1970s, I find that the estimated long-run response of the UK nominal interest rate to inflation was well below unity. Moreover, the real interest rate was permitted to be negative for most of this period. These results suggest that UK monetary policy failed to provide a nominal anchor in the 1970s. In the 1980s, control of inflation was more successful and, consistent with this, the estimates suggest a tighter monetary policy. This tightening was manifested in an increase in the average prevailing level of real interest rates, and a high degree of responsiveness to foreign interest rates, rather than in a stronger response to inflation. Indeed, the estimates in this chapter suggest that the long-run response of nominal interest rates to inflation remained below unity until the inflation targeting period 1992–97. For that period, the long-run responses of the UK nominal interest rate to inflation and the output gap are remarkably close to the values of 1.5 and 0.5 found by Taylor (1993) to be a good description of recent US monetary policy, and close to the recommendation for UK monetary policy made by Goodhart (1992).

A natural question before proceeding is what interest there is in characterising UK monetary policy in periods where it is non-optimal, such as the 1972–90 period of generally high inflation. A major reason is that a quantitative characterisation of policy helps to recover structural parameters describing the economy's price and output determination. For example, the decomposition of euro area inflation over 1980–99 by Smets and Wouters (2002) with a structural model requires specification of a policy rule, so that estimation can disentangle policy-rule parameters from behavioural parameters describing pricing and spending decisions. In a full-system estimation exercise such as undertaken in that paper, it may not be feasible to model all historical breaks in policy regime, so information about the quantitatively most important breaks in policy behaviour is useful. The estimates in this chapter indicate which are the quantitatively most important shifts in policy and so can aid future work on structural modelling of the UK economy.

2. GOODHART AND TAYLOR ON INTEREST RATE RULES

Goodhart (1989, pp. 130–31) pointed to an 'unhelpful dichotomy, between the theory and the reality of Central Bank operations'. On the one hand, he observed that both J.M. Keynes and Milton Friedman, when discussing 'practical policy matters concerning the level of short-term interest rates . . . had no doubts that these were normally determined by the authorities, and could be changed by them, and were not freely determined in the market. . .'. However, as he also noted, in analytical work, both positive and normative, these authors and many others (including users of the traditional IS-LM model) represented the monetary policy decision as entailing the choice of money growth rate. This was also true of much work on empirical monetary policy reaction functions, for example Barro (1977).

It is true that, as Goodhart and his fellow MPC members noted, 'for each path of the official rate given by the decisions of the MPC, there is an implied path for the monetary aggregates' (MPC, 1999, p. 169; see also Goodhart, 1987, p. 254), but the characterisation of actual central bank policy as a money-growth reaction function obscures many of the issues facing policy-makers. Central bankers' decisions in practice typically are concerned with whether to change the level of short-term nominal interest rates in the face of new information on the state of the economy. A decision to leave the nominal interest rate unchanged will, in general, not imply that money growth will be constant, since the rate of money growth consistent with a given setting of nominal interest rates will differ depending on the particular pattern of shocks hitting the economy. The money growth rate can therefore not be treated interchangeably with the nominal interest rate as the central bank's choice variable.

Irrespective of whether the choices of instrument and reaction functions made by central banks were wise ones, it was unsatisfactory that much work in monetary economics prior to the 1990s failed to characterise actual central bank practice accurately. Empirical work, as discussed in Section 1, requires estimation of structural economic parameters based on monetary policy behaviour that is modelled as realistically as possible. Judgements on the optimality of actual historical policy also require accurate characterisation of actual policy. For example, an evaluation of the relative merits of a fixed money growth rule and the interest-rate-oriented policies followed by actual monetary policy-makers requires that the latter be modelled with reasonable accuracy. Only then can one have an analytical framework that deduces the price level and output dynamics that arise from interest-rate-based monetary policies.

In many respects, however, much of the pre-1990s literature on monetary policy fell short of providing such a framework.[4] Much of the literature, as noted above, concentrated on reaction functions in which the money growth rate was the dependent variable. And when central banks' concern with interest rates was recognised in formal modelling, it was represented as the pursuit of rigidly pegged nominal interest rates, as in Poole (1970). UK monetary economists might have been expected to have a more realistic perspective, in light of Johnson's (1972, p. 233) observation that 'the tradition of British central banking and monetary theory . . . identified monetary policy with the fixing of the level of interest rates'. However, UK authors often represented this policy in macroeconomic models by the setting of interest rates at fixed levels irrespective of the state of the economy, just as Poole did. Kaldor (1982), for example, represented UK monetary policy graphically as a fixed nominal interest rate, with the nominal money supply provided perfectly elastically at that rate. As a characterisation of monetary policy at the monthly or quarterly frequency, this seems inadequate. As Goodhart (1987, p. 253) put it, 'I would dispute [the] repeated claim that the UK authorities have operated (implicit) interest rate targets . . . I cannot recall a period of open-loop fixed targets in the UK in the last 18 years, during which I was personally involved . . .'. Rather, Goodhart regarded it as more appropriate to model policy as '*closed-loop* targets for short-term interest rates, in which these were varied in response to contingent outcomes for exchange rates, the growth of the monetary aggregates, etc.' Indeed, it was this type of monetary policy reaction function that Goodhart used in his empirical work, for example Goodhart and Bhansali (1970).

To Goodhart, then, the appropriate representation of actual central bank policy was neither a money-growth-based reaction function nor a policy of rigid interest rate pegging; it was instead an interest rate reaction function according to which short-term rates were adjusted in a manner intended to provide macroeconomic stability. Different formulations of interest rate rules, of course, will have different degrees of success in delivering this stability, and Goodhart increasingly turned his attention to the appropriate form of the interest rate reaction function. Such a rule would capture the advantage stressed by Poole (1970) of not allowing money demand shocks to produce variability in output and inflation, by allowing the money stock, but not nominal interest rates, to rise in the face of a permanent fall in velocity. By the same token, the rule should not be one that allows runaway money growth, as would occur for example if the central bank attempted to hold real interest rates below their natural value. In July 1992, Goodhart proposed one scheme for setting interest rates:

> I have sometimes wondered whether, starting from zero inflation and 3 per cent nominal interest rates, there should not be a presumption that such interest rates should rise by 1½ per cent for each 1 per cent that inflation rises above zero, and that the Governor should be asked, say twice a year, to account for any divergence from that 'rule'. (Goodhart, 1992, p. 324)

An important property of such a rule, Goodhart noted, was that 'in order to raise real interest rates, nominal interest rates must be raised significantly more than the prior increase in the annualised rate of growth of the RPI . . .'.

Concurrently with Goodhart's proposal, Taylor (1993) showed that the behaviour of the US Federal Funds rate (the nominal interest rate used by the Federal Reserve as its policy instrument) was well described by the simple formula:

$$R_t = (r^* + \pi^*) + 1.5(\Delta_4 p_t - \pi^*) + 0.5\tilde{y}_t \qquad (7.1)$$

In equation (7.1), the nominal interest rate R_t is annualised and expressed as a fraction, $\Delta_4 p_t$ is annual inflation, and $\tilde{y}_t$ is the output gap (defined as $\tilde{y}_t = y_t - \bar{y}_t$, where y_t is log real GDP and $\bar{y}_t$ its potential level). π^* is the target for annual inflation, and r^* is the steady-state value of the real interest rate.

Taylor thus found that US monetary policy in practice conformed closely to the sort of rule regarded as desirable by Goodhart – namely, a nominal interest rate rule with a response of 1.5 to inflation. Relative to Goodhart's proposal, however, the rule also includes an output gap response. One might wonder why there was no such response in Goodhart's proposed rule. A first reason may have been the difficulty in settling on a measure of real aggregate demand that is available on a timely basis and that can be measured reliably. Obtaining accurate 'real-time' estimates of GDP and expressions of GDP data relative to an estimate of their 'natural' level, are not trivial issues, especially for the formulation of monetary policy, as stressed in Orphanides (2002). Another reason for Goodhart's omission of an output gap term may have been an expectation that a policy of stabilizing inflation would itself tend to keep output close to potential. This is consistent with the Governor of the Bank of England's (2001, p. 126) characterisation of inflation targeting as 'to keep overall demand in the economy growing broadly in line with supply-side capacity'. It is also consistent with the observation that the most serious output gap variations in the UK in the postwar period have been the result of policies that led to large increases in inflation (such as the Barber and Lawson booms), or have been a consequence of monetary policies that tried to rein in inflation after periods of excess demand (as in the early 1980s and early 1990s downturns). From this perspective, a separate response to the output gap in the interest rate rule may not be required, as inflation targeting would facilitate output gap stability.

In any case, Taylor's work has inspired much research on interest rate rules, and moved monetary economics in the direction sought by Goodhart. In particular, Ireland (2001) notes that, 'Following the publication of Taylor's (1993) original essay . . . monetary economists have come to appreciate that most central banks . . . conduct monetary policy by managing short-term nominal interest rates rather than some measure of the nominal money supply; in addition, monetary economists have come to appreciate that most central banks . . . systematically adjust their nominal interest rate instruments in response to output and inflation'.

In empirical work, rules such as equation (7.1) can be thought of as a simple approximation of actual policy behaviour, attempting to represent a complex process with a small number of parameters. In theoretical and policy-simulation work, a rule like (7.1) can be compared to the performance of other schemes, such as optimal rules, which use a wider information set.[5] In this light, it should be emphasised that it is not essential to the logic of the rule that the coefficients in (7.1) be 1.5 and 0.5. Indeed, experiments with interest rate rules in a variety of models have frequently supported higher values of one or both feedback coefficients in (7.1).[6] One reasonably general result is that it does seem desirable to have a (long-run) coefficient on inflation in the rule exceeding one, which helps to ensure that the Taylor rule delivers inflation equal to its target value (π^*) on average (see Taylor, 1999b). As noted above, Goodhart (1992) stressed this as an important property of an interest rate rule, and Woodford (2001) labels it 'the Taylor principle'.

Taylor's original paper emphasised the visual match of rule (7.1) with actual US interest rate behaviour. There have subsequently been attempts to fit Taylor rules to data using formal econometric procedures; CGG (1998, 2000) and Judd and Rudebusch (1998) do so for the US, and CGG (1998) also report estimates for the UK, Japan, France, Italy, and Germany. The principal departure these studies have found from equation (7.1) is strong support for a large positive coefficient on the lagged dependent variable. In money demand studies, the lagged dependent variable coefficient is often treated as indicating costs of adjusting money balances, but as central banks can adjust interest rates easily over short periods, the adjustment-cost interpretation is not applicable to estimated interest rate rules. Rather, the lagged interest rate coefficient has been interpreted as a 'smoothing' parameter, and an interest rate equation that includes such a term can be regarded (if it is dynamically stable) as one whose long-run solution is of the form given in equation (7.1).

The remainder of this chapter reports estimates of the UK monetary policy reaction function. It is important first to note an econometric issue that affects the interpretation of the results. This issue is whether it is legitimate to interpret the coefficients in econometrically estimated versions of (7.1) as policy reaction parameters. The estimates below avoid simultaneity problems by using instrumental variables (IV) estimation whenever current or expected future values of variables appear in the estimated equations. Even so, there are potential identification problems. For example, in the degenerate case where the central bank controls inflation perfectly, the resulting low variability of inflation may lead to insignificant estimates of the policy response to (expected) inflation. Fortunately, the data used in this chapter do seem to provide sufficient variation in inflation and the other explanatory variables to avoid this problem (see Nelson, 2000).

One feature of the present study that should be mentioned is that I make no attempt to interpret the intercept terms of the estimated policy rules. A standard approach is to interpret the estimated (long-run) constant term as composed of the sum of the steady-state real interest rate, r^*, and an 'inflation target', π^* – just as it is in equation (7.1). Typically, analysis of the constant term has proceeded by fixing the value of either r^* and π^* *a priori*, and then deducing the implied inflation target or equilibrium real rate; see Judd and Rudebusch (1998, pp. 7–8) for a discussion.

I do not follow this approach for two reasons. First, as I discuss further in Section 4, policy-makers in the 1970s relied heavily on devices other than monetary policy to control inflation. The UK policy-making environment in the 1960s and early 1970s, which Charles Goodhart's work helped to change, was a 'Radcliffean' one in which the importance of monetary policy for inflation outcomes was greatly underestimated.[7] It is therefore unlikely that, for such periods, analysis of the estimated monetary policy rule is sufficient to deduce the policy-makers' implicit 'target' for inflation. Instead of trying to disentangle either π^* or r^* from the estimated constant term, I simply report the ex-post real interest rate for each of the regimes for which I estimate policy rules.

The second reason why I do not attempt to interpret the intercept is that the variables I use, notably GDP, are revised data. And I use detrended output series obtained from trends fitted to the entire 1971–98 period. Thus, the output gap data are not the 'real-time' data available to policy-makers when they were making their decisions. As noted above, the analysis in Orphanides (2002) suggests that differences between the real-time and final data can have important consequences for the analysis of policy rules. In evaluating their consequences for the results in the present chapter, it is important to note that Orphanides' key finding for US data is that 'the bulk of the problem is due to errors in the measurement of potential output. As is now evident, real-time estimates of potential output [in the 1970s] severely overstated the economy's capacity relative to the recent estimates . . .'. For the UK, a similar overstatement appears to have occurred in the 1970s (Nelson and Nikolov, 2001). Official targets for real GDP growth were announced in the early and mid-1970s that seem, in retrospect, to reflect over-estimates of the UK's potential growth rate and/or the amount of spare capacity in the economy.

If the bulk of the difference between final and real-time data consists of one-sided and infrequently corrected errors about the output gap level, then my use of final data will mainly affect the intercept terms of the policy rules that I estimate, rather than the estimated response coefficients.[8] Again, this is a reason against undertaking a structural interpretation of the intercept terms, and concentrating instead on the estimated slopes. Nelson and Nikolov (2001) construct a quarterly real-time UK output gap series beginning in 1965. Below I check my estimates of quarterly reaction functions that use final data with estimates obtained using real-time output gap data, and verify that the policy reaction coefficients are not materially different.

3. EMPIRICAL ESTIMATES

This section provides estimates of interest rate policy reaction functions for the United Kingdom. Throughout, R_t is measured by the Treasury bill rate[9] (expressed as an annualised fraction), $\Delta_4 p_t$ is the annual percentage change in the Retail Price Index (spliced into the RPI excluding mortgage interest payments, RPIX, in 1974), and $\tilde{y}_t$ is measured by the residuals from a 1971

Q1–1998 Q4 regression of log real GDP, y_t, on a linear and a quadratic trend.[10]

Results using the full 1972–97 sample indicated that response coefficients exhibited considerable non-constancy (see Nelson, 2000), consistent with several breaks in monetary policy regime. Accordingly, the estimates reported here are for specific subsamples corresponding to different policy regimes: (a) July 1972 to June 1976: from the first full month of a floating exchange rate to the end of the pre-monetary targeting period; (b) July 1976 to April 1979: the monetary targeting period that preceded the election of the Conservative Government;[11] (c) May 1979 to February 1987: the period beginning with the election of the Thatcher Government; (d) March 1987 to September 1990: informal stabilisation of the sterling/Deutschmark exchange rate; (e) October 1990 to September 1992: membership of the ERM (a period for which I attempt no reaction function estimates); and (f) October 1992 to April 1997: the period of inflation targeting in the UK prior to the Bank of England receiving operational independence.

Other divisions of the 1972–97 period are possible, of course, and some alternatives are discussed below. But, especially compared to the US, many of the regime changes in the UK are notable for having been made explicit through public announcements – including those in 1976, 1979, 1990, and 1992 – and it seems worthwhile to exploit this historical information rather than use statistical criteria to determine the dates of regime changes. Let us proceed, therefore, to examine more closely the first regime, 1972–76.

3.1 1972–76

The first specification which I estimate for the 1972–76 regime is a backward-looking Taylor rule with lags of inflation, the gap, and the interest rate:

$$R_t = \kappa + \sum_{i=1}^{j} a_i \Delta_4 p_{t-i} + \sum_{i=1}^{j} b_i \tilde{y}_{t-i} + \sum_{i=1}^{j} c_i R_{t-i} + e_t. \tag{7.2}$$

Here e_t is a white noise disturbance. The presence of lags of R_t allows for interest rate smoothing. The long-run inflation and output responses are $w_1 \equiv (\sum_{i=1}^{j} a_i) / (1 - \sum_{i=1}^{j} c_i)$ and $w_2 \equiv (\sum_{i=1}^{j} b_i) / (1 - \sum_{i=1}^{j} c_i)$. I also estimate a forward-looking rule:

$$R_t = \kappa + a_k E_{t-1} \Delta_4 p_{t+k} + b_0 E_{t-1} \tilde{y}_t + \sum_{i=1}^{j} c_i R_{t-i} + e_t \tag{7.3}$$

with long-run coefficients $w_1 \equiv a_k / (1 - \sum_{i=1}^{j} c_i)$ and $w_2 \equiv b_0 / (1 - \sum_{i=1}^{j} c_i)$. Apart from the smoothing terms, specification (7.3) differs from (7.2) by restricting the influence of lagged information on monetary policy decisions to its effect on the conditional expectations of the current output gap, $E_{t-1}\tilde{y}_t$, and future inflation, $E_{t-1}\Delta_4 p_{t+k}$. Below I report estimates of (7.3) for alternative values of k.

The 1972–76 sample period consists of only sixteen observations, which might appear insufficient to produce reliable estimates. However, the information content of a data set depends not only on its length but also on the regressors' sample variation. As shown in Nelson (2000), inflation, detrended output, and the interest rate were exceptionally volatile in the four years to 1976, implying that the 1972–76 sample contains a large amount of information, which accounts for why the estimates of (7.2) given in Table 7.1 below are precise and interpretable.

Table 7.1 Interest rate reaction function estimates for the UK, sample period: 1972 Q3–1976 Q2

Specification	Long-run coefficient on: Inflation	Output gap	Smoothing coefficients Σc_i	SEE	Serial correlation lags 1–4: test (p value)
Equation (7.2), OLS,	0.124	0.570	0.274	0.0106	0.56
$j=2$	(0.077)	(0.198)	(0.213)		
Equation (7.3), IV,	−0.073	−0.045	0.683	0.0129	0.45
$j=2, k=0$	(0.325)	(0.665)	(0.213)		
Equation (7.3), IV,	0.095	0.156	0.577	0.0133	0.84
$j=2, k=1$	(0.201)	(0.440)	(0.235)		
Equation (7.2), OLS,	0.075	0.349	0.454	0.0138	0.83
$j=2$, real-time data	(0.104)	(0.242)	(0.211)		

Note: Numbers in parentheses are standard errors. For the IV estimates, the instruments are a constant and lags 1–6 of R_t, $\Delta_4 p_t$, and $\tilde{y}_t$.

Estimates of (7.2), using lag length $j=2$ quarters, are presented in Table 7.1.[12] The long-run estimated response to inflation is 0.12; while significantly above zero, this is very low in relation to Goodhart's (1992) and Taylor's (1993) coefficient of 1.5. Indeed, if one uses $R_t-\Delta_4 p_{t-1}$ as a rough guide to the real interest rate $R_t-4{\cdot}E_t\Delta p_{t+1}$, the estimate suggests that policy-makers permitted each 1 percentage point increase in inflation to reduce the real interest rate by over 80 basis points. In addition, the output response coefficient is large (0.57) and significant.

These results are consistent with descriptions of macroeconomic policy during this period (for example Campbell, 1993, p. 471; Goodhart, 1997, p. 403). The Heath Government maintained that it could stimulate output through expansionary monetary and fiscal policies, while holding down inflation through wage and price controls.[13] This reflected a view, initially shared by the Labour Government elected in 1974, that the inflation of the 1970s largely reflected autonomous wage and price movements, and that the appropriate policy response was to influence the prices of specific products, rather than focus on monetary policy.[14] Examples of the non-monetary attempts to control inflation include the incomes policy imposed by the Heath Government in 1972 and the voluntary incomes policy pursued by the Labour Government from 1974; the extension of food subsidies in the March 1974 Budget; and cuts in indirect taxation in July 1974.

In Table 7.1 I also estimate, by IV, the forward-looking version (7.3) of the Taylor rule, for horizons $k=0$ and $k=1$.[15] The estimates are considerably less precise and interpretable than those of (7.2). Thus, in the 1972–76 period monetary policy-makers appear to have moved the short-term interest rate mainly in reaction to past behaviour of real aggregate demand and, to a very limited extent, inflation.

All the results so far use revised data. To check the sensitivity of results to this, I reestimated (7.2) with the lags of $\tilde{y}_{t-i}$ replaced by ${}_t\tilde{y}_{t-i}$, which denotes the data available on the period $t-i$ output gap as of period t.[16] I also replaced the quarterly average series R_t with the end-of-quarter observation R_t^{end}, in keeping with the fact that GDP data for period $t-1$ were generally not available until late in period t. This 'real-time' version of (7.2) supported a lag-length choice of $j=2$; moreover, there was no evidence of sizeable period t reactions to data on period $t-1$ inflation or the output gap. Accordingly, I found that the following specification was adequate:

$$\underset{(0.021)}{R_t^{end}=0.060}+\underset{(0.211)}{0.454\,R_{t-1}^{end}}+\underset{(0.063)}{0.041\,\Delta_4 p_{t-2}}+\underset{(0.150)}{0.191\,{}_t\tilde{y}_{t-2}} \qquad (7.4)$$

$$R^2=0.504,\ SEE=0.0138.$$

The implied long-run responses implied are reported in Table 7.1, and are close to the final-data estimates of (7.2). The main difference is that the gap response is less statistically significant and somewhat smaller using the initial data. This may reflect policy-makers' reliance on a variety of measures of economic activity. To the extent that subsequent revisions bring GDP movements more into conformity with other activity measures, the final revised GDP series may be a better index of the activity variables that enter policy reaction functions in real time.[17]

3.2 1976–79

This regime begins with the announcement of targets for the monetary aggregate, £M3 (Sterling M3), in July 1976, and finishes with April 1979, the last month prior to the election of the Conservative Government. As this regime is shorter than any other that I consider, my estimation uses monthly data, measuring the output gap by quadratically detrended log industrial production.[18]

Results are reported in Table 7.2, starting with estimates of (7.2). These give insignificant and wrongly signed coefficients on both inflation and the gap. The table also reports estimates of the forward-looking specification (7.3) for various choices of k. Neither $k=0$ nor $k=3$ delivers interpretable estimates. A specification with three-quarters-ahead inflation ($k=9$), however, delivers a significant, correctly-signed inflation response, and an insignificant but correctly-signed gap response. As the table also indicates, $k=12$ instead of 9 delivers similar but somewhat weaker results.

Clearly, the results are sensitive to the specification chosen, but the best characterisation of the period seems to be that interest rates responded to expected annual inflation nine months ahead, with interest rate smoothing

Table 7.2 Interest rate reaction function estimates for the UK, sample period: July 1976–April 1979

Specification	Long-run coefficient on: Inflation	Output gap	Smoothing coefficients Σc_i	SEE	Serial correlation lags 1–12: test (p value)
Equation (7.2), OLS, $j=2$	−0.996 (0.489)	−1.082 (0.590)	0.231 (0.182)	0.0082	0.05
Equation (7.3), IV, $j=2, k=0$	−1.446 (1.443)	−1.099 (1.428)	0.928 (0.054)	0.0081	0.20
Equation (7.3), IV, $j=2, k=3$	−0.062 (0.068)	−0.812 (2.553)	0.369 (0.202)	0.0087	0.41
Equation (7.3), IV, $j=2, k=9$	0.622 (0.086)	0.111 (0.138)	0.602 (0.101)	0.0073	0.78
Equation (7.3), IV, $j=2, k=12$	0.559 (0.193)	−0.152 (0.312)	0.802 (0.071)	0.0080	0.37

Note: Numbers in parentheses are standard errors. In these regressions, $\Delta_{12}p$, twelve-month inflation, is used instead of $\Delta_4 p$, reflecting the use of monthly data. Correspondingly, j and k here refer to months, not quarters. For the IV regressions, the instruments used are a constant and lags 1–6 of R_t, $\Delta_{12}p_t$, and $\tilde{y}_t$.

and a small output gap response. The long-run inflation response of 0.62 is over four times the estimated 1972–76 response. Nevertheless, it is important not to overemphasize the tightness of policy over 1976–79. One reason why I find a rise in the inflation response compared to pre-1976 is that the nominal interest rate was cut aggressively (by over 900 basis points from late 1976 to early 1978) ahead of a fall in inflation from mid-1977 to late 1978. This easing reversed much of the progress achieved in reducing inflation. Reflecting the easier monetary policy, base money growth rose sharply from late 1977; inflation troughed at 7.6 per cent in October 1978 and continued to rise until May 1980 (when it reached 21 per cent).

Another reason for doubting the tightness of the 1976–79 policy is the average level of interest rates. Central banks' control over nominal interest rates gives them considerable leeway in the short run in affecting the behaviour of real interest rates. If one measures the real interest rate by $R_t - \Delta_{12}p_{t-1}$, the real rate did not become positive until June 1978; the ex-post real interest rate also only became positive in that month, and averaged -3.14 per cent over 1976–79. While this is higher than the -5.72 per cent ex-post real rate observed in 1972–76, it indicates a tendency until 1978 to hold nominal interest rates well below actual and prospective inflation.

3.3 1979–87

This regime followed the election of the Conservative Government in May 1979 and concluded with the Louvre Accord on exchange rates in February 1987. Throughout this period, monetary policy-makers stressed inflation control, and exchange rate floating was largely permitted. Arguably, the sample should begin in March 1980 with the announcement of the Medium Term Financial Strategy (MTFS) and end in October 1985 with the suspension of £M3 targeting. Large misses of the £M3 target were permitted as early as mid-1980, however, and the MTFS was revamped in 1982. It was also clear before 1985 that policy-makers did not regard £M3 overshoots as intolerable, provided other measures of monetary conditions did not indicate that policy was loose.[19] It may therefore be satisfactory to treat 1979–87 as one regime rather than subdivide it according to the attention given £M3.[20]

The estimation period is 1979 Q2–1987 Q1. Estimates of (7.2) are reported in Table 7.3. The estimated long-run response to inflation is 0.34, significantly positive but also significantly below unity. The long-run output gap response is 0.26. Table 7.3 also reports two versions of forward-looking rule (7.3). With $k=0$, the long-run response to the output gap is 0.16; to inflation, 0.38, close to the estimates of (7.2). The smoothing coefficient is also similar. The output gap response is not statistically significant

Table 7.3 Interest rate reaction function estimates for the UK, sample period: 1979 Q2–1987 Q1

Specification	Long-run coefficient on: Inflation	Output gap	Smoothing coefficients Σc_i	SEE	Serial correlation lags 1–4: test (p value)
Equation (7.2), OLS,	0.342	0.258	0.337	0.0112	0.22
$j=1$	(0.063)	(0.124)	(0.199)		
Equation (7.3), IV,	0.380	0.164	0.373	0.0099	0.68
$j=1, k=0$	(0.058)	(0.143)	(0.156)		
Equation (7.3), IV,	0.387	0.058	0.483	0.0105	0.75
$j=1, k=1$	(0.078)	(0.160)	(0.143)		
Equation (7.2), OLS,	0.308	0.118	0.323	0.0122	0.44
$j=2$, real-time data	(0.086)	(0.189)	(0.238)		

Note: Numbers in parentheses are standard errors. For the IV regressions, the instruments used are a constant and lags 1–4 of R_t, $\Delta_4 p_t$, and $\tilde{y}_t$.

but its presence in the equation is supported by monthly estimates.[21] Table 7.3 also shows that a horizon of $k=1$ delivers similar results to the $k=0$ case, and that estimates of rule (7.2) are little changed if real-time output gap data are used.[22]

These results leave us with an apparent anomaly. Inflation fell over much of 1979–87, and by February 1987 was down to 3.7 per cent. The results here indicate that this disinflation was achieved with a response of the nominal interest rate to inflation (w_1) below 1.0. Yet analysis of historical periods, such as CGG's (2000) coverage of the US, typically characterises disinflations as periods where w_1 exceeds unity.

Why, then, did UK monetary policy in the early 1980s achieve disinflation? The answer appears to lie in the high level of real rates. The Taylor rule approach often assumes that the average real rate over a given sample equals its steady-state level, with the latter typically assumed to be 2–4 per cent. For 1979–87, however, this position seems untenable: ex-post real rates averaged 4.66 per cent, about 750 basis points higher than their 1976–79 level. Thus while the *movements* of the nominal rate in response to inflation over 1979–87 were muted, the average prevailing *level* of rates was consistent with restrictive monetary policy. This is recognised by CGG (1998, p. 1054): 'Monetary policy boiled down to keep[ing] real rates steadily high over this period, even when inflation was low during the mid-1980s'.

3.4 1987–90

The period 1987–90 consisted of informal linking of the pound to the Deutschmark. This includes not only 'shadowing' of the DM (1987–88), but also the period 1988–90 in which UK monetary policy continued to track German policy. For example, in October 1989 the UK 'immediately followed' the Bundesbank's interest rate increase with an equal increase (Lawson, 1992, p. 951).[23]

I estimate on monthly data, March 1987 to September 1990. In the estimated specifications, as in CGG (1998), the UK rate responds to the German day-to-day nominal interest rate R_t^G, annual inflation, and the output gap. The implied backward-looking and forward-looking specifications are (7.5) and (7.6) respectively:

$$R_t = \kappa + \phi_G R_t^G + \sum_{i=1}^{j} a_i \Delta_{12} p_{t-i} + \sum_{i=1}^{j} b_i \tilde{y}_{t-i} + \sum_{i=1}^{j} c_i R_{t-i} + e_t \qquad (7.5)$$

$$R_t = \kappa + \phi_G R_t^G + a_k E_{t-1} \Delta_{12} p_{t+k} + b_0 E_{t-1} \tilde{y}_t + \sum_{i=1}^{j} c_i R_{t-i} + e_t \qquad (7.6)$$

Table 7.4 first gives estimates of (7.5).[24] There is a sizeable reaction to R_t^G, considerable interest rate smoothing, and a strong output gap response. There is apparently no response to inflation, however. In Table 7.4 I also reestimate (7.5) after deleting the inflation term. This is the preferred specification; estimates of (7.6) suggest that expected future inflation was not important. The results overall indicate that Bundesbank's monetary policy served as UK policy's nominal anchor. But domestic factors continued to be a consideration, indicated by the high degree of domestic interest rate smoothing, and by the positive output gap response.[25]

The estimates suggest a long-run response of UK to German rates of 1.11. This is nearly double CGG's (1998) estimate of 0.60. CGG's sample period was 1979–90, so their lower estimate seems to be a result of mixing a regime in which German policy was not a major influence on UK policy (1979–87) with one in which Bundesbank policy became a dominant consideration (1987–90). Estimation of (7.5) over May 1979–September 1990 gives a long-run R_t^G coefficient of 0.578 (standard error 0.268), while R_t^G is not significant if (7.5) is estimated over 1979–87.

An important question is why inflation took off in the late 1980s. Judged by the average ex-post real rate of 5.76 per cent, policy appears to have been generally 'tight' in this period, and Stuart (1996, Chart 4) finds that R_t was below Taylor's (1993) recommendation for only two quarters in 1986–88. Yet annual UK inflation rose over 5 points over 1987–90. One possibility is that both money growth and interest rates matter for aggregate demand, and that the outbreak of inflation was promoted by rapid money growth. In line

Table 7.4 Interest rate reaction function estimates for the UK, sample period: March 1987–September 1990

Specification	Long-run coefficient on:			Smoothing coefficients Σc_i	SEE	Serial correlation lags 1–12: test (p value)
	Inflation	Output gap	R^G			
Equation (7.5), IV, $j=1$	−0.036	0.453	1.136	0.518	0.0041	0.16
	(0.217)	(0.120)	(0.184)	(0.118)		
Equation (7.5), IV, $j=1$, inflation omitted	—	0.454	1.109	0.522	0.0041	0.16
		(0.119)	(0.088)	(0.115)		
Equation (7.6), IV, $j=1$, $k=0$	−0.094	0.409	1.247	0.522	0.0045	0.48
	(0.216)	(0.126)	(0.191)	(0.130)		
Equation (7.6), IV, $j=1$, $k=3$	−0.170	0.405	1.324	0.507	0.0045	0.57
	(0.185)	(0.122)	(0.183)	(0.131)		

Note: Numbers in parentheses are standard errors. In these regressions, $\Delta_{12}p$, twelve-month inflation, is used instead of $\Delta_4 p$, reflecting the use of monthly data. Correspondingly, j and k index months, not quarters. The instruments used are a constant and lags 1–6 of R_t^G, R_t, $\Delta_{12}p_t$, and $\tilde{y}_t$.

with this, base money and broad money growth suggest easy monetary conditions in 1986–88 (for example Congdon, 1992; Stuart, 1996, Chart 3).

3.5 1992–97

This period begins with the October 1992 shift to inflation targeting after the UK's departure from the ERM, and ends prior to Bank of England independence in May 1997. I use quarterly data, 1992Q4 to 1997Q1. Estimates of (7.2) are wrongly signed and insignificant. Far more plausible are the estimates of the forward-looking rule (7.3), particularly with $k=1$. The Taylor principle is satisfied; indeed, the long-run inflation and gap responses of 1.27 and 0.47 are remarkably close to the (1.5, 0.5) combination used by Taylor (1993) to characterise US monetary policy, and resemble Goodhart's (1992) recommended rule. Estimates on monthly data are similar, with long-run coefficients of 1.472 (s.e. 0.424) on inflation and 0.301 (0.068) on the gap.[26]

Table 7.5 Interest rate reaction function estimates for the UK, sample period: 1992 Q4–1997 Q1

Specification	Long-run coefficient on: Inflation	Output gap	Smoothing coefficients Σc_i	SEE	Serial correlation lags 1–4: test (p value)
Equation (7.2), OLS,	−0.323	0.534	0.475	0.0025	0.29
$j=1$	(0.525)	(0.138)	(0.109)		
Equation (7.3), IV,	0.576	0.597	0.389	0.0029	0.41
$j=1, k=0$	(0.544)	(0.149)	(0.118)		
Equation (7.3), IV,	1.267	0.470	0.288	0.0029	0.45
$j=1, k=1$	(0.468)	(0.131)	(0.116)		

Note: Numbers in parentheses are standard errors. For the IV regressions, the instruments used are a constant and lags 1−4 of R_t, $\Delta_4 p_t$, and $\tilde{y}_t$.

The average ex-post real rate over 1992–97 was 2.99 per cent, well below 1980s' levels. This largely must reflect factors beside monetary policy, such as a global fall in the steady-state real rate. But it is also possible that inflation targeting reduced ex-post real rates by lowering the risk of a sudden inflation outbreak. This suggests inflation can now be controlled without resort to real rates as high as 1980s' levels.

4. CONCLUSION

This chapter characterised UK monetary policy from 1972 to 1997 with Taylor-type policy rules. Estimation was on five separate regimes – with quarterly data for regimes of four years or more in length; monthly data otherwise.

Table 7.6 summarises the results. In some respects, they are in keeping with standard analysis of the Taylor rule. For example, the 1972–76 period of extremely high inflation is characterised by a near-zero response of nominal interest rates to inflation, in keeping with the 'Taylor principle' that inflation is only reliably controlled when this response exceeds unity. The low inflation period from 1992 is indeed characterized by a Taylor rule with a response above unity, and the form of the reaction function resembles that outlined by Goodhart (1992).

Table 7.6 Summary of reaction function estimates

Regime	Long-run inflation response	Long-run output gap response	Smoothing parameter	Ex-post real interest rate
1972–76	0.12	0.57	0.27	−5.72%
1976–79	0.62	0.11	0.62	−3.14%
1979–87	0.38	0.16	0.37	4.66%
1987–90[1]	0.00	0.45	0.52	5.76%
1992–97	1.27	0.47	0.29	2.99%

Note: 1. German short-term interest rate enters rule with long-run coefficient 1.11.

On the other hand, I did *not* find that periods of restrictive policy were necessarily characterised by a greater than unitary response of the nominal rate to inflation. Rather, policy tightenings were sometimes manifested in a sharp increase in the *average level* of the real interest rate. While long-run changes in the real rate tend to be due to changes in the economy's structure, monetary policy can influence the real rate heavily in the short run, due to inflation inertia. In particular, tighter monetary policy from 1979 contributed to a dramatic increase in the average real rate. The UK tightening was not reflected in an increase in the estimated inflation response, unlike the corresponding 1979 tightening in the US.

NOTES

* I am indebted to Christopher Adam, Alec Chrystal, David Cobham, Spencer Dale, Shamik Dhar, Charles Goodhart, Andrew Haldane, Paul Mizen, Glenn Rudebusch, Alison Stuart, John Taylor, Paul Tucker, and seminar participants at the Bank of England for helpful comments and suggestions. The views expressed in this chapter are the author's and should not be interpreted as reflecting those of the Bank of England or the Monetary Policy Committee.

1. Goodhart (1989) and Minford (1993) provide discussions of UK monetary policy covering the 1970s and 1980s. The pre-1970s period is discussed in Goodhart (1997).
2. Similarly, Muscatelli, Tirelli, and Trecroci (2002) present results for 1975–96, 1980–96, and 1985–96, and so do not consider the inflation targeting period separately. Adam, Cobham, and Girardin (2001) begin their study in 1985, so do not consider the 'Great Inflation' period of the 1970s or the early 1980s disinflation.
3. Post-1997 UK policy behaviour is analysed in Adam, Cobham, and Girardin (2001), Chevapatrakul, Mizen, and Kim (2001), and Martin and Milas (2001).
4. An early counterexample is McCallum (1981).
5. Chevapatrakul, Mizen, and Kim (2001) and Svensson (2001) criticize the value of Taylor rules due to the limited use they make of information.
6. See (for example) Henderson and McKibbin (1993) and the papers in Taylor (1999a).
7. For further discussion and references, see Goodhart (1997, pp. 399–400) and Nelson and Nikolov (2002).
8. Note that, since I divide the 1972–97 sample period into several regimes, the mean of the output gap measurement error can change across regimes without rendering inconsistent the estimated slope coefficients in the policy rules.
9. The actual interest rate used by the Bank of England as its instrument has varied over time, and has included Bank Rate (until September 1972), Minimum Lending Rate (1972–81), and the two-week repo rate (since 1996). The Treasury Bill rate has historically moved closely with these instruments, and is available for the entire sample period. For August 1992, the only month for which no observation on the bill rate is available, a value of 9.7 is used. This figure was obtained by assuming a 20 basis point spread above the 91-day rate (the 91-day rate was 20 basis points below the bill rate in both July and September 1992).
10. Quadratic detrending was also used in CGG (1998) and Peersman and Smets (1999). It would be desirable to construct an output gap series that takes into account stochastic variation in potential GDP. Such a procedure, however, may be vulnerable to misspecification of the production function and household preferences.
11. The broad money growth target for 1976/77 (initially for the M3 aggregate, later for £M3) was announced on 22 July 1976 (Bank of England, 1976, p. 296). The Conservative Government took office on 4 May 1979.
12. In Nelson (2000) I provide a more detailed presentation of the results, including the individual lag coefficients and experimentation with alternative horizons.
13. Over 1973–80, the Supplementary Special Deposits Scheme (the 'Corset') was periodically used as a quantitative control on the expansion of banks' balance sheets and therefore of the £M3 aggregate. However, it is likely that this device principally lowered the measured growth in £M3 artificially, without changing base money growth or interest rates, rather than genuinely restricting monetary conditions. The Bank of England (1982) acknowledged that the Corset 'tended to encourage the diversion of banking business into other channels'. See also Minford (1993, p. 423).
14. In keeping with this view, Sir Edward Heath has argued in his *Autobiography* that 'Our policy of expanding demand was essential to growth and employment and, therefore, broadly non-inflationary, on which basis inflation resulted largely from wage settlements' (Heath, 1998, p. 405).
15. The inclusion of regressors dated $t+1$ or later in principle introduces moving-average patterns into the equation's error term; however, autocorrelation in the estimated

residuals for these equations (as well as those for the other subsamples) does not appear to be significant.

16. The real-time output gap data come from Nelson and Nikolov (2001).
17. This statement refers only to the *fluctuations* in the gap series; it does not preclude the possibility that errors in the *mean* of the output gap led to policy mistakes.
18. Quarterly averages of this series have a correlation of 0.90 with the detrended output series over 1971 Q1–1998 Q4, and of 0.77 over 1976 Q3–1979 Q1.
19. See, for example, the accounts of this period in Goodhart (1989, p. 303; 1997, p. 408) and Minford (1993, pp. 409–12).
20. To check this, I added lagged annual £M3 growth relative to target as a regressor to (7.2), re-estimating over the period in which £M3 targeting was officially in force (1979 Q2–1985 Q3). The £M3 term had long-run coefficient 0.159, s.e. 0.114, with the other long-run coefficients $w_1 = 0.331$ (0.084) and $w_2 = 0.239$ (0.181), similar to the estimates in Table 7.3. One reason why £M3 growth does not enter is that policy-makers attempted £M3 control through overfunding, a technique designed, as discussed in Goodhart (1992), not to affect short-term nominal interest rates.
21. On monthly data from May 1979 to February 1987, the preferred IV estimates are:
$$R_t = \underset{(0.006)}{0.023} + \underset{(0.032)}{0.097}\, E_{t-1}\Delta_{12}p_t + \underset{(0.021)}{0.036}\, E_{t-1}\tilde{y}_t + \underset{(0.072)}{0.729}\, R_{t-1}.$$
Six lags of each variable plus a constant served as instruments. The long-run responses are $w_1 = 0.359$ (0.062), and $w_2 = 0.133$ (0.081).
22. The real-time data estimates of equation (7.2) in Table 7.3 are obtained from a regression of R_t^{end} on ${}_t\tilde{y}_{t-1}$, ${}_t\tilde{y}_{t-2}$, lags 1–2 of $\Delta_4 p_t$, and two lags of itself.
23. The 1987–88 period is distinguished by foreign exchange intervention by the UK authorities to stabilize the sterling/DM rate. But as Lawson (1992, p. 785) notes, this intervention was 'fully sterilized'. The intervention policy would thus not affect UK interest rates, and so is consistent with a constant interest rate rule for 1987–90.
24. Because the Nelson–Nikolov (2001) real-time output gap data are quarterly while the estimates in this section use monthly data, I do not estimate 1987–90 rules with real-time data. As documented in Stuart (1996), Nelson and Nikolov (2001), and elsewhere, errors in real-time UK GDP data were large in 1987–88. Stuart's (1996) Chart 4 suggests, however, that the real-time error is well approximated by one-sided mismeasurement of the level of the output gap – much like the 1970s real-time errors, which I found made little difference to UK reaction function estimates.
25. Adam, Cobham, and Girardin (2001) argue that US interest rates entered the UK monetary policy reaction function in the late 1980s. To test this, I re-estimated (7.5) adding the period t US federal funds rate as a regressor, with lags 1–4 of each variable and a constant as instruments. The long-run funds rate coefficient was insignificant (0.162, s.e. 0.211), while the long-run R^G coefficient was essentially unchanged (1.141, s.e. 0.170), as were the inflation and output gap coefficients.
26. On monthly data from October 1992 to April 1997, the preferred IV estimates are:
$$R_t = \underset{(0.005)}{0.007} + \underset{(0.263)}{0.620}\, E_{t-1}\Delta_{12}p_{t+3} + \underset{(0.031)}{0.127}\, E_{t-1}\tilde{y}_t + \underset{(0.091)}{0.579}\, R_{t-1}$$
Six lags of each variable and a constant served as instruments.

REFERENCES

Adam, Christopher, David Cobham, and Eric Girardin (2001), 'External influences and institutional constraints on UK monetary policy, 1985–2000', manuscript, University of St Andrews.

Bank of England (1976), 'Economic commentary', *Bank of England Quarterly Bulletin*, 16(3), 287–99.

Bank of England (1982), 'The supplementary special deposits scheme', *Bank of England Quarterly Bulletin*, 22(1), 74–85.
Barro, Robert J. (1977), 'Unanticipated money growth and unemployment in the United States', *American Economic Review*, 67(2), 101–15.
Broadbent, Ben (1996), 'Taylor rules and optimal rules', manuscript, UK Treasury.
Campbell, John (1993), 'U-turn: inflation', Chapter 26 of *Edward Heath: A Biography*, London: Jonathan Cape, pp. 468–83.
Chevapatrakul, Thanaset, Paul Mizen, and Tae-Hwan Kim (2001), 'Monetary policy: the predictive performance of Taylor rules versus alternatives for the United Kingdom, 1992–2001', manuscript, Nottingham University.
Clarida, Richard, Jordi Galí, and Mark Gertler (1998), 'Monetary policy rules in practice: some international evidence', *European Economic Review*, 42(6), 1033–67.
Clarida, Richard, Jordi Galí, and Mark Gertler (2000), 'Monetary policy rules and macroeconomic stability: evidence and some theory', *Quarterly Journal of Economics*, 115(1), 147–80.
Congdon, Tim (1992), *Reflections on Monetarism: Britain's Vain Search for a Successful Economic Strategy*, Cheltenham: Edward Elgar.
Goodhart, Charles A.E. (1987), 'Monetary policy: comment', in Rudiger Dornbusch and Richard Layard (eds), *The Performance of the British Economy*, New York: Oxford University Press, pp. 253–55.
Goodhart, Charles A.E. (1989), 'The conduct of monetary policy', *Economic Journal*, 99(396), 293–346.
Goodhart, Charles A.E. (1992), 'The objectives for, and conduct of, monetary policy in the 1990s', in Adrian Blundell-Wignall (ed.), *Inflation, Disinflation and Monetary Policy*, Sydney: Ambassador Press, pp. 315–34.
Goodhart, Charles A.E. (1997), 'Whither now?', *Banca Nazionale del Lavoro Quarterly Review*, 50(203), 385–430 reprinted in this volume with an extension as 'A central bank economist'.
Goodhart, Charles A.E., and R. J. Bhansali (1970), 'Political economy', *Political Studies*, 18(1), 43–106.
Governor of the Bank of England (2001), 'International and domestic uncertainties', *Bank of England Quarterly Bulletin*, 41(1), 125–8.
Heath, Edward (1998), *The Course of My Life: An Autobiography*, London: Hodder and Stoughton.
Henderson, Dale, and Warwick J. McKibbin (1993), 'A comparison of some basic monetary policy regimes for open economies: implications of different degrees of instrument adjustment and wage persistence', *Carnegie-Rochester Series on Public Policy*, 39(1), 221–318.
Ireland, Peter N. (2001), 'Endogenous money or sticky prices?', manuscript, Boston College.
Johnson, Harry G. (1972), 'The monetary approach to balance-of-payments theory', in Harry G. Johnson, *Further Essays in Monetary Economics*, London: George Allen and Unwin, pp. 229–49.
Judd, John P., and Glenn D. Rudebusch (1998), 'Taylor's rule and the Fed: 1970–1997', *Federal Reserve Bank of San Francisco Economic Review*, 74(3), 3–16.
Kaldor, Nicholas (1982), *The Scourge of Monetarism*, Oxford: Oxford University Press.
Lawson, Nigel (1992), *The View from No. 11*, London: Bantam.
Martin, Christopher, and Costas Milas (2001), 'Modelling monetary policy: inflation targeting in practice', manuscript, Brunel University.

McCallum, Bennett T. (1981), 'Price level determinacy with an interest rate policy rule and rational expectations', *Journal of Monetary Economics*, 8(3), 319–29.
Minford, Patrick (1993), 'Monetary policy in the other G-7 countries: the United Kingdom', in Michele U. Fratianni and Dominick Salvatore (eds), *Monetary Policy in Developed Economies (Handbook of Comparative Economic Policies, vol. 3)*, Westport, US: Greenwood Press, pp. 405–31.
Monetary Policy Committee (1999), 'The transmission mechanism of monetary policy', *Bank of England Quarterly Bulletin*, 39(2), 161–70.
Muscatelli, V. Anton, Patrizio Tirelli, and Carmine Trecroci (2002), 'Does institutional change really matter? Inflation targets, central bank reform and interest rate policy in the OECD countries', *Manchester School*, 70(4), 487–527.
Nelson, Edward (2000), 'UK monetary policy 1972–1997: a guide using Taylor rules', Bank of England Working Paper 120.
Nelson, Edward, and Kalin Nikolov (2001), 'UK inflation in the 1970s and 1980s: the role of output gap mismeasurement', CEPR Discussion Paper 2999.
Nelson, Edward, and Kalin Nikolov (2002), 'Monetary policy and stagflation in the UK', CEPR Discussion Paper No. 3458.
Orphanides, Athanasios (2002), 'The quest for prosperity without inflation', *Journal of Monetary Economics*, forthcoming.
Peersman, Gert, and Frank Smets (1999), 'The Taylor rule: a useful monetary policy benchmark for the euro area?', *International Finance*, 2(1), 85–116.
Poole, William (1970), 'Optimal choice of monetary policy instruments in a simple stochastic macro model', *Quarterly Journal of Economics*, 84(2), 197–216.
Smets, Frank, and Raf Wouters (2002), 'An estimated stochastic dynamic general equilibrium model of the euro area', ECB Working Paper No. 171.
Stuart, Alison (1996), 'Simple monetary policy rules', *Bank of England Quarterly Bulletin*, 36(3), 281–7.
Svensson, Lars E.O. (2001). 'What is wrong with Taylor rules? Using judgment in monetary policy through targeting rules', manuscript, Princeton University.
Taylor, John B. (1993), 'Discretion versus policy rules in practice', *Carnegie-Rochester Conference Series on Public Policy*, 39(1), 195–214.
Taylor, John B. (1999a) (ed.), *Monetary Policy Rules*, Chicago: University of Chicago Press.
Taylor, John B. (1999b), 'The robustness and efficiency of monetary policy rules as guidelines for interest rate setting by the European Central Bank', *Journal of Monetary Economics*, 43(3), 655–79.
Woodford, Michael (2001), 'The Taylor rule and optimal monetary policy', *American Economic Review (Papers and Proceedings)*, 91(1), 232–37.

Discussion of 'UK monetary policy, 1972–97: a guide using Taylor rules'

Paul Mizen

The focus of the chapter is the observation by Taylor (1993) that monetary policy setting relates to the short-term nominal interest rate not the growth of monetary aggregates, and that historically in the US, and for many other countries (c.f. Clarida, Galí and Gertler, 1998), the reaction function is a remarkably simple relation in three explanatory variables, the interest rate, the inflation rate and the gap between actual and potential output. In relation to this literature, Ed Nelson has put together an illuminating analysis of monetary policy that makes two very useful contributions to the literature.

First, the chapter illustrates that once again Charles Goodhart was a vital contributor to the development of a new research field, which in this case was the literature on policy reaction functions with the short-term nominal interest rate as the instrument. The chapter shows that in the late 1980s Goodhart was drawing on his experience within the Bank of England to bring monetary theory and analysis back towards the realities of monetary operations and practice. This entailed dispensing with the myths that monetary growth-based reaction functions and interest-rate targets were the basis for central bank policy. He explained that enlightened use of the interest rate had been addressed towards the intermediate targets of the day, whether they were growth rates of key monetary aggregates, the exchange rate, or inflation. Nelson's approach for the period before 1985 and after recognises that this was the case, and estimates separate reaction functions for each sub-sample accordingly.

The literature on interest-rate reaction functions has rightly been dominated by the name of John Taylor, but the desirability of a reaction function approach in central banking strategy with inflation as the main basis for feedback was put forward by Charles Goodhart before the article on Taylor rules was published. His approach did not include a direct role for the output gap, but presumably relied upon the knowledge that central bankers would be unlikely to act upon inflationary impulses without due reference to the balance of output in relation to capacity. The choice of inflation as the most important target was about to become the received wisdom, especially after the success of early inflation targeters. The *ex post* description of behaviour under this policy regime was to turn out to be similar if not identical to the interest-rate reaction functions described by Goodhart (1992) and Taylor (1993). Documenting the evidence in favour of Taylor rules in the inflation targeting period has been the empiricial contribution of this chapter.

Second, the chapter provides a careful and systematic analysis of the changing monetary policy regimes during the period 1972–97, blending economic commentary with econometric assessment. Nelson's approach differs from that taken by most previous authors, who took long samples of data over several monetary policy regimes (for example Broadbent: 1981–95; Clarida, Galí and Gertler: 1979–90; Adam, Cobham and Girardin: 1985–2000). The approach taken here has been to distinguish policy regimes and estimate the reaction functions separately for each sub-sample. This has some advantages since it allows regime-specific reaction functions to be estimated, and the coefficient estimates on the key explanatory variables to be interpreted more accurately. It also has some disadvantages in that the sample periods are often short, requiring the use of monthly rather than quarterly data to obtain a sufficient number of observations. The effect of adopting data at a monthly frequency is to introduce greater instability to the estimates of the coefficients in the reaction function as key choice parameters such as the forward-looking horizon are varied, and to obtain a higher coefficient estimate on the lagged interest rate (the smoothing parameter). The use of industrial production data rather than detrended GDP may also be part of the reason for these differences, particularly during the late 1970s when industrial disruption was a significant factor in the UK. Together the instabilities in the estimates of the function questions the usefulness of the Taylor rule at this frequency. Recent work by Chevapatrakul et al. (2001) suggests that monthly estimates of Taylor rules for the UK are more unstable, and less useful predictors of rate changes within-sample and out-of-sample, even for periods when the quarterly data suggest the Taylor rule is an appropriate description of the reaction function, that is 1992–present.

The chapter raises some interesting questions as it reviews the preferred reaction functions for each of the monetary regimes in the UK experence over the last thirty years. It prompts us to ask whether the Taylor rule should be estimated for the full sample? Given the fact that, for sub-samples of data, the Taylor rule coefficients are recovered only when the equation is estimated for the final sample period 1992–97, Nelson's answer seems to be negative. This then raises the question of whether it is useful to compare the actual policy rate against the predictions from a Taylor rule for the full sample? If the preferred reaction function includes variables that the Taylor rule does not contain, and finds that Taylor's chosen variables have coefficients that are insignificantly different from zero then one has to maintain *a priori* that the Taylor rule is optimal compared to the policy rule in force at the time to draw any useful information from the comparison. If instead one maintains that the actual policy reaction function adapted to meet the chosen intermediate variable of the day is the best estimate of the rule in force, then the comparison with the Taylor rule reveals the impact on the short-term interest rate of choices over the intermediate variable and not comparisons of rates to an 'optimal' value.

For the 1990s the chosen intermediate variable was the inflation forecast and this has yielded an estimated reaction function that conforms to the Taylor rule. Nevertheless we might still ask whether Mervyn King was correct in making his observation (press release 10 February 1999) that the reaction function that the Taylor rule is an *ex post* estimate of what any sensible inflation-targeting central banker would do? Although the reaction function for 1992–97 is discussed in relatively little detail in this chapter, presumably because it conforms to the Taylor specification and is therefore allowed to speak for itself, there is reason to believe that it would provide little guidance as an *ex ante* rule if estimated by the Bank of England at the required monthly frequency (c.f. Chevapatrakul et al., 2001). In-sample and out-of-sample forecasts of the next change in the interest rate prove to be remarkably static (opting for no change) compared to alternative reaction functions that embed other data that policy-makers on the Monetary Policy Committee would have access to on a routine basis. The answer to this final question suggests that even if the message of Nelson's chapter is that the Taylor rule is an accurate description of the policy reaction function under inflation targeting, it is still not particularly useful to a central bank intent on finding a guide to the future.

This is a fine chapter and a useful one for those interested in recent monetary policy experience in the United Kingdom. The chapter shows that the Taylor rule appears to be an acceptable description of events *ex post* for the period 1992–97 but has some limitations during the period prior to inflation targeting. Other reaction functions were in force at that time and perform better in describing events than the Taylor rule. I for one remain sceptical about the usefulness of the Taylor rule *ex ante* for policy-making, but few people are seriously suggesting that we should dispense with the services of Monetary Policy Committee members like Charles Goodhart in favour of a mechanical rule!

REFERENCES

Adam, Christopher, David Cobham, and Eric Girardin (2001), 'External influences and institutional constraints on UK monetary policy, 1985–2000', manuscript, University of St Andrews.

Broadbent, Ben (1996), 'Taylor rules and optimal rules', manuscript, UK Treasury.

Chevapatrakul, Thanaset, Paul Mizen, and Tae-Hwan Kim (2001), 'Using rules to make monetary policy: the predictive performance of Taylor rules versus alternatives for the United Kingdom, 1992–2001', manuscript, Nottingham University.

Clarida, Richard, Jordi Galí, and Mark Gertler (1998), 'Monetary policy rules in practice: some international evidence', *European Economic Review*, 42(6), 1033–67.

Goodhart, Charles A.E. (1992), 'The objectives for, and conduct of, monetary policy in the 1990s', in Adrian Blundell-Wignall (ed.), *Inflation, Disinflation and Monetary Policy*, Sydney: Ambassador Press, pp. 315–34.

Taylor, John B. (1993), 'Discretion versus policy rules in practice', *Carnegie-Rochester Conference Series on Public Policy*, 39(1), 195–214.

8. Goodhart's Law: its origins, meaning and implications for monetary policy

Alec Chrystal and Paul Mizen[1]

1. INTRODUCTION

Many distinguished economists have their name associated with some theory, concept or tool in economics. Obvious examples include: Giffen goods, the Pigou effect, Nash equilibrium, the Coase theorem, the Phillips curve, the Rybczynski and Stolper–Samuelson theorems, Ricardian equivalence, the Engle curve, the Edgeworth–Bowley box, Tobin's q, and the Lucas critique. However, very few economists are honoured by having their name associated with a 'law'. Charles Goodhart joins Sir Thomas Gresham, Leon Walras, and Jean-Baptiste Say in a very select club.

In this chapter we explain Goodhart's Law and the context in which it arose, and discuss whether it has the qualities that will help it survive over time. Mainly this requires that it can be adapted to new circumstances as the world changes. Gresham's Law, for example, was invented to describe the problems that arose from the artificial fixing of gold and silver prices but it turned out to have applicability to a wider range of monetary regimes wherever currency substitution was possible. Dollarisation in Equador, and other countries, would be a contemporary example of 'good money drives out bad'.

We shall focus particularly closely on the comparison between Goodhart's Law and the enormously influential Lucas Critique. It could be argued that Goodhart's Law and the Lucas Critique are essentially the same thing. If they are, Robert Lucas almost certainly said it first. However, while both Goodhart's Law and the Lucas Critique relate to the instability of aggregate macroeconomic relationships, we shall argue that there are significant differences. In particular, while the Lucas Critique has affected macroeconomic methods in general, Goodhart's Law has been more influential in monetary policy design – monetary targets are out and inflation targets are in.

2. WHAT IS GOODHART'S LAW AND HOW DID IT ARISE?

The original statement of Goodhart's Law can be found in one of two papers delivered by Charles to a conference in July 1975 at the Reserve Bank of Australia (RBA) (Goodhart, 1975a, b).[2] It reached a wider audience when the key paper was published in a volume edited by Courakis (1981) and then again in a volume of Charles' own papers (Goodhart, 1984). The context is very clear, but since the statement of the law was a (jocular) aside rather than the main point of the paper, the interpretation is open to some questions.

Throughout the post-WWII period up until 1971, sterling had been pegged to the US dollar (with major devaluations in 1949 and 1967) and monetary policy was dominated by this constraint. Exchange controls were in place and the main clearing (commercial) banks were subject to various direct controls on their balance sheet expansion. In August 1971, however, the US closed the gold window and temporarily floated the dollar. There was a short-term patch-up of the pegged rate system under the Smithsonian Agreement of December 1971, but sterling floated unilaterally from June 1972. Some alternative to the dollar as nominal anchor and some guiding principles for monetary policy in the new regime were needed.

Goodhart (1975a) outlines how research originating from the Bank and that of outside academics had indicated that there was a stable money demand function in the UK. The implication of this finding for monetary policy was deemed to be that the relationship could be used to control monetary growth via the setting of short-term interest rates, without resort to quantitative restrictions. The relevant section of the key paper reads as follows:

> The econometric evidence seemed to suggest that, one way or another, whether by restraining bank borrowing or by encouraging non-bank debt sales, higher interest rates did lead to lower monetary growth. In one fell swoop, therefore, these demand-for-money equations appeared to promise:
> (1) that monetary policy would be effective;
> (2) that an 'appropriate' policy could be chosen and monitored;
> (3) that the 'appropriate' level of the monetary aggregates could be achieved by market operations to vary the level of interest rates.
>
> . . . these findings, which accorded well with the temper of the times, helped to lead us beyond a mere temporary suspension of bank ceilings towards a more general reassessment of monetary policy. The main conclusions of this were that the chief intermediate objectives of monetary policy should be the rates of growth of the monetary aggregates, i.e. the money stock, in one or other of its various definitions, or DCE (and not particular components of these, such as

> bank lending to the private sector), and that the main control instrument for achieving these objectives should be the general price mechanism (i.e.. movements in interest rates) within a freely competitive financial system. (Goodhart, 1975a, p. 5)

The 'competition and credit control' reforms, which removed direct controls on bank lending, had been introduced in September 1971 and a dramatic surge in bank intermediation, leading to broad money growth rates in excess of 25 per cent, had resulted in 1972 and 1973. The conclusion drawn by policy-makers in 1973 was that the only option was to supplement monetary targets with direct controls on banks through Supplementary Special Deposits known as 'the Corset' (see Zawadzki, 1981). Modest interest rate changes seemed powerless in the face of this monetary expansion and the previously stable money demand function seemed to have broken down. This was clear well before 1975, but Goodhart (1975b) was a summary of the current problems of monetary management, as the title suggests.

Goodhart's Law is the statement missing from the square brackets in the quotation above. It says: 'Ignoring Goodhart's law, that any observed statistical regularity will tend to collapse once pressure is placed upon it for control purposes'. This makes the observation that previously estimated relationships (especially between the nominal interest rate and the nominal money stock–item (3) in the full quote above) had broken down. But as we shall see below this does not necessarily have any implications for the stability or otherwise of the demand function for real money balances, even though this was how the law was later interpreted.

The proximate meaning of the law is clear. Bank economists thought that they could achieve a particular rate of growth of the money stock by inverting the money demand equation that had existed under a different regime. But in the 1971–73 period this did not work, as it appeared that the old relationship had broken down. The 'law' states that this will always happen when policy-makers use such statistically-estimated relationships as the basis for policy rules.

The 1974–79 Labour Government introduced monetary targets, but they continued to attempt to hit them by means of direct controls in the form of the 'Corset'. When the Conservative administration of Margaret Thatcher took over as the UK government in 1979, monetary policy took a new turn. Chancellor of the Exchequer, Geoffrey Howe, labelled by his predecessor Denis Healey as a 'believing monetarist', attempted to target the growth rate of the money supply (£M3) by use of the official interest rate, after exchange controls were abolished in October 1979 and the Corset then became impossible to maintain. Targets were set for £M3 (broad money excluding balances in foreign currency) to lie in the range 7–11 per cent for the period 1980–81 falling by 1 per cent per annum to 4–8 per cent by 1983–84. In the event, however, money growth overshot its target by 100 per cent in the first two-and-a-half years. The abolition of exchange controls and the Corset (and the financial innovations that followed) meant that the relationship between broad money and nominal incomes fundamentally altered (see Goodhart, 1989).

Although it was becoming apparent by 1982 that the velocity trend had changed, partly because the relaxation of credit controls and exchange controls had redirected much foreign business back through the British banking system, Nigel Lawson, the new Chancellor appointed in 1983, reasserted his confidence in monetary targeting by publishing further growth targets often for several years ahead. The Medium Term Financial Strategy was largely unsuccessful, however (at least in controlling money growth), and this led to the conclusion that monetary targeting of all types was flawed. It was dropped in the summer of 1985 in favour of exchange rate shadowing.

Not only was the link from the policy interest rate to money unstable but so also was the link from (broad) money to aggregate demand. Monetary stability seemed (in some people's view) to be achievable by a fixed exchange rate in which the money supply was endogenous rather than by a money targeting policy. We return later to the issue of whether 'money' should have an active role in monetary policy. At this stage we just note the irony that Charles Goodhart is probably one of the few UK economists who does think that money matters and yet his law was repeatedly quoted in the 1980s to support the case for ignoring money entirely, or at least for monetary targets having no explicit role in monetary policy. We shall show some evidence on why this was the case in the next section.

A number of observations on the context in which the law arose are now appropriate. First, it should not have been too surprising, even at the time (1971–73), that removal of direct quantitative controls would lead to a surge of bank intermediation and that some adjustment period would follow. That this happened is not in itself evidence that the demand for money is in any sense unstable. Indeed, as Artis and Lewis (1984) have pointed out (and we revisit their results below), subsequent adjustments to prices, output and interest rates did return money balances relative to nominal GDP to their long-run relationship by the second half of the 1970s. The supply shock of a new operating procedure and abolition of credit rationing caused agents to acquire excess nominal money balances, but these were rapidly eliminated in the standard textbook fashion by bidding up goods and property prices – the 25 per cent plus money growth in 1972–73 led to 25 per cent plus inflation in 1974–75. Equally, the abolition of the Corset in 1980 could have been expected to lead to a surge of broad money growth in the early 1980s. That this surge happened at a time when the economy was heading into a sharp recession and inflation was falling in no way proves that money does not matter . . . it just indicates that it is not the only thing that matters.

Far from Goodhart's Law having an immediate impact on policy in the mid-1970s, events persuaded even politicians that money mattered and that money growth needed to be controlled in order to avoid excessive inflation.[3] Goodhart's Law only really came into its own as an influence on policy in the early 1980s when, following abolition of the Corset, broad money growth again surged. But, as noted above, this time the rapid growth of broad money coincided with a sharp recession and a decline in inflation, so the usefulness of monetary targets came into serious question. Simultaneously the financial markets experienced a period of deregulation and product innovation that altered the conventional role for money as a non-interest-bearing asset. Explicit targets were eventually dropped.

The second observation is that, notwithstanding the general loss of interest in money during the 1980s, there is plenty of evidence that there remains a plausible and stable long-run money demand relationship. Once allowances are made for the types of financial innovation that occurred in the 1980s, such as the introduction of interest-bearing current accounts and money market mutual funds, and some distinction is allowed between retail and wholesale balances the money demand function returns to normality. Were we to use a Divisia measure of money we would find that the correction for the effects of financial innovation would restore the stable money demand function, which is in any event evident using standard simple-sum aggregates within specific sectors, if not at the aggregate level.[4]

The third observation is that, while the apparent breakdown of the money demand relationship that led to the original statement of Goodhart's Law persuaded the authorities to return to the use of direct controls, there is a plausible interpretation of Goodhart's Law that would imply that such controls will not work for long. For example, let us suppose that over some period it were shown that the growth rate of broad money (M4) was a good leading indicator of inflation, so that the authorities decided to control the growth rate of banks' deposit liabilities by the fiat imposition of quantitative ceilings. Without other measures to control aggregate demand, the previously existing statistical relationship between broad money and inflation would be expected to shift as other channels of intermediation evolved, bypassing the distortions to the financial system. Indeed, this is exactly what happened in the second half of the 1970s, even though Goodhart's Law was intended to apply to the prior period when direct controls were absent. £M3 was controlled directly because that had been correlated with inflation (with a lag), but inflation picked up anyway and the controls were unsustainable once exchange controls were abolished. In many ways this is a better example of a statistical relationship breaking down when 'pressure was put on for control purposes' than the 1971–73 episode which spawned the original statement.[5]

A fourth and final observation at this stage is to note that, while there is plenty of recent evidence of stable money demand functions, it could be argued that this is only true because monetary authorities are no longer 'putting pressure on this particular statistical relationship for control purposes'. The focus on inflation targeting has killed off interest in stable (or otherwise) money demand functions. We are not aware of anyone having tested Goodhart's Law by comparing the stability of money demand functions in money-targeting countries with those in non-money-targeting countries. Whether stable money demand functions led to monetary targeting or the other way round is difficult to determine. The argument is always circular and counterproductive to the process of getting a fair test, because countries with the most stable money demand relationships are more likely to choose monetary targeting as a policy objective. But there is no evidence of which we are aware to suggest that monetary-targeting countries have *more* unstable money demand functions than others. Schmid (1998) argues that the Bundesbank's success can be attributed to the dominance of the universal banking system, and the low inflation environment that gave no incentive for banks to develop new financial instruments. Without significant deregulation and liberalisation of financial markets that had taken place elsewhere, German monetary policy was presented with fewer challenges because the basic financial relationships, including the money demand function, were essentially reliable.

3. THE ARTIS AND LEWIS RIPOSTE

In this section we re-examine the Artis and Lewis (1984) analysis with an updated data set. We calculate the inverse of velocity of circulation of money, using a measure of annual broad money defined by the Capie and Webber (1985) data series for £M3 spliced onto the official series for M2 (also known as 'retail M4') from 1982. The aggregate income series is based on national income up to 1948 and official GDP at market prices thereafter.[6] Plotting the resulting velocity series against the Consol rate (see Figure 8.1) shows that the money demand function (estimated over the period 1920–2000 excluding the data points for the years 1973–77) is remarkably stable. The fitted regression line is drawn in black. The regression line estimated by Ordinary Least Squares is:

$$\log(M/Y) = \underset{(0.046)}{0.305} - \underset{(0.026)}{0.538} \log(R) + \text{dummies}$$

R-squared = 0.852 ; F(5,75) = 86.327 [0.0000]
Standard error of equation = 0.103225; Durbin Watson 0.372; N = 81

This compares favourably to Artis and Lewis' estimate over 1920–1981 of

$$\log(M/Y) = \underset{(0.046)}{4.717} - \underset{(0.028)}{0.536} \log(R) + \text{dummies}$$

R-squared = 0.88; N = 58

Our regression line is remarkably similar in slope to the previous study, although the intercept differs due to the fact that our data series are scaled differently. As with the Artis and Lewis paper we can observe the disequilibrium period in the early 1970s on Figure 8.1 (which was removed using dummy variables before estimating the regression line).[7] The breakdown of the demand for money function is apparent during the period preceding the creation of Goodhart's Law, although the relationship quickly re-established itself

We now repeat this exercise but this time using the official M4 series instead of M2. The outcome gives a very clear illustration of why Goodhart's Law was widely quoted in the 1980s as being the explanation of why monetary targeting was inappropriate. Here we calculate inverse velocity using a monetary aggregate based on Capie and Webber's data up to 1963 then splicing with M4 to the present,[8] divided by the same income measure as before. We plot this against the Consol rate in Figure 8.2. The estimate of the regression line is calculated using a similar method and is compared to the data points. From 1982 onwards we can see a steady increase in the ratio of money to income for a given interest rate, which represents the effect of financial innovation. As the broader components of money included in M4 (but not in M2 and thus held mainly by firms and other financial corporations (OFCs)) offered more competitive rates of interest and/or sterling wholesale financial activity increased, so the stock of M4 increased relative to income. The set of data points clearly represents a different money demand function for the 1980s and 1990s which has shifted to the right, even though the demand function for retail deposits (M2) was broadly unchanged.

This shift we would argue is probably little to do with the use of M4 as a targeted aggregate but rather is the product of financial liberalisation and the rapid growth of wholesale money markets in London. In the Loughborough Lecture, the then Governor of the Bank of England, Robin Leigh-Pemberton (1986), identified the behaviour of financial intermediaries

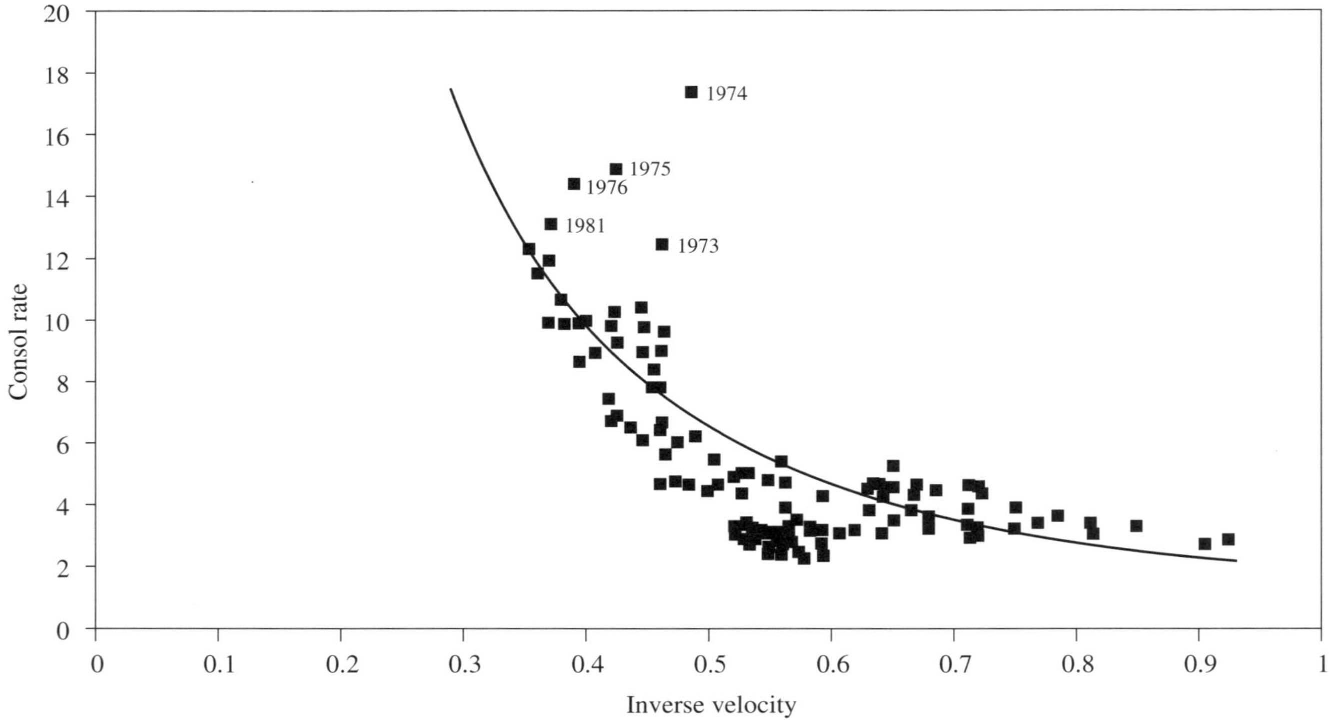

Figure 8.1 *Deviations from long-run money demand: 1973–81*

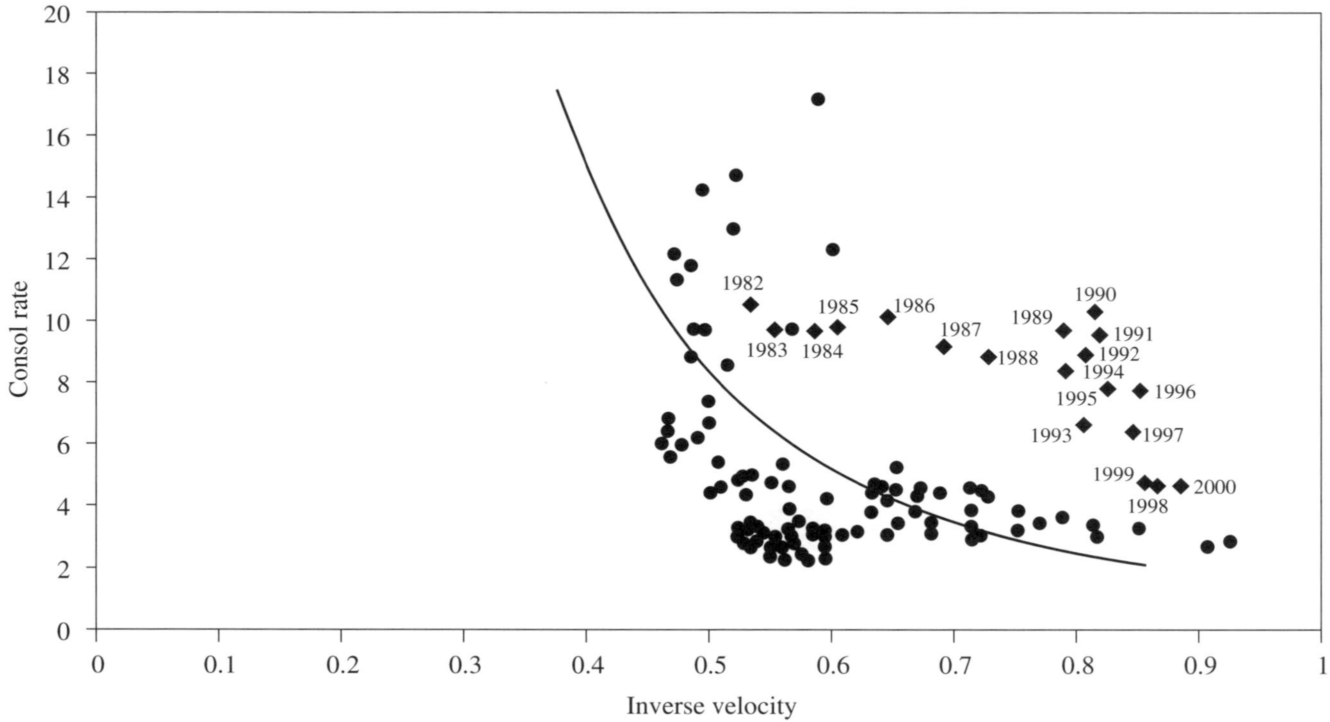

Figure 8.2 Deviations from long-run money demand: 1982–2000

(banks and building societies) and other financial intermediaries (OFIs such as securities dealers, investment institutions, and leasing companies, and so on) as largely responsible. Deregulation of the banking sector, and the removal of foreign exchange controls in 1979, encouraged banks to look for funds in the wholesale markets rather than from its retail-deposit base. OFIs increased both sides of their balance sheets from 1980, contributing considerably to the growth in broad money under much the same influences as the banks, with whom they were engaged in closer competition in existing and newly-developed markets as financial markets were liberalised. Together these factors increased the wholesale component of money balances in relation to income as revealed by a comparison of Figures 8.1 and 8.2.

4. GOODHART'S LAW AND THE LUCAS CRITIQUE

Goodhart's Law (1975) predates the publication of the Lucas Critique (1976), but the Lucas paper was presented at a Carnegie-Rochester conference in April 1973 and circulated more widely prior to publication (Savin and Whitman, 1992) so, if Goodhart's Law and the Lucas Critique are the same thing, Lucas said it first. What is reasonably clear is that both statements were arrived at independently and at a time when there were many big shocks hitting major economies – namely the general move to floating exchange rates in 1973 and the oil price shock. The question we address in this section is whether Goodhart's Law and the Lucas Critique could be different faces of the same coin.

Before we assess the relation between Goodhart's Law and the Lucas Critique we must consider earlier contributions by Heisenberg and Haavelmo. Heisenberg introduced a concept of invariance known as the Heisenberg Uncertainty Principle. This states, in the context of quantum physics, that the observation of a system fundamentally disturbs it. Hence, the process of observing an electron, which requires that a photon of light should bounce off it and pass through a microscope to the eye, alters the characteristics of the physical environment being observed because the impact of the proton on the electron will change its momentum. A system cannot be observed without a change to the system itself being introduced.

Perhaps an even more relevant and long-running literature is that in social science that discusses the problems of research on social interactions where both the observation of behaviour and the public reporting of it can change the behaviour observed. It is not just that people behave differently when they know that they are being watched, but also their belief systems can change when they later read what has been written about them. In a very clear sense, the intervention of researchers can change the nature of the relationships being studied.

Haavelmo (1944) offered observations on the problem of invariance applied to economics in his article 'The probability approach in econometrics'. The invariance issue is illustrated by the problem an engineer faces in attempting to record the relationship between use of the throttle and the speed of a car. Although he may observe that this relationship appears to be well defined for a level track under uniform conditions, it will alter when the conditions are allowed to vary. Nevertheless, there will be some conditions that are invariant even if other aspects of the environment change; examples include the physical laws describing gravitation, thermodynamics and so on. Haavelmo considered that there are degrees of 'autonomy' that define how likely it is that a relationship will vary with variation in the other conditions of the experiment. Physical laws are 'autonomous' in the sense that they do not change, but other relationships such as the relation between throttle and speed are variant or 'non-autonomous' to differing degrees. Autonomous relations have properties that appear to be laws, but non-autonomous relations do not.

In the field of economics, decisions of the private sector determine the state of the economic system, but the public sector, in the process of choosing and implementing policy actions, has an effect on the system itself such that the system is not invariant under different policy actions (or rules). Both Lucas and Goodhart have made the point in different contexts that modellers need to take into account the invariance (or lack of it) of each part of the model to variations elsewhere in the system.

The Lucas Critique takes this point and applies it to econometric modelling. Different policy-making behaviour influences the expectations of private agents and this changes behaviour in a rational-expectations model. The limitation of modelling exercises as a guide to policy arises from the fact that models typically do not allow for the impact of policy changes on the model itself. Lucas defines the evolution of the economy in the stylised form of the following equation

$$y_{t+1} = F(y_t, x_t, \theta, \varepsilon_t) \qquad (8.1)$$

where y_{t+1} is a vector of state variables, x_t is a vector of exogenously determined variables, θ is a vector of parameters to be estimated and ε_t is a vector of shocks; F is the functional form relating the state variables to their past, to exogenous variables and to shocks. The estimated relationships in the form of decision rules, technological relations and accounting identities are assumed to be immutable functions (F) with fixed parameter values (θ). If this were true, different settings the policy variables would generate different time paths for the exogenous variables, x_t, which could be compared and evaluated using some loss function.

The Lucas Critique notes that the historical conditions under which the model was estimated would *not* be invariant under different policy regimes and that the functional forms and parameter values will necessarily vary with different policy choices. If the policies were set using the known function $G(\cdot)$ of a vector of the state variable, a vector of parameters and a vector of shocks:

$$x_t = G(y_t, \lambda, \eta_t) \tag{8.2}$$

then the economy would generate the following sequence:

$$y_{t+1} = F(y_t, x_t, \theta(\lambda), \varepsilon_t) \tag{8.3}$$

such that the parameters of the model would be a function of the parameters of the policy-making process. Far from evaluating the implications of different policies using the historically estimated model (8.1) with F and θ, the consequences should be modelled using the policy rule (8.2) and response (8.3), which is dependent on the policy parameters chosen for (8.2). Hence Lucas and Sargent (1981) concluded that '. . . [historically-estimated policy invariant] econometric models are of *no* use in guiding policy'.

It is apparent from this analysis that the Lucas Critique is a statement about economic modelling and policy evaluation. It is a statement by a theorist about methodology of economic enquiry. The Critique makes statements about the inappropriateness of modelling an economy *as if* the structure were invariant across policy regimes, because expectations about policy choices will feed back to the crucial equations estimated in the model. Lucas proposes a remedy, through the development of the rational expectations literature and the related VAR modelling, a method that either uncovers the deep parameters of behavioural equations, or restricts itself to modelling the implementation of existing rules for fixed policy regimes in such a way that historically estimated models are not distorted (see Savin and Whitman, 1992). All of this is purely methodological, and refers to the way that modelling ought to be done.

The Lucas Critique develops a variation on the identification problem in econometrics, where the true structure of a system of economic relationships is unobservable from the available data because there are no independent variables to identify the individual equations. Economic models are described in such a way that policy choices and exogenous variables influence the future value of state variables, but the Lucas Critique reminds the modeller that even the structure and parameters of the model can change with different policy choices. Despite Haavelmo's prior claim to define the identification problem in the context of the invariance problem, Hoover (1994) indicates the significance of Lucas' work in a neat summary that notes 'Lucas was not the first to recognise the invariance problem explicitly, his own important contribution to it is to observe that one of the relations frequently omitted from putative causal representations is that of the formation of expectations' (p. 69).

So where does Goodhart's Law fit into this methodological setting? Is it just a variation of the insights of Haavalmo and Lucas? Goodhart's Law, as the discussion above has illustrated, arose in the context of a specific monetary control problem. In this sense, the Law is an application of the invariance problem to a particular institutional, monetary phenomenon. The observation arises from the performance of a 'statistical regularity', but lays down implications that follow from the application of policy based on these apparent regularities, rather than the guiding principles for econometric models. Nevertheless the idea is closely linked to the Lucas Critique by Goodhart himself,[9] and Goodhart in jest refers to his Law as a 'mixture of the Lucas Critique and Murphy's law' (p. 377).[10]

The distinctive feature of Goodhart's Law is its institutional application. The context is that of policy-making by the monetary authorities, for example the government or a delegated, and possibly independent, central bank, and the understanding of the channels of the monetary transmission mechanism. Although many of these channels operate through accounting identities, which are true by definition, some are based on statistical relationships, which can and do change. The Law observes that, although a statistical relationship may have the appearance of a 'regularity' by dint of its stability over a period of time, it has a tendency to break down when it ceases to be an *ex post* observation of related variables (given private sector behaviour) and becomes instead an *ex ante* rule for monetary control purposes. When stated in this way it becomes apparent that the essential feature of the Lucas Critique (and the more general problem of researchers' interventions in social science) – the lack of invariance of the system to the modeller/observer's interventions – is central to Goodhart's Law. Within the context of the monetary transmission mechanism, whenever the authorities attempt to exploit an observed regularity, the pattern of private sector behaviour will change as it observes that the authorities have begun to treat a variable that was previously an indicator of the policy stance (through some statistically defined relationship) as an intermediate target or objective of policy for control purposes.

A further distinctive feature of Goodhart's Law is that, whereas the Lucas Critique applies to changes in private sector behaviour induced by policy changes, Goodhart's Law in focusing on institutions of policy-making can induce other changes in public sector behaviour as well. For example, a government that has set itself the constraint of a monetary target may resort to hitting this target by means of changing its own fiscal behaviour. This change in fiscal stance will itself lead to further changes in private sector behaviour which reinforce the change in underlying statistical relationships. Thus Goodhart's Law is not just about directly induced changes in private sector behaviour. It is also about implications affecting other policy areas within the public sector, which then have yet further impacts on the private sector.

Goodhart's Law has been closely tied to the breakdown of the demand for money function. In part this is because the context in which Goodhart's Law first emerged, as the previous section has emphasised, was in relation to the poor performance of the demand for money function in the early 1970s. The breakdown of the relationship between interest rates and money growth (and perhaps also of the relationship between money and nominal incomes) was the basis for the original RBA paper published in 1975, as direct controls were relaxed and then replaced by the 'Corset', leading to unexpected behavioural changes by the banks. The link has also been supported by the fact that the most familiar application of the Law is given by the analysis of the 'monetarist experiment' of the Medium Term Financial Strategy in the early 1980s. Here the decision to use monetary aggregates as intermediate targets for policy-making in the United Kingdom coincided with a reversal in the velocity trend for broad money (£M3), which had not been anticipated. The assumption that the relationship between nominal incomes and money would be re-established was to prove unfounded (at least for aggregate M4) and the onset of financial innovations during the 1980s again altered the behaviour of the banking system and the public at large that further undermined any statistical basis for monetary targeting.

In discussion of the implications of changes in policy rules for the estimation of interest and income elasticities in the money demand function, Gordon (1984) shows that instability in the money demand function may be induced by policy changes such as the switch from interest rate to monetary base targeting. This is cited with approval by Goodhart in his discussion of the monetary targeting experiences in the US and the UK.[11] It is little wonder that Goodhart's Law has been associated so closely with money demand functions, but this is only one of its many applications.

5. THE LONG ARM OF THE LAW

Goodhart's Law is not only about the demand for money. In general application it refers to any 'statistical regularity', which is relied upon 'for control purposes', it is therefore equally applicable to a range of other behavioural statistical relationships. We could take the recent interest in the Taylor rule, for example. Some authors have considered that it should be treated as more than an estimate of the policy reaction function, and should be used as a guide for policy (Taylor, 2001). Others have evaluated the estimated function to explore its feasibility in this respect (Clarida et al. 1998; Nelson, 2000, and Orphanides, 2001).[12] We shall consider some of the issues relating to this point in this section.

The Taylor rule might be thought of as the present day equivalent of the 'stable' money demand of the 1970s. Proposed by John Taylor (1993), the Taylor rule has emerged as a simple but robust estimate of the monetary policy rule operated by a range of central banks. Clearly the rule has some major advantages in that it is simple, depends on only three variables that require data that are relatively easy to collect, and it provides a timely indicator of the instrument setting given inflation and output. Above all it seems to be able to explain the past history of monetary policy setting, particularly in the United States, but increasingly also for other G7 countries, following the taming of inflation by independent central banks using inflation targets (compare Clarida et al., 1998). While minor changes such as forward versus backward looking behaviour and closed versus open economy characteristics offer minor improvements, the basic rule appears remarkably robust (Taylor 2000, 2001). But how robust would this rule remain, with its parameter values of 1.5 on inflation and 0.5 on the output gap, if the relationship were to be used for control purposes?

The point where Goodhart's Law becomes relevant is when this 'statistical regularity' ceases to be an *ex post* summary of central bank behaviour (an estimate of the reaction function) in the context of flexible exchange rates, independent central banks and inflation targeting, but is adopted as a policy rule 'for control purposes'. In this guise the rule is liable to break down the moment a central bank decides to use the Taylor rule as the *ex ante* determinant of interest rate changes. But no central bank has chosen to set interest rates according to the Taylor rule criterion alone, so it is difficult to make an evaluation of the robustness on these grounds. Attempts to determine the robustness of the rule have therefore amounted to tests of the properties of the rule under different model assumptions (for example backward versus forward-looking models, closed versus open economy specifications and so on). In this respect the rule performs very well indeed (see Taylor 2000, 2001 for a review), but we are interested in whether the use of the rule for control purposes might alter its properties. The question is whether the rule would be reliable as a simple policy rule for *ex ante* rate setting. We can make some observations even in the absence of any evidence from its use for control purposes.

Ben McCallum (2000) has argued that if the Taylor rule is valid then we can arm a 'clerk with a calculator' in place of a monetary policy-maker. Svensson (2001) for one has argued that this is a dangerous step to take since a simple policy rule like the Taylor rule is an inappropriate description of current policy-making. The inflation forecast targeting approach adopted by most independent central banks is better understood as a commitment to a targeting rule. This is more than an instrument rule since the whole monetary regime is defined by the targeting rule and the instrument rule is only implied. The reaction function for the solved out system is model-specific, and allows for any extra-model information useful for meeting the objective and allows for judgment on the part of policy-makers. It is not a fixed-coefficient policy rule with an invariant relationship between a small group of variables. This would suggest that monetary policy should not be executed by clerks but by experts with relevant experience.

Sims (2001), in a review of Taylor's book *Monetary Policy Rules* (1999a), questions the lack of attention to the fit of the monetary policy rule and the 'uncritical acceptance of the notion that there has been clear improvement in monetary policy'. The Rudebusch–Svensson (1999) backward-looking model does not reject parameter stability even though monetary policy behaviour has not been stable during periods of the sample in the United States. Sims notes that there had been a major change to the Fed's operating procedures during the period October 1979–December 1982 yet this does not violate the Chow test for parameter stability when conducted (by Sims) on the full sample 1961:1–1996:2. This is explained by the fact that the differences in the interest rate behaviour 'are well within the range of sampling error'. While the finding is used by Sims to question the uncritical assumption that monetary policy-making has improved, it also shows that the Taylor rule may act as a stable summary of central bank behaviour even during periods when monetary policy-making is far from stable and changes to actual operating procedures induce considerable interest rate volatility. One of the more surprising results from the literature on Taylor rules is the stability of the parameter values *ex post*. The notion that the parameter values generated by Taylor's simulation exercise on US data should be so widely applicable to historical regimes reported by Taylor (1999b) or a range of monetary policy operating procedures is startling.

Consistent parameter values may not be the basis for good performance in setting rates, however. The performance of the Taylor rule as a predictor of the next rate change has been evaluated in-sample and out-of-sample in recent work by Chavapatrakul, Mizen and Kim (2001). There are three main conclusions that emerge from the paper. The first is that the Taylor rule, for all its durability at the quarterly frequency over a range of industrialised countries, does not emerge as a robust relationship at the monthly frequency with which UK monetary authorities set interest rates. Only for a very specific three-month horizon, with a quadratically-detrended output series, can the Taylor rule be replicated over the sample 1992–2001. More worryingly, the Taylor rule predicts base rate changes reasonably accurately within-sample, but it does so because the main prediction is 'no change' and this occurs about 70 per cent of the time. It has the same accuracy in forecasting as a stopped clock, which can also be right some of the time (twice a day). Out-of-sample, the same result holds, and alternative wider-information sets dominate the rule. This suggests that irrespective of whether the rule would remain robust to the decision to change its use for control purposes, its performance is inferior in rate setting compared to quite simple alternatives, let alone committee members who exercise judgement.

Of course, if central banks were very successful in applying a policy rule to offset shocks accurately, then the Taylor rule would certainly break down as a description of policy. This is because activity would be maintained at potential output and inflation would be exactly on target. Official interest rate changes would be unrelated to the output gap and deviations from the inflation target. Rather they would be closely related to the shocks that policy had been required to offset.

However, as Mervyn King has noted, there is certainly a great deal of common sense in the Taylor rule in retrospect in a world in which central banks cannot identify and offset shocks ex ante. 'Central banks that have been successful appear ex post to have been following a Taylor rule even if they had never heard of that concept when they were actually making decisions' (*Inflation Report* press briefing, 10 February 1999). Any sensible central banker should change interest rates in response to projected deviations of inflation from target and widening output gaps. However the difference between the use of the rule as a summary of past behaviour and as a predictor of future behaviour is considerable. Goodhart's Law suggests that a change in the use of the rule would tend to undermine the dependability of the statistical regularity. Fortunately no central banker has succumbed to the temptation to take this satisfactory *ex post* relationship between the short-term interest rate, inflation and output deviations from trend and attempt to use is as an *ex ante* guide for monetary policy-making, so perhaps the statistical regularity is safe.

6. WIDER IMPLICATIONS FOR MONETARY POLICY-MAKING

Goodhart's Law identifies the problem for monetary policy-makers as the unreliability of any statistical regularity that is subsequently used for control purposes. The question this raises is whether it dooms all statistical regularities to fail. Otmar Issing has reflected on this and concludes: 'If this theorem [Goodhart's Law] were generally valid, which Goodhart himself definitely does not claim, central bank policy would be faced by an additional and virtually insurmountable difficulty.' In a reversal of the logic generally applied to Goodhart's Law he then argues that, far from undermining the case for monetary targets, 'The vicious circle posited by Goodhart's Law can under certain preconditions be broken in the case of monetary targeting. By pursuing a steadfastly stability-oriented policy, the central bank can establish an anchor for inflation expectations and positively influence the stability of money demand' (Issing, 1997). Thus, he argues that a monetary target, perhaps acting as a twin pillar in an inflation targeting strategy, can pin down inflation expectations and establish the money demand function as a stable statistical relationship. The failure in the past was over reliance on the stability of the money demand function for the implementation of monetary policy. Issing's point is that the stable money demand function is an outcome of a credible monetary framework that embeds a monetary target or reference value, and whose focus is inflation expectations.

But was the problem to do with the particular choice of statistical relationship on which to depend? If we had chosen a different empirical regularity would we have faced the same problem? This is a question of the choice of instruments and targets. The historical record shows that the interest rate–money–output–inflation nexus was unstable and therefore the choice of money as an intermediate variable was an unfortunate one. Recent monetary thinking has taken the short-term interest rate as the instrument and the forecast of future inflation as the ultimate objective. This may be a better choice simply because there are many channels of transmission through which the interest rate can influence future inflation (see Bank of England, 1999), but also because inflation is the ultimate objective and not an intermediate target.

On the other hand monetary policy may have been more successful over the 1990s because we have abandoned 'statistical regularities' altogether 'for control purposes'. This is potentially where reliance on a simple policy rule for monetary policy setting rather than a targeting rule could upset the achievements that have been made. The development in the literature of robust, forward-looking rules takes us further from the simplest equations, and increasingly towards approaches that build in judgment and other information relevant to the policy-maker.

If the use of intermediate variables is always flawed then it is important for the ECB to assert that its monetary pillar is not intended as a target as such but rather as an anchor to inflation expectations over the medium term (see Issing, 1997; Issing et al., 2001). The role for central banks has been known for some time to be one of 'teaching by doing' in the realm of monetary policy. Artis et al. (1998) explain this point with the phrase 'do what you say and say what you do'. The influence of the policymaker should be positive: explaining the process and the outcomes ensures that the public builds trust in the independent central bank as a monetary institution. The gains from this trust are demonstrable in theory and in practice.

We have come some way from the circumstance in which the central bank takes the world as given and fails to recognise the importance of shaping expectations. Goodhart's Law, in as much as it resembles the Lucas Critique in the monetary policy sphere, is consistent with the implication that failure to recognise the importance of expectations over behavioural relationships will result in failure. The name of the game in the 1990s and beyond is to attach the public's expectation of inflation to the inflation target. Central banks are now in the business of shaping expectations rather than ignoring them.

7. CONCLUSIONS

The conclusion we draw from this chapter is that Goodhart's Law has many parallels in the world of physics, econometrics and economic modelling, but it has a unique niche to itself in the field of monetary policy-making. The development of the ideas can be traced to the breakdown of the demand for money function during the 1970s, when monetary targeting was in vogue, but we have shown that its application does not stop there. The concept of relying on a simple statistical regularity for policy purposes applies equally to the Taylor rule and other simple policy rules as it does to the demand for money function. Central banks should avoid the temptations that these apparently stable relationships pose for policy-making, remembering that the very same case was made in the early 1970s for the demand for money function. The role for central banks in the 1990s and beyond is to explain monetary policy, removing the mystique, and focusing expectations of future inflation on the inflation target. The operation of monetary policy involves the use of short-term interest rates in the pursuit of the final objective of monetary policy, and involves many different lines of transmission with a thorough explanation of the process. The temptation to squeeze this complex set of relationships into a simple statistical regularity that can then be used to set policy will recur, but Goodhart's Law is a warning against it. None of this, of course, implies that central banks can safely ignore 'money', and we feel sure that Charles himself would not wish his Law to be quoted solely with that end in mind. Inflation is inevitably about one thing: the value of money.

NOTES

1. We are grateful for comments and suggestions from Christopher Allsopp, Michael Artis, Forrest Capie, Charles Goodhart, Andy Mullineux, Simon Price, Daniel Thornton, Peter Westaway and Geoffrey Wood.
2. The original papers were reproduced in Volume I of *Papers in Monetary Economics*, Reserve Bank of Australia, 1975 under the titles 'Monetary Relationships: A View from Threadneedle Street' and 'Problems of Monetary Management: The UK Experience'.
3. Not all were persuaded, however. Denis Healey, the UK Chancellor of the Exchequer, was sceptical of monetarist theories and monetary statistics. Raising doubts about the ability of economic forecasters to predict accurate ranges for monetary growth, he claimed to have decided to 'do for economic forecasters what the Boston Strangler did for door-to-door salesmen – to make them distrusted forever'. The statistics on which the forecasts were based were received several weeks after the end of month collection date and were prone to revisions, so that new vintages of the monetary numbers could tell quite different stories to the early data. Goodhart recalls his experiences in the Bank of England, discussing the data on monthly growth rates in relation to a five month moving average as a guide to the trend:

   > The standard deviation from the moving average is large in relation to the calculated values of that moving average. We receive the data several weeks after the monthly make-up date. The noise in the series is so loud that it takes us several months to discern a systematic trend with any confidence. . . . So the movements in the series, when the systematic trends can be interpreted, tell you where you have been, not necessarily where you are going. That at least is something. (Goodhart, 1989, pp. 112–13).
4. See for example Drake and Chrystal (1994) and (1997), and Drake, Chrystal and Binner (2000).
5. There is a prior claim to have named the re-adjustment of a previously stable statistical relationship, known as the Le Chatelier (1888) Principle. This states that if a constraint is made on a system at equilibrium the system will adjust to overcome the effect of this constraint.
6. A consistent M2 series is only available from 1982, and M3 cannot be used after the mid-1980s owing to building society conversions.
7. The series used in this regression are non-stationary, so to deal with the potential spurious regression problem we estimated the relationship using the Johansen procedure for the sample 1920–2000. We found evidence of a single cointegrating relationship with slightly smaller intercept and slope coefficients than the OLS estimates.
8. The official series for M4 starts in 1963, so we are using the longest run of this available.
9. Explaining the monetary targeting experiments in the US and the UK and the reasons for them, Goodhart notes 'What finally caused the exercises to be abandoned was not the rise in unemployment but the increasing instability and unpredictability of the key relationships between money, and nominal incomes. Was this an inevitable concomitant of the introduction of such new rules and control methods, or was it just happenstance? In part it was, I believe, such a concomitant illustrating again the power of the Lucas critique and Goodhart's Law in this field' (Goodhart, 1989, p. 377).

10. Citation of Goodhart's Law outside of the world of academics and policy-makers has tended to emphasise the similarities to Murphy's Law at the expense of the Lucas Critique, usually with the benefit of hindsight.
11. More recently the US demand for money relationship has been rehabilitated to some extent. Lown et al. (1999) have shown that the unusual growth of the M2 aggregate in the US, and hence the uncharacteristic behaviour of velocity, was largely due to the financial condition of depository institutions. Revisions to the data accounting for capital constrained banks and thrifts remove the anomaly in the demand for money function. Equally, Carlson et al. (2000) allowing for depository restructuring that led households to readjust their portfolios towards mutual funds deals with the velocity shift of the early 1990s. This also reinstates the stable broad money demand function. Ball (2001) has a simpler solution still. By extending the data set beyond the 1980s the instability in parameter values is removed and an income elasticity of 0.5 and a negative interest semi-elasticity is restored.
12. Note that a number of papers consider the predictions of the Taylor rule against the actual outturn using historical or real-time data to evaluate the policy not the rule. Examples include Taylor (1999b), Orphanides (2000) and Nelson (2000).

REFERENCES

Artis, M.J. and M.K. Lewis (1984), 'How unstable is the demand for money in the United Kingdom?' *Economica*, 51, 473–76.

Artis, MJ. and M.K. Lewis (1991), *Money in Britain*, London: Philip Allan.

Artis, M.J., P.D. Mizen and Z. Kontolemis (1998), 'What can the ECB Learn from the Experience of the Bank of England?', *Economic Journal*, 108, 1810–25.

Ball, L. (2001), 'Another look at long-run money demand', *Journal of Monetary Economics*, 47, 31–44.

Bank of England (1999), *The Transmission Mechanism of Monetary Policy*, London: Bank of England.

Capie, F. and A. Webber (1985), *A Monetary History of the United Kingdom, 1870–1982*, London and New York: Routledge.

Carlson, J.B., D.L. Hoffman, B.D. Keen and R. Rasche (2000), 'Results of a study of the stability of cointegrating relations comprised of broad monetary aggregates', *Journal ofMonetary Economics*, 46, 345–83.

Chavapatrakul, T., P.D. Mizen and T. Kim (2001), 'Using rules to make monetary policy: the predictive performance of Taylor Rule versus alternatives for the UK 1992–2001', mimeo, University of Nottingham.

Clarida, R., J. Galí and M. Gertler (1998), 'Monetary policy rules in practice: Some international evidence', *European Economic Review*, 42, 1033–67.

Courakis, A.S. (1981), *Inflation, Depression and Economic Policy in the West: Lessons from the 1970s*, Oxford: Blackwells.

Drake, L. and K.A. Chrystal (1994), 'Company sector money demand: new evidence on the existence of a stable long-run relationship', *Journal of Money Credit and Banking*, 26(3), 479–94.

Drake, L. and K.A. Chrystal (1997), 'Personal sector money demand in the UK', *Oxford Economic Papers*, 49(1), 188–206.

Drake, L., K.A. Chrystal and J.M. Binner (2000), 'Weighted monetary aggregates for the UK', in M.T. Belongia and J.M. Binner (eds), *Divisia Monetary Aggregates: Theory and Practice*, Basingstoke: Palgrave.

Goodhart, C.A.E. (1975a), 'Monetary Relationships: A View from Threadneedle

Street' in *Papers in Monetary Economics*, Volume 1, Reserve Bank of Australia.
Goodhart, C.A.E. (1975b), 'Problems of Monetary Management: The UK Experience', in *Papers in Monetary Economics*, Volume 1, Reserve Bank of Australia, July (RD.LIB P332.5(063)d), available from RBA.
Goodhart, C.A.E. (1984), *Monetary Theory and Practice*, Basingstoke: Macmillan.
Goodhart, C.A.E. (1989), *Money, Information and Uncertainty*, Basingstoke: Macmillan.
Haavelmo, T. (1944), 'The probability approach in econometrics', *Econometrica.*
Hoover, K.D. (1994), 'Econometrics as observation: the Lucas critique and the nature of econometric inference', *Journal of Economic Methodology*, 1, 65–80.
Issing, O. (1997), 'Monetary Theory as the Basis for Monetary Policy: Reflections of a Central Banker', http://www.international.se/issingitaly.
Issing, O., V. Gaspar, A. Angeloni and O. Tristani (2001), *Monetary Policy in the Euro Area*, Cambridge: Cambridge University Press.
Le Chatelier (1888), *Annales des Mines*, 13(2), 157.
Leigh-Pemberton, R. (1986), 'Financial change and broad money', *Bank of England Quarterly Bulletin*, December, 499–507.
Lewis, M.K. and P.D. Mizen (2001), *Monetary Economics*, Oxford University Press.
Lown, C.S., S. Peristiani and K.J Robinson (1999), 'What was behind the M2 breakdown', FIS Working Papers, 2–99, Federal Reserve Bank of New York, August 1999.
Lucas, R.E., Jnr and T.J. Sargent (1981), *Rational Expectations and Economic Practice*, London: Allen and Unwin.
McCallum, B.T. (2000), 'The present and future of monetary policy rules', *NBER Working Paper No. W7916.*
Mizen, P.D. (1994), *Buffer Stock Models and the Demand for Money*, Basingstoke: Macmillan.
Nelson, E. (2000), 'UK monetary policy 1972–97: a guide using Taylor Rules', Bank of England Working Paper No. 120, July.
Orphanides, A. (2000), 'Activist Stabilization Policy and Inflation: The Taylor rule in the 1970s', FEDS working paper 2000–13, Board of Governors of the Federal Reserve System, Washington DC, February 2000.
Orphanides, A. (2001), 'Monetary policy rules based on real-time data', *American Economic Review*, 91(4), 964–85.
Rudebsuch, G.D. and L.E.O. Svensson (1999), 'Policy Rules for Inflation Targeting', in J.B. Taylor (ed.) *Monetary Policy Rules*, NBER, Chicago: Chicago University Press.
Savin, N.E. and C.H. Whitman (1992), 'Lucas critique', *New Palgrave Dictionary of Money and Finance*, Murray, Milgate and Eatwell (eds), Basingstoke: Palgrave.
Sims, C.A. (2001), 'Review of *Monetary Policy Rules*', *Journal of Economic Literature*, 39, 562–66.
Schmid, P. (1998), 'Monetary policy: targets and instruments', in S.F. Frowen and R. Pringle (eds), *Inside the Bundesbank*, Basingstoke: Macmillan.
Svensson, L.E.O. (2001), 'What is wrong with Taylor rules? Using judgement in monetary policy through targeting rules', http://www.iies.su.se/leosven/papers/JEL.pdf.
Taylor, J.B. (1993), 'Discretion versus policy rules in practice', *Carnegie-Rochester Conference Series on Public Policy*, 39, 195–214.

Taylor, J.B. (1999a), *Monetary Policy Rules*, NBER, Chicago: Chicago University Press.
Taylor, J.B. (1999b), 'A historical analysis of monetary policy rules', in *Monetary Policy Rules*, NBER, Chicago: Chicago University Press.
Taylor, J.B. (2000), 'Alternative views of the monetary transmission mechanism: what difference do they make for monetary policy?', *Oxford Review of Economic Policy*, 16, 60–73.
Taylor, J.B. (2001), 'The role of the exchange rate in monetary-policy rules', *American Economic Review Papers and Proceedings*, 91, 263–67.
Zawadzki, K.K.F. (1981), *Competition and Credit Control*, Oxford: Blackwell.

Discussion of 'Goodhart's Law: its origins, meaning and implications for monetary policy'

Charles Goodhart

While I am grateful to Alec Chrystal and Paul Mizen for their paper, nonetheless I feel that they treat the subject with more respect than it really deserves. It was, after all, only a throw-away line, but it is no doubt better to be remembered for a jest, than not at all. And it does have some merits.

One of the events that I best remember in the Bank was towards the end of 1973, when broad money, sterling M3 as it was then, was growing at a rate that was causing all kinds of public, political and press commentary, and problems. The request came down from the Prime Minister that we in the Bank were to control the rate of growth of the money stock, but we were to do so in a way that did *not* involve any increase in interest rates. Moreover, the Bank had recently, in 1971, introduced the new regime of 'Competition and Credit Control' whereby, with exclamations of self congratulation, we removed all the direct controls, the quantitative ceilings on bank lending. So what were we going to do? Anyhow John Fforde left this particular problem in my lap, and I came up with the 'Corset', which was just sufficiently complicated and based on incremental changes in interest-bearing (eligible) liabilities (IBELs), so that it was not immediately apparent to everyone that this was just another rather fancy quantitative direct credit control. But, anyhow, that was the way that money stock growth was controlled in part in 1974–75, and then it was used again at the end of the 1970s.

We had another of these kinds of wheezes for monetary control in the mid 1980s. This one was not primarily my own invention; at least I cannot remember it being mine. This was the over-funding exercise. Now the point of this digression, in relation to what Alec and Paul have written, is that when those in charge, in this case the monetary authorities, put enormous weight on a particular statistic, then the authorities may well change their own behaviour, as well as that of the private sector. The Lucas Critique is about the authorities changing their regime, and then the private sector reacts and adjusts. What I like to think is a tiny bit of added value of Goodhart's Law is that in such cases, when the authorities put a great deal of weight on a particular statistic, they are quite likely to behave in a way that will actually distort that statistic, in order to keep it close to the politically determined objective. Such distortion is almost, by definition, bound to lead to a change in the observed relationships; the public sector changes its own behaviour, as well as the private sector.

Another of the events which I recall well relates to the abandonment of monetary targets in the UK in the late 1980s. I was against monetary targets of the kind that the Conservative Government, and Mrs Thatcher, brought in when they came to power in 1979; and for the same kind of reasons that Lars Svensson has argued. The reason basically is that the ultimate objective that you want to try to control is inflation. If you do this through an intermediate target, where the relationship is uncertain, all that you will effectively add will be the noise in the demand for money function, and, therefore, it must be less efficient than going straight to an inflation target. So I was perfectly content when the government abandoned its emphasis on sterling M3. What shocked me then, and continues to disturb me, is that a government, and some key members of that government (and I would include Nigel Lawson here), who had previously put enormous weight on the argument that what was essentially needed, and the only thing that was needed, and the key to control of the economy, was to control aggregate sterling M3, then reversed course completely to the extent of ignoring monetary data altogether. When they decided that £M3 no longer should be the target, then in about two years they were ignoring it entirely; it was given zero weight and zero attention. While I agree that, because of the inevitability of various behavioural changes (for example of the kind that I have already mentioned), and of uncertainty due to innovation, and so on, you cannot see for sure what is happening simply by looking at any single monetary aggregate, equally the idea that there is *no* information in the monetary aggregates, and that there is *nothing* to be gained from examining and interpreting them is entirely wrong.

It is true that, when a central bank sets interest rates, money is, therefore, in some sense, not a complete sense, but in some sense, endogenous. When the authorities set interest rates, which is, of course, what we always do, that means that the monetary base becomes an endogenous variable; the banks can have as much monetary base as they want at that given rate. But the monetary aggregates are not *completely* endogenous, because shifts in the banks' keenness to make loans, changes in risk appetite, changes in their own liquidity preferences, changes due to shifts in regulatory capital, and so on, will have effects on the growth of money and credit. So, for any given interest rate and current developments in incomes and other factors, there will be changes in both credit and money, different from those expected on the basis of demand for money functions. Those 'residuals' (relative to the demand for money function given by the policy-determined interest rate and what is happening to income, and so on), need to be examined carefully to assess what they mean. Sometimes the Bank of England, and the Monetary Policy Committee, have decided that they do not mean very much. That was the case, for example, in response to what were massive shifts in the Other Financial Intermediaries' deposit balances (which quite frankly baffled the MPC and baffled me, and I had not seen any decent analysis, or even a description of what was going on in this instance, until Alec and Paul wrote a Bank of England Working Paper on this subject in December 2001). But in other cases, and at other times, the information from the monetary aggregates is important, and indeed can be crucial. If I was in Japan now, I would consider what is happening to bank credit to the private sector and to M2 almost my most important statistical guide. Especially with interest rates stuck close to zero, it is extremely important to see what is happening to the banking system, in terms of where you think the economy is going to go in future. There are other cases where real interest rates are almost indecipherable, for example under hyperinflation and when one has little idea what inflationary expectations may be. Under those circumstances, one of your only guides is monetary, and credit, growth. It really was a profound shock for me when so many of those people who had said that 'the only guiding star of the world is to be M3', after they discovered that M3 was *not* a perfect guide, went on to behave as if, since it was not perfect, it was totally useless. Both positions were, of course, wrong. And that is all that I want to say about Goodhart's Law.

9. A cost of unified currency

Nobuhiro Kiyotaki and John Moore*

1. INTRODUCTION

Until recently, Charles and I (Kiyotaki) taught a graduate monetary economics course together. Charles usually taught first in the autumn, and then I taught in the spring. The course was a popular one. The students seemed both to enjoy and to get puzzled by the contrast between us, in content and style. When students put questions to Charles, he always had answers. When they put questions to me, I often had to ask myself, 'Do I know the answer?' This short chapter, written jointly with John Moore, is in part the result of such a question.

The question can be phrased: 'In a hypothetical world where there are no country-specific macroeconomic shocks and so no need for independent stabilization policy, is having a unified currency always better than having separate national currencies?' A standard argument for separate currencies is that each country can pursue an independent monetary policy for stabilizing its national economy (assuming that monetary policy can and should stabilize an economy). A usual argument for currency unification is that it stimulates the trade of goods, services and assets. Thus it looks obvious that, if there is no need for independent stabilization, a unified currency would be better. But is it so obvious? We would like to present a counter-example.

The environment we have in mind is a world with many types of goods and many types of people. Each person is specialized in producing one particular type of good, but consumes another type. No two people find each other's products attractive. And, because of trading frictions, there is no central marketplace at which multilateral trades can be arranged. Instead, people randomly meet in pairs: they have to trade bilaterally. In this situation, money is essential to overcome the lack of double coincidence of wants. People cannot barter goods for goods, but they can trade goods for money. Although people don't want money per se, they accept it because it can be used to buy what they do want.

In this world, there are two symmetric countries. Each type of good comes in three different varieties, and in each country, each type of person has the choice: either to make a 'local' variety of his type of production good, a variety that is attractive to some other type of person from his own country but not to anyone from the other country; or to make a 'generic' variety that is attractive to that other type irrespective of nationality, although (to someone from his own country) less attractive than the local variety.

To make our point most sharply, we ignore geography in the sense that we assume a person is equally likely to be matched with a 'foreigner' as with someone from 'home'. A priori, one might think that, without spatial differences between the countries (reflected in a bias towards meeting someone from one's own country), a unified currency would certainly dominate two national currencies.

Indeed, the recent literature on money in an international matching framework, which allows for spatial differences between countries, reaches the conclusion that having a unified currency is preferable to having multiple currencies, insofar as inferior equilibrium allocations that are possible with multiple currencies are ruled out with a uniform currency. See, for example: Matsuyama, Kiyotaki and Matsui (1993); Trejos and Wright (1996); Zhou (1997); Ravikumar and Wallace (2001). Of course, an equilibrium in which people treat the multiple currencies on a par mimics a unified currency equilibrium. So the set of equilibrium allocations with a unified currency is nested inside the set of equilibrium allocations with multiple currencies.[1] The question is: Are there any *desirable* equilibrium allocations which multiple currencies can achieve but which a unified currency cannot? These papers suggest that the answer is no.

However, these papers do not have people choosing the variety of good that they produce, as we have in mind: the choice of either producing a local variety or producing a generic variety. We find that once such a production choice is allowed for, a uniform currency may no longer be preferable. Specifically, we will show that for an open set of parameters:

1. With a unified currency, only generic varieties are produced (because they can be sold more quickly).
2. With two national currencies, there is an equilibrium in which only local varieties are produced (by making a generic variety a producer would increase the chance of acquiring foreign money, but foreign money could only be used to buy foreign local varieties that are unattractive to him).
3. The two-currency equilibrium in which local varieties are produced strictly Pareto dominates the equilibrium with a unified currency.

In brief, there is a cost to having a unified currency: it can lead to too little specialization.

2. MODEL

Time is discrete, and continues forever. There are $k \geq 3$ distinct types good at each date, all indivisible. And there are k types of a continuum of agents with equal population size. For each type of agent, $i = 1, 2, \ldots k$, half come from one country and half come from another. For each type of good, there are three varieties: two local varieties peculiar to the two countries; and one generic variety common to both countries. Type i agents derive utility h from consuming a unit of their local variety of type i good; they derive utility ℓ, where $0 < \ell < h$, from consuming a unit of the generic variety of type i good; and they derive zero utility from consuming any other good, including the variety of type i good peculiar to the other country.

Instantaneously after consuming either a local or a generic variety of type i good, type i agents can choose to produce exactly one unit of type $i + \ell$ good – either their local variety or the generic variety. (Type k agents produce type ℓ good.) An agent can produce, store and carry one unit of his product without cost. But he cannot produce without first consuming, and he cannot store anyone else's product.

In every period, all agents meet pairwise at random, and each agent's trading history is private information. Each agent maximizes his expected discounted utility with discount factor $1/(1+r)$, where $r > 0$ is the common subjective interest rate.

In addition to goods, there is perfectly storable fiat money in fixed aggregate supply. Money is indivisible and cannot be stored more than one unit at a time. At each date a proportion m of each type of agent from each country hold one unit of money, but no goods. Everyone else holds no money, but holds one unit of their production good (the variety depends on the previous production choice).

We consider two alternative monetary regimes:

Unified Currency: a single currency is held by money holders.
National Currencies: money holders hold currency that is peculiar to their country.

We focus on steady-state Nash equilibria in which: first, each agent chooses his strategies of trade, consumption and production to maximize his expected discounted utility, taking as given the strategies of the other agents and the inventory distribution of money and products across agents; second, the strategies and the inventory distribution are stationary.

We start by considering a unified currency equilibrium in which only generic varieties are produced. At the end of each period, let V_g and V_m denote the expected discounted utilities of, respectively, a goods holder (without money), and a money holder (without goods). The Bellman equations are:

$$V_g = \frac{1}{1+r}\left\{\frac{m}{k}V_m + \left(1 - \frac{m}{k}\right)V_g\right\} \tag{9.1}$$

$$V_m = \frac{1}{1+r}\left\{\frac{1-m}{k}\left(\ell + V_g\right) + \left(1 - \frac{1-m}{k}\right)V_m\right\} \tag{9.2}$$

Equation (9.1) says, with probability m/k, the goods holder next period meets a money holder who consumes his product, and hence there is trade: he switches from holding goods to holding money. With probability $1-(m/k)$, the goods holder does not meet a consumer of his product, or meets a consumer of his product who has no money; either way, there is no trade. Equation (9.2) says, with probability $(1-m)/k$, the money holder next period meets a person who holds his consumption good, and hence there is trade: he enjoys utility ℓ from consumption then instantaneously produces with a view to selling in future. With probability $1-[(1-m)/k]$, the money holder does not meet a producer of his consumption good, or meets a producer of his consumption good who already holds money; either way there is no trade.

Rewriting these equations, we have:

$$r\,V_g = \frac{m}{k}\,(V_m - V_g) \tag{9.3}$$

$$r\,V_m = \frac{1-m}{k}\,(\ell + V_g - V_m). \tag{9.4}$$

Equation (9.3) says the return on holding goods is equal to the expected gain from trading to become a money holder. Equation (9.4) says the return on holding money is the expected gain from trading to consume and then instantaneously producing to become a goods holder.

Solving (9.3) and (9.4) for V_g and V_m, we obtain:

$$r\,V_g = \frac{1-m}{k}\,\frac{m}{1+rk}\,\ell, \tag{9.5}$$

$$r\,V_m = \frac{1-m}{k}\,\frac{m+rk}{1+rk}\,\ell, \tag{9.6}$$

$$V_m - V_g = \frac{1-m}{1+rk}\,\ell. \tag{9.7}$$

From (9.7), we learn that $V_m > V_g$, so that a goods holder *is* willing to give up his product to acquire money. We also learn that $\ell + V_g > V_m$, so that a money holder *is* willing to give up money to acquire the generic variety of his consumption good.

To confirm that this is an equilibrium with a unified currency, we have to check that no-one strictly prefers to make the local variety rather than the generic variety of his product. But if a producer were to make a local variety, he would only be able to sell it to people from his own country, which would halve the probability of trade without increasing the price; at the end of the production period, his expected discounted utility, V'_g say, would be the solution to

$$r\,V'_g = \frac{m}{2k}\,(V_m - V'_g). \tag{9.8}$$

Comparing (9.3) and (9.8), we see that $V'_g < V_g$: no-one wants to produce a local variety in a unified currency equilibrium.

Next, we consider an equilibrium with two national currencies where only local varieties are produced. Because production is specialized to the local variety in each country, nothing is traded with foreigners. Each country's money circulates exclusively among the citizens of that country. In the absence of international trade, we call the equilibrium 'autarky', and denote it by a superscript a. (It is not proper autarky, of course, since there is trade among agents from the same country.) The equations corresponding to (9.3) and (9.4) are now:

$$r\,V^a_g = \frac{m}{2k}\,(V^a_m - V^a_g), \tag{9.9}$$

$$r\,V^a_m = \frac{1-m}{2k}\,(h + V^a_g - V^a_m). \tag{9.10}$$

Comparing (9.9) and (9.10) with (9.3) and (9.4), the differences are: first, since only half of all matches are between agents from the same country, the frequency of trade is halved; but second, the utility of consumption increases from ℓ to h. From (9.9) and (9.10) we have:

$$r\,V^a_g = \frac{1-m}{2k}\,\frac{m}{1+2rk}\,h, \tag{9.11}$$

$$r\,V^a_m = \frac{1-m}{2k}\,\frac{m+2rk}{1+2rk}\,h, \tag{9.12}$$

$$V^a_m - V^a_g = \frac{1-m}{1+2rk}\,h. \tag{9.13}$$

From (9.13), we learn that $V_g^a < V_m^a < h + V_g^a$, so that people *are* willing to engage in this trading pattern.

To confirm that autarky is an equilibrium with two national currencies, we have to check that no-one strictly prefers to make the generic variety rather than the local variety of his product. By producing one unit of the generic variety, an agent could, at best, sell it for one unit of home or foreign money, depending on the nationality of the person to whom he sold it. (He might not be able to sell it all, because potential customers would prefer to wait to spend their money on local varieties from which they derive higher utility.) But in a two-currency equilibrium, he could use foreign money only to buy varieties of goods that are local to foreigners – varieties that yield him no utility. That is, only home currency is valuable to him.[2] Moreover, he can be guaranteed of receiving home currency from his home customers if he produces their local variety. Therefore, at best, there is no benefit from switching to produce the generic variety (and there would be a loss if the generic variety weren't acceptable to his home customers).

To construct our counter-example, we need to identify when an autarky equilibrium in which only local varieties are produced (an equilibrium satisfying (9.11) and (9.12)) dominates an equilibrium in which only generic varieties are produced (an equilibrium satisfying (9.5) and (9.6)). Precisely, we pose the question in the following way. Suppose the difference between two currencies is only in their colour. Starting from the equilibrium with two national currencies, suppose that, immediately after consumption but before production, everyone became 'colour-blind' and in effect switched to the equilibrium with a unified currency. Under what circumstances would everyone be strictly worse off? This boils down to asking when would $V_g^a > V_g$ and $V_m^a > V_m$. From (9.5), (9.6), (9.11) and (9.12) we see that this happens if and only if

$$\frac{h}{\ell} > \frac{2(1+2rk)}{1+rk}. \tag{C1}$$

Condition (C1) says that if the utility of the local variety is high enough relative to the utility of the generic variety, then everyone is better off in a world in which only local varieties are produced – despite the fact that fewer trades occur, because a producer has to be matched with a consumer from his own country. From now on, let us assume that condition (Cl) holds.

As we discussed earlier, in a world with two currencies – here of different colour – there is always a colour-blind equilibrium which mimics a unified currency equilibrium allocation. To clinch our argument, we need to see if there are circumstances under which the reverse is not true, in that a unified currency equilibrium cannot mimic the *superior* autarky allocation of a two national currency equilibrium. Is it ever the case that two national currencies are *necessary* to implement the Pareto-dominating equilibrium allocation?

In a world with a unified currency, suppose only local varieties were produced, as in autarky. Then discounted utilities will be given by (9.11) and (9.12). To knock this out as an equilibrium, suppose that:

$$\ell + V_g^a > V_m^a. \tag{9.14}$$

Inequality (9.14) implies that if at some date an agent with money were to meet someone with a generic variety of his type of consumption good, he would be strictly better off trading then, rather than waiting for a local variety. But this implies that a producer could sell a unit of generic good for one unit of money to anyone who consumes his type of product, irrespective of their nationality. Hence it would be strictly better to produce the generic good than to produce the local good: the number of potential customers would be doubled, and there would be no drop in price. In short, if inequality (9.14) is satisfied, autarky cannot be implemented with a unified currency.

From (9.13), inequality (9.14) is equivalent to:

$$\frac{h}{\ell} < \frac{1 + 2rk}{1 - m}. \tag{C2}$$

Condition (C2) says that if the utility of the local variety is not too high relative to the utility of the generic variety, then money holders will be willing to seize an opportunity to buy a generic variety rather than wait for a local variety, which in turn takes away any incentive to produce local varieties.

Notice that conditions (Cl) and (C2) are compatible if and only if

$$m > \frac{1 - rk}{2} \tag{9.15}$$

Inequality (9.15) is not hard to satisfy. For example, it is automatically true if $k > 1/r$.

We have proved the following result.

PROPOSITION: Under conditions (Cl) and (C2):

1. With a unified currency, the only stationary monetary equilibrium has generic varieties produced and traded internationally.
2. With two national currencies, there is a stationary monetary equilibrium in which local varieties are produced and traded locally (autarky).
3. The autarky equilibrium with two national currencies strictly Pareto dominates the equilibrium with a unified currency.

3. DISCUSSION

How dependent is our counter-example on the peculiar assumptions that we have made concerning the indivisibility of goods and money, and the fact that agents cannot hold more than one unit of money at a time? In effect, we have robbed the model of price variation: all trades have to be one unit of good swapped for one unit of money. Given this, producers always have an incentive to increase the size of their market if they can. In particular, with a unified currency, producers strictly prefer to make a generic variety because it can be sold to twice as many customers, without any reduction in price.

Had price variation been possible, producers might be tempted, even with a unified currency, to make a local variety because it yields customers a higher utility and hence might be sold at a higher price.

In a Walrasian market, variations in price across products would elicit efficient production choices. However, in a Walrasian market, there would be no need for money.

By explicitly modelling trading frictions, we admit a role for money but at the same time distort relative prices and hence production choices. Our counter-example shows that in this non-first-best world, there can be a role for several currencies, to mitigate such distortions. In general, this conclusion is robust to allowing for variation in price by, for example, considering a model with divisible goods. We conjecture that our counter-example does not ultimately hinge on our assumptions about the indivisibility of money or the upper bound on individual money holdings. Loosely speaking, with more flexibility there will be a narrower set of parameters for which a counter-example can be found; but, provided there are still trading frictions, the set will stay non-empty.

We should end with a note of caution. Our analysis should not be used naively in a policy debate as an argument in favour of maintaining national currencies. All we have done is to find an example in which currency unification inhibits specialization: people are induced to produce generic varieties rather than local varieties. However, it must always be borne in mind that non-unification is likely to inhibit trade in all other goods. If the problem of a unified currency is too little specialization in certain goods, then, if feasible, this would be best remedied by a targeted policy – for example promoting the production of those goods – rather than by maintaining national currencies. The choice of currency may be too blunt an instrument, given that it affects every part of an economy.

NOTES

* We thank Kiminori Matsuyama and Neil Wallace for a stimulating discussion following a seminar presentation by Neil of his paper with B. Ravikumar, 'A Benefit of Uniform Currency'. Our choice of title reflects that discussion. We also thank Sudipto Bhattacharya for his thoughtful comments.

1. Other papers demonstrate a positive role for multiple currencies to create small change: see, for example, Aiyagari, Wallace and Wright (1996) and Cavalcanti (2000). But as Ravikumar and Wallace (2001) point out, this may be an artifact of assuming that money is indivisible and there is an upper bound on individual holdings. Kocherlakota and Krueger (1999) provide a different rationale for multiple currencies: to permit agents to signal private information about their preferences concerning the source, by country, of the goods to be consumed.
2. He cannot swap foreign money for home money in a currency exchange, because in equilibrium each country's citizens exclusively hold their own currency. No-one from his home country would accept foreign money.

REFERENCES

Aiyagari, S.R., N. Wallace and R. Wright (1996), 'Coexistence of Money and Interest-Bearing Securities', *Journal of Monetary Economics*, 37, 397–419.

Cavalcanti, R. (2000), 'The Color of Money', mimeo, Pennsylvania State University.

Kocherlakota, N. and T. Krueger (1999), 'A Signaling Model of Multiple Currencies', *Review of Economic Dynamics*, 2, 231–44.

Matsuyama, K., N. Kiyotaki and A. Matsui (1993), 'Toward a Theory of International Currency', *Review of Economic Studies*, 60, 283–307.

Ravikumar, B. and N. Wallace (2001), 'A Benefit of Uniform Currency', mimeo, Pennsylvania State University.

Trejos, A. and R. Wright (1996), 'Search-Theoretical Models of International Currency', *Review*, Federal Reserve Bank of St. Louis, May/June.

Zhou, R. (1997), 'Currency Exchange in a Random Search Model', *Review of Economic Studies*, 64, 289–310.

Discussion of 'A cost of unified currency'

Sudipto Bhattacharya*

It is always an enjoyable task to discuss a contribution by two colleagues as creative as John and Nobu, and this is especially so on the poignant occasion of a Festschrift in honour of Charles Goodhart, whose research has done so much to communicate European contributions on monetary and central banking issues to the world at large. This poignancy is only heightened by this paper, titled 'A cost of unified currency', being presented inside the auditorium of the Bank of England, around the time when the new euro currency is just coming into force across large swaths of the Continent and in Ireland. Both from a pragmatic as well as from a theoretical perspective, a rigorous scrutiny of seemingly facile arguments for the dominance of a unified medium of exchange should be welcomed. Modern models of trading processes with frictions ought to be subjected to the same kinds of robustness tests vis-à-vis their efficiency (and other properties) as was done for the classical Walrasian (and then Arrow–Debreu) models with incomplete markets, by eminent economists such as Oliver Hart (1975). In particular, it is imperative that the functioning of such trading processes be analysed under some degree of *ex ante* heterogeneity among agents in their tastes and/or endowments; in their chapter, Nobu Kiyotaki and John Moore have examined just such a scenario.

In the Kiyotaki–Moore (hereafter KM) model, agents trade with fiat money in the absence of any 'double coincidence of wants', for k types of goods produced by a continuum of agents of whom half come from one country and half from another. Each type i good has three varieties: a generic one yielding utility ℓ to all agents of type i, and two local varieties produced in country A (respectively B) yielding utility $h > \ell$ to type i agents in country A (respectively B) only and $0 < \ell$ to all other agents. A type i agent of either country can only produce a good of type $(i + \ell)$ of a generic variety, or of the local variety of that country. For simplicity it is assumed that, in between times of consumption, each such infinitely lived agent can instantaneously produce only one unit of its feasible good of chosen variety, and then wait to trade it for a single indivisible unit of the money that is relevant to purchase its own unit of consumption good, via a random matching process among all agents. All agents apply a discount factor $r > 0$ per period, and a good-holding agent trades in each such period with probability m/k, where m is the proportion of agents holding money, under a unified currency regime and with probability $m/2k$ under a national currency ('autarky') regime. In the latter regime, no agent gains by selling his good for a unit of foreign currency which he cannot use to buy his preferred consumption good, if the goods being produced in equilibrium are of the national varieties.

KM show that there exist parameter values such that (i) with national currencies an equilibrium of producing the local variety in (by producers of) each country exists, which (ii) Pareto-dominates the equilibrium payoffs from producing and trying to sell the generic variety everywhere, despite the lower probability of trading in each period, but (iii) such a 'specialised' outcome cannot be a Nash equilibrium with a single currency, because each individual producer is tempted to switch to the generic variety of its type of good in order to be more likely to trade per period. The condition for (ii), of strict Pareto-dominance of the 'autarkic' equilibrium, is

$$\ell/h < (1+rk)/\{2(1+2rk)\} < \tfrac{1}{2} \qquad \text{(C1)}$$

whereas the condition for (iii), of a strictly profitable deviation from the situation of h-goods production by all others with a single currency is written by KM as:

$$\ell/h > (1-m)/(1+2rk) \qquad \text{(C2)}$$

This is compatible with condition (C1) for $(1-m) < (1+rk)/2$, or $m > (1-rk)/2$, which is clearly satisfied for all $m > 0$ if $rk > 1$, implying large trading frictions, or for all $rk > 0$ if $m = \tfrac{1}{2}$, which is the level of m that maximises the *ex ante* expected utility over goods- and money-holders in all of these symmetric search equilibria.

These conditions are derived without assuming that the (specialised) equilibrium with national currencies entails any changes in the relative or absolute frequencies with which one meets foreigners from the other country: Marmite sellers from UK search for their countrymen in the polyglot crowd in Oslo, which contains Norwegians who prefer their goat cheese spread! This strains the matching interpretation of the trading mechanism, since currencies and trading restrictions usually pertain to their geographic locations (countries) rather than to the nature of the good being traded. More important, the condition (C2) for a profitable deviation from the specialised production outcomes with a single currency requires only that the trading partner of the deviant matched (by type) producer is better off by exchanging her unit of fiat money for a unit of the generic good, as compared to her expected payoff from waiting for the next match with a non-deviant producer of her preferred variety. This form of the condition, for a mutually beneficial trade off the equilibrium path (obviously so for the deviant), is clearly a by-product of the simplifying assumptions of only one indivisible unit of money being storable, or being tradable for one unit of any variety of the good being offered in trade. It may be argued that a more complete post-matching bargaining process on a type of good is needed to fix the terms of trade across money and goods. While the ramifications of doing so in equilibrium pertain largely to the determination of a nominal price level, or several prices across many currencies as in Trejos and Wright (1996, op. cit.), here we are solely concerned with providing some flexibility in the partitioning of the gains from trade off-equilibrium.

To this narrower end, one may postulate a technology of production whereby a buyer matched with a seller producing a good she did not expect to encounter in equilibrium may demand more units of the good in return for her indivisible unit of money. Under a simplifying assumption regarding the production technologies, a transaction that arises based on such demands may be viewed simply as a transfer of utility units from the seller to the buyer which results in their off-equilibrium post-trade value functions satisfying some applicable (Nash) bargaining model. One example of such a technology is the following: any local variety can be produced in only one unit per period without cost, whereas the utility cost of producing q units of a generic variety is given by the function $C(q) = \ell \text{ Max } \{q-1, 0\}$. Note that, since trade takes time and the future is discounted, no producer will gain by producing more than one unit of a generic good in an equilibrium with a single currency when others are producing only one unit. However, for a deviant from a conjectured single-currency equilibrium in which all others are producing local varieties, her matched buyer is likely to demand $q>1$ units for her money, so that the gains from trade relative to the ongoing options of waiting for future matches are split across the buyer and the seller in the same proportions as these would have been on trading in equilibrium. In other words, using the notation of the KM chapter and dropping the superscript 'a' for the local-variety allocation:

$$r\,k\;Vg\hat{} = m[Vm - Vg\hat{} - \ell(q-1)] \tag{1}$$

and

$$[\{\ell q + Vg - Vm\}/\{Vm - Vg\hat{} - \ell(q-1)\}] = [\{h + Vg - Vm\}/\{Vm - Vg\}] \tag{2}$$

where $Vg\hat{}$ is the value function of a (one-shot) deviant generic good producer.

Now, the condition (C1) for Pareto dominance of the local variety production and trade outcome remains unchanged, but that for the existence of a strictly profitable deviation from this strategy profile under a single currency, $Vg\hat{} > Vg$, represented in the condition (C2) above, changes as follows. As shown in the KM paper, for the local variety production and trading strategy profiles, agents' value functions are given in their equations (9.11) and (9.12) by:

$$Vg = [\{(1-m)\,m\}/\{2rk\,(1+2rk\}]\,h \qquad (3a)$$

for the non-deviant producer with good to sell, and

$$Vm = [\{(m+2rk)\,(1-m)\}/\{2rk\,(1+2rk)\}]\,h \qquad (3b)$$

implying

$$[Vm - Vg] = [\{2rk/m\}\;Vg] = [(1-m)/(1+2rk)]\,h \qquad (3c)$$

Using equations {(3a), (3b)} to substitute for $\{Vg,\ Vm\}$ in equations (1) and (2), one may calculate the values of $q > 1$, and hence of $Vg\hat{}$ for the deviant. We wish to determine if the condition required for the resulting $Vg\hat{}$ to (strictly) exceed Vg is consistent with the condition (C1) above.

To that end, we first add unity to each side of equation (2) to obtain that:

$$[\{Vg - Vg\hat{} + \ell\}/\{Vm - l(q-1) - Vg\hat{}\}] = [h/\{Vm - Vg\}] \qquad (2')$$

so that if $Vg\hat{} > Vg$ then it must be the case that

$$[\ell/h] > [\{Vm - \ell(q-1) - Vg\hat{}\}/\{Vm - Vg)] \qquad (4)$$

Substituting in the numerator and the denominator of the right-hand side of (4) from the equations (1) and (3c) respectively, we obtain that the condition for $Vg\hat{} > Vg$ is:

$$[\ell/h] > [\{(rk/m)\;Vg\hat{}\}/\{(2rk/m)\;Vg\}] > 1/2 \qquad (C2\hat{})$$

This *clearly contradicts the condition (C1) above*, thus implying that if the strategy profile of all agents producing local varieties, and trading with half of the matching frequency as compared to producing the generic varieties and trading these, yields a Pareto superior outcome, then it will also be a Nash equilibrium even under a single currency allowing unfettered trading between all pairs having strictly positive gains. Our assertion holds under a specific technology for producing more than one unit of the generic variety being available off the equilibrium path of unit production of the local varieties, and it is based on a Nash-type bargaining solution among the matched traders determining the sharing of the gains from trade between a buyer and a seller.

How is one to interpret this result, beyond it being just one of many 'robustness tests' that could be applied to assertions about the likely efficiencies of different currency regimes? On a 'positive', perhaps imperialistic, economic policy note, one might assert that the lesson of the Kiyotaki–Moore paper is a linguistic one, that even agents with tastes sharply biased towards local goods ought to learn the language of the other agents amongst whom they live/travel, well enough to carry out the alternating offers bargaining (see Binmore, Rubinstein and Wolinsky, 1986) that would allow them to thwart the potential-deviant foreigner peddling generic goods of lower utility. (One is tempted to mention the example of a disappointed Auslander in St Germain hoping for a large glass of Mosel, asking for 'drei' of a generic Orvieto and, on being told that it is 'nein' (dry that is), leaving disgusted with the silly bargaining antics of the locals!)

However, an alternative interpretation, one that diminishes the force of any critique or qualification implicit in this discussion, is at least as appealing. Perhaps Kiyotaki and Moore tie their hands too tightly by assuming that a national or single currency equilibrium in which a local-varieties production pattern might be sustained does not also lead to changes in the relative frequencies with which agents would meet their own country folk as opposed to foreigners. Indeed, if each agent literally consumes only one type of good as modelled, then in either of the local-varieties production equilibria above they ought to be doing their searching only in their own country, thus meeting agents from their own country twice as often as the KM model allows them to do in such an equilibrium. That would clearly affect the upper bound in the condition (C1); its right-hand side would now be unity! However, this is clearly an extreme case insofar as nobody would propose a unified currency unless there were gains to be had by trading across countries that could not be attained locally. Hence, a more complete comparison of the scenarios that KM wish to contrast may indeed require an explicit model incorporating (a) agents having convex preferences over both local and global types of goods, (b) costs of setting up currency exchanges charging bid-ask spreads or commissions, and (c) agents' meeting patterns that respond to the gains from trade they would achieve from trading with locals versus with foreigners. This intriguing and lucid paper of Kiyotaki and Moore may thus be pointing us towards a rich set of extensions of extant search-theoretic models of trading and price determination.

NOTE

* Instructive calculations carried out with Nobu Kiyotaki and helpful remarks from John Moore and Marcus Miller were both very useful.

REFERENCES

Binmore, K., A. Rubinstein and A. Wolinsky (1986), 'The Nash Bargaining Solution in Economic Modelling', *Rand Journal of Economics*, 17, 176–88.

Hart, O. (1975), 'On the Optimality of Equilibrium When the Market Structure is Incomplete', *Journal of Economic Theory*, 11, 418–43.

10. Money and the monetization of credit

Martin Shubik*

1. INTRODUCTION

> In Utopia all greed for money was entirely removed with the use of money. What a mass of troubles was then cut away! . . . Who does not know that fear, anxiety, worries, toils and sleepless nights will also perish at the same time as money? What is more, poverty, which alone money seemed to make poor, forthwith would itself dwindle and disappear if money were entirely done away with everywhere. (Thomas Moore, *Utopia*, Book II, p. 149)

What are the basic distinctions among a money, a near money and a money substitute? When is an individual's IOU note as good as cash? Under what circumstances can an economy get along without a governmental issue of money? What does the economy described in Saint Thomas Moore's *Utopia* have in common with the Arrow–Debreu treatment of the competitive economy?

Where does information, knowledge, 'know who' and expertise play a role in monetary economic theory? How accurate is our knowledge of individual wealth? When and how does it serve to back credit? What is credit and what role does it play in the functioning of markets?

The goal in this chapter is to consider and discuss these questions and to consider how a measure of the degree of monetization of the potential credit in any economy might be constructed. An attempt at mathematization is left for separate work, however, a simple example is presented in the Appendix and some crude statistics are presented in support of this approach.

Goodhart (1998) in a stimulating article discusses the very different approaches to the existence of money between the cartalists who stress the power of the state and those who stress the private sector (he chooses the appellation 'Mengerian') market-oriented response to minimizing transactions costs. It is my belief that both of these approaches have a large element of truth in the development of a government money and large institutional near-monies and credit facilities. The unifying theme is the role of networks and information combined with custom and law for enforcement.

2. MONEY, GOODS, MARKETS, PEOPLE AND MARKET MECHANISMS

> The Congress shall have Power To lay and collect Taxes . . .
> To borrow Money on the credit of the United States; . . .
> To coin Money, . . .
> To provide for the Punishment of counterfeiting the Securities and current coin of the United States;
> To establish Post Offices and Post Roads;
> (Excerpts from Article I of the Constitution of the United States)

The competitive equilibrium analysis of the price system concentrates on goods, individuals and firms as the primitive concepts with the endowment of goods given. The existence of an equilibrium set of prices is established. Total trust or a timeless trade is implicitly assumed. The strategic market game approach (Shubik, 1999) differs from that of the competitive equilibrium in the introduction of an explicit role for money and for markets as price formation mechanisms. The stress is on process, mechanism and a playable game. A playable game requires rules and the rules are a product of both custom and law.

A useful way to consider money, markets and market mechanisms is as follows. Represent any good or financial instrument by a point. An arc connecting any two points may be regarded as a market. At a finer level of detail there is a black box associated with each arc which contains a market mechanism which specifies precisely how a price is formed in that market. A commodity or paper financial instrument serves as a money if it has arcs which connect to all other points. Figures 10.1a, b, c and d illustrate an economy with 4 goods and 0, 1, 2 and 4 monies.

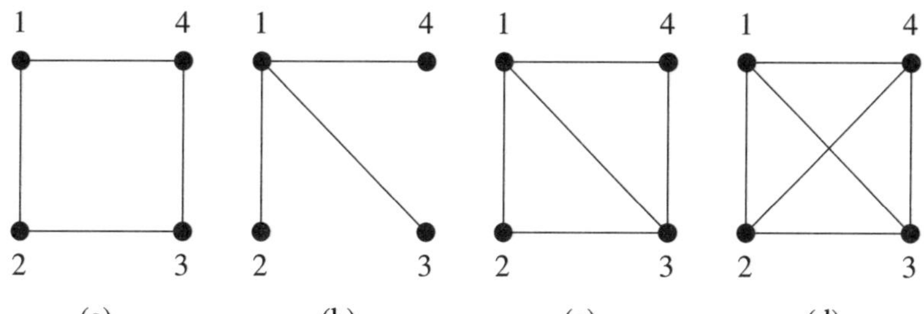

Figure 10.1 Monies and markets

The 'black box' contains the specific details of the market institutions and clearing devices. Thus, for example, details concerning whether a specific market utilizes a double auction mechanism and has a clearing house attached are in the black box. Dubey, Mas Colell and Shubik (1980) showed that with a continuum of agents the details concerning the specifics of mechanism could be ignored at equilibrium. When the continuous approximation to the finite number of agents cannot be justified, the mechanism matters.

When discussing the money supply the term 'near money' is often used to refer to a financial instrument which will be accepted as a means of payment in almost all transactions. Thus a cheque drawn on a well-known and reputable bank or a major credit card may serve as a near money.

A money substitute is an instrument such as a gasoline or department store credit card which substitutes in the short term (often 30 days) for a cash payment in a specific market.

A somewhat difficult question is how small a community can support a money. There are instances where prisoners have utilized cigarettes, or towns or special communes have issued their own currencies based on labour units or on redemption in the national currency. But they tend to depend on the specifics of the structure of the environment in which they are embedded and tend to be highly transient. In particular they tend to be special communities within and dependent on a larger ongoing society.[1]

3. CREDIT, INFORMATION AND NETWORKS

In essence all inside money is credit. Fiat money is an asset, a paper gold.[2] 'Credo' or 'I believe' is essential to the successful acceptance of any money or near money. Trust and belief are critical. In turn they depend on the social and individual evaluation of information leading to reputation. Information is highly influenced by three basic factors. They are: space, time and network connections and visibility.

Much of human behaviour is local both in time and space. The growth of communication methods have reinforced the importance of an information net connection which overcomes physical distance. Every individual has a 'know-who network'. In 1700 immigrants to the United States had friends and family in 'the old country' and to some extent were in contact with them by sea mail or by a rare ocean voyage. The telegraph, the telephone and now the web have radically changed the importance of space in message communication. In a less radical manner physical space has been shrunk by the railway, the automobile and the jet aircraft. Yet for much of day-to-day life physical distance is a critical consideration.

In travelling, for example, in spite of being able to see pictures of a hotel, or reproduction of a menu, this information is a poor substitute for knowing someone whose judgement you trust, who knows your tastes and has stayed frequently in the hotel and eaten at the restaurant in question. Locality both in space and time are still critical in the micro-economics of evaluation.

The influence of modern communication has, for many purposes, elevated the *network* to a level of importance on a par with space and time. In particular the network is emerging as a key feature in the financial world and in the evolution and evaluation of credit. For some purposes of communication the appropriate measure of distance is no longer a linear measure but the number of nodes in a communication net connecting *A* to *B*. In some instances the symmetry or lack of symmetry in the strength of the connection *A* to *B* or *B* to *A* may be of importance. A 'know-who net' between friends or family may tend to be symmetric. But the relationship between a government agency and a private citizen or between two individuals at different levels in a hierarchy is nonsymmetric.

A useful way to look at the individual is as an entity belonging to several different nets which serve different purposes, such as family, friends, professional, religious, economic and political. Depending on the stimulus and activity the individual agent's attention and activity switches among these nets. For the most part organizations are devoted primarily to only one of these purposes.

3.1 Fiduciaries, Intermediaries and Instruments

Most economic decisions are made by fiduciaries. The decisions are based on informal or formal group actions. Even most of consumer decisions are made by one member of the family buying for the family. Family saving (which can be regarded as passive lending) and family financial investment is heavily in mutual funds and pension funds where the individuals and families are passive investors having implicitly if not explicitly acknowledged their lack of competence in investing directly except in durables such as houses, automobiles and other consumer durables.

The intermediaries offer aggregation of funds, efficient transactions, expertise, and supervision of portfolios. Except for a small part of the saving population who are rich or sophisticated or both, the savers or 'passive investors' are served by mass market standardized financial products. The financially small investor may own a nonstandardized financial instrument if he invests in his brother-in-law's new firm or his close friend's business or if he is being hoodwinked into a fraudulent IPO.

When he or she procures a large loan such as a mortgage the homeowner signs a legal document more or less standardized by the state, but possibly adjusted by the lawyers and 'personalized' with the specification of the property in question. The mortgage may be flowed through in a large package of mortgages to be cut up, wrapped into special groups and sold independently much like processed chicken in the supermarket. Drumsticks or long maturities here; wings or a high risk package there. At this stage both the mortgage and the chicken have lost their individuality.

By far the largest primary financial markets are for instruments being sold by financial and/or nonfinancial corporate fiduciaries to each other. Here the rule is that the larger the transaction, the more complex and nonstandardized and the more frequent the dealings between the agents the more likely the transaction will be face-to-face, not via a mass anonymous market. The trade will be a hand-tailored transaction with a highly specific information content, even though the package may involve fungible instruments such as bonds and stock of both parties.

The concepts of anonymity and fungibility depend on social, legal and political context and the fineness of perception. The most anonymous of means of payment is a cash payment with no receipt and no witnesses. In the context of everyday business a payment by cheque or credit card is, in essence, anonymous. It is not anonymous from the point of view of leaving a 'paper trail' to track down illicit trade or socially unacceptable behaviour, nor is it anonymous if it is utilized in customer lists or credit card payment credit evaluations.

The competitive market functions the best under mass anonymous transactions (see the axioms of Dubey, Mas-Colell and Shubik, 1980), yet the credit markets function best with the availability of an analysed dossier on each individual. When there are masses of individuals to be serviced for credit standing, the personal touch of the local banker will be replaced by some form of more or less automated scoring system. Furthermore, in economic transactions involving only a few years the commercial code, the laws of contract and the force of custom are givens. This includes the power to enforce and to punish violation.

3.2 Family, Friends and Finance

The sociological phrase '6 degrees of separation' refers to the feature of human communication networks that there is probably a 'know who' network with no more than six links which can connect any two individuals on the globe.[3] More important than the existence of a tenuous web of links is how the links are reinforced to produce a solid connection which may lead to new behaviour and a modified or new institution. Both frequency and intensity conspire to 'thicken' or solidify the social and economic connections. A good example is provided by the history of many merchant bankers (see Wechsberg, 1966, for an entertaining popular description). An individual in opening a retail establishment builds up a far larger net than he might have purely socially. If he is a good merchant he will have many repeat customers (thickening of the links) and will be able to assess how to grant his customers credit. As his reputation grows and his assessments of credit granting turn out to be profitable he may expand his lending beyond consumption loans and may give up his non-financial activities.

In general private individuals and single proprietors do not have a sufficient number of links, a large enough reputation or the credit assessment ability and resources to be able to go heavily into the credit granting business. If they lend at all it is not their IOU notes that they lend but whatever bank credit or government money they possess. Good collateral is an effective substitute for individual credit assessment. This is why a single individual with little initial capital, who is able to do a reasonable job on evaluating objects for pawn and lends only a fraction of their discounted worth, can become a pawnbroker.

Physical force is also a substitute for the need for credit assessment; the numbers racket seller may extend credit to some of his gamblers knowing that his enforcers provide a sufficient threat that he will be repaid.[4] Legitimized force plays its role in the governmentally specified rules governing trade and the economy.

Individuals who are famous or notorious, such as movie stars, pop singers, football players, some billionaires, top politicians or Mafia family leaders have extremely large 'know who' nets but the nets are essentially all unidirectional and the reinforcement is unidirectional, that is, anonymous individual *A* knows the star and may learn more about him or her, but the star knows nothing whatsoever about the individual. This net has economic value to the celebrity, it may be used as a source of credit and she can become an avenue of transmission in advertising and public relations.

An estimate of the lower and upper bounds on the size of the individual 'know-who' net for most individuals is of the order of 4,000 +/− 1,000. The guesses are constructed from my own information and informal discussions with friends. Somewhere between 500–5000 links per individual has been suggested by Charles Kadushin (2000) elsewhere.[5] The questions raised by the attempt to describe the net are regarded as more important than the numbers guessed. The reader is urged to construct his or her own estimates. There are studies in sociology by Milgram (1967), Granovetter (1973), Boissevain (1974), relevant to this. It is unlikely that anyone has exceeded acquaintanceship with more than 25,000 individuals whose names and faces he recognizes and who know him.

Considering only the individual's economic life, we divide it into consumption and production segments. Thus the economic 'know-who' net consists of stores, tradesmen, medical facilities, brokers, banks, employers and others, who for most individuals are at most a few hundred. Much of the network data concerning economic institutions either does not exist in a form utilizable for this discussion or does not exist at all. We can hazard guesses and hope that the case can be made for the eventual gathering of this type of information (see White, 2001).[6]

3.3 Credit Evaluation

Money and credit are based on an intermix of information, trust and power. In particular, for the most part the relationship between a borrower and lender; the insurer and the insured or the customer and the department store is nonsymmetric. The individual chooses the bank or a major store through some combination of reputation, location and chance and establishes a more-than-one-time relationship by experience. The reputation of an ordinary citizen or small business is not immediately known to the large institution. It must rely on some form of information gathering and evaluation. Since the 1950s in the United States the techniques of quantitative methods in credit evaluation and management have increased considerably (see Rosenberg and Gleit, 1994) along with the growth of consulting and specialist credit evaluation firms such as Fair Isaac Company and credit bureaux such as Equifax, Experian and Transunion.

Much of the mass credit evaluation is for consumer credit associated with the various types of credit cards available. The old 3 Cs of commercial banking, '*Character, Competence* and *Collateral*' are expanded and specialized.

An estimate of the cost of a mass consumer credit assessment may be somewhere between 5–25 cents per capita depending on sample size, frequency of updating (such as 6 times a year for some credit cards), with many billions of credit decisions per annum, based on these evaluations. The borrowing limit is for the most part below $15,000. Different estimates can be made by a credit company both concerning the creditworthiness and the potential profitability of a card holder. A private individual in 2001 could obtain his or her own credit profile commercially in the US for $12.95.

The automated evaluation programs have recently been extended into small business lending where the sums may be as high as $500,000. As the individual amounts borrowed become larger the evaluation process becomes less anonymous and more hand-tailored. A due diligence study of a firm in a merger or acquisition can easily involve many millions in accounting, legal and investment banking fees.[7]

Credit assessment may be done by scoring procedures, but also much of it comes about as a byproduct of contractual relationships of varying force. An individual in opening either a bank account or a broker's account enters into a contract and after a few years a 'track record' is more or less established.

4. SOME CRUDE STATISTICS ON THE COMMUNICATIONS STRUCTURE OF TRADE AND CREDIT

Some crude figures concerning the network and geographical structure of individuals and economic activity are given. The estimates come primarily from the 1999 Statistical Abstract of the United States (SAUS).

4.1 The Agents to be Distinguished and some Magnitudes

The population of the United States in 1996 was approximately 270,300,000 and in 1998 was composed of around 102,500,000 household units averaging 2.62 persons per unit with around 200,000,000 voters (SAUS, 490). Essentially all of these units contained some member who recognized the existence of the government of the United States and its power and reputation. Most households have individuals who recognize their state government and some (but not too many) may know the name of the mayor or an alderman in the town in which they dwell.

In 1996 there were 4,631,000 corporations, 1,654,000 partnerships and 16,956,000 individual nonfarm proprietorships (SAUS, Table 861). Among the corporations 841,000 had receipts of over a million dollars and accounted for a little under 95 per cent of the total receipts of $14,890 billion. The top 80,000 partnerships had receipts of over a million dollars and accounted for 88 per cent of receipts of $1,042 billion. The top 71,000 proprietorships accounted for only 19 per cent of receipts of $844 billion. Averaging over all members the size ratios of corporations: partnerships: proprietorships was 68:13:1. The size spread among the institutions which accounted for 95 per cent of all trade is far larger.

An indication of the financial size of the government sector is given by their revenues and expenditures. In 1996 when GNP was $7,674 billion (SAUS, 727):

- The Federal government revenues and expenditures were $1,573 billion and $1,705 billion.
- State government revenues and expenditures were $967 billion and $860 billion.

- Local governments revenues and expenditures were $804 billion and $794 billion.

Dividing group income by the size of the group and normalizing so that the size of the individual income is 1 we obtain a rough comparison of financial size in Table 10.1.

Table 10.1 A comparison of financial size

	Numbers	Expenditure	Unit finance size	Size
Fed	1	1.57E+12	1.57E+12	55,387,324
States	50	9.67E+11	1.93E+10	680,986
Local	85,000	8.04E+11	9.46E+06	333
Individual	270E+6	7.66E+12	2.84E+04	1

The Federal government weighs in at around the income of 55,000,000 individuals while the state governments on the average are around 680,000. Together all levels of government expenditures are more than 40 per cent of GNP.

The sizes of distributors and wholesalers relative to population was approximately 1:170:520, while for banks in the USA it was 1:30,700. Averages are frequently misleading, but for brevity and consistency it is worth giving them with the warning as to where the worst distortion is located. For example. although there may be several stock markets in the US as a good approximation only two account for over 90 per cent of the trade by any measure. Furthermore for virtually all of the financial institutions the top ten account for a considerable percentage of the economic activity.

4.2 Space

The land size of the United States is around 3,536,300 square miles. It has existed as an independent country since 1776 or for 225 years. In 1996 the number of Metropolitan Statistical Areas (MSA) in the United States was 274 with an aggregate population of 211,900,000 or around 79 per cent (SAUS, Table 40). 91,000,000 lived in the top 12 metropolitan areas in 1997. Much of day-to-day living is local, although the Web is making inroads into retailing and financial markets are more and more Web phenomena. Where we live matters considerably in social, political, work and general economic life.

4.3 Financial Institutions, Intermediation and Information

Any competent text on financial institutions notes the important functions of intermediation and lists various reasons for intermediation. These include: aggregation and pooling, divisibility, flexibility in maturity, greater liquidity and good accounting. These services are provided by size, expertise, location and network connections.

The financial processes are as much production processes of an economy as is the manufacture of steel. Although it is true that much of information, once produced can be replicated easily, for example a song or a lecture can be tape-recorded many times at little cost, thus the analogy between a normal consumer or producer good and information may be poor. This however is not so for many of the purposes of credit evaluation. A credit evaluation is not unlike a driver's licence or a licence plate. They are products with network acceptance.

The financial institutions may be regarded as factories dealing generally in information transmittal, aggregation and disaggregation, but more specifically in information evaluation. In some industries the network increasing returns to scale arguments are well known (see for example Arthur, 1989, 1994), but it is still an open question in the study of the banking industry (and other financial institutions), given the importance of both networks and location, as to whether increasing returns hold until there is only a surviving monopolist. It is my belief that even without legal constraints banking tends to an oligopolistic, not a monopolistic structure because of the blend of geographical space, network connections and expertise.

5. THE DYNAMICS OF CREDIT ASSESSMENT

A credit constrained closed economy can be viewed via an essentially static analysis with an extra set of credit constraint parameters on each individual and institution. The meaning and genesis of these parameters provide the link to dynamics and to the conventional analysis. They also tie into the full five Cs version of the original three Cs of credit assessment. They are Character, Competence, Capital, Collateral and Context. The last two cover guarantees from others and the relevance of macroeconomic overall assessment of the economy.

In a large economy much borrowing is quasi-anonymous in the sense that it is essentially on a mass basis to consumers, homeowners, small firms, car buyers all of whom, from the point of view of the lenders, are a large anonymous set of risk classes. The individual is considered as a member of a risk class not as 'Mr Jones'. Because loans involve the linking of at least two time periods they, of necessity, call for a paper trail (or its computerized equivalent). The members of the mass of small borrowers all have a relatively small 'know-who network'. In general few of them are known to more than a few thousand individuals, most of whom do not know them in the context of an economic net.

6. CREDIT CONSTRAINED EXCHANGE AND PRODUCTION ECONOMIES

A way of estimating the potential for monetization of credit in the economy is by comparative statics which takes as given the communication and goods and services nets and several different scenarios for the overall state of the economy. These provide the justification for placing the cash flow constraints on a standard equilibrium model of a multi-period economy. The cash flow constraints, in turn, are eased by the granting of credit and credit depends on collateral and valuation. Valuation depends on specific detail considered in the context of the overall state of the economy.

6.1 Network Simulation or Analysis

Given a fixed institutional and macroeconomic context, a modification of the multistage general equilibrium analysis is sufficient to describe the credit conditions in an economy for a few years. The modification requires period-by-period cash flow constraints which are imposed in varying degrees on each individual according to the assessment of that individual's creditworthiness. If we regard the creditworthiness measure of each individual as a parameter given as a datum of the model then there is a natural upper and lower bound to the credit structure of the economy. The upper bound is the standard Arrow–Debreu economy with only one final budget constraint. The lower bound is the no credit situation where each individual has to balance the books each period.[8] A measure of the difference between the outcomes provides a valuation of trust or credit.

At a more basic level (and hence the title of this chapter) we may wish to ask where do the creditworthiness parameters come from? They are derived from the information and knowledge network of the economy.

When the modeling of process is attempted the rules of the game must be given and these rules implicitly describe institutional structure. The contrast between the Cartalists and Mengerians referred to by Goodhart (1998) is not an 'either/or' choice. Depending upon the starting point in history selected there is an intermix of the currently formal rules reflected in the laws (especially the enforcement of contract) and the body of custom and practice which is always at work modifying the laws.

6.2 Network Assumptions

This section is devoted to considering the nature of the network and information structure required for the simulation of a network model to study the monetization of credit. This level of description is somewhat different from that of the general equilibrium model and from most macroeconomic models. The primitive elements are: Natural persons; Legal persons and the Government. From the point of view of economic activity we need to consider several networks. They are subsets of the 'know who network'.

The 'know who network'

Each agent of the three agent types may be considered as a node in a network. An arc connecting any two points indicates that A knows B if the arc is directed from A to B, say in the form $A \rightarrow B$. If B also knows A then the arc is described by $A \leftarrow\rightarrow B$.

Knowledge of others, acquaintanceship and friendship are all multidimensional phenomena, but from the viewpoint of finance and credit extension the 5 Cs provide a good basis and the credit evaluation programs are devoted to reducing the many dimensions to one, or at least a few. Furthermore the laws of contract provide incentives for disclosure and compliance.

In particular in the relationship between A and B, intensity and duration of interaction may be of importance. Thus the concept of old friend or acquaintance implies some length of time of interaction, but a more intense relationship with the former than the latter. A's knowledge of B who is a senator or film star may be purely one way. A may have read a biography of B and have a fairly good character assessment of B, but B may not even know of the existence of A.

A specialization of the 'know who network' is to limit the net to economic concerns.

Properties of a credit system

> In God we trust, all others pay cash. (Old American saying)

In the development of mass market economics and finance more and more the trend is to make everyday personal consumption decisions anonymous from the point of view of the supplier. The local banker, retailer, restaurant or tailor are replaced by chains with branches or franchises. Only a small part of the 'higher end' of the market merits explicitly personal service. In contrast with individual consumer behaviour in an anonymous or impersonal market, large financial deals or corporate investments are made by fiduciaries often meeting face-to-face and hand-tailoring rather than mass-producing the transaction. The fact that a large transaction is usually made by fiduciaries in the context of legal and accounting requirements increases the content of self-conscious optimizing behaviour.

Underlying the credit-granting mechanisms in a society are several basic properties:

Economy

1. *Symmetry:* This is a normative property which requires that all individuals who fit the same profile under a credit assessment system are treated identically in both credit arrangements and in the law.
2. *Optimality:* A credit arrangement must be perceived as benefitting all parties.

Information costs and evaluation

1. *Reputation:* This includes two of the classical 5-Cs, Character and Competence; both are a function of the length of history on and 'track record' of the individual.
2. *Loan length:* a. The longer the loan, the less certain the repayment; b. the longer the loan the more difficult the evaluation (*ceteris paribus*).
3. *Expertise:* Primarily because economists do not have a satisfactory theory of expertise there is a tendency to leave it out of consideration in economic theorizing. But much of finance is not merely an exercise in nonsymmetric information, but in perception. As such the role of the financier is not merely to have a finer perception or a refinement of the information sets of the layman, but to understand the dimensions and quality of risk in ways not perceived by others.
4. *Credit rating and due diligence:* Mass markets for small amounts of credit for consumption call for automated evaluation scoring for classes of essentially anonymous borrowers, this covers the majority of consumers. Credit markets for production tend to be less and less anonymous as the loan size and size of the institution increase.
5. *Context:* This is one of the 5 Cs and in the actualities of credit granting summarizes the influence of the socio-political macroeconomic aspects of the situation when the loan is being made.[9]

Collateral and contracts

1. *Information and collateral:* The larger the validated collateral, the less the need for knowledge of Character and Competence.
2. *Paper, goods and liquidity:* Collateral usually represents one's own or one's guarantor's capital in paper form. Individuals who mortgage their houses, in general, live in them, but those who borrow from pawnbrokers surrender the physical asset. If the mortgage is repaid the use of the house has not been interrupted, but its use as collateral has provided the means of obtaining the needed liquidity.[10]
3. *Contract, custom and enforcement:* The structure of the economy is in constant evolution, but in any small interval of time the rules of the game are more or less given.

Network considerations

1. *Credit and non-face-to-face nets:* The ability to make mass consumer loans with little or no security and no face-to-face assessment requires that the issuer or sponsor have a visibility to large numbers as well as a favourable reputation. The minimum size for such an institution is undoubtedly dependant on many institutional parameters, but it appears that at the minimum the net of recognition is many thousands.
2. *Credit and face-to-face nets:* The number of entities required for the issue of information-intense lending is as low as two. Two large entities such as two international oil companies, if they have a continuing relationship can net their trades without bankers. In essence they accept each other's credits as bank money substitutes.
3. *Integration and merger as money substitution:* The large institution provides its own internal net, trust and enforcement structure. The corporation is able to net its internal credit arrangements with some flexibility as to when it has to balance the books.

6.3 The Credit Potential of the System

In the Appendix a simple example of two-period trade is calculated to illustrate how, at the level of a simple general equilibrium model the information, evaluation and communication system requirements are considerable. The information and evaluation differences between this and the same markets using cash is noted. The fact that we use a credit system given the costs of evaluation may be regarded as a measure of the value of credit.

'Moneyness' is a slippery concept to measure as is seen by the construction in the United States of M1, M2 and M3. Given these crude aggregates, when we compare them against the GDP we find a somewhat variable velocity. In the last twenty years the velocity associated with M1 has increased by around 14 per cent and both the velocities associated with M2 and M3 have varied by over 10 per cent. The variability is in part associated with the aggregates represented both in GDP and in the definition of the monetary aggregates. All forms of credit used as a general or local liquid means of payment need to be included in velocity calculations. But many forms of credit which might substitute for government or bank money are in control of subgroups or special nets in the economy. When circumstances change they may have a 'know who network' slack of possibly as high as 20 per cent. It is suggested that a way to estimate the variation in the creation of credit and in velocity would be to examine the strategic opportunities among six sets of agents: individuals, nonfinancial businesses, financial institutions, local government, federal government and the foreign sector. One may consider the 36 cells of interaction, for example among individuals there are the opportunities for slow payment and barter; among firms netting and slowing of accounts receivable; between the federal government and individual economic units there is the whole battery of government policy on the interest rate, taxation, subsidy and spending, each of which in part influences velocity.

Table 10.2 The velocity of monetary aggregates

	GDP/M1	GDP/M2	GDP/M3
80	6.82	1.74	1.39
85	6.75	1.67	1.30
90	6.96	1.75	1.38
95	6.45	1.99	1.57
98	7.79	1.93	1.41

The government, even in a repressive dictatorship has never been a control monolith. The more a subgroup trusts its members and the more autarkic its needs are, the more it is in a position to substitute its means of payment and hence change the velocity measures.

6.4 Credit, Money and Everyone a Banker?

A somewhat esoteric, but nevertheless serious, set of questions in economic theory is: Do we need a central bank? Could we run an economy with private banks or even individuals issuing their own money? (See Black, 1970, for example.) Are government bankruptcy laws needed, or can the free market take care of default? The practical financier or director of a central bank might regard the questions as frivolous; but at the same time they fall in the same category as the Modigliani–Miller claim that under certain highly counterfactual conditions that corporate financial structure will not matter.

The careful mathematical analysis of Arrow and Debreu; the less careful but more institutional commentary of Modigliani and Miller and the utopian writings of Thomas More all share the implicit abstraction of a world with perfect trust and costless information. They provide an unwitting basis for a wishful thinking ideology concerning the virtues of an idealized competition that has never existed and will never exist in a world where information, knowledge, cognition and perception are not costless.

When a phenomenon is said to work in theory, but not in practice, what is implied is that the theory is not sufficient to cope with the reality. Both Arrow and Debreu and Modigliani and Miller's results serve as the upper benchmarks for the ideal welfare world with perfect trust. It is also easy to mathematize the other extreme for a lower benchmark with no trust and no credit whatsoever. The complex world of money and credit, replete with a needed complex body of law and lawyers to adjudicate incomplete contracts, lies between the two.

In the example in the Appendix a credit assessment of each individual is given as a parameter of the game. But this one number M is made up of three numbers with immediate credit evaluation interpretation. $M = \eta\rho^* a^*$ where a^* is the estimate of *capital and collateral* held by an individual, p^* is the *context* of expected price, and η, the 'haircut' can be considered to reflect the assessment of *character and competence*. In the one play game an equilibrium dependent on the parameters will exist. But the credit evaluators might wish to adjust their evaluations in the light of the new market information. Given the high dimensionality of the estimates[11] the demonstration that this will converge to a consistent rational expectations equilibrium is doubtful.

7. CONCLUDING REMARKS

In More's *Utopia*, along with the perfect Arrow–Debreu world, there will be no government or outside money as perfect trust, common knowledge and information prevails. Even there a numeraire might be needed if prices are utilized. In this perfect world each individual issues his or her own credit or inside money. The world is so perfect that the accounting for debts outstanding for several decades among billions of individuals are recorded and balanced without costs or problems. All are their own bankers. All credit is monetized as the clearing house has a perfect dossier on all for all time.

In the world that we live in both inside and outside money exist, taking advantage of different information net structures, different levels of trust and due diligence and different levels of enforcement against default.

Even if we were to accept the idealization that all individuals and institutions could issue their own paper, in a world where a government exists and by any reasonable economic measure is hundreds of thousands to millions of times larger and more well known than the individual,[12] if all agents are in a position to issue their own currency the government will issue its currency and due to its network recognition that form of credit will become the dominant money. The acceptance of any individual's or institution's IOU notes as generalized purchasing power will be a matter of network acceptance and this is more or less how the monetary and credit system works. IOU notes which have a large enough acceptance become a money. Anyone can issue IOU notes, but they only become a money when they are broadly accepted. Apart from the government having the largest recognition network, its ability to tax and to issue more IOU notes secured by its full faith and credit also helps. But even then it is not necessarily enough. Both money and credit are manifestations of trust. A broad network recognition is necessary but not sufficient to support a money. Universal trust requires universal recognition, but universal recognition does not imply universal trust.

APPENDIX

There are three lengths of loan which merit formal mathematical modeling. They are: 1. the transactions or clearinghouse loan; 2. the short-term loan and 3. the long-term loan. They can be considered as a 0, 1 or 2 period loan. When *A* and *B* immediately exchange value for value utilizing some form of clearing arrangement there may be a brief interlude when one or both have given up some form of value and have not yet received the payment which is 'in the mail', the float or the clearing house. There are deep legal and technical clearing house problems in covering the few minutes or hours where one or more positions are not covered but in general clearing risks are not great (see Shubik and Slighton, 1997; Goldman Sachs, 1996; BIS, 1996; Summers, 1994). However we confine our remarks to short-term borrowing represented by two periods with a one period loan between them. New phenomena emerge in long-term borrowing represented by a three period economy with the possibility for a two period loan. An important credit distinction among 0, 1 and 2 periods is (to a good approximation) the occurrence of 0, 1 and more than 1 unforeseen exogenous or endogenous events such as accidental or intentional default. With two periods the opportunity to create a second level of paper appears.

Two Period Trade

What does and what should the trading and credit network look like? For simplicity we consider a symmetric model. In doing so we lose the considerable network distinctions between small and large firms. Furthermore the intrinsic power and information asymmetry between consumer and retailer or consumer and banker is not illustrated explicitly, but is manifested in the network information conditions assumed. In fact in a large modern economy the relationship between buyer and seller is often nonsymmetric. Rather than claim realism in the sense of a close representation of an actual retail market our empirical test is to set it up as a playable experimental game. With this caveat the model suffices to illustrate the network, information and evaluation aspects of trade and credit. Figure 10.2 shows a many person modification of the Edgeworth bargain that is straightforward to formalize and analyse. A closer abstraction of retail trade and credit requires far more differentiation of actors. In a reasonable retail model the agents to be considered explicitly are the customers, the retail establishments, the banks, clearing arrangements and credit evaluation agencies together with the central bank and the employers of the customers modelled implicitly if the full circular flow of resources is to be illustrated.

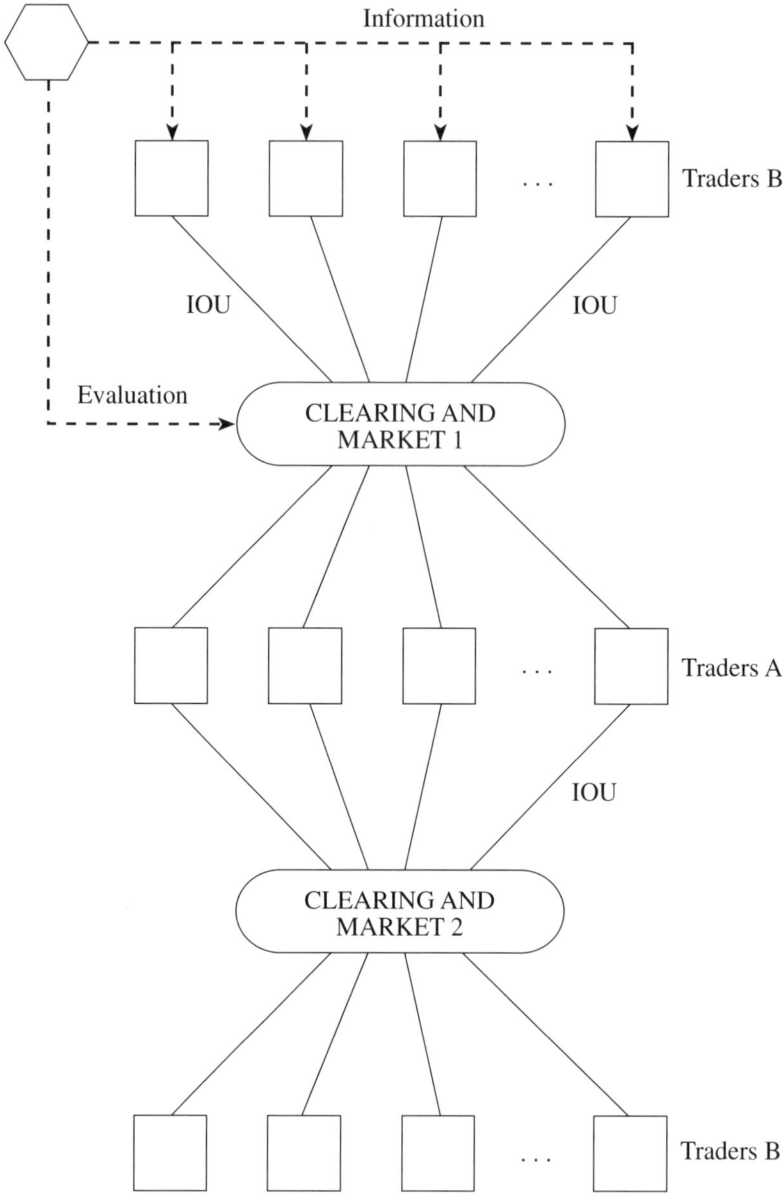

Source: Shubik (2001).

Figure 10.2 Trade with credit evaluation and a market mechanism

In Figure 10.2 the two sides are both modelled as traders. The *B*s buy from the *A*s in period 1 and sell to the *A*s in period 2. This is a far cry from the complexity of a retail market with consumer-customers and retailers often far larger and more connected than the individual buyer. However the structure in Figure 10.2 'stacks the cards' in favour of considering everyone being able to issue their own credit. Even so in any attempt to play a game with more than, say, 10 agents per side, the game designer is going to need to consider clearing arrangements. Complexity and communication are kept low by the introduction of two 'black boxes', the credit evaluation agency which provides the credit evaluations and the market mechanism (see Shubik, 1999, Chs 5 and 6) which provides price generation, trades and clearing.

We provide a simple example of the type of model discussed in Section 6 where we consider a typical trader of Type *A* and of Type *B*.

There are two periods and one perishable commodity each period and spot markets only. Traders of Type *A* are endowed with $2a$ units of the first period good and nothing in the second period. Traders of Type *B* have nothing in the first period and $2a$ units of the second period good. Symbolically the initial endowments are for Trader *A* $(2a,0)$ and for Trader *B* $(0,2a)$.

All of the traders have the same utility function which is of the form:

$$u(x_1,y_2) = 2\sqrt{x_1} + 2\sqrt{y_2} \tag{10.1}$$

If we attempt to utilize this model as a playable game several more features must be specified. They are the level of common knowledge between the traders, the existence of a numeraire and the rules concerning default. We assume common knowledge and the existence of a numeraire. Call it 'the Ideal'. It need have no physical existence, but it immediately takes on utilitarian value if the default penalty is unpleasant and the intensity of the default penalty is linked to the size of the default measured in units of Ideal. The unit of societal punishment is some form of disutility measure whose scale we might call the 'Bentham'. Thus the dimensions of the bankruptcy penalty are 'Benthams/Ideal' (or BI^{-1}). We may modify the utility function to reflect the default condition to be:

$$u(x_i, y_i) = 2\sqrt{x_i} + 2\sqrt{y_i} + \mu[\text{Default size}] \tag{10.2}$$

where μ is a parameter which can be interpreted as the marginal disutility of default.

We first comment on a two-person economy. It is difficult to conceive of a two person society. But the closest to the two-person situation we might get is two socialized individuals, say undergraduates in a bargaining experiment. The referee can control whether they have known each other previously and whether or not they bargain face-to-face. The Edgeworth (1932) two-person analysis implies face-to-face bargaining with an exchange of two current goods determined without a price signal ahead of time. Here we could conceive of an experiment using two freshmen with the first move made by Trader *A* at the start of the first semester and with the second move made by Trader *B* at the start of the next year when they come back as sophomores (if they come back and the experimenter is still there and the notes from the first part of the experiment can be found). Credit requires some form of contract between the two traders.

In Shubik (1999) trade utilizing either fiat money or gold has been discussed. Implicit in the discussion was the assumption that all payments were in cash and all individuals recognized and accepted gold or fiat. When neither gold nor fiat exist trade must depend on inside money. We may introduce a parameter to reflect the overall degree of trust between Trader *I* and Trader *J*, or more realistically if there are many traders of each type and they are trading through a more or less anonymous market, we may assume that in any random pair traders do not know each other, hence the trust parameter is that of the bank or, in the game, the referee. This parameter can be considered as the 'credit assessment' parameter. As argued above, it is determined for each individual by information and network considerations.[13] We select a parameter η where $0 \leq \eta \leq 1$.

Actual trade is embedded in time. There is usually a history of the market. For instance the last market price is known. For purposes of credit evaluation we need to be able to estimate the individual's assets and their expected value. If a^* is the estimate of the quantity of assets held by an individual and p^* the expected price, the amount $\eta p^* a^*$ can be considered to be the size of the credit line as estimated by the banker. Here the η can be regarded as the 'haircut' or the discount on the valuation of the asset given for the borrower's protection. If we wish to consider a playable game where each trader is his own banker then we must assume that in a mass market at least the market clearing agency is aware of the reputation and creditworthiness of each individual i in the suggested limit of the amount $\eta_i p^* a_i^*$ on the acceptability of the individual's paper.

We can see immediately the upper and lower bounds of full credit and no credit in this exchange. Full credit can be simply portrayed by the standard general equilibrium solution. Due to the simplicity of the example we can solve by inspection. The utility to each is initially $2\sqrt{(2a)}$ and the final utility for each is $4\sqrt{a}$.

When $\eta = 0$ no trade will take place and the final utility is the same as the initial autarkic solution. In this simple instance the utility functions being all the same we have a simple measure for the value of trust going from the no trust instance to the full trust of general equilibrium.

The credit constrained equilibrium solution

Model 1: It is sufficient to consider the instance of trade without active default to illustrate the influence of the credit constraints. In order to do so we merely solve a credit constrained general equilibrium model. This amounts to solving the two expressions of the form:

$$u(x_1, y_1) = 2\sqrt{x_1} + 2\sqrt{y_1} + \lambda_1[2ap_1 - p_1x_1 - p_2y_1] \tag{10.3}$$

and

$$u(x_2, y_2) = 2\sqrt{x_2} + 2\sqrt{y_2} + \lambda_2[2ap_2 - p_1x_2 - p_2y_2] + \lambda_3[\eta p_1{}^*a^* - p_1x_2] \tag{10.4}$$

where the extra constraint in the second equation reflects the credit restriction. We obtain nine equations of the form:

$$\begin{aligned}
\frac{1}{\sqrt{x_1}} &= \lambda_1 p_1;\\
\frac{1}{\sqrt{y_1}} &= \lambda_1 p_2;\\
\frac{1}{\sqrt{x_2}} &= (\lambda_2 + \lambda_3) p_1;\\
\frac{1}{\sqrt{y_2}} &= \lambda_2 p_2;\\
x_1 + x_2 &= 2a;\\
y_1 + y_2 &= 2a;\\
2ap_1 &= p_1x_1 + p_2y_1;\\
2ap_2 &= p_1x_2 + p_2y_2;\\
M &= \eta p^*a^* = p_2y_2
\end{aligned} \tag{10.5}$$

Solving we obtain:

$$p_2 = \frac{2a - M}{M} \tag{10.6}$$

and

$$\lambda_1 = \frac{1}{\sqrt{2a - M}};$$

$$\lambda_2 = \lambda_1 \sqrt{\frac{M}{2ap - M}} \tag{10.7}$$

$$\lambda_3 = \frac{1}{\sqrt{M}} - \lambda_2$$

with

$$x_1 = 2a - M; \quad x_2 = M; \quad y_1 = \frac{M^2}{2a - M}; \quad y_2 = 2a - y_1 \tag{10.8}$$

We may check to see that when $M = a$ we obtain the competitive equilibrium solution with

$$x_1 = x_2 = y_1 = y_2 = a; \quad \lambda_1 = \lambda_2 = \frac{1}{\sqrt{a}}; \quad \lambda_3 = 0; \quad p_1 = p_2 = 1. \tag{10.9}$$

When $0 < M < a$ the credit constraints become binding. (When $M = 0$ there is no trade and λ_2 is not defined.)

Model 2: Two-person trade with gold or fiat as money

Gold: We can modify Model 1 by introducing an ideal gold. Such a gold would be the equivalent of a transferable utility. Thus we can imagine a new playable game where each trader has an initial endowment as follows. Type A has $(2a,0,M_1)$ and Type B has $(0,2a,M_2)$ where the utility function for each is

$$u(x_i, y_i) = 2\sqrt{x_i} + 2\sqrt{y_i} + m_i \tag{10.10}$$

where gold appears as a perfect money with linear utility.

The pattern of trade is essentially the same as in Figure 10.2 with the deletion of the credit assessment as the cash payment in gold makes it unnecessary.

Fiat: When fiat is used instead of gold. If the individuals trust the government to the extent that each believes that the other will accept the currency then the system with fiat (Kiyotaki and Wright, 1989; Bak, Nørelykke and Shubik, 1999) requires no extra information beyond the knowledge that all will accept the fiat. The distinction between the ideal gold and the acceptable fiat can be illustrated considering two matrices. The first is an intrinsic valuation matrix and the second is an acceptance matrix. Any pair of matrices represents i's estimate of j's acceptance and valuation.

$$\begin{bmatrix} 1 & 1 & 1 & \cdots & 1 & 1 \\ 1 & 1 & 1 & \cdots & 1 & 1 \\ \vdots & & & \ddots & & \\ 1 & 1 & 1 & \cdots & 1 & 1 \end{bmatrix} \begin{bmatrix} 1 & 1 & 1 & \cdots & 1 & 1 \\ 1 & 1 & 1 & \cdots & 1 & 1 \\ \vdots & & & \ddots & & \\ 1 & 1 & 1 & \cdots & 1 & 1 \end{bmatrix} \qquad \begin{bmatrix} 1 & 1 & 1 & \cdots & 1 & 1 \\ 1 & 1 & 1 & \cdots & 1 & 1 \\ \vdots & & & \ddots & & \\ 1 & 1 & 1 & \cdots & 1 & 1 \end{bmatrix} \begin{bmatrix} 0 & 0 & 0 & \cdots & 0 & 0 \\ 0 & 0 & 0 & \cdots & 0 & 0 \\ \vdots & & & \ddots & & \\ 0 & 0 & 0 & \cdots & 0 & 0 \end{bmatrix}$$

Acceptance Valuation Acceptance Valuation

Ideal Gold as Money Fiat Money

NOTES

* I wish to acknowledge the able and enthusiastic research assistance of Sam McCarthy.

1. See a recent example of the issue of the simec by Professor Auriti in Guardiagrele, Italy reported in the *New York Times*, January 30, 2001 by J. Tagliabue.
2. All credit has an offset; but some injections of government money need not have an offset (other than force or guile). Fiat money is not redeemable, it is an asset like gold and may have no offsetting instrument. The financial system as a whole may be nonsymmetric. It does not need to net to zero; but under appropriate conditions it can be shown that in an infinite horizon stationary state the economy is cash consuming and in the limit, symmetry is approached (see Shubik, 1999, Chs. 11 and 15). The nonsymmetry is a feature of the dynamics and is related to the financing of the float and the selection of the numeraire and bankruptcy penalties.
3. If each knew the same number of individuals in a tree or hierarchy structure one would only require a little more than 1800 connections per individual for a 6 degrees of separation span to cover the world population.
4. There is a popular dialogue worth noting. COLLECTOR: Pay up! DEBTOR: I cannot pay, I have no money, it is like trying to get blood from a stone. COLLECTOR: What makes you think that you are a stone?
5. Website reference.
6. Just before this paper was fully finished I visited Harrison White and had the pleasure of obtaining the file set for his forthcoming book on Markets from Networks. Although his stress is on production rather than consumption or finance, the approach is allied to the discussion here.
7. A rough estimate can be obtained from observing that the investment banks in the United States earned around \$12 billion in 2000 for around 4,000 deals.
8. At its simplest each individual i might have a creditworthiness parameter η_i where $0 \leq \eta_i \leq 1$, but in a more complex network world the parameter might be η_{ij}, that is i's credit rating with j.
9. The understanding of the relevance of context is critical to all applications. A study of proverbs indicates that many of them occur in pairs which appear to contradict each other, yet depending on context each may be right. Thus we have: 'Look before you leap' and 'He who hesitates is lost'.
10. An interesting open question concerns what are the limits of 'paper on paper'? As economies become more complex more instruments are invented. The common stock overcame the indivisibility problems caused by joint ownership of large assets. Warrants are second level paper and calls on warrants are third level paper. In a world without transactions, information or computation costs there appears to be no logical limit, but in actuality two to three levels appear to be sufficient.
11. For n individuals there are $3n$ parameters without the added difficulties caused by the presence of exogenous uncertainty and production.
12. For the United States the government is roughly 55,000,000 times wealthier and at the least 300,000,000/5,000 or 60,000 times more well known.

13. Fifty years ago the determination might have involved a local banker for small loans, currently a credit evaluation firm may supply the banker with an evaluation.

REFERENCES

Arthur, W.B. (1989), 'Competing technologies, increasing returns and lock-in by historical events', *Economic Journal*, 116–31.

Arthur, W.B. (1994), *Increasing Returns and Path Dependence in the Economy*, Ann Arbor, MI: University of Michigan Press.

Bak, P., S. Nørelykke and M. Shubik (1999), 'Dynamics of money in a market economy', *Physical Review* E, 60(3), 2528–32.

Bank of International Settlement (BIS) (1996), *Security of Electronic Money*, Report by the Committee on Payment and Settlement Systems and the Group of Computer Experts of the central banks of the Group of Ten countries, Basle, August 1996, © Bank for International Settlements.

Black, F. (1970), 'Banking and interest rates in a world without money', *Journal of Bank Research*, 9, 20.

Boissevan, J. (1974), *Friends of Friends: Networks, Manipulators and Coalitions*, London: Basil Blackwell.

Dubey, P., A. Mas-Colell and M. Shubik (1980), 'Efficiency properties of strategic market games: an axiomatic approach', *Journal of Economic Theory*, 22, 339–62.

Edgeworth, F.Y. (1932), *Mathematical Psychics: An Essay on the Application of Mathematics to the Moral Sciences* (original, 1881), London: London School of Economics.

Goodhart, C.A.E. (1998), 'The two concepts of money: implications for the analysis of optimal currency areas', *European Journal of Political Economy*, 14, 407–32.

Goldman Sachs (1996), Symposium on Risk Reduction in Payments, Clearance and Settlement Systems, New York.

Granovetter, M.S. (1973), 'The strength of weak ties', *American Journal of Sociology*, 78, 1369–80.

Jevons, W.S. (1875), *Money and the Mechanism of Exchange*, London: Macmillan.

Kiyotaki, N. and R. Wright (1989), 'On money as a medium of exchange', *Journal of Political Economy*, 97, 927–54.

Milgram, S. (1967), 'The small world problem', *Psychology Today*, 1, 62–7.

Rosenberg, J. and A. Gleit (1994), 'Quantitative methods in credit management', *Operations Research*, 42(4), 589.

Shubik, M. (1999), *The Theory of Money and Financial Institutions*, Cambridge, MA: MIT Press.

Shubik, M. (2001), 'Money and the monetarization of credit', Cowles Foundation Discussion Paper No. 1343, New Haven, CT: Cowles Foundation for Research in Economics, Yale University, p. 17.

Shubik, M. and R.L. Slighton (with the collaboration of G.J. Feeney) (1997), *The Defense Implications of the Recent and Future Changes in the World Monetary and Financial Systems*, mimeo, New Haven, available from the author.

Summers, B.J. (ed.) (1994), *The Payment System: Design Management and Supervision*, Washington, DC: International Monetary Fund.

Wechsberg, J. (1966), *The Merchant Bankers*, Boston, MA: Little, Brown.

White, H.C. (2001), *Markets from Networks*, Princeton, NJ: Princeton University Press.

Discussion of 'Money and the monetization of credit'

Anne Sibert

The contribution of this entertaining chapter is to provide a storehouse of ingredients for concocting theoretical and empirical models of financial networks. Some of the ingredients are schemes for classifying things, such as maturity of assets or time frames for modelling. Other ingredients are data, such as the cost per capita of a mass consumer credit assessment, a variety of figures from the 1999 *Statistical Abstract of the United States*, and the number of personal connections required for 'six degrees of separation' to span the globe. One of the most interesting data sets is the author's mixture of guesses and estimates about the size of various types of networks that an individual belongs to and the intensity of the corresponding bilateral relationships. Martin Shubik suggests that a way the numbers in the chapter might be used is to measure the acceptability of different types of credit in exchange for goods and services.

The models the author apparently envisions could be used to address many questions of current importance. Technology and the regulatory environment now allow the private-sector issuance of e-cash, the electronic cousin of the banknote, and this has fostered interest in the role of inside money. A number of issues arise. Do we need a central bank to provide a medium of exchange? Is the co-existence of inside and outside money optimal? Are we likely to end up with many types of inside money, trading at different discounts? How important are the networks that clear and settle inside money systems? How does the increased importance of bank and non-bank issued inside money affect monetary policy, financial stability and the central bank's ability to collect seigniorage?

Given their importance, there are relatively few theoretical attempts to answer these questions. Two examples are Cavalcanti and Wallace (1999) and Williamson (1999). The results of these papers suggest that inside money regimes are preferable to outside money regimes. However, their specification of inside money regimes is quite abstract. For example, in Cavalcanti and Wallace (1999) a generic inside money is issued by 'banks' whose trading histories is known. A less abstract formulation of credit issuers, possibly along the lines suggested by Martin Shubik, may be needed to provide really satisfactory answers to this and the other questions listed above.

It is the task of comment writers to quibble. One problem with the chapter is that, although the author begins by asking what the important differences between money, near money and money substitutes are, he fails to draw much distinction between inside and outside money. At one point he appears to believe there is little difference, other than the nature of the issuer, saying, 'In essence all money is credit.' Thus, the use of an asset as money depends on the likelihood that the issuer of the asset can be compelled or feels obliged to redeem the asset.

I disagree with this view; an essential feature of money – at least fiat money – is that it is not credit. Wallace (1980) emphasises that a defining trait of fiat money is inconvertibility; an issuer does not promise to convert it into anything else. In both Wallace (1980) and Kiyotaki and Wright (1989), money has value, not because of the reputation of the issuer, but because there are self-fulfilling beliefs that it will be acceptable in trade for goods. The government may attempt to 'back' fiat money by legal tender laws and requiring its use in paying taxes, but these actions are meaningless if the currency does not already have value.

Martin Shubik argues that there is a unifying theme in the development of both government money and inside money and this is networks and information combined with the roles of custom and law for enforcement. I would say that this is true for the development of credit markets and the use of credit as a medium of exchange, but it is not so obviously true for fiat money. Thus, the dominant models of the micro-foundations of money – the search-theoretic models (for example, Kiyotaki and Wright, 1989) and the spatial-separation models (for example, Townsend, 1980) – have no explicit role for information or legal systems.

REFERENCES

Cavalcanti, R. and N. Wallace (1999), 'Inside Money as Alternative Media of Exchange', *Journal of Money, Credit, and Banking*, 31(3), 443–57.

Kiyotaki, N. and R. Wright (1989), 'On Money as a Medium of Exchange', *Journal of Political Economy*, 97(4), 927–54.

Townsend, Robert M. (1980), 'Models of Money with Spatially Separated Agents', in John H. Kareken and Neil Wallace (eds), *Models of Monetary Economics*, Minneapolis, MN: Federal Reserve Bank of Minneapolis, pp. 265–304.

Wallace, Neil (1980), 'The Overlapping Generations Model of Fiat Money', in John H. Kareken and Neil Wallace (eds), *Models of Monetary Economics*, Minneapolis, MN: Federal Reserve Bank of Minneapolis, pp. 49–82.

Williamson, S. (1999), 'Private Money', *Journal of Money, Credit and Banking*, 31(3), 469–91.

Index